1999

Fertile Ground, Narrow Choices

Fertile Ground

Studies in Rural Culture

Jack Temple Kirby, editor

The University of North Carolina Press

Chapel Hill and London

Narrow Choices

Women on Texas Cotton Farms, 1900–1940

Rebecca Sharpless

Designed by April Leidig-Higgins

Set in Minion by Keystone Typesetting, Inc.

Manufactured in the United States of America

The paper in this book meets the guidelines for
permanence and durability of the Committee on
Production Guidelines for Book Longevity of the
Council on Library Resources.

Library of Congress Cataloging-in-Publication Data
Sharpless, Rebecca. Fertile ground, narrow choices:
women on Texas cotton farms, 1900–1940 / by
Rebecca Sharpless.

p. cm.—(Studies in rural culture)

Includes bibliographical references and index.

ISBN 0-8078-2456-9 (cloth : alk. paper)

ISBN 0-8078-4760-7 (pbk. : alk. paper)

1. Rural women—Texas—History—20th century.

2. Cotton farmers—Texas—History—20th century.

3. Texas—Rural conditions. I. Title. II. Series.

HQ1438.T4S53   1999   98-23630

305.4'09764'091734—dc21   CIP

03 02 01 00 99 5 4 3 2 1

In memory of my grandmothers,

Mary Rebecca Lynch Frierson and Annie Mel Allen Sharpless

contents

Preface xi

Acknowledgments xxi

Introduction
Women, Cotton, and the
Crop-Lien System 1

1 Women, Daughters, Wives, Mothers
Gender and Family Relationships 17

2 Keeping Warm, Keeping Dry
Housekeeping and Clothing
in the Blackland Prairie 69

3 Living at Home
Food Production and Preparation
in the Blackland Prairie 109

4 Making a Hand
Women's Labor in the Fields 159

5 Life Beyond the Farm
Women and Their Communities 189

6 Staying or Going
Urbanization and the Depopulation
of the Rural Blackland Prairie 219

Notes 249

Bibliography 293

Index 311

maps, illustrations, and tables

Maps

Map 1. Major physical features of the Blackland Prairie of Texas 5
Map 2. Counties of the Blackland Prairie of Texas 6
Map 3. Moves of the Rice family, Hunt County, Texas 10

Illustrations

Spring plowing, Williamson County 3
Mother and children at a cotton wagon, Kaufman County 50
Board and batten tenant farmer's house, Ellis County 86
Landowner's daughter weighing cotton, Kaufman County 185
African American church on the open prairie, Ellis County 201

Tables

Table 1. Number of Tenants and Landowners in Four Blacklands Counties, 1900–1940 8
Table 2. Average Age of Farmers' Wives at First Marriage in Four Blacklands Counties, by Ethnic Group, 1900 and 1910 18
Table 3. Average Number of Births and Surviving Children Born to Farmers' Wives under Age Forty-Five in Four Blacklands Counties, by Ethnic Group, 1900 and 1910 40
Table 4. Months of Field Work Women Performed Per Year, by Ethnic Group 165

Table 5. Percentage of Women Performing Farming Tasks, by Ethnic Group, in Hill County, 1921 166

Table 6. Literacy Rates for Women under Age Forty-Five in Four Blacklands Counties, by Ethnic Group, 1900 and 1910 194

Table 7. Change in Numbers of Tenants and Farm Owners in Four Blacklands Counties, 1930 and 1940 234

Table 8. Population Growth of Towns in Four Blacklands Counties, 1900–1940 236

Table 9. Population Growth of Major Blacklands Cities, 1900–1940 237

Women's Memories,
Women's Stories

> When everything else has gone from my
> brain—the President's name, the state capitals,
> the neighborhoods where I lived, and then my
> own name and what it was on earth I sought,
> and then at length the faces of my friends, and
> finally the faces of my family—when all this
> has dissolved, what will be left, I believe, is
> topology: the dreaming memory of land as it
> lay this way and that.
> —Annie Dillard, *An American Childhood*

As Bernice Bostick Weir stands on the front porch of her white-painted bungalow in McLennan County, Texas, she gazes northwest to the Stampede Valley. The rolling prairie stretches before her, only a few houses and trees marking the grazing lands between her home and the distant horizon delineated by the passing freight cars of the Santa Fe Railroad. Recalling her arrival in that place as a bride in 1919, she remembers the landscape differently: "When Pat and I married, fifty acres was a family plot. The Briscoes lived over here and they had six children; the Johnsons lived over there, and the Watsons lived right down here. And the Newmans lived over there, and Newmans lived up here."[1] The Blackland Prairie in Bernice Weir's memory is thickly populated with farm families, the rich, dark soil covered with cotton. As Weir remembers the vistas of her early adulthood, she is recalling a landscape, in Pamela

Grundy's apt phrase, "patterned by people."[2] Weir's memories are configured by her relationships with other people, as her marriage, the births of her children, and the deaths of loved ones provide the structure upon which her recollections hang.

For others, the landscape has become less distinct with the passage of time. The Blackwell sisters, Louise and Deenie, drove through northeast Navarro County looking for their childhood homes. They wrote, "We were able to identify some of the hedgerows, bridges, and other landmarks, to pinpoint where the small farms had been; but only one house of some six or seven of our childhood memories remained. It stood in isolation about a mile from the public dirt road we travelled on, and was obviously being used as a hay barn. Gone were all the houses, gardens, school houses, churches, fruit trees, pecan trees, and berry patches—all levelled to make room for Coastal Bermuda grass for the Hereford cattle which now dot the entire landscape."[3] For the Blackwells, children of sharecroppers, all of the physical manifestations of their culture are gone. The prairie cotton farms of their childhood remain in their memory, however, as lively, vital places, where their father farmed other people's land and their mother kept careful watch over her nine children.

This is a book of memories turned to stories, from women such as Bernice Weir, Louise Blackwell Dillow, and Deenie Blackwell Carver, who lived on cotton farms on the Texas prairie before 1940. The concept of the family plot—an expanse of soil subdivided to meet the needs and test the resources of an individual family unit—neatly encapsulates the two defining aspects of women's lives of the Texas Blackland Prairie: farming and family. The use of stories is highly appropriate for reconstructing the world of these women, for, as Bettina Aptheker has observed, women order their experiences in part through personal narratives: "Stories are one of the ways in which women give meaning to the things that happen in a lifetime, and the dailiness of life also structures the telling, the ordering of thought, the significance allocated to different pieces of the story."[4] In the telling, women represent themselves and those dear to them in terms of everyday activities. Such personal stories, as Shula Marks comments, help "move us beyond the aridity of an unpeopled political economy, to the ambiguities of everyday life."[5]

In this particular work, all of the stories are public. I found no collections of personal letters or diaries to reconstruct women's internal lives. Nor have I discovered any contemporary writing by women about themselves except the letters written for publication in regional agricultural newspapers. The three chief types of sources for this study, autobiographies and written memoirs, oral history interviews, and sociological reports, all were produced for public consumption, in T. L. Broughton's words, "at the juncture of the public world of announcement and the private work of self-analysis and meditation."[6] Women write and speak in the public realm of private matters.[7]

The most extemporaneous of the three types of sources are the written autobiographies or memoirs that people of the Blackland Prairie generated to tell their stories. Historically minded older residents have set down their recollections, primarily to instruct younger generations on how life used to be. These memoirists were a self-selected group, well aware of their own historicity, who had time to write and most of whom possessed the financial means to have their memoirs printed for their families and friends.[8] The volumes have found their way into libraries haphazardly. The memoirs cited here were generated by men and women in almost equal numbers, but they total less than a dozen: a tiny percentage of the millions of Texans who lived on cotton farms before 1940. Only one of the writers, Eddie Stimpson, is black.

The few rural women who have chosen to write their memoirs appear to have transcended the alleged female difficulty of claiming "the authority of individual personal experience, asserting unique knowledge of that unique subject, the self" and making their autobiography "the dynamic process of recorded choice."[9] Many of these autobiographers are recording their personal perspectives on processes now long past: how to make butter, how to hoe cotton, how they walked miles to school. These women lack the intense inner dialogue marking many of the professionally published autobiographies that are the subject of most autobiographical theory. As Patricia Meyer Spacks astutely observes, many female autobiographers are artists who demand public attention: "The housewife seldom offers her life to public view."[10] The "housewives" in this study have offered their lives to us, but it is their outer lives and not their inner ones. They are motivated by the desire to teach their grandchildren how materially different life was. The implicit message may be: Look what we had to endure. You come from strong people. And look how easy you have life by comparison. These memoirs focus, as Spacks remarks, "not on the narrating self, but rather on the outer world of people and events: the memoir writer's intention is not self-examination." With careful reading, however, a researcher can discover much from the written memoir. The memoirist's "vision of the outer world is as much a projection and refraction of the self as the autobiographer's. The manifest content of the memoir may be different, but the latent content is likewise self-revelation."[11]

The second type of evidence, oral history, is a multilayered recording of experience. The complexity of oral history lies in its interactive nature: one person telling her story to another. The telling is affected by a large number of factors, including the ethnicity, class, and sex of the teller and of the listener. The interviewing methodology also affects the outcome of the interview. Despite its complicated nature, oral history is probably the most valuable tool for studying the lives of rural people, the single best opportunity to discover the thoughts and motivations of those who will not write their memoirs. Except for some family photographs, none of the women whom I interviewed had extensive papers. Without oral history, their lives might remain absent from the historical record.[12]

I personally conducted some of the interviews between 1990 and 1995. I found my interviewees strictly by word of mouth, by asking persons likely to know older women in rural areas. This procedure may have skewed the interviews slightly, as I talked only with people who knew someone in my circle of acquaintances. In many ways, however, I believe that the stories of these people reflect the experiences of farm women throughout Central Texas. While each woman's experience is unique, there is a commonality to the experiences that resonates throughout almost every interview. Like the Latin American *testimonios* discussed by Doris Sommer, the women's interviews represent more stories than just their own. Many times, they are the stories of the women's mothers in particular and hence have "collective subjects."[13]

Opinions vary widely on the topic of oral history methodology.[14] Some theorists, particularly those who work with politicians and businesspeople, advocate an aggressive interviewing approach that allows the interviewee to "get away with" nothing. Others suggest almost complete passivity on the part of the interviewer, basically allowing the interviewee to shape her own narrative without interference.[15] In selecting a methodology, I chose a middle ground between the two approaches. I used the same very general interview outline for each person, and I guided the interviews, especially asking follow-up questions to elicit more detailed information. At the same time, I tried diligently to encourage each interviewee to tell her story in her own words, without my interference with the narrative. The interviews adhered fairly closely to the outlines, with each person patiently answering my most minute query. Between my prodding for details, however, the interviewees sometimes burst forth in torrents of narrative, and those eloquent words form the crux of this study.

None of the women whom I asked to be interviewed appeared to be surprised at being asked, and none refused or seemed even slightly suspicious.

They stated repeatedly that they were happy to help me. Our interviews were filtered through a variety of factors. The most ubiquitous difference between us was age: all of the narrators were fifty to sixty years older than I. My life experiences, begun in the Cold War, shared little chronologically with theirs. Another was educational level. Two people, Myrtle Dodd and Inez Folley, graduated from college. The rest had not finished high school and one, Luz Hurtado, had no formal education. I was completing and then had completed the Ph.D. degree. Ethnicity became yet another factor, something that bound me to the Anglo narrators and separated me from the African American and Mexican women. Language, too, separated me from the Mexican women, who spoke the language of their birth country. The translator for the Spanish-language interviews was a university undergraduate student, and her presence, while necessary and most welcome, put yet another layer of distance between the narrators and me. (The afternoon that we interviewed Adelaida Almanza and Cayetana Navarro together—in the kitchen of the nursing home where they were living—and listened to them swapping stories of learning to make tortillas was one of the most fun and gratifying that I have spent in many years of oral history interviewing.) The characteristic that most of us shared was gender, as all of the interviewees except Dovie Carroll were female. Most of the women wanted to know, first, if I were married, and when I answered affirmatively, asked if I had children. Rather than enter a discussion that might alienate them, I would reply that my husband had two sons. The presence of offspring (albeit in their twenties and living far from their father) seemed to satisfy the requirement of motherhood. The list of variables goes on: some Baptist, some Roman Catholic, all Christian; some financially comfortable, some poor. And yet, it seems, rapport came easily. Possibly it was because the interviewees' experiences reflected those of my father and his older sisters, echoing stories that I had heard all of my life. Perhaps I should have been more skeptical or more aggressive with my questioning, but I approached these people in their eighties and nineties feeling honored that they would spend their time with me, recalling events of sixty, seventy, eighty years before.

All of the people whom I interviewed were able to describe events in their youth in vivid detail. Because of these people's ability to recall details, the interviews that I conducted were deep rather than broad: a relatively small sample, with no fewer than three interviews per person and, in the case of Dovie and Etta Carroll, as many as seven. While I remain generally pleased with the interviews, I have deeply regretted lost opportunities to discuss such subjects as sexuality, and now, several years later, I also have wished that I had asked different questions about morality and community ethics. The opportunities for oral history research are fleeting, however, especially when working, as I was, with a population born between 1900 and 1915. We rarely get second chances.

This study also uses oral history interviews conducted by others, mostly under the auspices of the Baylor University Institute for Oral History and the oral history program at Texas A&M University–Commerce. The Baylor interviews fall into three groups: those conducted by volunteers for the Junior League of Waco for their project History of the Woman in Waco; those conducted with men who had grown up on farms and become successful in their chosen field of employment; and those conducted to document the careers of retired Central Texas teachers. Rural childhoods were only a beginning point for most of these interviews, reflected through lives of professional and personal achievement. James Conrad and his colleagues at TAMU-C also interviewed retired teachers and citizens of the Greenville area who reflected on their rural roots, which are closer, in Hunt County, than in the more urbanized Waco area. The questions were often not those I would have asked, but the interviewees comment helpfully on their rural backgrounds nonetheless. Unlike interviews that the researcher conducts herself for her own purposes, these interviews resemble other archival materials in that one takes what one finds and does what one can with them. They require looking behind the positivism of most of the answers to impart meaning beyond mere description. But they provide valuable insights into young people on Texas farms.

Moving into the realm of interpretation and shaping an overall narrative from interviews and memoirs became the most daunting task once the interviews were transcribed. As Elizabeth Hampsten observes, in writing someone else's life story, we fear "cannibaliz[ing] the lives of others" and must dare ourselves to "have anything serious to say. The mere desire to give form and therefore meaning to others' lives or their writing is, if you think too much about it, forbiddingly arrogant. We should be warned by the Pygmalion myth."[16] One of the most difficult aspects of this study has been granting myself the authority to back away from the materials, to analyze them according to my formal training as a scholar, which has brought knowledge about the political and economic context in which the women of the Blackland Prairie lived, and to draw conclusions from the materials.

Much of the difficulty stems from knowing the interviewees personally, having shared long afternoons and received gifts of crocheted doilies and homemade plum jelly. Shula Marks comments: "[Historians] may well be structured and caught up in the very processes we are trying to analyze. This is particularly the case when we record the stories of living subjects, in whose lives we inevitably become a part."[17] In my view, the writer must work to remain faithful to the intent of the interviewee while remaining distant enough to maintain perspective, to challenge the oral source material just as one would a written source. In all honesty, I never came across any material in any oral history in this research that I did not believe was accurate or valid from the teller's perspective. I sincerely hope that I have represented accurately the truths and insights given to me through the generosity of the women whom I interviewed and by those interviewees who shared their thoughts with others.[18] At the same time, I realize that the women in the Blackland Prairie did not live in vacuums but rather in the midst of national currents. As a result, I have worked to bring the larger movements in southern economic and social history into the interpretation. As Marks concludes, "If the dilemma is inescapable, the endeavor is nonetheless worthwhile, for it is through the presentation of the life story that we can try to capture both the internality of experience and the externality of structure. By intervening between subject and reader in the presentation of self, we grapple with the central problem of human agency."[19] I have to avoid thinking that I can see these women's lives more clearly than they do, but I must also use the knowledge that I have to put them into context with each other.

The third significant body of documentation for this study comes from rural reformers in the 1920s and 1930s, when social workers sent by the State of Texas and the U.S. government wrote extensive reports on the conditions of life in the Blackland Prairie. The work of three women in particular stands out: Ellen Nathalie Matthews and Helen Maretta Dart, who traveled throughout Central Texas in 1920 for the U.S. Department of Labor Children's Bureau; and the inimitable Ruth Alice Allen, who from 1928 to 1930 made an extremely thorough investigation of Central Texas women's roles in cotton cultivation, published by the University of Texas Bureau of Research in the Social Sciences. These sociologists and social workers conducted their investigations with keen eyes, and their observations provided much rich detail for this study.

Such sociological accounts, which have quantitative aspects to them, are close to contemporary accounts of rural life before World War II. The researchers assumed pathology because of rural poverty, and they approached their subjects as problems to be solved. They apparently tried not to condescend to the women with whom they talked, however. They, and their male counterparts who investigated land-tenure problems, endeavored to retain an even tone in their writing. Occasionally they could not resist showing their horror at the iniquities of rural life, viewing farm women through their "discerning, discriminating middle-class gaze."[20] But the body of documentation that they left is irreplaceable and invaluable.

This study has two aims: to analyze the physical conditions of women's lives in the cotton South and to discover how they coped with a reality that was bleak for many. The physical conditions are easier to see and write about, although the subject has remained relatively untouched by historians. No single source has discussed the physical existence of farm women's lives in the American South. And while much has been written on postbellum cotton cultivation and its demise, little has been done to examine the lives of women within southern cotton culture. Anthropologist Marjorie Shostak writes, "[W]e should make every effort to overcome obstacles, to go out and record the memories of people whose ways of life often are preserved only in those memories. And we should do it urgently, before they disappear."[21] Between 1900 and World War II, rural life in Central Texas changed from that of small farms joined by dirt roads, impassable after every rain, to that in which the majority of the residents had left the farms and moved to urban areas. The memories are fading rapidly, as young brides of the 1920s are now women in their nineties with middle-aged grandchildren.

The way of life described here was filled with routines, many of which were undone almost as soon as they were done: A typical farm woman cooked a meal, fed her family, washed the dishes, and began preparations for the next meal; washed clothes, knowing that next week the clothes would be dirty again; drew water with the full realization that she would soon use her supply and have to draw more.[22] But each of these actions was laden with importance, for the welfare of a woman's entire family depended heavily upon this labor-intensive work. Bettina Aptheker has described this type of cyclical, nonlinear existence as "dailiness," in which women's work is usually a process and seldom a conclusion.[23]

Within this nonlinear cycle, how did women survive and occasionally thrive in such situations? To depict these women as superhuman is to do them a disservice, for, as Laurie Mercier has observed about farm women in Montana, tributes to selfless farm women "often glorify rather than document the women's experiences."[24] I have chosen to view them as women who usually worked hard, tried their best, and sometimes failed in their attempts to create comfortable lives for their families and for themselves. Historian Wayne Flynt has commented that for Alabama poor whites, "striving, not accomplishment, often became their legacy."[25] Like the people about whom Flynt wrote, most of the women in this study never gave up, despite the tremendous odds against their accomplishing anything that the world at large would notice. This study attempts to discover why women in the rural South resemble "the ghostly army of good women" about whom Carolyn Steedman writes in England who endured "scrubbing the Lancashire doorstops until they dropped, babies fed by the side of the mill, bringing the money home, getting the food to the table, never giving in." Steedman declares, "There is no way of not working hard, nothing but an endurance that allows you to absorb everything that comes by way of difficulty, *holding on* to the grave."[26]

Farm women comprised the largest part of the adult population in Texas until 1940 and in the American South until 1960. The analysis of rural women's daily, mundane lives reveals much about early-twentieth-century southern culture, for, as folklorist Fred Kniffen once observed, little can be understood about the human condition by studying only what is unique.[27] Farm women rarely led exciting lives, and very few became famous. Yet the study of them gives new insights into the twentieth-century South. To borrow from the poet and novelist Gwendolyn Brooks, rural women resembled the brilliant yellow flowers taken for granted every spring day: "Dandelions were what she chiefly saw. Yellow jewels for everyday, studding the patched green dress of her backyard. She liked their demure prettiness second to their everydayness; for in that latter quality she thought she saw a picture of herself, and it was comforting to find that what was common could also be a flower."[28]

acknowledgments

This kind of project brings about indebtedness to many, many people. I am happy to acknowledge those who assisted in this work. The librarians of Central Texas gave much to me and to this study. Thanks to the staffs of the A. Frank Smith Jr. Library Center at Southwestern University; the Nicholas P. Sims Memorial Library, Waxahachie; the Archives, Sterling C. Evans Library, Texas A&M University; the Still Photos Division of the National Archives; the Prints and Photographs Division of the Library of Congress; and the Center for American History at The University of Texas at Austin, especially Trudy Croes, Ralph Elder, and William Richter. I am deeply indebted to the staff of the Texas Collection at Baylor University: Ellen Kuniyuki Brown, Linda Claridy, Dorothy Copeland, Kathleen Hinton, Kent Keeth, Eric Morrow, Michael Toon, Richard Veit, and Christina Wright. Also in the Baylor University library system I am very grateful to all the good people in government documents and the interlibrary loan office, whose work in many ways made this study possible.

I owe a special thanks to the best folks in Commerce, Texas: James Conrad, archivist at the James Gee Library at Texas A&M University–Commerce, and Kyle Wilkison, superb historian of Texas agriculture. Jim has been an extraordinary help to me and to others in amassing and making accessible his archive of rural history. Kyle has my enduring gratitude for his insight, his remarkable generosity in sharing his research, and his treasured friendship.

Those who led me to my oral history interviewees helped me immeasurably: Mary Carroll Bridges, Emily Calvary, Robert A. Calvert, Margie Lopez Cintron, Robert and Evelyn Smajstrala Cunningham, Linda Fraga, George Harrison, Hazel Hight, Nan Holmes, Marguerite Hendrick Owen, Phil Sanchez, and Rufus B. Spain. I am especially thankful to those who patiently shared their time and their memories with me through our interviews, hour after hour: Adelaida Torres Almanza, Etta Carroll and Dovie Carroll, Alice Owens Caufield, Myrtle Calvert Dodd, Inez Folley, Luz Sanchez Hurtado, Cayetana Martinez Navarro, Inez Adams Walker, and Bernice Bostick Weir. Without their memories and their words, this study simply would never have been. Several of them have died since our times together, and the memory of them makes this work particularly poignant for me.

My debt remains large to my graduate committee at Emory University, who guided this study as a dissertation and whose interest has been unwavering: Dan T. Carter, Elizabeth Fox-Genovese, and especially Allen Tullos, who instigated the transition from dissertation to book. T. Lindsay Baker and Robert A. Calvert read the entire manuscript, while Jack Temple Kirby, Lauranett Lee, Robert McMath, Thad Sitton, and Nan Woodruff commented on various parts of it as conference papers. Rosalie Beck, Carol Holcomb, and Lois Myers gave valuable critiques, and I am most grateful to the anonymous reader for the University of North Carolina Press, whose insightful, thorough reading made the manuscript much stronger. At the UNC Press, Jack Kirby, David Perry, and Lewis Bateman kept the faith through the slow periods of revision, and Mary Caviness offered sharp-eyed editing and many kindnesses. I also want to pay homage to the three women whose work most heavily influenced my thinking: Margaret Jarman Hagood, whose tender yet unsentimental portrait of North Carolina farm women first inspired this study; Ruth Allen, whose insightful study of Central Texas lent much weight to my discussions; and Ellen Ross, with her splendid study of family and poverty in Victorian England.

Colleagues and friends at the Baylor University Institute for Oral History provide intellectual stimulation, companionship, and tolerance for me every day. I give thanks for Kathryn Blakeman, Hilary Gardner, Carol Holcomb, Jaclyn Jeffrey, Peggy Kinard, and Lois Myers. The University Research Committee at Baylor funded the Spanish-language interviews. Baylor undergraduate Lelis Idalia Nolasco excelled in translating at the sessions and then transcribing the interviews with Spanish-speaking women, while Nancy Gladen expertly edited the Spanish transcriptions. Also at Baylor, Vice Provost for Academic Affairs Dianna Vitanza provided both encouragement and released time to aid the completion of this project.

My friends and family have lived with this work for many years now. Theresa Furgeson McClellan, Carrie Caldwell Jiménez, and Carolyn Reed Devany have modeled for me the joys and trials of balancing motherhood and other activities. Suzanne Marshall, Ann Short Chirhart, and Zhao Jianli have remained constant while engaging in their own scholarly work. Phyllis and Bill Falco have personified the concept of neighbor. I have benefited beyond imagination from the love, interest, and faith of my family, especially my parents, Helen Frierson Sharpless and Garland Sharpless; my brother, Lester Sharpless; my nephew and niece, Joshua Ables and Jennifer Pitts; and my stepson, Richard Charlton. Finally, there is Tom Charlton, my husband. I will never find words to thank him enough for all that he is and all that he does, but I plan never to stop trying.

Fertile Ground, Narrow Choices

introduction

Women, Cotton,
and the Crop-Lien System

Kathryn Peacock Jones, known as Kate, grew up on a cotton farm that her father owned in Red River County, Texas. In her eighties, Jones wrote her memoirs of her childhood for her family. She recounted, from a distance of sixty years, the story of her sister Ruth's marriage in 1919: "Ruth married Roy Sartain on June 15, 1919. We were all hoeing cotton on Saturday morning, and at noon when we quit, six of us stood our hoes against a dead tree in the field. Ruth married the next evening on Sunday, and when we five went back to the field, Ruth wasn't there; I cried and I feel sure Jewel [her other sister] did too. When we went to the house for lunch, we cried again."[1]

Ruth Peacock Sartain's marriage illustrates one of the most important truths of life on the Blackland Prairie of Texas before World War II: The cotton crop did not stop for marriages, and it only occasionally paused for births and deaths. Women were wives and mothers, but many were agricultural laborers as well. The Peacocks followed their usual routine that weekend, like millions of families throughout the South, and returned to the fields on Monday less one daughter. Her sisters missed her keenly as they began their work, an activity in which they identified strongly with one another. A second, obverse truth also emerges: Like many of their peers, Ruth and Roy Sartain married at the height of chopping season, refusing to wait until the field work became less hectic. People went on with their lives in spite of the cotton crop. Despite the need for their labor in the fields, women also carried out such traditional female tasks as cooking, sewing, and child care.

Cotton growing relied heavily on women. While most historians have written of the relationship between men and cotton, women also had involvement with the staple crop that ruled the Lower South for more than a century—aptly nicknamed King Cotton for its despotism. Between the invention of the cotton gin in 1793 and World War II, the demands of the cotton crop shaped the lives of women, men, and children, black, white, and, later, Mexican. If a woman lived in the cotton belt that stretched from South Carolina to Texas, she knew its agriculture well. The seasons of work in the fields dictated the rhythms of all other aspects of life. And a family's success or failure in the cotton market determined the material well-being of the entire family, delimiting the re-sources that a woman had to perform her traditional tasks: housing, clothing, food, and time itself. Because cotton cultivation required the labor of entire families, furthermore, the great crops of the early twentieth century could not have been cultivated without women's active participation in agricultural labor and in caring for other family members who worked in the fields. Women depended on cotton agriculture, and cotton depended on women.

The relationship of southern women to cotton probably dates to its experi-mental cultivation in the early eighteenth century.[2] By the end of the eighteenth century, as cotton spread westward, slave women routinely performed field work in cotton, many doing tasks identical to men's and sometimes in greater quantities.[3] Although evidence is much sketchier, women in white yeomen farming families, too, probably worked with the antebellum cotton crop; Steph-anie McCurry has thoroughly documented the routine field work of women in the South Carolina Low Country. Southern society, however, disapproved of white women working in the fields. According to McCurry, "Women's work in the fields, although customary, was customarily ignored and even denied."[4]

Following the Civil War, freedwomen remained in the fields as they had in previous decades.[5] No study yet exists of the impact of the Civil War on the labor of white women. We may speculate, however, that with the increasing number of white men becoming tenant farmers and sharecroppers, the need for field labor by their wives and daughters became ever more intense. While the transition remains undocumented, we know that by the early twentieth century, the majority of white women in the cotton belt performed at least some field work, as did almost all African American women.

Spring plowing, Williamson County, March 1940 (Photo by Russell Lee, courtesy of the Library of Congress, LC USF-34-35683-D).

By 1900, when this study begins, women were an integral part of the cotton economy in at least three ways. They participated in the commercial economy by contributing literally incalculable amounts of direct agricultural labor— incalculable because most of the time their labor mingled with that of the rest of their family, and they seldom received separate payments. They created a domestic economy by sewing, cooking, taking care of gardens, and raising poultry and livestock. In so doing, they saved their families precious cash, sidestepped the usurious credit system, and enhanced their diets beyond the basic cornmeal and pork. Some also participated as petty-commodity producers, selling butter and eggs for cash. And finally, in bearing and rearing children, women reproduced not only the farms' primary labor force but also the people who would carry their family lines forward. Most adult women in the rural South performed a combination of all three activities, simultaneously serving as housewife, mother, and field worker.

This study documents the roles of women in cotton by examining one specific geographic area, the Texas Blackland Prairie, a funnel-shaped expanse of chocolate-colored clay that extends down the eastern third of Texas between the mixed pine forests of East Texas and the treeless expanses of the southern

Great Plains.[6] Opened to widespread cotton cultivation in the 1880s with the arrival of the breaking plow and the railroad, by 1900 the Texas Blackland Prairie occupied an important niche in American cotton farming. With its distinctive, extremely productive soil and a growing season of approximately 245 days, the Blackland Prairie was the site of intensive cotton cultivation from Reconstruction until World War II, producing as much as 6 percent of the United States' annual cotton crop in the early twentieth century.[7] The Blackland Prairie stands distinct from other parts of the South because it is more fertile, more arid, more ethnically diverse, and has a discrete economic history. Yet it was equally poor, racist, and sexist. The economic and social relations shaped by cotton cultivation in Texas strongly resembled others throughout the South, and women's lives shared much in all cotton growing areas.

In many ways, the women on southern cotton farms before 1940 resembled rural women in various other areas of the United States, as described by Joan Jensen, Deborah Fink, Glenda Riley, Nancy Grey Osterud, and other scholars.[8] Most farm women in the United States before World War II married, had children, and spent most of their time feeding and clothing their families and taking care of their homes. The division of labor on early-twentieth-century American farms varied widely, as women often actively participated in outside farm labor. Nationally, many American farm women, to use the phrase of Veronica Strong-Boag, "pulled in double harness," performing all of the house-related duties and also working in the fields.[9] Some received assistance with their housekeeping from the men in their families; to the women, however, belonged the longest hours of work and the most double tasks.[10] Farm women contrasted strongly with urban women, who were relegated to the role of nonproducing consumer as electrical appliances, processed foods, and other conveniences became available. Rural women remained highly productive, with eggs, butter, garden produce, preserved fruits and vegetables, clothing, cotton picking sacks, bed linens, and innumerable other tangible goods to show for their efforts. Rural women proved essential to their families' economic survival in ways that few middle-class urban women could match.[11]

Despite such nationwide similarities, southern rural women lived in a world distinct from those found in other farming sections of the United States. They differed from farm women in other parts of the nation primarily because of

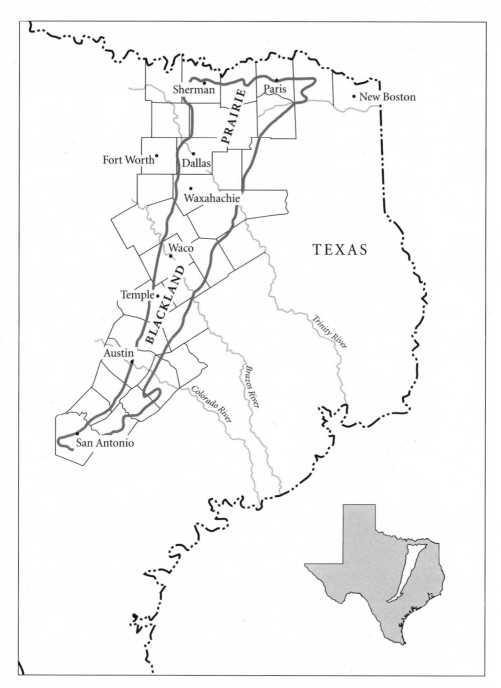

Major physical features of the Blackland Prairie of Texas

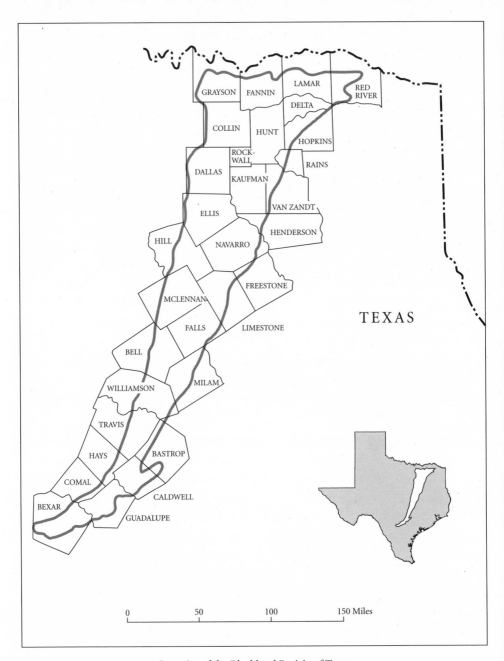

GRAYSON
FANNIN
LAMAR
RED RIVER
DELTA
COLLIN
HUNT
HOPKINS
ROCK-WALL
DALLAS
KAUFMAN
RAINS
VAN ZANDT
ELLIS
HENDERSON
HILL
NAVARRO
FREESTONE
MCLENNAN
FALLS
LIMESTONE
BELL
WILLIAMSON
MILAM
TRAVIS
HAYS
BASTROP
COMAL
CALDWELL
BEXAR
GUADALUPE

TEXAS

0   50   100   150 Miles

Counties of the Blackland Prairie of Texas

three factors: the South's poverty, its racial diversity and racism, and its tight constraints of gender. This study examines the gendered roles of women within one poor, racist society.

The economic deprivation of the South played a major role in the region's distinctiveness. Although other areas of the United States also witnessed tenant farming and sharecropping, the population of the rural South suffered most deeply from the effects of a system where the many farmed land owned by the few. Despite the fertility of the Blackland Prairie, many of its people lived in poverty as deep and in circumstances as meager as those described in the Deep South by James Agee and others.[12] Only a few rural people gained wealth from the land, and most of the truly prosperous lived in the region's numerous towns.

Farmers of the Blackland were thoroughly entangled in the crop-lien system. From Reconstruction until 1930, both the absolute numbers and percentage of tenants among all farmers in the Blacklands rose steadily. They increased 24.3 percent between 1880 and 1920, a rate almost twice as high as the average increase for the entire United States.[13] By 1920, almost three-quarters of all farms in the Blackland Prairie were operated by tenants.[14] Table 1 depicts the growth of tenancy between 1900 and 1930 and the decline brought by the New Deal between 1930 and 1940 in four selected Blackland Prairie counties.

What exactly did the crop-lien system mean for a farm family? First, it meant that the family gave up part of its crop in return for use of the farmland and sometimes a year's worth of supplies. In standard practice, a tenant farmer, who furnished his own tools and work stock, paid the landowner a third of the corn crop and a fourth of the cotton crop, giving rise to the phrase "farming on the thirds and fourths." A sharecropper, who furnished only his own labor and that of his family and depended on the landlord to supply everything from seed to mules, split the crop down the middle with the owner in an arrangement called "farming on the halves."[15]

Below the sharecroppers, occupying the lowest position in the tenure system, were the farm laborers, landless people who worked for minimal wages. Some worked only seasonally, while others performed odd jobs on the farms year-round. They had little autonomy, and wages were meager. A laborer in Ellis County reported that he worked for seventy-five cents or a dollar a day in 1913, along with his wife and five children, and ended the year $127 in debt.[16] Many African Americans and the great majority of Mexicans, most of whom were recent immigrants, fell into the farm-laborer category.[17]

TABLE 1. Number of Tenants and Landowners in
Four Blacklands Counties, 1900–1940

	1900	1910	1920	1930	1940
Ellis					
Owner	2,040	1,778	1,680	1,358	1,486
	(34.2%)	(30.7%)	(29.2%)	(22.4%)	(37.8%)
Tenant	3,918	4,005	4,086	4,682	2,435
	(65.7%)	(69.2%)	(70.8%)	(77.5%)	(62.1%)
Hunt					
Owner	2,458	1,926	1,941	1,652	1,679
	(41.4%)	(32.4%)	(38.0%)	(28.0%)	(37.7%)
Tenant	3,478	4,011	3,185	4,238	2,765
	(58.6%)	(67.5%)	(62.0%)	(72.0%)	(62.2%)
McLennan					
Owner	1,985	2,083	1,924	1,858	1,894
	(37.9%)	(35.9%)	(34.3%)	(28.1%)	(42.9%)
Tenant	3,253	3,781	3,750	4,752	2,518
	(62.1%)	(64.1%)	(65.7%)	(71.9%)	(57.0%)
Williamson					
Owner	1,761	1,828	1,853	1,452	1,556
	(40.0%)	(40.8%)	(40.4%)	(29.5%)	(39.4%)
Tenant	2,642	2,647	2,737	3,461	2,385
	(60.0%)	(59.2%)	(59.5%)	(70.4%)	(60.5%)

Sources: *Twelfth Census of the U.S.*, 1900; *Thirteenth Census of the U.S.*, 1910; *Fourteenth Census of the U.S.*, 1920; *Fifteenth Census of the U.S.*, 1930; *Sixteenth Census of the U.S.*, 1940.

The relationships between landowners and the people who farmed their land were complex and multifaceted, varying with circumstance and personality. Landowners had great latitude in deciding who would farm their land. In the Blackland Prairie, the birthrate remained higher than the rate of rural-to-urban migration until the Great Depression, and more people wanted land than could have it. An owner, therefore, could pick and choose, dismissing a tenant or sharecropper for little or no reason at all. Tenants and sharecroppers likewise had little to tie them to a given farm, and perhaps one of their greatest prerogatives was leaving the previous year's farms in December, looking for better places. Relationships could be dissolved from either direction: "The connection between landlord and tenant, as a rule, is transitory, neither party being willing to continue the connection if either finds the least objection to it."[18] A variety of circumstances might cause a family to move: the sale of the land, a cranky landowner, a disagreement between the landowner and tenant.[19] One 1930 study determined that two-thirds of the sharecroppers in Texas had occupied their farms for less than two years. Sharecroppers moved every 2.3 years and tenants every 3.5 years. The poorer the family, the more likely it was to move. As little as most share tenants owned, their few possessions kept them slightly more stable than croppers who had nothing.[20]

For many Blackland Prairie families, these biennial moves became a way of life. The migration of the Rice family in Hunt County provides a good example. Lee Rice was born in 1901 on a farm owned by T. C. Foster in the Liberty community, where his father farmed on thirds and fourths. In 1902, the growing family, which eventually included twelve children, moved to a farm between Liberty and "what is now Ardis Heights." These farms, according to Rice, varied in size from fifty to one hundred acres.[21] In 1903, Rice's maternal grandfather, Grandpa Chambliss, bought a 160-acre farm four miles southwest of Greenville, the county seat, and built an extra house for his daughter's family. The Rice family lived there three years, then shifted to Greenville for a year, where the father did street work for the city. In 1906, they went back to Grandpa Chambliss's farm. They remained there until 1909, then left and made one crop at "the Mansfield farm." Returning to Grandpa Chambliss's in 1910, Rice recalled, "Papa made one crop and Grandpa lost the farm. When he made payments on the farm he trusted the real estate man to give him credit for the payment. He never did ask for a receipt. Finally the payments became so large he couldn't pay them." Grandpa Chambliss moved to a farm one mile west of his old home, and his daughter's family took their possessions to Bethel, "100 yards East of the Bethel church." They made two crops there, 1911 and 1912, then moved to the Hayter farm, "200 yards West of the Bethel Church. We made one crop here, 1913. Then we moved back down East of the church. We made one more crop here, 1914. Then we moved from Bethel to six miles northeast of Greenville, on the Cassel farm halfway between Liberty and Jacobia." On the eighty-acre Cassel farm, the Rices finally came to rest, living there fifteen years.[22] Rice does not say why the family stopped moving. Perhaps enough of the children were reaching the size that a landlord would consider them valuable laborers. Maybe his father found a landlord with whom he could work in a satisfactory way. Or perhaps Rice's father simply gave up trying to find the better life that many tenants fruitlessly sought. Each of these

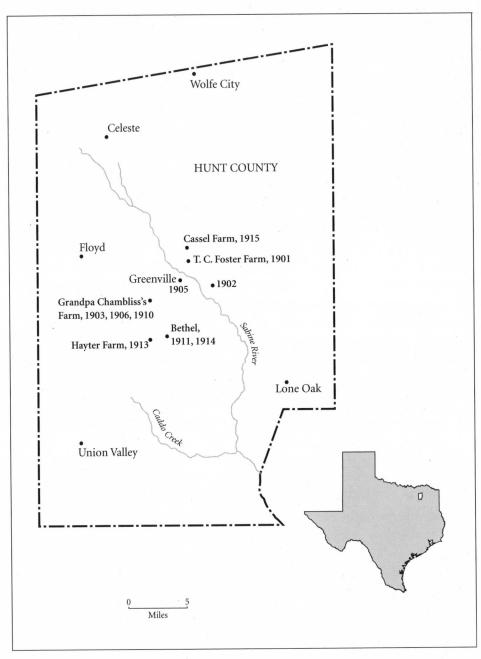

Moves of the Rice family, Hunt County, Texas

Introduction

moves challenged the wives and mothers, who found themselves adapting to changing circumstances and new environments, settling their husbands and children into different houses and different patterns of interactions.[23]

Credit formed the core of the crop-lien system. Farm families lived from harvest to harvest, most quickly spending the little cash that they received from their cotton crop and then borrowing money to tide them over until the next harvest. In some instances landlords "furnished" their tenants and sharecroppers with necessities such as food and feed, providing access to a furnishing merchant for other goods, and deducting the expenditures with interest from the tenants' cotton crops at the end of the year. In most areas, a general store extended credit to nearby farmers and provided farm families with groceries, clothing, hardware, and medicines. Smaller merchants handled dry goods and groceries as well. The cost of store credit was exorbitant, sometimes twice as much as prices for goods bought with cash.[24] The credit system was fraught with abuse, particularly on the part of landowners who cheated their tenants out of their rightful parts of the crops by manipulating accounts and charging usurious interest rates on advances.[25]

The inequalities of the crop-lien system led to a stratified society throughout the Blackland Prairie. A sample of 350 households from the Hunt County tax rolls reveal that in 1900 and 1910, 13 percent of county residents had no taxable property whatsoever. Conversely, in a sample of 250 households in 1910, the 4 wealthiest households (.01 percent) in the survey had greater combined wealth ($60,495) than the bottom 158 (63 percent) of the other county residents put together ($57,931).[26] Frank Locke, recalling his boyhood home at the turn of the twentieth century in southern McLennan County, clearly remembered the strata: the top, consisting of those who owned four to eight hundred acres of land, educated their children, and maintained their homes carefully; those next to the top, smaller landowners, who had adequate housing, whose children were required to work but went to school nonetheless; in the bottom half, tenant farmers, who owned their own teams and implements; and approaching the bottom, sharecroppers and farm laborers who were indebted to the landowners for years.[27]

Blacklands residents themselves seldom openly acknowledged class differences. In a 1920 survey of farmers' attitudes in Travis County, less than a third of the respondents—owners and tenants, white, black, and Mexican—replied that social inequality existed. Those few who acknowledged class differences blamed the uneven distribution of wealth and the tenant system for their division.[28] In Ellis County, researchers found a "tendency, slight, yet distinct, to discriminate socially between landowner and tenant." Some landowners denied the existence of any discrimination, declaring that their children would marry into tenant families, while others regretfully admitted the cleavage, and yet a third group of landowners accepted the differences "as a matter of course."[29]

The distinctions between the various types of farmers could be subtle or broad. Despite their loud protests to the contrary, landowners stood apart, theoretically independent of anyone else's will (but actually often dominated by their bankers, their cotton brokers, and the world cotton market), and their possession of the land that they worked or rented out definitively separated them from the other two-thirds of their neighbors. Even the most affluent tenants were not worth as much financially as the poorest landowners. Likewise, the most well-off sharecroppers were not worth as much as the poorest tenant farmers.[30] Disparities between tenants and sharecroppers, although perhaps not obvious to the casual observer, definitely existed.

The success of the cotton crop depended on numerous uncontrollable variables, including the weather and the world cotton market. Prices determined in faraway places such as New Orleans and London affected whether a woman could buy school shoes for her children in any given year. Young Kate Peacock Jones found out quickly just how the cotton market could have an impact on her life. She and her husband, Enos, hoped to use the proceeds of their cotton crop in 1920 to move out of his father's home and onto a farm of their own, an important step in building their own family life. During the boom time after World War I, Enos Jones sold three bales of cotton from his father's Red River County farm for forty cents a pound. Then prices plummeted. He held three bales until the next spring, hoping that the prices would rise. They did not, and Enos received little for his cotton. The young couple's dream of moving to a farm of their own was dashed by the market failure.[31]

In this world of poverty and limited choices, bound by the movement of their husbands and the fortunes of the cotton crop, women worked to carve out their lives as best they could. Every action that a woman took that kept them from the furnishing merchant defied the credit system. And every lock of cotton that she picked implicated her into compliance with the economic status quo.

The second factor that distinguished rural women of the South was the racism that pervaded their segregated society, dividing the females just as it did the males. Like poverty, racism existed elsewhere in the United States, but the legacy of slavery and the anger over Reconstruction created a milieu in which bias against African Americans was extremely strong. Southern black women lived in a world where racism circumscribed almost all of their movements. The ever-so-slight blurring of racial boundaries during Reconstruction had hardened quickly, and by the turn of the twentieth century, the limits of a segregated society were firmly in place in Central Texas. White women, too, were affected by racism, sure that no matter how poverty-stricken they might be, they still ranked above their black neighbors. In Texas, the dominant Anglo population also extended their prejudice against the German and Czechoslovakian immigrants who arrived in the late nineteenth and early twentieth centuries, and even more against the Mexican immigrants who came in increasing numbers throughout the early twentieth century. The common experiences of gender eased the situation for a few black and white women who developed relationships if not true friendships, but in the Blackland Prairie as in all of the South, segregation and mutual distrust were the rule rather than the exception among women of various ethnic groups.

Racist attitudes in Central Texas arrived with the earliest settlement by U.S. emigrants. For approximately ten thousand years, Native Americans occupied the prairie with only each other to be concerned with. By the early nineteenth century, most of the Native Americans in the Blacklands belonged to two groups: the Tonkawas and the Wichitas, which were a subgroup of the Caddo. From the west, the Comanches occasionally made their presence felt throughout the Blackland Prairie.[32] Although Spanish explorers claimed all of the area later known as Texas for the crown in the early sixteenth century, for most of their three-hundred-year dominion they expressed little interest in their territory north of the San Antonio River. Between 1745 and 1751, the Roman Catholic Church built three missions in present-day Milam County, but in 1758, after a series of difficulties, the Spanish retreated to San Antonio and ended their efforts to colonize northward for more than half a century.[33]

The first Euro-Americans to inhabit the prairies were yeoman farmers from the Upper South, who began arriving in parts of the Blackland in the 1820s.[34] Bringing white people's diverse ways to the region, they forced the Native Americans to the west, until the remnants of the Wichitas were removed to Oklahoma in 1859.[35] The Comanches, too, were removed to a reservation in Indian Territory in 1867.[36]

As they moved the Native American population out, white settlers brought approximately twenty-two thousand chattel slaves to the region with them between 1840 and 1861. By 1860, slaves comprised widely varying proportions of the population in Blacklands counties, from a low of 8.7 percent in Hunt County to a high of 39 percent in McLennan County, probably because of that county's Brazos River–bottom plantations.[37] An undetermined number of slaves, probably in the tens of thousands, also were brought to the region from the southeastern United States during the Civil War as their masters "refugeed" them, hoping to escape the war and keep their human possessions in bondage as long as possible. In several Blackland Prairie counties, the slave population more than doubled between 1860 and 1864. The prairie did not lend itself to large-scale plantation agriculture, however, because of transportation difficulties and the toughness of the native sod, and Blacklands slaves comprised only 12 percent of the state's total slave population, much of which concentrated in river-bottom plantations near the Gulf of Mexico.[38]

The fighting during the Civil War that decimated much of the Lower South left Texas almost unscathed, and the white population of the region increased dramatically in the years after the war. Emigration from the eastern United States to the Blackland Prairie surged as white southerners seeking to leave their war-ravaged homes came to Texas. Between 1861 and 1878, the population of Texas increased fivefold, and that in the northern Blacklands grew tenfold. Of the postwar immigrants to the northern part of the prairie, more than half came from Arkansas, Tennessee, Alabama, or Mississippi, with another 20 percent arriving from Missouri, Louisiana, or Kentucky.[39] All of the immigrants brought with them hopes, prejudices, and traditions that would shape the future of the Blackland Prairie.

Members of other ethnic groups also came to live on and work the dark clay. After the Civil War, more than twenty thousand freedpeople populated the Blacklands counties, primarily in the bottomlands. Following emancipation in June 1865, most of the freedpeople stayed nearby, working as farm laborers. As the prairies opened, some African Americans sought their fortunes on the grasslands, and by 1920, African Americans made up between 10 and 22 percent of the population of various Blacklands counties.[40] As the reputation of the Blackland Prairie's fertile soils spread, other non-Anglo groups began to contemplate life on its expanses. German and Czechoslovakian (mostly Moravian) immigrants started arriving in the Blacklands as early as 1876, lured by Texas steamship and railroad agents.[41] Once families became established, many wrote back to Europe, describing Texas in positive terms, and other relatives followed and began farming nearby.[42] The Germans and Czechs often settled together, frequently sharing a single Roman Catholic church among the Protestant Anglos.[43] The immigration persisted until 1914, when World War I closed American borders and postwar immigration quotas made sure that they stayed closed.

The last major ethnic group to settle in the Blackland Prairie came from Mexico. Before 1910, Mexicans emigrated to Texas in small groups or as individuals, laboring primarily as migratory agricultural workers in the land that they called "la Tierra Negra."[44] The Mexican Revolution of 1910 spurred emigration, and Mexican citizens began arriving in Texas not as seasonal workers but as permanent residents.[45]

Mexican immigrants moved slowly up from the Rio Grande and in 1920 made up 4.1 percent of the permanent population of Williamson County in the southern Blacklands, 1.8 percent of McLennan County and 1.3 percent of Ellis County in the central part of the region, and only 0.5 percent of Hunt County, near the Oklahoma border.[46] The immigration continued steadily throughout the 1920s, unaffected by the laws that had stifled movements from Eastern Europe. Often denied work as tenant farmers or even sharecroppers, many Mexicans suffered from deprivation as bad as that which affected African Americans.[47]

Within this world of cotton and the crop-lien system, separated from one another by racial tensions, lived millions of Texas women. Like women throughout history, women in Central Texas lived "contingent lives."[48] The dictates of the cotton economy constrained their lives, its labor demands shaping the rhythms of work each year. That economy in turn was shaped by the quirks of the world textile market and the vagaries of the weather. To a significant extent, women's personal choices in life were also limited by many factors: by legal limitations that kept them as inferior citizens, by societal expectations that dictated that they marry at an early age, by lack of birth control that ensured repeated cycles of pregnancy and childbirth.

Farm women in Central Texas contested or acquiesced to their limitations for a variety of reasons, with innumerable means. Within circumstances far beyond their control, they shaped their own lives and those of their families in powerful ways.[49] The family, the locus of almost all women's lives, serves as the beginning point for investigating rural women's lives and their impact on the twentieth-century South.

chapter *one*

Women, Daughters, Wives, Mothers

Gender and Family Relationships

"To be a [southern] woman has meant, for most, to be a woman among their people," says Elizabeth Fox-Genovese.[1] Like their counterparts elsewhere in the South, many farm women in Central Texas before World War II lived their entire lives among a network of kin, heavily influenced by the other women in their families. Most began life as daughters of farm people, taught by female relatives to carry out their duties. They married, often while they were still in their teens, and began having babies within a year of their marriage. By the time that a farm woman reached her thirtieth birthday, she might have five or six children, and she might continue pregnancy and childbirth for another fifteen years. As old age and widowhood approached, a woman might begin to speculate about who would watch over her in her last years, hopeful that her children and grandchildren would care for her as she had cared for them. Within the sweeping cycles of birth, life, and death, a woman knew that her life was shaped by her sex and defined by her connections as a daughter, wife, and mother. Her experience contrasted greatly with those of her husband and sons even as their choices had great impact on her life. This chapter examines the experiences of women enmeshed within their families.

When a woman in the Blackland Prairie married, she was following the cultural expectations of rural southern society. Census data for the region show that the women's average age at first marriage was nineteen. In rare cases, a girl

TABLE 2. Average Age of Farmers' Wives at First Marriage in Four
Blacklands Counties, by Ethnic Group, 1900 and 1910

| | 1900 | | |
	White	Black	White and Black, Combined
Ellis	19.38	18.88	19.21
Hunt	19.98	19.32	19.76
McLennan	19.51	18.66	19.22
Williamson	19.01	18.58	18.86
	1910		
	White	Black	White and Black, Combined
Ellis	19.15	18.96	19.08
Hunt	19.03	18.70	18.92
McLennan	19.33	18.64	19.10
Williamson	19.48	18.58	19.18

Sources: *Twelfth Census of the U.S.*, 1900; *Thirteenth Census of the U.S.*, 1910.
Note: N=100 white women and 50 black women for each county.

might marry as young as ten or eleven, or a woman might delay marriage until
her midthirties. Black women tended to marry slightly younger than white
women, by about six months. The mean for both groups, however, was in the
late teens. Table 2 illustrates the average age of marriage for farm women in
four Blackland Prairie counties.

Girls of all ethnic groups were brought up with the expectation that they
would marry. Mary Hanak Simcik recalled "baptism clothes, and go-to-
communion, and brides and grooms and all that stuff" as a Czech Roman
Catholic child making doll clothes.[2] In the African American community near
Robinson, McLennan County, Alice Owens Caufield remembered the hope
chest of her aunt Emma Owens Mayfield, whom Alice and her sister Peaches
"idolized": "I can remember Aunt Emma's hope chest with all them beautiful
gowns. Like it was embroidered with the ribbon running. And she always had
the neatest things. Aunt Emma was neat and everything had to be just right."[3]
Despite her parents' and brother's status as sharecroppers, Emma Owens gathered pretty clothes in preparation for her marriage, and her young nieces
watched with intense interest.

Popular amusements reflected the expectation of marriage. Among Anglos
in the early twentieth century, one of the most widespread activities for young
people was an event known as a play-party, in which participants played so-

Gender and Family Relationships

called ring games, singing and clapping a rhythm while moving about the room.[4] Many different versions of the ring game existed, and most of them involved the pairing off of young couples.

In his autobiography, folklorist William Owens carefully described the ring games in which he participated while teaching school near Honey Grove, Texas, in the early 1920s. Owens recorded the words to the song and motions to the dance of a ring game called "Going to Boston," in which a very young couple publicly declared their sentiments about each other:

Come on, boys, let's go to Boston,
Come on, boys, let's go to Boston,
Come on, boys, let's go to Boston,
To see this couple marry.

We formed two lines, the boys facing the girls. The head couple, the girl from the eighth grade, the boy from the ninth, promenaded down the back between the lines while we sang:

Ha-ha, Arthur, I'll tell your papa,
Ha-ha, Arthur, I'll tell your papa,
Ha-ha, Arthur, I'll tell your papa,
That you're going to marry.

It was Arthur Halliburton, with a flush in his face, a laugh on his lips, a tenderness in his hand for the girl at his side. He left her at the head of the line and led the boys around the girls. Then it was Jennie Linn's turn to promenade with him, as we sang:

Ha-ha, Jennie Linn, I'll tell your mama . . .

She let us know by the pride in her step, the flash in her eye, that she cared only for Arthur. She led the line of girls around the boys and, when she came back to Arthur, they grasped hands and he guided her to the foot of the line, where they stood hand in hand while we sang:

Now they're married and living in Boston,
Now they're married and living in Boston,
Now they're married and living in Boston,
Living on chicken pie.

They had paired off. They were glad for the others to see they had paired off.[5]

Despite their young ages, Arthur and Jennie Linn were beginning a courtship under the careful scrutiny of their peers. The projected "marriage" involved moving away from the farm. "Boston" could be Boston, Texas, a small community not far from Texarkana, or the large northeastern city, where, undoubtedly, none of the singers had ever been. Although the song indicates some parental disapproval ("I'll tell your papa"), the "marriage" apparently becomes a satisfactory, if not luxurious, situation. The young couple lives on chicken pie, a typical Sunday southern meal.

Marriage was the expected outcome for both of these near-children. Folklorist Owens moved to Dallas at the end of the school year, so we do not learn of the result of the courtship. But many young people married while still in their teens. Another popular Texas ring game, "Weevilly Wheat," featured the lyrics to the well-known American folk song "My Pretty Little Miss." "My Pretty Little Miss" declares that she will go crazy if she doesn't find a young man by her sixteenth birthday, upcoming the next Sunday.[6]

With marriage as the norm, rural Texans viewed being an "old maid" as a highly undesirable fate, and community amusements reflected this distaste. William Owens recorded a song called "The Old Maid," which he classified as a humorous work. The song was known throughout Texas, and it classified an old maid's objections to all of her possible suitors:

> I would not marry a man that was tall
> For he'd go bumping against the wall;
> I'll not marry at all, at all,
> I'll not marry at all.

> Chorus: I'll take my stool and sit in the shade
> I'm determined to live an old maid.
> I'll not marry at all, at all,
> I'll not marry at all.

> I would not marry a man that preaches
> For he'd have holes in the knee of his britches;
> I'll not marry at all, at all,
> I'll not marry at all. (Chorus)

> I would not marry a man that was small,
> For he'd be the same as no man at all;
> I'll not marry at all, at all,
> I'll not marry at all. (Chorus)

> I would not marry a man that was rich,
> For he'd get drunk and fall in the ditch;

> I'll not marry at all, at all,
> I'll not marry at all. (Chorus)

The song could have an infinite number of verses, with local variations in names and situations. It declares the peculiarity of a woman who chooses not to marry, especially with her superficial reasoning and scorn for virtually all types of men. The willingness to "sit in the shade," out of the sunlight of a nuclear family, marked the old maid's withdrawal from the mainstream of society. The classification of this song as humorous demonstrates just how ridiculous people of the Blacklands found the option not to marry.[7]

Emma Guest Bourne remembered a school program from her childhood in the 1890s in the Detroit community, Red River County, called "The Old Maid's Convention." The program served as a warning to the young girls taking part in it: "There were about twenty of us girls dressed like the old maids of many years ago. We were bemoaning the fact that we were old maids and there seemed no chance for our ever capturing a husband." The "old maids" were approached by a man who introduced himself as "Mr. Makeover," explaining that "he had a machine that would turn us old maids into pretty young girls." One by one, the old maids entered a "large box-like contraption with a handle which he could turn at will." When the first old maid emerged from the box, she had become a "changed being, dressed in a beautiful long flowing costume of soft, pale, blue, material, followed by the others in succession dressed like the first." Professor Makeover then played a march on his machine and the young girls showed their appreciation "by marching in circles around him singing joyful songs."[8] Bourne's guileless recollection of "The Old Maid's Convention" many years later indicates that the community apparently recognized easily the stereotypical character of the ugly old maid. The people of Detroit received unquestioningly, under the auspices of an educational institution, a performance in which a single male character could turn a handle "at will," save an entire group of young women from the awful fate of being unmarried, and then get them to march to a tune of his own playing.

Most young people, then, entered their teens expecting to find their life mates within a few years, and courting rituals enabled them to mingle with possible partners. Young Anglo-Americans met at group activities such as community singings or play-parties, carefully chaperoned by older family members and neighbors. As historian Nancy Grey Osterud has pointed out, meeting in community settings provided young couples with chances to get to know one another without appearing too obvious.[9] Lucille Mora Perkins and her future husband, Louis John Perkins, "the catch of the community," courted through community activities in 1916 and 1917:

> On Sunday evenings, we had singing. . . . Every Sunday, we'd go to a differ-ent home, in the evening from possibly, say, seven o'clock on to about nine o'clock or ten o'clock, depending. Then we didn't have cars. We had buggies and horses. So I had met Louis at the church that day and, of course, he wanted to know if we could go to a singing that night. I said, "By all means. Sure. We'll go singing." So here he comes with his buggy and horse. That buggy was shined up. It was just sparkling. . . . So really, that evening, then about 6:30, 6:45, we went to the singing. We had a piano, organ, wherever we were going. . . . Of course, there is where I met so many of the people, you see. So from then on it was almost a regular thing.[10]

After the group activities, buggy rides provided a place of privacy for a couple that rarely existed in parents' small houses with many siblings or in a home where the teacher boarded. According to Frank Locke, strict rules governed the buggy rides; the couple had to be going somewhere, with a "specified and approved destination." In some locales, couples could ride together for plea-sure on Sundays only.[11]

Bernice Porter Bostick Weir met her first husband, Pat Bostick, at a party in 1916, but their courtship was altered by a new invention, the automobile:

> Well, my uncle that lived down here in the Liberty Hill community—he had the girl that's my age—and I'd come up here and they had lots of parties up here at night where the whole family would go, the mother and the daddy. Well, I'd come up to Uncle Bruce's, and he'd hitch up to the wagon and we'd all go wherever the party was. Everybody else was that way. And so I met Pat at a party. But the first time I ever went with him, I didn't have a date. He had Grandma's car, a little Ford. And we's up here at church. And he and Lilburn Newman, which was a neighbor there—they were real close and went with different girls together—Lilburn never had any way to go and Pat did, you see. And so Pat was with Sadie and I was supposed to go with Lilburn. And when we went to get in the car, Pat grabbed me and put me on the back seat and Lilburn and Pat's girlfriend had to get on the front seat. And that was our first date together.

Gender and Family Relationships

As the owner of the car, Pat Bostick pressed his material advantage to persuade his male friend to switch dates with him: "He told Lilburn he could drive. Lilburn loved that because he didn't have a car to drive at home." He used his physical advantage to "grab" young Bernice and place her where he wanted her. Pat Bostick may also have employed the age difference to persuade his future bride to join him; she was barely sixteen, and Pat was twenty-four: "I considered him a man and I was just a little girl."[12]

Several studies have shown that the rules of courtship changed with the coming of the automobile. As a young woman wrote to a male companion in 1923, "You can be so nice and all alone in a machine, just a little one that you can go on crazy roads in and be miles away from anyone but each other."[13] In the Blackland Prairie, parents tried to counteract the effects of the car by retaining an amount of control over the young, unmarried adults' activities: "You's supposed to come in at a certain time, of course, which we always did, it seemed to me like," Myrtle Dodd said. "We'd always talk to Mama about where we's going and where we expected to get back to. And when we started going to Waco to the show, that's pretty bad if you—they probably set up and worried till you got back."[14]

Young Roman Catholic men of Czech descent used a ritual method of showing their approval of chosen young women. A series of washing ceremonies took place around Easter, indicating the beginning of courtships. On the day after Easter, Mary Simcik recalled, "the young men would go and wash the eligible girls' faces. If you were lucky he would come early Monday morning while you were still in bed and wash your face." This action would "show that they were stuck on the girl, to show his affection."[15] In some areas, the young men washed the women's faces on Easter morning, and the young women in turn washed the men's faces on the day after Easter.[16] Around the community of West, a cleansing ritual in a young woman's bedroom, at a traditional time of annual spiritual rebirth, marked the start of a new relationship.

Guarding women's morality was a major concern of rural Blacklands residents, as it was throughout the South, and premarital sex for women was ostensibly forbidden. Parents especially retained strong ideas about how their daughters should dress.[17] At the turn of the century, girls wore knee-length dresses until they were nine or ten. After age ten, they covered their knees and wore floor-length dresses with several underskirts.[18] More modern styles, however, revealed more of the female form, much to the dismay of parents trying to rear their daughters correctly. Myrtle Calvert Dodd's teacher designed a dress for a school program that raised the concern of parents. About 1917 Dodd was in the seventh grade, just entering puberty, when her class was assigned to perform a Maypole dance. She said, "I'll never forget. Mother made a dress and didn't want us to wear it. It was made of crinoline. And it had ruffles. And my father said it's just not enough for us to wear. He didn't want us to wear them, either. And it had straps, you know, on the shoulder. And they's blue and green; Lillian's [her sister] was green and mine was blue. And we had to go to school to get the material; the teacher bought it. They thought it was too skimpy, you know." But youth prevailed, and the Calvert sisters danced the Maypole with bloomers dyed to match their blue and green outfits. Their father had spent his limited money and their mother her valuable time sewing dresses to please the teacher despite their own misgivings.[19]

In many households, the morality of dress extended to footwear and the importance of keeping one's feet covered. Alice Owens Caufield remembered her grandmother's warnings about the necessity of wearing shoes: "I thought that those who were barefooted was just careless. Grandmother taught us a certain morals. If you wore shoes—like folks would wear a shoe and it's clicking on the back of your foot every time you pick up your foot like these strapless shoes we wear now. And she said decent women didn't let shoes flap on their feet. You had to be very careful about your neatness and cleanliness."[20] Troy Crenshaw echoed Caufield's grandmother's teaching: "After puberty, girls, and even many boys, hesitated to expose bare feet outside the family."[21] The taboo of bare feet had class overtones, for the most impoverished families had difficulty obtaining shoes. "Decent" people, however, would find the means to keep their women's feet covered.

Women bore the burden of maintaining morality, and "nice" girls did not engage in sexual relations outside of marriage. Sexually active, unmarried females brought great scorn to their families. Frank Locke observed bluntly: "The double standard was much in evidence."[22] Troy Crenshaw vividly wrote of the moral imperatives that laid the blame for illicit sexual activity squarely at the feet of the women. His mother preached to her young sons, citing "the trashy Rape family across the creek," which lived close geographically but far beyond the pale of acceptability. The oldest Rape daughter first showed her "loose character" by driving by the Crenshaw household early one morning in a state of obvious intoxication with a "middle-aged rake." Their Hunt

County community was horrified when her younger sister "brought on the ruin of Ned," the oldest son of a farmer up the road. According to Mrs. Crenshaw's interpretation, Ned lost his moral bearing when his mother died and "his poor father could not cope with a house full of motherless children." In the eyes of the community, the second Rape daughter seduced Ned, became pregnant, and coerced him into eloping with her.[23] To Miss Rape alone went the blame for the relationship and marriage; poor motherless Ned was helpless in the face of such feminine wiles. Mrs. Crenshaw used the Rape girls as a cautionary tale to warn her young sons away from such women and also cemented her role as moral arbiter for her family; she would help them avoid Ned's fate.

While mothers could be fairly explicit in talking with sons, they faced the difficult task of safeguarding their daughters' moral reputations without revealing any details about sex or reproduction. They did so with cryptic warnings, as Mary Hanak Simcik commented: "And there was one thing Mama never told me anything about—sex—ever. She never talked about anything like that to me. The only thing she told me, 'Don't ever take a ride with anybody you don't know. . . .' We used not to be afraid of strangers; but still, I was warned."[24] Fathers guarded their daughters in a more direct way. Frank Locke remembered that "the most universal code" of behavior for men concerned their wives and daughters: " 'Don't bother my women-folk.' It didn't happen very often, but if a farmer's home was 'broken up' or his daughter 'ruined,' he got his shotgun and went looking for the guilty man."[25]

Despite the community mores, sexual crimes did occur. In Hunt County in 1906, for example, a man who was reputed to be a traveling minister tried to rape the daughter of his host's neighbors.[26] Many times, ostensible concern for the sanctity of their property and their women became the excuse for mob violence as Texas men engaged in the all-too-common practice of lynching. More than one hundred lynchings occurred in Texas between 1900 and 1910 alone, most of them in the eastern third of the state.[27] Throughout the Blackland Prairie, as elsewhere in the South, the majority of lynch victims were African Americans, often paying the supreme price simply because of the color of their skin or the alleged misdeeds of a relative. One of the most horrific incidents, which produced nationwide attention, was the 1916 stabbing and burning of seventeen-year-old Jesse Washington, an illiterate African American farmhand accused of murdering his employer's wife in Robinson, McLennan County. A crowd of more than ten thousand people watched the lynching on the lawn of the city hall in Waco, the county seat.[28] In lynchings, racism and sexism combined into deadly conflagrations.

Young couples often moved into marriage without a great deal of planning or forethought. With short courtships, they were apparently ready to marry and were looking for suitable mates. "Those were the days the boys didn't see so much of the girls before getting married," R. W. Williams of Hunt County commented. "A date every other Sun. seemed about sufficient."[29] Etta and Dovie Carroll were seventeen and eighteen, respectively, when they married in 1921. They had met through a mutual friend when Etta was down from Oklahoma, visiting her grandmother in Waxahachie, the county seat of Ellis County. She recalled, "I went back home. Then I got a letter from Dovie, and we kept corresponding and we married then March 15, 1921." Dovie Carroll remarked, "So we just got to writing and well, when she was here, I'd go to see her." "We wrote to one another, and then he asked me to marry him," Etta Carroll continued, "so I come down here and we married." Bride and groom knew little about each other's backgrounds; Etta Carroll commented, "When I was down here visiting my grandmother, why, I met some of his folks then. But other than that, I didn't even know where he lived, you might as well say."[30]

In many cases, a young Anglo woman married outside of her immediate circle of acquaintances, choosing a mate from a surrounding community but not from her own community. Few married childhood sweethearts, preferring young men whom they met in their teens. For young women from tenant farms, their families' mobility almost ensured that they would not be near acquaintances from childhood. For landowners' daughters, who might live nearer to relatives, marrying out of the community served as a form of exogamy, extending the network of kin into farther reaches of the county. Emma Bourne recalled: "Ours had been a small world. . . . We knew that Greenville was up that way somewhere too, for that is where father found mother and where our kinfolks lived and often came to see us."[31] Bourne's family, its scope limited to northeast Texas, expanded from Lamar County into Hunt County through marriage. African American, Mexican, and Czech young people had fewer choices for mates, expected as they were to marry within their own ethnic group. Interracial marriages were illegal between African Americans and Anglos, and almost nonexistent between Mexicans and Anglos or Mexicans and African Americans. In southern Travis County after World War I, an

"American" woman who married a Mexican man was completely excluded by her community.[32]

Mexican men sometimes returned to their native land to find wives and bring them to the United States. Adelaida Torres Almanza was a native of San Luis Potisí, Mexico. She met her future husband, who had migrated to McLennan County from Mexico to find work, when he returned to Mexico to visit relatives in 1925. Juan Almanza made it clear from the outset that his bride would come with him to Central Texas. Seventy years later, she recalled, "I felt bad because of the people that had to stay, but at the same time I loved him and I knew that I had to come here. He let me know from the beginning that he wasn't from there and that he had to come back to live here."[33]

Inez Adams Walker, an African American, met her husband when he became a tenant on the farm where her family already lived: "We was on a farm, on the same farm, and he lived in the back on that farm and I lived up close to the road. He used to come by there and pass me and we finally got acquainted with each other. He was staying with—his mother married a man back behind there and he'd travel through our yard all the time." Despite the daily contact, the young couple had to make a formal acquaintance. W. T. Walker finally wangled an invitation to call through a male friend who was courting Inez's older sister, and the two married a year later.[34]

Eddie Stimpson recalled that racial segregation affected courtship practices in Collin County in the 1920s: "The boys and girls was very much acquainted because they all lived nabor to each other. They got to see each other whin they walk those three to seven mile to school together." The long walk to the African American school afforded ample time to observe a potential mate. Work patterns, too, could give young people a chance to see each other: "The courting some time would get plenty serious in the cotton patch or corn patch. Once the boys and girls could figger out how to get away from there parent, they would say, Dad or Mom, I'm going to the other end and chop or pick my way back."

Stimpson's own parents met in the cotton patch in 1927. His father was a man of nineteen, a sharecropper in his own right since the age of twelve. His mother was barely thirteen, not the oldest but the largest of four sisters. Stimpson asked his mother why she had married his father. She replied,

My and his famley were picking cotton and Eddie, your father, came through the cotton field one day. He seen me and talk to me and the others. And he was a good look man. He told me he was going to marrie me. He went and ask my father and mother for me and we got married. . . . It had been very hot in the cotton field, dragging that sack, and this man came by and I no him because we were all nabors. I was a little shy but I think I was glad. And whin he told me he was going to marrie me, it did both scare me and kinder made me feel good. First thing I thought about, I would be able to leave home like all girl wish. And I would be able to get out of the cotton patch. Well, I was able to leave home, but I never got out of the cotton patch.

Stimpson's grandfather gave his blessing to the marriage of his young daughter for economic reasons: "Times were hard. There were no money and mom father was glad to get rid of a girl especially to some one who had a job and was a worker."[35]

Most marriages were based on romantic love or something resembling it, and young people generally chose mates independently of their families. Desire to possess Blacklands farms led some people to extreme measures, however. In eastern Johnson County, barely touched by the Blacklands, members of the Stricklin family still recall the story of their Grandmother Benton, who, around the time of World War I, forced her daughter Bertie to break up with her fiancé whose family owned a sandy-land farm. Her only objection to the young man apparently was the type of ground his family occupied. Grandma Benton insisted instead that young Bertie marry a Blacklands farmer whom she did not love.[36] The Benton family raised their social status by affiliation with Blacklands owners at the cost of the dreams of their daughter.

In the Blackland Prairie, as elsewhere, the course of love sometimes encountered problems. In Hunt County, it was common practice for a boy to "fool" a girl in the community, as R. W. Williams recalled: "This meant that the boy would be engaged to the girl and many times when time arrived for the wedding the boy just simply failed to appear. Other times he would carry her along in her belief that they were going to be married and then tell her just a few days before the time that he was only fooling." Williams did not give the motivation for "fooling," but perhaps cold feet were the most forgivable of reasons. He did express a great distaste for such "deceptions" as old ways that were best left behind.[37]

The popular Texas folk song "Bury Me Beneath the Willow" depicts the heartbreak caused by an untrue lover. According to folklorist William Owens, the song was well-known throughout Texas and was usually sung in harmony by two women, a soprano and an alto. The lyrics depict a young woman mourning herself to death over her broken engagement:

Tomorrow is our wedding day,
God only knows where he may be;
He's gone to seek another bride,
And now he care no more for me.

Chorus: Oh, bury me beneath the willow,
Beneath the weeping willow tree,
And when he knows where I lie sleeping
Perhaps he will then think of me.

My heart is broken, I'm in sorrow,
Weeping for the one I love,
For I know I ne'er shall see him
Till we meet in heaven above. (Chorus)

The willow is the traditional symbol of sorrow. Apparently the sad tale of the jilted young woman resonated among the young women who sang the song, accounting for the song's widespread popularity.[38]

Kate Peacock feared the worst when she was planning her marriage to Enos Jones at the justice of the peace's office in Red River County in the early 1920s. She kept the wedding arrangements a secret because a friend of hers had been left at the altar, and "I just couldn't see any use in telling it until we were actually married."[39] Enos, like most grooms, did appear, and the wedding went through successfully. But grooms deserted their prospective brides often enough to create doubt in young women's minds.

A few weddings that occurred among Anglo couples in the Blacklands were elaborate, centered around large dinners. The typical event, however, was a very small affair, marked perhaps by a new dress for the bride and a ceremony involving only the wedding couple and a few friends.[40] Small weddings reflected the seriousness of purpose that pervaded farm life, with little time to play, and the limited financial resources for entertaining. Dovie Carroll remembered his marriage to Etta Hardy in 1921: "Well, it happened all at oncest. In other words, I met her at the train that evening, late that evening, me and my brother-in-law, and we went to the courthouse and got the license and then went on College Street there to the Methodist church." They spent their wedding night at his father's house, seven miles south of Waxahachie, where the wedding had taken place.[41]

The occasion of Bernice Weir's marriage to Pat Bostick was made memorable primarily by the weather:

It was the second of February, and it had rained all that winter. We didn't have even gravel roads then, and it was slushy, slushy. And he and a neighbor boy borrowed his brother's Hupmobile, and it had running boards to it, and all the way to Temple that mud and slush was hitting up underneath the running boards. And we left home right after—I guess close to one o'clock, and we were married at 2:30 at the parsonage—First Christian Church parsonage in Temple. . . . We came on back down to my family's and they had a little cake and coffee and stuff like that.[42]

Czech weddings, in contrast, throughout the first half of the century were almost always intricate, all-day affairs, with church ceremonies, dinners, and dances—much to the chagrin of the Prohibitionist, nondancing Baptist and Methodist Anglos around them. Czech Texans prized their community celebrations, which included virtually all like-minded inhabitants of the area; since Czechs tended to marry only other Czechs, both families would be involved in staging the party. Communal celebrations allowed people to strengthen their bonds with one another as well as to forget their cares with dancing, food, and liquor. In Czech communities such as Tours, in McLennan County, relatives of the bride and groom began cooking two or three days in advance, starting with pies and cakes the first day, noodles and bread on the second, and the more perishable dishes on the last. On the Saturday before the wedding, two men, "the groom's men," washed and decorated the "nicest buggy available" and went from house to house in the community, extending invitations to the wedding. Each invited house gave them a drink of beer or whiskey, and the men had "more than enough" before the task was done. If a community lacked a dance hall, the bride and groom bought from a lumberyard enough wooden boards to lay out on the ground, usually outside the bride's home, as a platform for eating and dancing.

The wedding mass took place early in the morning, and from Tours bridal parties often went to the nearby town of West to have their photographs taken. Many of these photographs survive, revealing formally dressed, somber-faced young people. Before World War I, perhaps half of the brides in the Tours area of McLennan County continued the European tradition of wearing dark dresses. By about 1915, however, virtually all of the brides had shifted their preferences to American-style white or pastel-colored wedding dresses, even shortening the skirts as current American fashions dictated. The grooms' attire remained largely the same throughout the decades; the young men appeared in dark suits and white shirts with high, stiff collars.[43]

Dinner followed at noon for the immediate family and special guests, with large quantities of chicken soup, two kinds of meat, vegetables, and bread. Few families owned enough plates and flatware to accommodate such a crowd, so guests ate in shifts and the women who were helping serve washed the tableware between each group. The wedding couple and their guests spent the afternoon visiting and in the early evening spread the leftovers from the noon feast. The dance at the bride's home or a community dance hall, led by local musicians, began soon thereafter. The partygoers danced the lively polka throughout the evening, accompanied by accordion music. At midnight, a ceremony often took place for removing the bridal veil, accompanied by the song "Uz mou milou" ("Now My Dear One") or "Svobodo, Svobodo" ("Freedom, Freedom").[44]

The lyrics to "Uz mou milou," a duet sung by a male and a female portraying the groom and bride, delineate gender roles in the Czech community:

> "To the church door now they lead my dear one;
> This time, O maiden dearest, this time thou art mine."
> "No, not quite yet, my most beloved;
> I am mother's still, not thine."
>
> "To the altar now they lead my dear one;
> This time, O maiden dearest, this time thou art mine."
> "No, not quite yet, my most beloved;
> I am mother's still, not thine."
>
> "From the altar now I lead my dear one;
> This time, O maiden dearest, this time thou art mine."
> "Now I am thine, my most beloved;
> Not my mother's now, but thine."[45]

"Uz mou milou" depicts a passive bride being led to the church and the altar by an impersonal "they." The groom is eager to possess his virgin ("maiden") bride, as he has apparently been unable to in the past: "This time thou art mine." The bride apparently comes to the altar willingly, addressing the groom as "my most beloved." But she clings to the vestiges of her girlhood throughout the wedding service, claiming her status as her mother's property. Not until the wedding service is concluded does the bride transfer her allegiance from her mother to her new husband, who then leads her away. The fact that the mother, not the father, "possesses" the bride may indicate the relatively strong position of married Czech women in Texas. But the young bride herself is virtually powerless, shifting from her mother's rule to that of her new husband.[46]

In the African American community in Collin County, weddings were simple affairs held after church. Eddie Stimpson recalled that the wedding of his aunt Senie in the early 1930s took place on a Sunday morning right after church service: "The announcement was made that there's a wedding on this morning. My aunt and my uncle were to walk down the isle together. . . . After the preacher, Sister Riddle, finish, the bride and groom walk back down the isle together out the door. There were people line up outside and some type of seeds were thrown at the cuple. . . . The cuple drove to her husband famley home as was usual with newly weds."[47]

Once the wedding celebrations were over, the serious work of making a marriage began. In the early part of the century, some communities observed the postnuptial traditions of the pounding and the shivaree. For a pounding, neighbors and family brought food to help the newlyweds set up housekeeping. (The name "pounding" came from the practice of bringing gifts of staple foods—flour, sugar, and so on—by the pound weight.) At a shivaree, friends of the couple surrounded the home where they were spending their wedding night, awakening them with shouts and playing loud music until the couple invited everyone inside for refreshments. Frank Locke remembered that in McLennan County the shivarees were "frequently unappreciated, often resisted, but usually ended with everyone being invited in for a jam session, dancing or a continuation of the noise and hoopla."[48] The few Czech couples who had small weddings were sometimes given shivarees, but unlike their demanding Anglo counterparts, the serenaders themselves brought beer, sandwiches, and other treats.[49]

Many couples relied heavily on their parents to provide for their necessities, either by setting them up in housekeeping or by allowing the newlyweds to live with one set of parents for a year or so. In most cases, the bride left her own family and went to her husband's farm or that of his parents, a tradition common in many societies that, according to anthropologists, "allow[s] men to appropriate women's labor and solidify male dominance."[50] Tullia Ischy remembered, "Maybe they'd just stay at home a year after they got married and farm with their daddy. I know two of my brothers did and then after that, they rented land to get a start and it taken quite a bit to get started farming."[51]

Almost every young woman moved directly from her parents' house to that of her husband, never living on her own. Some single young men, in contrast, worked as "hands" on other people's farms, often that of relatives, and tasted some autonomy before setting up their own households.[52] A woman marrying a man who had lived apart from his parents might have to rely especially heavily on him in learning to be half of an independent couple. The separation from family sometimes proved traumatic for young women, especially when poor roads made returning home for frequent visits unlikely. Kate Peacock Jones recalled the separation of her sister Jewel, who married in the early 1920s, from her parents and sisters: "It was very sad to me when Jewel married too, as she married a man, Lee Hegler, who lived at Hubbord, about 12 miles from our home, and that was too far. Jewel would not get to come on Saturday nights to visit us."[53] Jewel Peacock Hegler may have joined the circle of her in-laws' family as she left that of her birth. But homesickness undoubtedly made many young women question their decisions to marry.

Bernice Bostick Weir endured a rough transition from her status as daughter to daughter-in-law and wife in 1919. She moved seven miles from her parents' home to that of her mother-in-law, Texanna Eleanor White Bostick, whom she had not previously met. Weir's first husband, Pat Bostick, had lived alone with his widowed mother for seven years on her land, and the older Mrs. Bostick reacted coolly to the teenage bride. Weir recalled her reception with pain more than seventy years later: "And you know, I never had met his mother. And she and my brother-in-law's wife was in the kitchen. They's cooking up a storm like they's going to have a big feast or something. So Pat took me in and introduced me to them and I don't know whether it was that day or the next day I called her 'Mother' and she turned and she said, 'I'm not your mother.' So I never did call her 'Mother' any more. It was always Mrs. Bostick till the children came along and then I said 'Grandma Bostick' all the time."

Weir felt like a visitor in her new home, recalling that her mother-in-law retained the role of chief housekeeper: "She always had a garden and raised chickens and things like that. And she always went ahead. I was just a little girl there. . . . I was reared to mind, and I always minded her and everything."

A highly flexible woman, Weir passed lightly over her mother-in-law's shortcomings. She subtly indicated, however, that getting along with her mother-in-law took great effort. Weir's sister-in-law was either unwilling or unable to win their mother-in-law's affection, but Weir succeeded: "She was a wonderful mother-in-law and I loved her and she loved me. We never had any fusses or words or anything. But she and her other daughter-in-law would go years at a time and wouldn't speak, visit or anything. I don't know why they got that way."

After less than a year of living together, Grandma Bostick decided to leave the newlyweds and their newborn son on the farm, and she moved to the nearby community of Moody. "When I married and came into the home, why, she lived there—that was February, and she lived there until December," Weir continued. "And she went to town and bought her a house. She said it wasn't right. She said, 'My pleasures are not yours and yours are not mine.' Said, 'It would be the best for me to go to town.' "[54] At age sixty-three, Texanna Bostick, a woman who had survived the deaths of her husband and four of her seven children, began her new life as a townswoman, and her nineteen-year-old daughter-in-law became the new generation of farmwife.[55]

Bernice Bostick Weir and her mother-in-law were not alone in their awkward efforts to adjust to one another. On the other side of McLennan County, Anton and Rosie Filer Berger married in 1923 and moved in with his mother, Anna Berger. As the people of Tours tell the story, Anna Berger would not allow twenty-three-year-old Rosie to do any cooking in her household, despite the older woman's limitations. One day when she was at home alone, young Rosie decided to defy her mother-in-law's ban on her cooking and made several loaves of bread. The family enjoyed the bread, "but Anna would not praise her daughter-in-law." The next day Anna Berger told Dorothy Huber, with whom she took cows to pasture every morning, "Rosie baked the best bread I have ever eaten. I could have eaten it all up." Huber apparently reported the praise back to the household, and Rosie Berger became chief baker in the household. With increasing rapprochement between the two women, Anton and Rosie lived with Anna four years before moving to their own farm.[56]

In contrast to the Bosticks and Bergers, some mothers-in-law and daughters-in-law lived in harmony from the beginning. While the Bergers were trying to work out their lives in Tours, Ben and Josephine Schroeder Uptmor lived nearby with his mother, and the two women developed "a real friendship . . . that remained for the rest of their lives."[57] Etta Carroll's mother-in-law loaned her sewing machine and helped Etta make clothing for their children while Etta and her husband, Dovie, lived in a small house on his father's farm after their marriage in 1921.[58] Young women living apart from their birth

Gender and Family Relationships

families benefited mightily from cordial relationships with the women in their husband's families.

As they set up their households, couples also struggled to establish their relationships within the marriages. Women, under the southern patriarchal ideal, were supposed to be subject to the will of their men—their fathers, husbands, and, finally, in their widowhood, to that of their sons. Isolated on single-family farms, women who lived in nuclear family units found themselves subordinate in many ways to their men.[59]

Within a framework of legal subordination, female children received strong messages in their socialization process. They observed their mothers and realized the importance of women's contributions, as Geneva Berry-Robbins of Williamson County pointed out about her mother: "She worked along side my dad to make ends meet to feed their family."[60] But many girls early recognized the double demands that women faced. Families expected female children to work as hard as their brothers outside the house, and then perform house-related chores as well. While many male children did field work, few engaged in such tasks as washing dishes or minding younger siblings, as female children did. "Most of the time [the boys'] job was working in the field and tending to the stock and all, and the girls' jobs was cleaning the house, and helping them," Inez Folley, from Limestone County, remarked. "But they didn't help us much."[61] As a rule, women were to perform their own work without assistance from the men.

Because cotton was such a labor-intensive crop, however, men frequently needed the women's help with the outdoor farmwork. Such conditions brought difficulties to women on two counts: their husband's resentment and a lack of respect for housework. For a poor farmer, his dependence on his wife may have reinforced his sense of inferiority, already drummed into him by the tenant system, because he could not survive economically without the direct help of a woman. He may have deeply resented the system that forced him into needing a woman's help, when farming was supposed to be a man's work, and being reminded of his need for his wife may have made the insult all the deeper. For a farm woman, the pressures of the farm itself may have denigrated the perceived value of housework. Except in the most extreme circumstances, the cotton crop and the livestock took precedence, regardless of anything else occurring in the family's life. Asked about his assistance when his children were newborns, Etta

Carroll's husband, Dovie, responded: "I helped all I could, but still I had to milk and feed and work in the field, this, that, and the other, so it kept me busy on the outside, too."[62] The economic life of the farm could not stop for babies. To an insensitive observer, women's contributions in house and garden might be ignored, for they usually did not bring in either cash or credit.

Because their labor was essential to the family's economic survival, some rural women may have commanded more power and respect than their consuming urban counterparts. Despite their economic importance, however, the majority of women in the Blacklands apparently had only limited opportunity for self-determination. The situation in Texas compares to that investigated in Nebraska by Deborah Fink, who observed that within propertyless families any equality between men and women tended to be an equality of powerlessness. Although field work could potentially have served as a liberating force for women, it was instead often a part of the family wage, combined with the wages of all other family members.[63] In the Blackland Prairie, as elsewhere, women's field work had little effect on their authority in their families. They remained subordinate to the men.

The rewards for rural women's intense labor failed to reflect the amount or value of the work that they performed. Just because the farms and their husbands desperately needed them did not mean that farm women in the Blacklands or anywhere else enjoyed special regard or privilege. Rural sociologist Carolyn Sachs has observed, "Interdependence does not necessarily equal equity. In fact, control of farms has historically been under the male head of the household."[64] And Joan Jensen found in New Mexico that farm women recalling their lives in the 1920s and 1930s "complain of husbands as 'partners' who uprooted the family when they decided to move, and as 'managers' of the partnership who ran families into debt, leaving women no alternative but divorce or acquiescence."[65] Situations in which women were relatively powerless particularly held true in the tradition-bound South. Despite the importance of women's work, men retained most formal power throughout the South, furthering the legendary southern patriarchal structure.[66] And pervasive poverty rendered less consequential the material benefits that women's efforts might have brought in other, less stricken areas of the United States.

Two accounts by men of their families at the turn of the twentieth century strengthen the stereotype of the delicate white southern woman submitting to her man at any cost, echoing the findings of historians such as Joan Cashin in the Old Southwest.[67] In recalling his family's move from Alabama to Texas,

G. L. Vaughan commented, "Mamma's co-operation was more a matter of compelling circumstances than of choice. She was much too far away from her beloved kindred in Georgia than she wanted to be. Papa was determined to get to Texas. Mamma, a devoted mother, would do many things against her choice to hold the family together."[68]

Mamma Vaughan strongly resembles the reluctant immigrants often portrayed in Western American history, as Elizabeth Jameson has pointed out. Jameson argues that the often-quoted diaries and letters expressing women's pain at leaving family and friends behind give only one side of the story and that many women may not have feared the move as much as is commonly believed.[69] G. L. Vaughan may have expressed his mother's emotions accurately, but he may also have been carried away by stereotype.

Frank Locke remembered, from the turn of the twentieth century, his father as the head of the household, "rugged, patriarchal, and individualistic," while his mother was "a great, rural woman" whose virtues "justified our love and adoration for her." The son praised his mother's "delicate nature, abhorrence of the uncouth, sense of fairness, diplomacy as a peacemaker, established set of values, a love of nature—'God's little creatures'—and dumb brutes . . . her attention to duty, love for her family, compassion for the sick and suffering, love of God and country, belief in the Bible—'I believe every word of it.'" So great was Mrs. Locke's sense of delicacy that she cooked but refused to eat the doves that her sons shot, declining to ingest "God's messengers of love and peace."[70]

Yet not only sentimental men recall their fathers' authority in the family and their mothers' giving natures. Myrtle Calvert Dodd, anything but sentimental, definitely named her father when remembering who headed the household: "I guess you'd call it my daddy. We all listened to him more . . . especially as far as the work was concerned. Most of the time it was help—he'd say, 'You're going to help your mother,' about certain things. My mother, you know, was hard of hearing, and she just depended on him."

Robert Calvert decided when his children were old enough to do field work and when to buy household appliances, including a stove and a sewing machine, and determined that his children would have better lives than his. "I'll guarantee you one thing," Myrtle Dodd declared, "my father saw that we was taken care of what we ought to have if it was at all possible. He wanted an education so bad hisself and didn't get to get it." He also decided when it was time to move to another farm, changing assignments frequently, as tenant farmers often did, despite the qualms of his wife: "He'd usually ask her what she thought about it. . . . 'Well, I don't know,' she'd say. 'I dread moving,' or, 'I hate to do this, that, and the other. But if that's the best, why—' "

Occasionally the family tried to exert pressure on Robert Calvert's decisions, to no avail: "When we moved to the other side of Hewitt, there was a lot more land—black land, better farm land. But the Stribling place sold and we wanted our father to buy it and he said, well, there wasn't enough land there, and part of it was poor land and he didn't like the water situation because the water that pumped from the windmill on the branch—if it didn't rain, it went dry and then you had to draw water for the stock and all." For her father, each move meant "better each time most of the time. Boys were bigger and he wanted a bigger situation, and he got it. But the house was not as nice" on the new place.[71] Robert Calvert obviously cared for his family very much and apparently did not intentionally tyrannize them. But he usually got his way.

Perhaps because of the forces of modernization that were creeping into rural society, younger generations shared more in decision making than did older couples. Young women who went to town could see their urban peers holding jobs and living outside of parental supervision, and they could see independent young women making decisions autonomously. Rural women continued to capitulate frequently to their husbands' wishes, however. Like the Calverts, Bernice and Pat Bostick also clashed over their land situation. In 1925, as a young man with a growing family, Pat Bostick paid cash for 130 acres across the road from his existing farm. His wife, who was twenty-four years old at the time, had had other ideas: "There's a place back over here that came on the market that I wanted him to buy so bad and everything, and I had it figured out how we could pay for it. But it would've taken all of our surplus money and he wouldn't—It would've been about a hundred acres."[72] Pat Bostick shared his business information with his wife—"I always knew what was going on, seemed like"—and she vigorously gave her opinions. Nevertheless, the husband ultimately made the final decisions about acquiring additional land.[73]

Other couples who married after World War I shared more decisions. Dovie and Etta Carroll discussed almost every matter of consequence on their farm, from the purchase of household goods to child discipline. When recalling who disciplined the children, Dovie Carroll responded, "One as much as the other. If I was out in the field, why, she'd do all of it and if I's at the house, me and her both, both of us would."[74]

Decision making also varied with ethnic group. According to Clinton Machann, the leading historian of Czech Texans, Czech families shared the responsibility for making important decisions, and a woman, particularly a

Gender and Family Relationships

starenka (grandmother) might wield "considerable influence" in the household. Czech women appear to have borne great responsibility for determining their families' fates, as stories from the Tours community show.[75] Overall, however, married women remained subject to the wills of men, who reserved the right to make the major decisions for their families.

As a young bride was adjusting to her new role as wife, she often found herself also adapting to a second new role: mother. Little girls were socialized to expect motherhood, receiving baby dolls as presents, and their expectations were soon met.[76] For most women in the Blacklands, motherhood followed within the first year of marriage. Bernice Weir, married at age eighteen, remembered her first pregnancy: "I got pregnant right straight. I had the baby in nine months and two days, and Billy Pat [her younger son] said one time, said, 'Well, I wondered. I knew you got married in 1919 and had a baby that year and I wondered if you had to get married or what happened.' I said, 'No. I didn't have to get married, and I wasn't pregnant when I married. . . .' Oh, I liked to have cried my eyes out. I didn't want to be pregnant."[77]

In the Blackland Prairie, as in most agricultural societies, many adults viewed numerous children as additions to the workforce, and the birthrate for farm people exceeded that of townspeople.[78] In the early 1920s, landlords frequently asked prospective tenants about the sizes of their families, assuming that the larger the family the more promptly the crops would be tended. Not infrequently, landlords turned down tenants whose children they considered too young or too few to meet the labor requirements of the farms.[79] Women in the Blacklands held to the traditional view of children as economic assets, even if caring for the children exhausted their bodies and minds. Reformers frequently expressed astonishment at the number of women who had to stop and count to determine how many children they had. As sociologist Ruth Allen observed in the lower Blacklands, "Every American could at least 'count up' and tell how many she had, but several Mexicans and Negroes did not know to how many children they had given birth."[80]

Table 3 illustrates, first, the average number of births to farmers' wives still in their childbearing years and, second, the number of surviving children of those women, in four Blackland Prairie counties, drawn from the manuscript census. For white women in 1900, the average was 4.31, while African American women were averaging 5.02 births. Each of these women had the potential of having yet more children, for the numbers reveal only the previous births and

TABLE 3. Average Number of Births and Surviving Children Born to Farmers' Wives under Age Forty-Five in Four Blacklands Counties, by Ethnic Group, 1900 and 1910

| | 1900 | | | | | |
| | White | | Black | | White and Black, Combined | |
	number born	number surviving	number born	number surviving	number born	number surviving
Ellis	4.47	3.67 (82.1%)	5.04	4.12 (81.7%)	4.66	3.82 (81.9%)
Hunt	4.51	3.70 (82.0%)	5.56	4.42 (79.5%)	4.86	4.08 (83.9%)
McLennan	4.09	3.50 (85.5%)	4.66	3.48 (74.7%)	4.56	3.49 (76.6%)
Williamson	4.20	3.68 (87.6%)	4.84	3.68 (76.0%)	4.41	3.68 (83.4%)
Average	4.31	3.63 (84.4%)	5.02	3.92 (78.2%)	4.62	3.76 (81.5%)

| | 1910 | | | | | |
| | White | | Black | | White and Black, Combined | |
	number born	number surviving	number born	number surviving	number born	number surviving
Ellis	3.73	3.23 (86.6%)	3.76	2.92 (77.7%)	3.74	3.12 (83.6%)
Hunt	3.92	3.34 (85.2%)	4.98	4.14 (83.1%)	4.27	3.65 (85.4%)
McLennan	3.81	3.35 (87.9%)	5.14	4.16 (80.9%)	4.25	3.62 (85.1%)
Williamson	3.99	3.69 (92.5%)	4.32	3.34 (77.3%)	4.10	3.57 (87.1%)
Average	3.86	3.40 (88.1%)	4.55	3.64 (80.0%)	4.09	3.49 (85.3%)

Sources: *Twelfth Census of the U.S.*, 1900; *Thirteenth Census of the U.S.*, 1910.
Note: N=100 married white women and 50 married black women for each county.

Gender and Family Relationships

the number of children in any given household at one time, not total fertility rates. These figures, nonetheless, are well above the national average of 3.54 in 1900, demonstrating the higher fertility of rural women.[81] The numbers of births declined slightly in 1910, falling to 3.86 for Anglo women and 4.55 for African American women.

Statistics, of course, tell only part of the story. Each woman enumerated on the manuscript census had her own pattern of childbearing and child rearing: for example, the twenty-four-year-old mother in Ellis County in 1900 who had married at sixteen and in eight years of marriage had borne six children and buried three, the thirty-five-year-old Williamson County mother working to make her house stretch to house the nine children whom she had borne in twenty years of marriage, or, conversely, the McLennan County woman who in 1910 had been married fourteen years but at age thirty-four had borne no children. Childlessness was relatively rare. Of the 1,200 women sampled, only sixty-one—5.08 percent—of those who had been married three years or longer were childless. This figure is significantly lower than the national average, which in 1910 was 14 percent. In a society that placed a premium on children as workers, and with rural women's limited access to methods of contraception, voluntary childlessness was almost surely unheard of, and a childless woman was almost definitely the object of pity by her neighbors.[82] At least one "barren" woman tried "to avoid a lonely old age by mothering an orphan girl," but the foster daughter provided little comfort in later years.[83]

Few parents explained the cycle of human life to their daughters, even though they probably had ample opportunities to see animals reproducing on the farm. Troy Crenshaw remembered that a pregnant woman ceased going out in public "as soon as maternity dresses no longer concealed the secret in her protruding front."[84] Older children usually went to relatives or neighbors while their young siblings were being born, and they were generally excluded from the intense goings-on surrounding the arrival of a new baby.

Bernice Weir recalled chiding her mother for not informing her about her sister's impending birth in 1915, only four years before her own marriage: "Years after that, I said, 'Mama, why didn't you tell me? I was fourteen years old, and why didn't you tell me that we's going to have a baby?'

"She said, 'Oh, well, I thought that girl that you'—her name was Cassie Gunn—'I thought sure Cassie had told you all about it.'

"I said, 'Mama, Cassie never told me anything at all about anything like that.' So Mama—she was reared back when everything was kept under the blanket."[85]

As Bernice Weir's mother surmised, some young women in the Blackland Prairie did receive their sex education from their peers. Inez Folley, bundled off to relatives while her mother gave birth to her numerous younger siblings, commented, "Well, at that time little girls didn't know anything about that. They didn't know where babies came from, and it was a secret. . . . Whenever we got back, we had a little new baby. And of course, we thought the doctor brought him to them. We didn't know anything about it. I can remember whenever my friend told me, and it was just a big shock, because I didn't know where babies came from. I guess I was nine or ten years old."[86] Many young women would not ask their mothers for information, as Louise Blackwell Dillow recalled: "I remember well the first time I heard the word 'spaghetti.' When I asked its meaning, my older sisters began to snicker and tease me as they often did, and suggested that I ask Mama. Of course they were pulling my leg but for years I was convinced that 'spaghetti' was a forbidden word. I was not about to ask my mother what it meant."[87] This code of silence meant that young women sometimes faced their first sexual experiences and childbearing with fear. For Cayetana Martinez Navarro of McLennan County, the impending birth of her first child brought terror: "A neighbor told me that the baby was going to come out the same place it went in, and I was very scared." She added wryly, "And after that I had a baby every two years."[88]

Blacklands residents recall with mixed emotions the frequent births of more children. Older children often resented the toll that childbearing took on their mothers, perhaps articulating ideas that their mothers hesitated to utter aloud. Audie Murphy was the seventh of twelve children. According to his biographer, Murphy recalled his parents' procreation "with a kind of contempt—directed at his father, not his mother. Of his father he said, 'Every time my old man couldn't feed the kids he had, he got him another one.'"[89]

Hester Calvert had nine babies in thirteen years, and her oldest child, Myrtle, viewed the last arrivals with considerable skepticism: "When Milos, the next-to-the-youngest brother, was born, that was six of us. I thought that was enough. I was getting old enough, you know. Grandmother tells it—I don't remember telling it—that I said to her, 'We didn't need these last two.' Nadine [the baby] was sick and I was having to help take care of the little brother, Royce."[90] Hazel Beauton Riley told of her sister's displeasure at Riley's birth in 1905: "Since a new baby came to their house every other year, this latest one was decidedly old hat to her. She knew how much work babies caused, more washing, more ironing, more water-carrying, more everything."[91]

Only occasionally did parents openly disavow the children they had borne. Elizabeth Williams Estes, from a wealthy landowning McLennan County family, recalled the dismay of a Mexican father at the birth of his daughter:

> I remember we had a Mexican family living there. . . . Blas had eleven children while he lived there; ten of them were boys, and my mother would go down when Rosa would be expecting her child momentarily and help her. The last one was a little girl, and Mother said, "Oh, she was the sweetest little thing," rosy-cheeked and black hair and black eyes and just a darling child. And she kept telling Rosa how beautiful she was and how fortunate; and she told Blas Trevino, was his name, how fortunate now they had the little girl. So that afternoon when Blas came up to milk, he called my father out, "Mr. Peeler, Mr. Peeler," Daddy went out; and he said, "Miss Gippy [Estes's mother, Gibson Denison Ross Williams], she lika da little girl." Blas said, "We have no use for little girls; we give her to Miss Gippy." . . . Then my mother had a terrible time explaining that she already had a little child and that she couldn't take care of another one.[92]

The new father embodied the legendary chauvinism of the Mexican male, effortlessly proffering his firstborn daughter to his boss's wife as one might a stray kitten. He also appeared shortsighted, since many Mexican women worked prodigiously in the fields. Surely Gibson Williams's explanation of already having one child to care for seemed like a lame excuse to someone with eleven children. Yet the Mexican immigrant's would-be gift may have reflected the unspoken sentiments of many fathers upon the birth of a girl child, whose field work had to be defended against a disapproving society and whose virtue would have to be guarded until she married. All babies, boys and girls, required more attention, with the mother dividing her finite time "between father and child, and between children, the breast baby and the knee baby."[93] A tired mother had ever less time for the father with the birth of each child.

Despite exhaustion and lack of privacy in crowded houses, couples managed to maintain sexual relations, resulting in frequent pregnancies and births. Among many Blacklands families, birth control remained uncommon until World War II. Women used cycles of breast-feeding to limit their pregnancies, but lactation merely spaced births two years apart. In both the upper and lower Blacklands, tenants rarely used artificial birth control such as condoms or diaphragms, available in the 1920s and 1930s. Older African American women in particular reacted strongly against even the idea of birth control, responding time and again, "What else did the Lord put women here for?"[94] Childbearing did have its limits, however. After delivering her tenth child, the doctor gave Lou Thomas Folley a stern ultimatum. Folley's daughter, Inez, recalled the birth of her sister, Finis: "You know what Finis means? If you looked it up in a dictionary, it'd say, 'the end,' and she was the last baby my mother had. And her doctor named her. He said, 'Mrs. Folley, I'm going to name this baby. Its name is Finis. That means that's the end of it. This is the last one you're going to have.' And it was."[95] Inez Folley did not know how the doctor ended her mother's rhythm of pregnancies, but his prediction held true.

Sheltering children from sexual knowledge apparently presented a greater concern to parents than did actual birth and child rearing. The frequency of pregnancies created casual attitudes about the real processes of gestation and childbirth, although pregnancy and childbirth were major causes of death in young women across the United States at the turn of the twentieth century.[96] Even among relatively affluent, landowning families, prenatal care was minimal. Bernice Weir remembered: "I just got so sick at my stomach I vomited every time I'd eat anything. I didn't know that you did that way, but that's what happened to me. You know, back then you didn't go to the doctor unless you'd get sick or something. And the doctor usually came to the house. Had to call the doctor out there one time on account of my legs cramping so. And I called him again another time. And that's the only time the doctor saw me till the baby was ready to be born."[97] When Myrtle Dodd's mother, a tenant farmer's wife, almost miscarried her ninth child, she had little choice but to keep on with her household chores: "She couldn't stay in the bed. There was too many of us."[98] For women who worked in the fields, pregnancy usually brought little or no respite from physical labor, particularly for members of Eastern European or African American families.[99]

While three-quarters of Anglo women used physicians to attend their births by the late 1920s, more than half of the African American and Mexican women employed midwives, and numerous women from each group had no professional assistance with their births. In 1925, Inez Adams Walker gave birth to her first daughter, Bertha Mae, in rural Milam County with the help of a midwife:

"We had old ladies that they'd go get and they'd see after you."[100] As many studies of childbirth have shown, midwives often administered births equally or more competently than doctors, and in some areas the practice continued into the 1930s.[101] In Limestone County, Lou Thomas Folley delivered babies for black and white women alike: "I guess you would call her a midwife, because she helped—even to the Negroes, she helped bring their babies in the world," her daughter remembered. "She'd go from place to place where they could—if it was close enough to where she could walk or where they could come and get her and take her. But she worked as a midwife. She didn't get any money for it; it was all free gratis. But there's one family that she helped to bring their tenth child into the world."[102]

Among German settlers in McLennan County, Maria Mousberger Rauschhuber answered the call of the parish priest, who announced that the community needed another midwife. She trained as a midwife in Omaha, Nebraska, in the late 1890s. Rauschhuber could not practice her skills on herself and died from uremic poisoning in 1907 following the birth of her twelfth child.[103]

Mexican families often employed the talents of a *curandera*, or folk healer. Adelaida Torres remained skeptical of the skills of the local *curandera* who attended the births of many of her neighbors: "I had seven kids and I didn't go to the *curandera* for any of them. Everybody would say that she was a good *curandera*. And I would say, 'No, she's not a good *curandera*. It's just luck. God is helping her and that's why everything comes out all right.' If she was a good healer, it was only because God helped her."[104] But countless other families depended on the services of *curanderas* to deliver their children and take care of their illnesses.

When Etta and Dovie Carroll were expecting their first child in 1922, they chose to have a doctor's care at the birth rather than a midwife's. Etta Carroll commented, "I just was always raised to go to the doctor, and he [her husband] was too." The doctor rode out seven miles from Waxahachie to the Carrolls' one-room house. Physicians' care came at a cost, however. When Hazel Beauton Riley was born in 1905, her father paid a Dr. Armstrong from Biardstown five dollars for her delivery.[105] By the late 1920s, an African American woman in the lower Blacklands paid doctors $45 and $75 for her first two births, then paid midwives $5 and $7.50 for her next two.[106] For landless farmers, using a doctor could reinforce their dependence upon their landlords. The daughter of a Hill County doctor recalled the system by which her father and uncle collected their fees for delivering babies:

They got beat, you know, so much. So many bills were never paid, so finally my uncle got very weary of this and he would make this itinerant have the owner of the farm underwrite the expenses. He'd say, "Will Mr. So-and-so stand for this bill?" And if the man would say yes, well, my uncle and my father would go. . . . Of course, the owners of the farm didn't always stand good for it, but this kept them from getting beat out of many of their fees and, too, that made the least itinerant sharecropper feel some sense of responsibility. . . . He refused, then, at times to go and thus he began to educate people to make advance arrangements, if their wife was going to have a baby. If they were any part of a man, they could make arrangements.[107]

Only the rarest of births took place in hospitals. The wealthy Westbrook family, which owned several thousand acres in southern McLennan County, arranged for young Marguerite to spend the weeks prior to the births of her children in the 1920s in the city—once in Austin and once in Waco, where her babies were born with the latest obstetrical care. After each of the births, the Westbrooks hired a nurse for six-week periods.[108]

Many young mothers were already well acquainted with the tasks of child care, having been responsible for younger brothers and sisters for much of their lives. Some relied on female relatives to come at the time of birth, giving the new mother rest and sharing mothering skills. At times, relatives traveled long distances, indicating the importance of this cross-generational training and support. Following her great-grandson's birth in May 1922, Etta Carroll's grandmother came from Oklahoma and stayed with the young family, letting Etta rest in bed for a full ten days. After the grandmother's death, Dovie Carroll's aunt took her place at the births of the Carrolls' other five children.[109] When Arbie Marie Rampy was born in 1906, her maternal grandparents and an aunt traveled 150 miles to attend the birth, because all other available help was in the field picking cotton.[110] Neighbors, too, assisted as best they could, and women registered their gratitude in telling ways. Bernice Weir remembered, "There were some people that lived up above us on the hill and their names was Brewster. And Mrs. Brewster was with Mama when Alice was born, and her name was Alice. So that's the reason that—where she got her name."[111]

Many women did not receive adequate postpartum care, particularly after their first births, and resumed their household and field tasks very soon after childbirth, creating complex gynecological problems for themselves in later years. Numerous older women considered the lack of proper care during pregnancy and childbirth to be one of the worst features of farm life. They observed that the long-term cost of the damage to their health rendered meaningless the short-term savings on medical care during their pregnancies.[112]

Giving birth to a child soon became the least of a mother's worries, as concern for providing for its physical needs and giving it attention and discipline quickly overtook her memories of birth pains. While most births turned out successfully, with both mother and child surviving, premature or otherwise weakened babies faced long odds without sophisticated neonatal care. In the 1920s, an estimated 10 percent of the children born in Texas died before their first birthdays.[113] As Table 3 demonstrates, children in the Blackland Prairie fared poorly. In 1900, between 13 and 18 percent of children born to white mothers had died, while 19 to 26 percent of the black children did not survive. The situation improved slightly in 1910, with the white death rate declining to 8 to 15 percent and the black deaths standing at 17 to 23 percent. The census does not reveal how the children died or at what age, but the stark fact remains: During the first decades of the twentieth century, one out of every five children in the rural Blacklands did not survive. In African American families, the numbers could be as high as one out of four.

Even though they often had numerous other children, mothers mourned for their lost little ones. Grieving women wrote to their "sisters," fellow readers of the *Semi-Weekly Farm News*, to lament their children. In February 1910, Mrs. Ruthie Owens of Salado, Bell County, wrote: "On October 14 God saw fit to take from us our darling baby boy. . . . Oh, sisters, how hard it was to have to give such a sweet little boy up, but God knows best. His name was Robbie. . . . Four days after his death I was stricken with paralysis and haven't been able to talk well since and can not use my right hand to sew with. I would be so thankful if some sister would send in a remedy for paralysis."[114] Owens tried to accept what she perceived as the will of God, but her body apparently rebelled against such acceptance. Mrs. Lorena Gardner of Blooming Grove, Navarro County, also attributed the death of her small daughter to the will of God and relied on her religious faith to sustain her through the loss: "The 9th of last June we had to give up our darling baby girl, not quite 7 months old. Oh, how hard it was to part with her, but I have the consolation that I have a darling waiting on that beautiful shore, and by God's help I intend to meet her there."[115] Gardner's vision of life after death presented a hope for a joyous reunion with her baby daughter.

Bernice Weir depended on her religious faith and on her surviving children to cope with the deaths of her two older children, both young adults, only months apart. She recalled, "You know, the Lord promises you that he won't put more on you than you're able to bear, so I guess we had the promise. We had the other children. They were both in high school, and they just kept us busy. Keeping busy is better for you than sitting. It was awfully hard—and to this day, we're never over it; I don't guess we'll ever be over it."[116]

When Stacy Lee Carroll died of scarlet fever in 1927, his mother also consoled herself with her surviving children and with her work. She had been seriously ill herself, and the doctors wanted to keep her confined to the house. But she rebelled: "Well, if you had other things to see about, then you had to hold up on account of each other and then do for them. And they said, 'Now, don't get out in the sun and do anything this year. You stay in the house.' Well, that spring after he died—that summer, I went to the field and helped a little bit. Just get out the house, take the children with us."[117]

Women dealt with their loss in other ways as well. Some showered their love on other children, as Bernice Weir remembered: "Mama had a cousin that just had a daughter my age, and she lost her when she's about three years old. And she said that she caught that dysentery from a cat; now, I don't know if that's true or not but the cat died and then the little girl died. Well, she was real foolish about me because I was her child. And she made lots of my clothes."[118]

When Troy Crenshaw's sister Carrie died, their mother used her grief to demonstrate her frustration at their family's inability to give their children all of the material possessions that they wanted. Carrie had wanted a pair of white shoes to match those of her singing partner at the annual Odd Fellows picnic, and their father had denied her request because he thought it extravagant. Two months later Carrie died, "and her heartbroken mother told the funeral director to lay her out in white shoes. He urged that the usual burial in stocking feet is more suggestive of lying down to rest and that shoes would not even be seen in the casket. But the child in whom Mother saw herself more than in any of her other children went to rest in white shoes beside her grandmother."[119] Mrs. Crenshaw had not successfully used her influence while Carrie lived, but she upbraided her husband into providing for her in death.

Feeding and caring for numerous children could have occupied all of farm women's time had they the opportunity. Almost all women in the Blacklands breast-fed their babies. Bernice Weir remembered, "I nursed my babies and I slept with them on my left arm until they's a year old," sharing the bed with her and their father.[120] Occasionally a baby would have trouble digesting its mother's milk, as Myrtle Calvert Dodd remembered about her sister: "We liked to not raised Nadine, the youngest one. Had to go to Temple with her and get—poison had gotten into her system. She was the tiniest, ugliest little thing and made the prettiest woman you've ever seen. My father took her to Temple to a doctor and he got her on Mellin's food. We'll never forget—she couldn't digest; had to take her off the breast, you know. Couldn't find anything that would digest."[121] Mellin's food was one of several commercially produced nutritional supplements that helped mothers who could not nurse their babies. It had to be purchased at the store, either with cash or on credit. A baby who would not nurse then became not only a worry but also an added expense.

Frail children also became ongoing sources of concern for their mothers. Norma Blackwell was, according to her younger sisters, "skinny, frail, and finicky-eating." Mrs. Blackwell gave her second-born privileges that the other eight children jealously observed: "A child who appeared hungry or sick was the child who received the most attention. Norma was frequently allowed to eat a piece of cake while it was still warm, while the others had to wait until dinner-time."[122]

Trying to care for a child while doing housework or field work could become a mother's foremost frustration. Mothers commonly tried to control their children with verbal threats that betrayed the stress of trying to rear a family amid the prevailing poverty of the region's farm people. Several people recalled hearing African American mothers warning their children away from danger with a specific phrase: "You gets away from that well! You might fall in and you knows I ain't got no money to bury you with!"[123] If living with many children was hard, sending them to the graveyard was harder.

Eddie Stimpson recalled his mother's cautionary tales for her children, including her headstrong younger daughter, Bessie Lee: "If there is any thing I can remember well, that is remember day in and day out, the care and concern Mother had for us kids and Dad. It didn't make no diffrence whin or what time it was. Every time one of us walk out that door Mother wanted to no where we were going and what time would we be back. . . . She would take time and caution us what danger was ahead especial going across the road, to the store or creek to play in water. She had a safety tip for us all. Of course it did not matter with Sister Bessie Lee. She was going to do something wrong, time she got out of Mom site. Any way this is why Mom would all way say, You be good Bessie Lee. . . . You stay close to Eddie Jr., girl."[124]

Mother and children at a cotton wagon, Kaufman County, July 1936
(Photo by Arthur Rothstein, courtesy of the Library of Congress, LC USF-34-5172-E).

Most of the time mothers coped with child care as best they could, alternating it with other tasks. Bernice Bostick Weir's baby daughter amused herself while her mother ironed: "I'd set her in a box and Pat's shaving mirror was at least twenty inches long, and I'd hang that on the safe door and she'd just play with herself and all. . . . She'd entertain herself."[125] Attempting to cook with toddlers around sometimes resulted in disasters, and many families recall vividly stories about spoiled food, probably because the loss of food was so impressive to them. Jimmie Sowell's baby brother dumped a box of water softener into a grape pie intended for company, and Myrtle Calvert Dodd's younger sister ruined an entire pot of potato soup with a sliver of Ivory soap.[126]

Gender and Family Relationships

At age four Louise Blackwell Dillow fell into the ten-gallon bucket of lard that she stepped on, trying to reach the peanut butter. She pointed out her mother's mixed reasons for concern at the time of the mishap: "Although my mother was usually quiet and soft-spoken, her wild shrieks at the sight of her child almost drowning in lard could be heard throughout the countryside. I never was sure if Mama was more upset about the horrendous mess, the very real physical danger of my drowning in oil, or the loss of ten gallons of lard some four or five months before hog-killing time."[127] Families later retold these stories with amusement, but such incidents undoubtedly lacked humor for the mothers who had to prepare more food. Mothers working in the fields found child care a particular challenge, as we shall see.

Disciplining large numbers of children could also try parents' patience and energies. Many Blacklands families used corporal punishment on stubborn children, girls and boys alike. While fathers played major roles in disciplining children, mothers administered the razor strap or switch as well. Dovie Carroll observed,

Well, most all of fathers back in those days, they didn't tell you but one time to do something, and if you didn't do that, well, the next time he tells you to do something, you done it. . . . My daddy didn't say much; he just tell you to do so-and-so and if you didn't do it, when he'd come in, he'd say, "Son, why didn't you do what I told you to?" Of course, I'd tell him I's playing or something, well, I'd always say till he went in the house. When he went in the house, it might be an hour or something like that, regardless; he had a double razor strop hanging up by the mantel of the fireplace and he'd get that, why, the next time he told you, you'd do it.

The Carrolls continued these disciplinary practices with their own six children, both parents administering whippings as they saw the need.[128]

African American families in McLennan County believed in strong discipline of children to make worthy adults. Alice Owens Caufield explained her grandmother's view, which Caufield also held:

I'm speaking of my grandmother, who said, "You break the sapling while it's young." And when he grows up, he doesn't forget. You teach the sapling to honor your father and your mother and then thy days will be long upon the land. He learns to honor the family and it grows out. He learns to respect and love everybody. But that teaching is going to have to be as you grow up. Don't wait till you get up here [raises hand high] and think you can break one doing just the way he want to do, been doing it all of his life. You gotta say no; you gotta be firm, and if they bend the sapling while it's young and spare not the rod—if he's never had a whipping down there, you think he's going to take a whipping after you get him up here? He's not.

As a child, Caufield felt the sting of her grandmother's disapproval: "She was short and plump and them laps I used to sit upon—like you going to roll off. But she had enough lap to roll you across and give you a good whipping on your hiney. She'd whip you with the broomweed. That was her discipline club. She broke that root part off and you had that little thing that was going to sting. And I can remember getting whippings from her, being the oldest, and whatever she'd tell you to do, you'd have to do it. Discipline was the order." Millie Stimpson, too, required her children to select their own switches, and "if you came back with one too small, you went and got another one until you got enough to plait together."

African American mothers in Central Texas, as elsewhere, shared child discipline. In Caufield's childhood, the multiple mother figures were members of their Masonic auxiliary, the Heroines of Jericho: "They guided their young folks, and anybody who knew right could guide anybody's child and tell them, 'You're doing wrong, so don't do that.' The members were close. The parents worked together. These women wasn't fighting each other. You know, when you go to lodge meeting, you might bring up child discipline or what so-and-so and I told thus-and-so, and that mother will say, 'Anytime you see one doing wrong, you just let me know.' And when he gets home, he's supposed to get a whipping. And you got one. The parents were together on upbringing the children."[129] This type of shared mothering was common in the African American community. It replicated patterns forced by slavery, in which correct behavior could be a matter of life or death, and children learned that family responsibilities extended to the community.[130]

Mothers from all ethnic groups spent considerable amounts of time keeping their families healthy. Some practiced preventive medicine, tying bags of asafetida (commonly pronounced "asfiddity"), a strong-smelling gum resin, around their children's necks to ward off colds and to ease the pain of teething. Inez Walker described the asafetida bags that were common not only in her African American household but many others: "Make a little bag and sew that asafetida up in it and put a little string on it and put it around their neck. They said it help it when they're teething and everything 'cause a lot of times babies have fever when they teethe."[131] Many women also gave their children's "systems" thorough spring cleanings with standard castor oil, Black Draught, or "a ghastly amber colored liquid" called "three sixes." Some African American families also used a tea made from a local plant known as balmonia, as Alice Caufield recalled: "It looks kind of like a lily. And it's not quite purple—maybe it's a little on the orchid side. And it's a little bell concern. It grew out on that prairie. She would give us balmonia tea, and there was always some kind of tea they going to give you in the spring to clean you out. Always. It would work you."[132]

When the preventions failed, entire families might become ill. Myrtle Dodd recalled measles taking down the older children in her family of eight: Her mother said, "'I'll declare, we had the measles up till spring!' One would get well and another would take it."[133] A caregiver had a few common remedies at her disposal, either made from materials already on hand or from plants grown especially for cures. For those who succumbed to colds despite the obnoxious asafetida resin, poultices of turpentine, kerosene, and lard in flannel bags sometimes eased congestion, while turpentine and/or kerosene mixed with sugar stifled coughs. African American mothers made tea from dried cow dung and soup from crow meat to combat colds.[134] From slippery elm bark women made a buffer for the bitter doses of quinine used to treat several maladies. They grew madeira vine to combat boils or "risens" and a malady known as "sore eyes."[135] Fat meat and turpentine were combined to treat superficial wounds, while sulfur, meat, and grease assuaged the "seven-year-itch" and sugar mixed with soot stanched bleeding.[136] Mexican women grew medicinal herbs in their gardens, including *hierba buena* (mint), *hierba anís* (anise), and *ruda* (rue). Tobacco, snuff, and laundry bluing eased the pain of insect stings.[137]

Many families from all ethnic groups also used commercially manufactured medicines. Early in the twentieth century, some Blacklands families used aspirin to relieve pain, while others had no access to any kind of commercial pain reliever until after World War I. Bottles of chill tonic (Grove's or Febreline were the most popular brands) eased the symptoms of malaria, along with hot bricks or heated irons and piles of bed covers. Other store-bought remedies included castor oil, liniment, and salve, all available from the traveling "Watkins" or "Rawleigh" salesman for cash or barter.[138] As a young teenager, Alice Owens Caufield suffered terribly from menstrual cramps and headaches, and her stepmother administered a well-known patent medicine, Wine of Cardui, to break the headache and bring on a delayed menstrual period. Other young women suffered through menstrual cramps with only warm cloths to ease the pain before aspirin became common.[139] But simple remedies failed to cure some of the region's most debilitating diseases: malaria, typhoid, hookworm, pellagra, tuberculosis. These health problems lingered well into the 1930s.[140]

The physical and emotional consequences of repeated pregnancies and childbirths showed on many rural women before World War II. Sometimes the weariness of motherhood had almost imperceptible effects. Kate Peacock Jones remembered that her mother sang to her older children but not so much to the younger ones, and explained, "I know she was pretty occupied with her housework" by then. Her father, by contrast, never gave up playing his French harp.[141] Audie Murphy wrote that one of his earliest memories was of his mother as a "sad-eyed, silent woman" who "toiled eternally." When Murphy's next brother was born in 1926, "the responsibility for taking care of Audie, now two, fell to Corinne, the oldest child, who was sixteen." The mother, said to have been pretty once, seemed old and sickly.[142]

Throughout the Blacklands in the early twentieth century, the basic family group consisted of a mother, a father, and their children. Families frequently lived within a circle of kin, however, and relatives moved in fluid groups in and out of each others' lives. Most Anglo-American and Eastern European immigrant families lived as independent units, extending their households only in times of great need. Newly married couples might live with one set of parents for a while, especially the parents of the groom, and aging relatives frequently came to stay with their younger kin. More often, several generations of one family lived close by but not under the same roof.[143] In Red River County, Emma Bourne's childhood home was physically linked with paths to her paternal grandmother Guest's and to her aunt's and uncle's homes.[144] Separate families might own adjoining farms, as older members of the Carroll clan did in southern Ellis County, or younger family members might rent from relatives, as Dovie and Etta Carroll did.[145] Almost always, these kin networks were patrifocal; a woman left her own family's circle and joined that of her husband.

Many of these families created tight social networks. A slight majority of the women surveyed in the lower Blacklands remained in the counties of their births, while another 21 percent hailed from elsewhere in Texas.[146] Those who remained physically close to their birth families or those of their husbands might be able to depend on relatives for company and assistance. The women—sisters, in-laws, cousins—at times shared sewing, cooking, child care, and gossip. The Porter family in which Bernice Bostick Weir grew up from 1901 to 1919 exemplified both the good and bad sides of family networks. She recalled,

> There's a big bunch of us. I had two cousins that was born the same year I was. One was in March and I was in June and the other one was in October. They'd always be there, you know. Uncle George and them lived just up above us there and Uncle Ed and them lived down in the pasture. He had a little farm down in the pasture, down—it was a lane that led down there from Grandpa and Grandma's place. . . . We were always close. We had this one aunt that—she was sweet and good one Christmas and maybe we wouldn't see her the next Christmas 'cause she's mad at something or somebody or herself one; I don't know which. . . . We never knew what kind of a mood we's going to find Aunt Eula in.

Sometimes relatives could be loving and nurturing. At other times, relatives interfered and talked about each other. Weir continued, "My uncle—Papa's baby brother lived up on the hill from us and when Pat and I went to get married, we all had party lines. I was eavesdropping, and I heard Aunt Mytie say, 'Oh, have you seen today's paper?'

"Whoever it was she was talking to said, 'No. Why?'

"She said, 'Oh, Bernice is going to get married.'

"She said, 'Well, who in the world is she going to marry?'

"She said, 'Well, I don't know what it is, but it looks like a Bohemian name.' We always laughed about Pat being a Bohemian."[147]

Aunt Mytie may have been gossiping only because she was angry at having been left out of the inside information on her niece's engagement. But the idea that she promulgated had potentially severe social repercussions. In 1919, an Anglo marrying a Czech would have been unheard of in Bell County. Immigration laws were slamming the doors shut on further arrivals, and the Ku Klux Klan was flexing its muscles against immigrants and Roman Catholics. Very few Czechs married outside of their ethnic group until after World War II.

In the Tours community, family backbiting drove one young couple to the perimeter of the kinship circle. Martin and Agnes Jupe Schroeder married in 1914 and rented from her parents for the next six years. One of Agnes's sisters began "carrying tales" and stirring up trouble between the Schroeder and Jupe families. The situation became so bad that Martin Schroeder swapped farms with his brother-in-law and moved his wife away to escape the family meddling.[148]

African American families often combined households under the same roofs, as did Mexican families. For both groups, these actions reflected their financial difficulties. In the lower Blacklands in the late 1920s, sociologist Ruth Allen found that individual African American households sheltered an average of 7.02 people, all usually related to one another, and not necessarily through the father's line. One household, for example, consisted of two sisters and their husbands, one child, and the sisters' mother and grandmother. The largest group in Allen's sample, nineteen people all living in the same house, was composed of a mother, two grown daughters, three grown sons, the sons' wives, and two of the sons' children. The women shared the household tasks, distributing the responsibility of feeding and clothing large numbers of people. Single women, too, could be part of a household unit in an extended family situation. At the same time, Mexican family groups encompassed even more people, with 8.17 as the average number of household members.[149] While these joint living conditions may have eased housekeeping tasks for non-Anglo women, the situation also exacerbated the crowded living conditions in Blacklands houses, discussed in the following chapter. Few houses in the region were built to accommodate fifteen, nineteen, or even thirty residents.

A significant number of family groups from all ethnic backgrounds contained orphaned children or those whose mothers had died. Single fathers relied heavily on female relatives, especially grandmothers, to care for their children. Julia Roberts Hardeman, an African American from a family of nine children in Hunt County, recalled: "My mother died when I was too young to remember. He [her father] just reared we kids by the help of his mother and my mama's mother until she passed away."[150] Dovie Carroll's mother, Mattie Carroll, died of tuberculosis in 1906, leaving four children between the ages of three and twelve. "My aunt, they owned a farm that adjoined ours. . . . And so she helped see after the children," Carroll remembered. "Of course, my oldest sister, she done the best she could seeing after us all, but my aunt, she'd come down there and see after us and, of course, she kept me up there quite a bit."[151] The experience of Dovie Carroll's sister trying to be a mother at the age of twelve demonstrates Nellie McKay's observation that the death of the mother is also "the death of the child."[152] When her mother died, her own childhood ceased, and she assumed responsibility beyond her years in caring for the younger children in the family.

To a limited extent, child care crossed the boundaries of race. Few women in the Blackland Prairie had regular assistance with child care from hired servants as did many of their counterparts in the Southeast. But since neighbors assisted with child care, Hester Calvert took care of the three children of Bird Moore, an African American laborer on their farm, so that he could work in the fields after his wife's death in childbirth.[153]

Sisters, grandmothers, and aunts all took motherless children into their own homes as well as helping widowed fathers with child care. Frequently, they added the new children to families already quite full. One of the most remarkable examples of helping with extended family was the household of Beulah Buffington and Joseph David Berry of Milam County. Beulah Berry grew up at the turn of the twentieth century in a group of sixteen children: five from her mother's first marriage, six from her stepfather's first marriage, and her five half-brothers and -sisters. J. D. Berry was one of a family of ten children. According to the Berrys' daughter, Geneva Berry-Robbins, the couple had some of Beulah's younger sisters or J. D.'s brothers and sisters living with them from the time of their marriage in 1905. They continued sheltering young relatives, and with six biological offspring of their own, the Berrys had children in their home for forty years, until their last daughter left home in 1945.[154]

At times, a single father relinquished the care of a child until he remarried, then took the child back. In the Tours community, for example, Otillia Guggenberger Uptmor and her husband, Anton, took in newborn Theodore Rauschhuber after his mother's death in 1899. They added Theodore to their own family, which included several very young children, one of whom was still being breast-fed. "When she [Otillia Uptmor] had gone to the home to view the body of the young mother, she heard the baby crying in the next room. He was hungry and would not take the bottle. She immediately nursed him and he fell asleep." The Uptmors kept Theodore until he was five, and then his father took Theodore with him to Oklahoma.[155] Bird Moore's young daughter, taken at birth by an aunt after her mother's death, stayed with her aunt over her father's protests several years later.[156]

For young Anglos and African Americans, remarriage after the death of a spouse was common, but a shortage of suitable partners prevented Mexican widows from remarrying as readily.[157] Second marriages between people with offspring resulted in crazy-quilt families of her children, his children, and their children, much like the Buffington-Lumpkin family from which Beulah Berry came. A woman such as Rosina Macicek Vrba of Tours could find herself serving as mother to ten children, four from her husband's first marriage and six from her own, or like Dovie Carroll's stepmother, also named Etta Carroll, who had one child of her own and four stepchildren to care for.[158] Some of these families got along, and others did not. The Gunn-Keaton family, discussed below, provides an extreme example of a blended family that failed.

Many women found themselves rearing children alone for various lengths of time. In the early twentieth century, death claimed men in a variety of ways, from farming accidents to blood poisoning to tuberculosis, leaving women to make their own ways with their children. In the lower Blacklands in the late 1920s, 6.4 percent of the white women, 14.0 percent of African American women, and 12.3 percent of Mexican women studied were widows, either "indeed" or through desertion.[159] Many times, broken marriages forced women, or allowed them, to exert forceful leadership roles in their families.

Widowhood or divorce made many women single heads of households. In a 1925 Hill County study, 14 percent of the white landowning farms were headed by women, while in Hunt County in 1910, white widows headed 2.1 percent of the tenant households. Each of the tenant women had at least three children at home over the age of eighteen who would bring sizable amounts of farm labor into the family economy.[160] The trends of landownership indicate that more affluent women were more likely to remain on the farm after their husbands had died, with some control over the family resources. Tenant women, on the other hand, had more tenuous existences and may have remained in rural areas, but not necessarily as head of households. They may have stayed with their children or other relatives instead of trying to make a living on a rented farm.

Some widows maintained high levels of control in their lives after their husbands' deaths. Although Texanna Bostick, for example, may have felt forced out of her home by her son's marriage, she retained a great deal of influence in her family. Lou Thomas Folley nursed her husband, debilitated by the loss of a lung and Bright's disease, for fourteen years, during which time he managed to sire ten children. When he died in 1919, she was left with the children on their Limestone County farm.

Despite the fact that Edward Green Folley had needed assistance even in dressing himself, he had not prepared his wife for her widowhood. Inez Folley recalled, "She had to do more providing for us because my daddy didn't leave her any instructions of what to do and she just had to learn the hard way." With the combined efforts and exceptionally hard work on the part of every family member, the Folleys managed to keep their farm, and Lou Folley remained there another fifteen years, eventually passing the land on to one of her sons.[161]

In Hunt County, Effie Slemmons of the Lone Oak community was widowed in 1912 at age thirty, eight months pregnant. Her husband's death left her with five children under the age of fourteen and heavily in debt. Almost single-handedly, Slemmons sold enough eggs, milk, and cotton to pay off the debt and even make a down payment on a hundred acres of land to be purchased from her late husband's brother. In 1917, she built a new house for her family using recycled lumber. According to relatives, Slemmons succeeded because of her hard work and her extreme frugality. Her daughter-in-law, Addie Jo Slemmons, remembered that after Effie skimmed milk with a large spoon, there was nothing left except "bluejohn," very thin, almost transparent milk with a bluish cast.[162] Effie Slemmons's story, like that of Lou Folley, demonstrates that determined women could sometimes make their ways as unmarried people in the Blacklands.

Other widows depended on their relatives and neighbors to assist them. Inez Adams Walker remembered that when her uncle died, her father took care of his brother's widow and children.[163] Many communities observed patterns of charity that would allow families to gain income with perhaps a measure of dignity. Custom dictated that the poor be allowed to keep the proceeds from "scrapping" cotton, or going over the field for the last time after picking and gathering what leftover bits of cotton they could for the little cash it would bring. The Hunt County community of Commerce condemned the local doctor, landowner, and Ford dealer, Warren B. De Jernett, who broke these unwritten rules of charity and took a third of the cotton that a widow and her small children had scrapped from his fields. An anonymous writer acidly recalled the incident, which probably occurred in the 1920s: "That stingy act really showed his true colors and I always felt that he was a prime candidate to be a secret republican voter for he certainly had the morals to suit their party affiliation. He would fleece anybody that he got the chance to do, yet he lived in a big new mansion made of brick and still owned the other fine house next to the old Day Elementary school that was good enough for any rich man. He just always coveted a few more dollars than he already had. People were fairly well against the good Doctor after that, though. It really hurt his reputation."[164] Communities acted in concert to protect the weak, and De Jernett broke the rules of community charity.

Some marriages ended before the death of a spouse through desertion or divorce. Others persisted despite great misery. Determining the levels of spouse abuse in the Blacklands is impossible, but it certainly existed in forms ranging from verbal abuse to murder. Gladys Everett, a Baptist minister's wife, wrote of being invited to a noontime meal at the home of a woman whose husband was "not a Christian." When Everett and her minister husband arrived at the house, the wife asked the husband to put his dog in another room. During the very tense dinner, the woman requested from her husband a second helping of roast beef. Everett recalled, "He looked at her, eyes glaring and voice trembling and burst forth with, '— —, you made me shut my dog up because of your preacher but you are not going to eat all of the meat up from him, you've had enough, eat some 'taters.' She did with tears in her eyes. Before the dessert he fed the dog the remainder of the roast." The wife then apologized to Everett as they washed dishes together, "saying he was so set in his wicked ways, he just couldn't behave." This wife endured humiliation in front of her minister, a person of status in the community, and one can speculate that the private abuse must have been even greater. The marriage had lasted a long time, however, for they had a thirty-five-year-old son "with the mind of a twelve year old."[165]

Other families followed the patterns of ambivalence that often marks abusive relationships. Troy Crenshaw recalled the time that a widow with five children moved into a tenant home near their house in Hunt County. One Sunday morning, the oldest daughter appeared at the Crenshaws' door, asking permission to use the telephone to call the sheriff. She told the Crenshaws that the family had left Oklahoma to "get shut" of the man who had been "dogging" their mother and "he's found us." The sheriff's car stopped a few hours later. Toward sunset the man and the woman he had been accused of dogging were seen strolling arm in arm with three younger children following behind. The family returned to Oklahoma a few months later.[166]

In Collin County, Millie and Eddie Stimpson alternately enjoyed and suffered through almost twenty years of marriage. Eddie Stimpson worked hard at farming, but he had a taste for liquor and other women, which his wife found difficult to tolerate. Millie Stimpson coped with her anger in a number of ways. When she had time and was "feeling blue," she took her troubles to the nearby creek, saying, "I got to get out of this house for a while. . . . I don't feel too good." She "would grab her poles and head for the creek. She would all way say, I'm going fishing where I can have some peace." Presumably, fishing brought her relief through sitting quietly near a small stream, perhaps the location of the only shade trees amid the cotton fields. Fishing also provided food for her family and so became a positive action. Millie Stimpson used her energy to cope with her frustrations toward her husband. As her son said,

I can remember whin my mother would get depress about no money, not much food, and my dad would not come home till late. She would start

Gender and Family Relationships

reading a while, walking the floor, cleaning up where she had all ready clean, humming a song. Then she would go out on the porch and gaze out across the western horizon, and start singing, 'Nobody Know the Trouble I See,' and 'In the Even Whin the Sun Goes Down, I Hate to See That Even Sun Go Down.' She would just stand there looking at the sun. I guess us kid sense some thing not right and no better than to bother her. Soon she would feel better. If Dad had not come home, we would eat, and sit out on the porch until Dad come home or bed time. Then we had our Bible study, say our prayers and to bed.

Millie Stimpson left her husband at least twice in the first ten years of marriage, taking her children to her parents' home in the small city of Sherman. The second time, when the cotton needed chopping, Eddie Stimpson "finely beg mom back." At last, she reached the end of her patience. One night she left her two young daughters at home alone while she and Eddie Jr. walked five miles to catch his father in a romantic liaison. The son wrote, "We went to the house where Dad was visiting a woman. We peep in the window. The woman was sitting in Dad lap. Mom kick the door down. The woman ran out the back door and Dad got up and stroll on out to the car, Mother and I behind him." To her son's amazement, Millie Stimpson was angered to the point of violence: "Whin we got back home Mom jump out of the car, run into the house, got the shot gun and as Dad come in the door she raise the gun to shoot him, and Ruth and Bessie Lee standing beside her jump and swung down on the barrel. Without Ruth and Bessie Lee, Dad would have been shot gun dead, but all the shots went into the floor." The drastic action had its desired effect: "After that Dad was a good boy for years."[167]

Despite all of the disagreements and bad behavior, Stimpson recalled, his father never struck his mother, and the shotgun scene may have been all the more impressive because of the violence where none had been before. Some marriages, however, concluded in a crescendo of domestic violence. In Hunt County, Bob Bird, a well-to-do farmer from the Mohegan community, killed himself in front of his family after arguing with his wife. The Birds had had "family trouble," and the wife showed a "badly gashed face" to the investigators, a result of Bird's whipping her before shooting himself.[168]

In Bell County, the affluent Gunn family, owners of a 277-acre farm near the town of Holland, lived in discord for fifteen years before the family's violent dissolution in 1920. The documents concerning the Gunns' recurring legal battles depict a family in torment. In 1905, Sarah Keaton, a widow with four sons and two daughters between the ages of three and twelve, married James N. Gunn, a widower with three daughters between the ages of eight and twelve. The Gunns then had five children of their own.[169] For the next decade and a half, Sarah and James Gunn continually quarreled with their stepchildren as well as with each other, and Sarah reported that her husband began "unkind, harsh, and tyrannical conduct toward her" shortly after their marriage. As the children reached adulthood, each left the chaotic household, with one Gunn daughter and one Keaton daughter even taking up residence together, away from their parents.

The discord between Sarah and James Gunn reached the crisis stage in October 1919. According to Sarah Gunn, James, "without any just cause whatever, cursed and abused" her, "slapped and struck her with his fist, threw her violently on the floor, struck her with a conch shell, beat and bruised her, and drew a pistol and threatened [her] with death, if she did not leave the premises." She left in the company of one of her daughters, venturing out into the darkness to seek shelter at a neighbor's house. A few days later, Sarah filed for divorce from James, telling her attorney that he had "repeatedly threatened to take her life."[170]

Before the divorce was completed, however, Sarah and James Gunn reconciled, and by the spring of 1920, Sarah had abandoned the divorce suit and gone back to the farm.[171] Matters soon deteriorated further, and on 8 November 1920, James Gunn shot and killed Sarah and her twenty-three-year-old son, Hobart "Jack" Keaton. His attorneys argued that James Gunn acted in self-defense, fearing that Jack Keaton was going to kill him. The Bell County jury, however, found Gunn guilty of murder and sentenced him to ninety-nine years in prison. Sarah and James Gunn left their five minor children, the youngest of whom was two years old when her mother died. The Gunn estate, valued at sixty thousand dollars, was broken up and much of it used to settle legal fees.

Because most domestic violence went unreported, one can only speculate about its extent in the early twentieth century. Sarah Gunn's willingness to publicize her husband's abuse was unusual, and he may have perceived her revelations in the course of the divorce suit as betrayal. Perhaps his sense of betrayal even provoked him to commit his ultimate act of violence, although he steadfastly maintained that he felt that his own life was threatened by Jack Keaton.

Rather than going through a public breakup like the Gunns', many dissatisfied husbands simply left. In 1923, one marriage in five in Texas ended in divorce, but many of those seeking such legal recourse may have been urban dwellers. Farm people may have preferred less formal separations, with disgruntled husbands just disappearing.[172] The number of desertions followed ethnic lines. In the late 1920s, surveyors found few white women separated or divorced from their husbands, reported "a comparatively large number of deserted wives" among African Americans, and characterized the deserted woman as "becoming a pathetically and surprisingly common figure among the Mexicans."[173] On rare occasions, the wife left the husband. Conrad Grellhesl frequented the saloon in Leroy, McLennan County, and became abusive when he drank. In 1926, his wife, Mary Seith Grellhesl, divorced her husband after the birth of their ninth child and moved to the town of West.[174]

Among rural Anglo-Americans, a strong stigma still existed against divorce throughout the first half of the twentieth century. Bernice Weir, married to her first husband for more than thirty years, commented, "I always said I believed marriages are made in heaven. I believe that you know your mate when you meet them. And when you take the vows, I believe you ought to stay with them."[175] Myrtle Calvert Dodd remembered that in the McLennan County community of Hewitt, there "wasn't no such thing as divorce then. Never heard of it—or separating."[176] Around Waxahachie, near the big city of Dallas, divorce was more common, although not particularly welcome, as Etta Carroll recalled: "Oh, yes. People divorced." Dovie Carroll added, "We knowed some, but very few. Very few back in those days." He recalled that people in the community "didn't appreciate it much, but they still was friends to them." Etta Carroll said, "We treated them just like we always—We said, 'That's their business and not ours.'" Dovie Carroll concluded, "You didn't hear too much divorces back in them days. Very few."[177] The Carrolls characterized their own marriage as peaceful, Etta Carroll commenting: "We always worked in harmony. If you can't, why, just sit still until you get over it."[178]

Czech Americans and Czech immigrants documented cases of divorce in spite of the Roman Catholic Church's vigorous teaching against it. The widowed Caroline Gast married Johann Jupe in 1902 and moved to the Jupe homeplace from Westphalia, a German settlement in Falls County. The marriage did not work out, and she received the Jupe family home and forty acres in the settlement, while Johann moved in with his son and daughter-in-law. In 1917, August Maler was robbed near West and left to be dragged to death by his horses, leaving his wife of twenty-three years, Elizabeth Richerzhagen Maler, a well-to-do widow. The next year, Elizabeth, aged thirty-seven, married twenty-eight-year-old John Debbendener. The marriage was "a disaster," as John was apparently only interested in spending Elizabeth's money. He began to accumulate debts and left Tours on a train to escape his creditors. A local citizen observed, "That was the best ticket Elizabeth ever bought."[179]

In many cases of desertion, separation, and divorce, alcohol abuse appears to have been a major factor. In virtually all cases, the abusive alcoholic was the husband and father. World War II hero Audie Murphy was born into an extremely poor family near Celeste, Hunt County, in 1924. Audie, the seventh child, was sixteen and living in Hunt County when his alcoholic and irresponsible father, Pat Murphy, "simply walked out of our lives and we didn't hear from him again." According to the family, he had tried to get Josie Murphy, his wife, to go with him to West Texas, looking for more opportunity and different prospects. She refused to leave the Hunt County area, where her aging parents lived, and Pat took off without her. Josie Murphy died shortly thereafter of heart disease, leaving her smallest children to go into an orphanage south of Greenville. Her famous son bitterly recalled in 1956, "She died when she was in what should have been her vigorous years. Her story, including her early death, is not unusual in the history of a sharecropper's family, particularly when the sharecropper himself runs off, leaving his wife to take care of their children—in Mother's case, nine of us."[180]

In a remarkably candid local history (1988), Sister Mary Elizabeth Jupe chronicled the foibles and failings as well as the triumphs of the German and Czech families of Tours, McLennan County. According to Jupe, alcohol played a large role in fomenting discord in the small crossroads surrounded by cotton farms. Women like Anna Jupe Uptmor assumed the role of family leader when their husbands, for whatever reason, proved incapable of doing so. Anna Uptmor's husband, Henry, did "not tak[e] his responsibility as bread winner too seriously," and Anna became "the organizer, the planner, the provider." Henry was more interested in playing his accordion, and Tours people recalled his being "so drunk that he could hardly stand up, but he never missed a note."[181]

Frances Podsednik, who immigrated from Czechoslovakia and came to the area near West, also in McLennan County, in 1904, remembered the liquor problems of the men in her community: "They drank too much, I don't know if from the Old Country they would drink, they were mean to their wives, some of them. The women didn't drink, the men did, but the women didn't. They hate it, because the men that would drink was mean. My sister hate it, the men would get drunk and say such ugly things. She could kill that man when he be like that."[182] Alcohol abuse crossed ethnic lines: Vera Allen Malone, an

African American, recalled that her father, who was "a good farmer," had "one habit which was very bad, and that was he drank a little bit. And a lot of times he would drink too much; and when he would drink too much, of course, then he wasn't doing anything much. Sometimes that'd be for a day or two."[183]

Sometimes whiskey only threatened marriages rather than destroying them as women took matters into their own hands. When her husband, Albert, did not come home, Pauline Wanke Weinberger hitched up the buggy, went to the saloon where he was regaling his comrades with tales, and took him home.[184] Mary Olsovsky Uptmor left her husband, Louis, in a battle over his home brew during the Depression. Louis wanted to make home brew, probably corn whiskey, to bring in a little extra cash, and Mary opposed the project because she thought men would squander money on drink rather than spending it on their families. "When persuasion failed, she packed her suitcase, took the youngest child, and bought a ticket to Oklahoma where her dad lived. Louis had one of the children to write a pleading letter to her to come back. After she felt that she had made her point, she returned. There was no whiskey brewed on that Uptmor place."[185]

Dramatic episodes were the exception, not the rule, for marriages in rural Texas in the early twentieth century. How many marriages were actually loving and happy is impossible to determine, but most couples stayed together. Mutual need bound them, and a substantial number of couples reached old age together.

Many older farm people tried hard to remain independent and maintain their own households. Those who owned their land were sometimes able to remain in their homes by renting out their farmland or by having younger relatives come live with them. Tenants, on the other hand, usually lost claim to places to live when they could no longer work in the fields. Even as many of them had spent their working lives moving from tenant farm to tenant farm, they spent their old age rotating among their children, as Etta Carroll said: "First one of them, and then the other, because they didn't have any homes."[186]

Families expanded to take in their older members just as they adjusted to accommodate extra children. Sometimes the adaptation could be difficult. Flake Burnett of Hunt County remembered his grandfather, Jim Burnett, attempting to live with one of his daughters, "but he was a stormy kind of an old man."[187] Karen Gerhardt Britton wrote of hearing her female relatives whisper about the mistreatment of her elderly great-grandmother in Ellis

County. The stories of the great-grandmother's abuse by her daughter caused "great sadness and even greater rage" among the other women of the family, but an attempt to save the great-grandmother created a permanent schism in the family.[188]

Myrtle Calvert Dodd recalled her family's stretching to include grandparents from both sides of the family. Both her paternal and maternal grandmothers alternated living among several of their children in southern McLennan County, "and as soon as that one left, the other one would come." Reflecting on the addition of grandparents to a family with eight children, Dodd said, "Well, it was hard. When they came, why, we had to make room for them, of course. Really, now, I don't know how they did it. But we did. . . . My grandfather was eighty years old, and Grandmother was thirteen years younger. Still able to have kept house. But you know, then they just thought you's supposed to live with your kids."[189]

Such changes in the family structure and living arrangements must have been disagreeable for everyone concerned at times. Busy mothers like Hester Calvert had to make room in their homes for the older people and help them feed and clothe themselves. But breaking up housekeeping and becoming dependent on their children also proved a strain on women who had had their own households for forty or fifty years or longer. Myrtle Dodd remembered her grandmother's efforts to fit in and not cause trouble despite her misgivings about her daughter-in-law's performance as a wife and mother: "Now, my grandmother knew to hold her tongue, but I've heard her say, 'If I's so-and-so, I wouldn't do so-and-so. I wouldn't let my younguns do so-and-so.' I've heard her say those things, but not to my mother. But she knew when to say and when not to say. Very diplomatic."[190]

Most families took care of their own, even outside the immediate family. Josie and Cornelius Crenshaw took in various relatives, as their son remembered: "Two daughters of an older brother of their Aunt Josie came for a summer visit that lasted until one of them died of consumption a year later. Although Cousins Ida and Edna had seen much better days, they were like Robert Frost's Hired Man, who came back home to Warren and Mary to die: they had no other place to go, and so my parents had to take them in." The cousins stayed only a year, but Josie Crenshaw's widowed and childless sister, July, "half deaf and palsied," lived with the family for fifteen years. Aunt July and her sister did not enjoy the most cordial relationship. Mrs. Crenshaw felt better, however, after Aunt July was rebaptized; "the petty domestic irritations that her sister had caused her through the years lessened as the two reflected that they were now together at last as sisters in the New Testament Church."[191] Only the most unfortunate people ended their lives alone. Some of them, mostly female, spent their last days at county-run paupers' farms. Flake Burnett, the son of the superintendent of the Hunt County farm, observed of the farm, "It was a good place for them except the loneliness and the neglect of the families. It made it pitiful but then you find the same thing out here in our nursing home, they're still neglected, forgotten."[192] After years and years of hard work, the ultimate calamity came for women isolated from their family circles.

Within their networks of family, women in the Blacklands lived as wives, mothers, daughters, and sisters, defining themselves in their relationships to others. They operated not within separate spheres from their menfolk but in overlapping circles. Many married women directed as much energy as they could toward the physical nurture of those families, working to provide homes as comfortable as limited financial circumstances would permit. Chapter 2 will examine the ways in which Blacklands women endeavored to shelter and clothe their families and themselves.

chapter *two*

Keeping Warm, Keeping Dry

Housekeeping and Clothing
in the Blackland Prairie

When blues singer and Blacklands native Leadbelly recorded his plaintive rendition of "The Boll Weevil" in 1936, he mournfully repeated the unwelcome insect's persistent longing for a permanent home.[1] Like the boll weevil, tenant and sharecropper families in the Blackland Prairie moved from farm to farm, looking for a place to settle. "Home" in America of the early twentieth century was a complex concept, made even more so in Central Texas by the crop-lien system. To the landowners, home meant the place that they looked forward to passing on to their children. The tenants and sharecroppers knew that they would in all likelihood not be in the same place in five years.

Some of these folks' notions of house and home may have transcended class lines, however. Houses, as physical structures, were actual barriers against the outside, places to keep their families dry when rain poured, shaded when the sun blazed, and sheltered when blue northers howled down out of the plains. Keeping the outside out was a constant battle, whether against dogs, chickens, insects, or ever-present mud or dust, and women fought tenaciously to maintain the boundaries. At the least, home was a physical presence, a leaky roof over a family's head. At the most, it was a psychological haven, the location where family members could come together and feel loved and secure.[2]

Home was essentially a private place, although in most cases the house was actually owned by someone outside of the family. For sharecroppers and tenants, the house came with the land and was only occasionally a part of the consideration in the choice of property to farm for the next season.[3] Most women had little say in choosing these houses, but once the family moved in, the care and upkeep of the house became the jurisdiction of the mother. Many women subscribed to bourgeois ideals of cleanliness, dearly bought with scarce water and harsh lye soap. Keeping the house orderly was one way in which a woman could gain some sense of agency in her life. She could not control the weather or the world cotton market. She usually would not have the means of getting her family out of debt. But she could try to keep her house straight and clean. For a poor woman, the home was an area of relative autonomy, where she worked directly for the welfare of her family rather than the profit of the landowner.[4]

Women on the Blackland Prairie often shared field work with the men, but in most cases housework was the women's domain exclusively.[5] Household work usually has one primary feature, regardless of the race, class, or sex of the person performing the work: the goal of making a house and its inhabitants cleaner, more weatherproof, more comfortable. Beyond this ultimate intent, however, housework changes from household to household with several factors. One, of course, is a woman's bent toward domestic activity. In the rural Blackland Prairie, as in every other location, some women simply enjoyed housework, while others disliked it or preferred other enterprises. Social pressure, too, may have determined the ways in which women kept house, as young girls were socialized into understanding the purported importance of an orderly house.[6] Family size also affected both the amount of housework to be done and the number of helpers available to a wife and mother in the form of older daughters or extended family. Myrtle Dodd, the oldest of eight children, recalled, "It was my job to see that the younger ones had their clothes all ready to go to school and to make beds and—we kind of had to straighten up everything before we left because my mother—like I've told you, she had to sew—she nearly always had a baby and there's just too much to do. We just dare not leave without our beds made."[7] For many women in the Blacklands, their families' incomes determined how they kept house. A woman who did not have to do field work could devote more time to indoor chores, and women in more prosperous families had more conveniences such as running water to ease their work. Some landowners' wives were assisted by African American tenants' or sharecroppers' wives, who consequently had even less time for their own families' chores. Eddie Stimpson praised his mother's industriousness that led her to clean house for other families: "I can give my mother and father high praises for being good providers. . . . She didn't mind wrapping us kid up and go scrap the little cotton left on a burr, or walking for five mile to do house work for a cupple of doller."[8]

Even women who worked only in the house kept rigorous schedules, with numerous meals to be cooked, many clothes to be made and washed by hand, and animals to be fed and tended; those who performed both field work and housework had to manage their time all the more carefully just to get everything done. They labored to provide the most basic requirements for themselves and their families: shelter, clothing, and food.

Most Blacklands families in the early twentieth century lived in houses of one of three styles: Cumberland, double pen, or single pen. All three of these styles gave witness to the origins of the Blacklands population in the southeastern United States, for they descended directly from Anglo-American folk architecture of the Middle Atlantic region. A Cumberland house, the most common, was a two-room rectangle with an exterior door into each room on one long side, following a floor plan that originally occurred commonly in middle Tennessee and the Cumberland plateau. The next most popular type was the frame double pen, a simple two-room rectangle with gables on the ends. A single pen consisted of one square room with aligned front and rear doors and a fireplace in the middle of one gabled wall.[9] Others lived in frame dogtrots or shotgun-style houses, styles dating back well before the turn of the century. Most people in the Blacklands lived in houses that began with one or two rooms, compared to their counterparts in other parts of the United States, where farmhouses contained an average of seven rooms.[10]

More prosperous families lived in larger, more comfortable houses. The "central hall house," which peaked in popularity around 1900, featured four rooms, two on each side of the hall. The style most popular with landowning families after 1910 was the gable bungalow, which had three rooms with gables facing front and back. Home builders along improved highways, with close ties to urban areas, favored the gable bungalow, while those less influenced by the city preferred other styles, such as the hip bungalow and cross-gable houses. But almost two-thirds of the residents in these areas before 1940 lived in either Cumberland, single-pen, or double-pen houses—houses that began with only one or two rooms.[11]

Kitchens were sometimes added to two-room houses. These were called shed rooms, and they often stretched across the back of a two-room house. Alice Owens Caufield recalled her family's tenant house in southern McLennan County: "I can remember a bedroom, another bedroom, and then over on that side, like you're building the shed room, that was the kitchen; it was a long kitchen."[12] Less than ten miles away, Bernice Weir remembered how common shed rooms were: "I suppose it was just kind of a shed room across the back because that's the way so many of the houses were in that day and time for renters."[13] Adding a shed kitchen removed the hot stove from the house and may have decreased the danger of fire, but it also isolated women's work from the rest of her family, making it difficult to watch small children or communicate with others.

Most of the houses were made of wood, usually pine imported by rail from East Texas, Arkansas, or Louisiana. Many were of board-and-batten or box-and-strip construction, a single-layer construction that was extremely permeable in cold weather.[14] Most had masonry pillars or wood blocks for foundations; some had fencing across the crawl space to shut out chickens, dogs, and other would-be occupants, as "only low-life people allowed dogs in the house," according to Frank Locke.[15] Multiple porches, sometimes as many as three per house, shielded many houses from the hot Texas sun.

The quality of housing varied widely. In 1920, researchers placed the value of landowners' homes at twice that of tenant farmers and three times that of sharecroppers.[16] In Hunt County one observer marked the contrast: "Most of the farmhouses are unpainted four- or five-room frame buildings, but a few are substantial and well kept. Many of the tenant houses have only two or three rooms."[17]

The poorest houses were "little more than hovels hardly fit for human habitation," with dirt floors and visible cracks between the exterior boards.[18] While most were constructed new for the purpose, some tenant houses were recycled slave quarters.[19] A disgruntled farmer wrote to University of Texas researchers shortly before World War I: "I am going to give you a description of the house that I am in while I am writing this letter. It is a four-room shack, two big rooms 14 X 14; two little side rooms, 8 X 14, just boxed and stripped; no overhead ceiling; no shutters inside; no strips inside; three windows, 8 X 10 light; no porch and there is plenty of cracks in the outside walls that a half-grown rat can run through."[20] Eddie Stimpson recalled that one house that his parents occupied as sharecroppers had "a lot of rats, big ones." He also remembered lying in bed, looking at the stars through the holes in the tin roof of the house.[21]

In contrast, many landowners lived in comfort, if not with the ease of townspeople. When Kate Peacock Jones married in 1920, she and her husband moved in with his father until they could set up their own household. She recalled her father-in-law's house: "To me it was the nicest and prettiest house in the country. It was on high ground, with a big grass lot out front, with a big gate to go in and out and a yard fence. It had two large rooms about 18 feet square and a big wide hall between the rooms with a smaller room behind each large room." The house had back and front porches and one fireplace with "a nice mantle." The large kitchen had a new "Home Comfort Range." The house was made of "extra good pine lumber." The inside walls and ceilings were beaded board "that looked almost like varnished furniture," while the pine exterior was always painted white.[22]

The wealthiest landowners built fine homes commensurate with their economic status. The Westbrook family, whom one neighbor remembered as "richer than all the rest of the people down there put together," owned almost 4,500 acres in McLennan County in 1910, and they built a series of elaborate houses on their acreage, which extended into neighboring Falls County.[23] When the McLennan County home of the Peeler Williams family burned in 1909, Williams brought in brick for the replacement house on railroad cars and built walls three bricks thick. His daughter remembered that Williams's African American tenants hauled the brick and did a "great portion of the construction work." The final cost of the home came to just over five thousand dollars.[24]

At times, houses underwent changes in status as they aged. Such shifts indicate mobility on the owners' parts as well as that of the tenants. When Bernice and Pat Bostick built their new bungalow in the late 1930s, their old house across the road became a tenant house, although it needed repair. Bernice Bostick Weir commented, "We rented out a little land and people lived in it, just the same."[25]

Millie Birks Stimpson celebrated when her husband gained permission from their landlord to move from the shotgun-style house that they occupied in their early years of marriage to "the big house." Her son recalled, "I think whin Mom got word we could move she carried all she could by hand that day with Ruth and me tottling along with her, each trip probly with a little bag or bucket helping out. . . . Mother were so proud. She scrub the floor, paper the house all over. It was like the beginning of a new life for her. She were happy about all the room she had. She let out a sound, Wow, a Home at last!" Millie Stimpson considered this house a major improvement in their lives despite the leaky roof that meant that the family had to use "tub and bucket, pot and pan to catch the water" and even move the bed to keep from getting wet during every rain.[26]

Sociologist Ruth Allen frequently found African American and Mexican tenant families in old homesteads that had been abandoned by the landowners and left "to fall about [the tenants'] ears." She reported some rooms unfit for use, others used to store seed and feed, and some left empty because of a lack of furniture.[27] In Navarro County, a six-room Cumberland structure built about 1901 boasted interior wainscoting and exterior fish-scale shingles, indicating high status. But the pattern of room enlargement and the artifacts later found around the house showed that the house was used as housing for itinerant Mexican workers, its walls plastered with a 1928 Spanish-language newspaper.[28] The willingness of Mexican laborers to accept poor housing made them welcome to some farmers. Landowners in the lower Blacklands began hiring Mexican tenants with the knowledge that they would work even more cheaply and could demand even less than African Americans. This pattern appeared in Central Texas in the late 1920s: "It is true that the Mexican will put up with housing accommodations which the American tenant will not be asked to put up with. It may also be true that the Mexican will be more under the control of the owner than any other tenant."[29] In Hunt County, too, owners replaced both black and white tenants with pliable Mexican workers, as a local graduate student reported at the time: "White and negro cotton tenant farmers cannot compete with the Mexican—they cannot accept his standard of living. Cotton planters who employ Mexican help feel even less responsibility toward them than they do in the case of negroes, and much less than in the case of white men and their families."[30]

Almost all Blacklands houses were built with the goal of keeping their occupants cool in the Texas summer, but, as the newspapered walls indicated, the cross-ventilation made many houses uncomfortable during winter cold spells. Some well-to-do farmsteads had two fireplaces, one on each end of the house, and the majority of owners had brick or stone fireplaces.[31] By the 1920s, most houses were heated by stoves that burned wood or coal, although some people continued to depend on fireplaces.[32] Bernice Weir recalled the coal-burning heater in her first home as a bride in southern McLennan County in 1919: "Of course, you know, we didn't have any kind of heat then except the heater and the cookstove, and our winters were so much worse then than they are now. They had had a fireplace in that house but it had been closed up because they said their legs burned up and their backs froze to death."[33] Although the stoves were an improvement, Adelaida Torres Almanza observed that they

Housekeeping and Clothing

were still inadequate for large families. Her extended family lived in a McLennan County house with only canvas in the windows instead of glass, and the family huddled around the heater for warmth. She remembered: "Since there were so many of us the heater wouldn't be enough. My father-in-law would sit there, and my sister-in-law, and this other sister-in law, and this little kid, and I didn't have a place to sit in front of the heater, and it was very cold."[34] Almanza did not indicate why she was excluded from the circle around the fire, but perhaps as the most recent bride she had the least entitlement to a spot at the stove. Coal had its own set of problems, as Myrtle Dodd remembered: "My mother hated coal because it made everything so dirty."[35] Coal also required money with which to buy it.

Sometimes wood was no more plentiful than coal, proving scarce on the prairie grasslands. In northern Hunt County, affluent farm families purchased two- to three-acre lots in the Sulphur River bottoms so that they could have an adequate supply of oak or pecan firewood in the winter.[36] In McLennan County, Mexican immigrant women left their homes in the cities and chopped firewood for more prosperous families.[37] To conserve firewood, Etta Carroll remembered, she and her family watched their consumption carefully: "We let our fire die—go out at night. And you didn't keep the whole house warm; after we got the big house, we'd shut off doors."[38]

Owners constantly added to or subtracted from their houses. As archaeologists David Jurney and Randall Moir observe, "A home was never complete. The basic modular form of each dwelling represents the original intent, and possibly the family size, of the builders. Subsequent additions indicated how family size changed or rooms shifted in function by adding rear kitchens due to greater affluence, reduced lumber costs, or advancing technology."[39] The first home of Frank Locke's family near Lorena, McLennan County, in the 1890s, was of box-and-strip construction, consisting of two large rooms and two shed rooms. Next, the family added two eighteen-by-twenty-foot rooms, one above the other. A few years later, they built on a parlor, a "dormitory" for the boys, and two porches.[40] Their home reflected their stability as part of the landed class.

Blacklands families tended to be large, and homes were frequently cramped. In Hill County in 1920, for example, social workers found overcrowding "considerably more common" than supposed. One family of ten living in a two-room house and another with eleven in three rooms were not "isolated cases." Most white families lived with about one room per person, and 25 percent lived with two persons or more per room. Black families were considerably more crowded, as more than three-quarters lived with more than two persons per room and only 2 percent averaged fewer than one person per room.[41]

With such congested conditions, general living areas frequently served double duty as bedrooms, each room being purely functional. Myrtle Calvert Dodd recalled the tenant house that her parents shared with their eight children on the Stribling farm near Hewitt, in McLennan County, around 1910:

> The front bedroom would have been, really, the living room, most people, and it was when they had company. It was mine and my sister's room. And the next room had two beds in it, and my mother's and father's room was the one that came out on the ell. It had two beds, too. And usually the youngest one or two slept on one of those beds and my parents slept on the other one. And the boys' room was back of the kitchen and run up to the bathroom. It had two beds in it, too. I know it did, because whenever Leroy, this cousin of mine, came to live with us, he had one of the beds and two older boys had the other.[42]

The Sanchez family in Bastrop County used each of their three rooms as a bedroom, segregating their four girls into one, their four boys into another, and the parents in the third.[43]

More prosperous homes had sitting and dining areas apart from the sleeping quarters, but sharing bedrooms was still common. The Locke home, a few miles from the Stribling farm, had two large upstairs bedrooms: one with three double beds for the girls and the other with four double beds for the boys, plus one downstairs bedroom with two double beds. Bernice Weir's two daughters slept in the room with her and her husband, while their two sons slept in the other bedroom. In the summer, entire families moved outdoors. The Collier family simply moved all of their chicken-feather mattresses out on the porch.[44] "Of course, when the weather got hot, my dad had a big old tent," Dovie Carroll commented, remembering his boyhood before World War I. "We put four beds under it. He put that up out in the yard and we'd sleep out there through the summer under that tent. It was made out of canvas. Put up beds out there."[45]

For migrant workers, temporary conditions were often absolutely wretched. In Hill County in 1920, U.S. government investigators found a Mexican family of six and two single men living in a one-room shack. Seven Anglo-Americans lived in a tent barely covering three beds, while another tent sheltered ten people. In the farmhouse on the property, where the owners had moved out to let pickers have the house, a family of four lived in one room, a family of six lived in two rooms, and a single man lived in the hall between. Among African American families, conditions were also dreadful; the agents commented, "Practically every negro family had 'doubled up' with some other family and quarters were very crowded."[46] Bernice Weir recalled housing six African American women and one man in a one-room house on their McLennan County farm, and the Lockes lodged families in their machine shed.[47]

As Troy Crenshaw, a farmowner's son, pointed out, with large numbers of people living under one roof, "friction did sometimes generate sparks."[48] A tired mother at the end of the day might have to settle not one or two but three or four children into a single bed. Family members had little privacy or individual space. Parents sharing beds or bedrooms with small children may have found that sexual intimacy came at a premium, although the large size of families indicates that most managed to maintain intimate physical relations despite the presence of older children. For some women, the loneliness of a long cotton row may have been preferable at times to a small house overflowing with one's kinfolk and progeny.

Women tried diligently to make even the poorest housing as comfortable as possible, working with materials at hand. Luz Sanchez Hurtado remembered her mother stretching cotton ducking across the open rafters of their tenant house in Bastrop County, making an interior tent to protect her family from the numerous leaks in the roof.[49] Decorating a house with cracked walls and broken windows required imagination and improvisation, and oftentimes what might have appeared to be ornaments were in fact attempts to keep out the weather. Lee Rice recalled one of the numerous houses that his tenant-farming family occupied in Hunt County before World War I and his mother's attempts to make it livable:

When we moved to the Cassel farm the house did not have any underpinning, there were holes in the floor. Wind blew up through those cracks. Mama didn't have any money to buy a new rug, so she decided to make a rug to cover the floor. She borrowed a loom. The neighbors gave her their old clothes. She cut and tore these clothes into one inch wide strips. She sewed these strips together and wound them into balls, of ten inch diameter. When she thought she had enough balls (dozens!) she and Papa set up the loom and we started weaving rugs. It took a long time, but Mama finally had enough rugs to cover the floor of our living room. The neighbors gave her their old newspapers. We put a half dozen layers of paper down on the floor then the rugs on top of the papers. That made an airtight floor.[50]

Mrs. Rice was making an investment in her family's long-term well-being, for the Cassel farm was the place where they stayed after moving ten times in twelve years. Perhaps her labor indicated a determination to stay, or perhaps they had already decided to settle on the Cassel farm and she was trying to make the best of the situation.

Landowning families seldom had to resort to such measures to seal their floors. Frank Locke remembered that his family's parlor floor was covered with "matting, a popular, imported vegetable fiber floor covering, thirty-six inches wide and in varied colors and patterns. Fastened to wood floors with matting tacks. It sold for twenty-five cents to sixty cents per yard." The rest of the floors in their McLennan County home were bare pine, scrubbed once a week.[51] The Bostick family first had plain wooden floors, then added linoleum on the kitchen floor and finally acquired an Axminster rug for the front bedroom that doubled as a parlor.[52]

Dirt was an integral part of farm life, coming into the house as dust in dry weather and as mud in wet times, often mixed with manure. Many families cared for their floors fastidiously, sweeping their wooden floors every day and mopping them frequently. If water were plentiful, they brought it to the houses in barrels on slides from the wells or other water sources. More commonly, they used soapy water left from laundry. Myrtle Calvert Dodd recalled, "Plain old plank floors. And Mama scrubbed them. She'd scrub them with lye water, then rinse them off. They'd be as clean. In the wintertime, she didn't used to do them as much she wanted to, but in the summer we did them, oh, nearly every week. Nearly every Saturday. That was a job, because we had company on Sunday lots of times, and if we knew company's coming, we sure had to do it."[53] In Navarro County, the African American Langham family made do by using plain ashes when lye was in short supply.[54]

Interior walls varied in materials from rough planks to beaded board to fancy wallpapers for the well-to-do.[55] Many farm women improvised wall coverings for their board-and-batten structures, where the thickness of only one piece of lumber separated interior and exterior. With purposes both aesthetic and practical, they brightened wooden walls darkened by years of soot from lamps, fireplaces, and stoves, and provided extra sealing against cold and rain. Some used homemade whitewash, made of quicklime, water, lard, flour, and salt, to plaster interior walls.[56] More common for tenants' homes was the use of newspaper and magazine pages as interior insulation and decoration. Fordyce Sims, the son of a Dallas County sharecropper, recalled his excitement when he went to Cedar Hill with his father at age eight and saw real wallpaper on the walls of their rooming house. "To paper where we were living," wrote Sims, "Mother used pages of newspaper on the boxing plank walls, making paste of flour and water. I learned to do some of my reading on those papers."[57]

Some women put in hours of painstaking work in decorating houses that they might occupy a few years at best. Sociologist Ruth Allen found Mexican women using creative methods in their tenant homes, employing the meager materials at hand to satisfy their longing for beautiful surroundings. One had taken the pages of a jewelry catalog to paper her walls, covering one wall with pictures of silver goblets and another with images of clocks, while another woman papered the walls of three rooms with hundreds of "some kind of bank statement divided with blue lines," fitting each piece exactly to the adjoining piece so that the lines matched.[58] And one Hunt County Anglo woman attempted to bring color into her house by decorating the interior walls with "crayon drawings of brown horses on sheets of pale-green, lined paper, torn from a pencil tablet."[59]

In the Blackland Prairie as elsewhere throughout the nation, decorative items, like rugs and window coverings, often carried strong messages about the class position and level of "refinement" in a home.[60] Window coverings in particular were decorative rather than functional in an area where houses were far enough apart not to require any shelter from the curious eyes of neighbors or passersby. In Tours, McLennan County, two members of the Jupe family illustrate differing attitudes toward home decorating. Gertrude Holecek's family owned the store in Tours, and she grew up "accustomed to beautiful things." When she married John Jupe, Gertrude Holecek Jupe made matching bedspreads and curtains for their farm bungalow, ensuring a decor that she believed was proper but that most likely seemed superfluous and even pretentious to her neighbors. For Anna Jupe Uptmor, on the other hand, housework was of secondary importance after field work, and her windows had no curtains. But when her three daughters married, she made curtains for every window in their new homes.[61] Perhaps she wished for them lives with less field work than hers and symbolized her desires with window coverings that further separated the outside from the inside.

On the other side of the county, Bernice Bostick Weir faced her mother-in-law's disapproval for her curtains, which were purely ornamental: "The kitchen over there had two windows and three doors to the kitchen. And Grandma never did have any curtains in her kitchen at all, and when she moved out, I put curtains up there. She said, 'Well, you just ruined your kitchen. You darkened it where you can't see.' But it looked prettier anyway. That was what I wanted."[62] For the Folley family, in Limestone County, no shades seemed necessary. "We had homemade curtains that we made and put around in the dining room and in the parlor," said Inez Folley. "But in the bedrooms we didn't have curtains. You didn't have to pull the shade out in the country. You didn't have any close neighbors."[63] The family had greater needs than privacy, and the Folleys chose to spend their little money on other than aesthetic desires.

Alice Owens Caufield remembered the class prejudices exhibited by her cousins and the way they demonstrated their supposed superiority through their home:

> Those who had big living rooms and red carpet from wall-to-wall like the Austin—I had an aunt to marry into the Austin family, and they would talk about Old Man Dan Austin. He had the big house at Downsville with red carpet from wall to wall and all the fine stuff. My aunt—my mother's sister married into that family. The black Austins have always felt that they were very important people. All the Austin children, my first cousins, they felt very important. Brags. I never did brag about anything. Maybe they felt they had the best team or the best—whatever they were, they were just top, just like people are today. High ideas, I guess.[64]

With their wall-to-wall red carpeting as a tangible sign of their higher position, the Austin children felt superior to others of their race.

When most Blacklands inhabitants recall the furnishings in their homes, they tend to remember the number of beds in the house and little else. Often women made their own mattresses and pillows of lint cotton, hay, or chicken or goose feathers, and home demonstration agents sometimes carried out mattress-making workshops. Commercial mattress manufacturers also used families' own cotton to make new mattresses.[65] Among fastidious housekeepers, the beds received much attention, as Bernice Weir remembered: "Every week the beds were to be sunned; the mattresses were to be carried out."[66] In the warm Blacklands climate, the fight against insect infestation could not be let up for long. Mary Ann Collier Campbell remembered, "Chinches (bed bugs) would get in the folds of the mattresses and on the springs. Everyone in

Housekeeping and Clothing

the country had these little bugs. . . . They were dealt with by taking a little piece of rag dipped in kerosene and dabbing every fold and corner of the mattress. . . . These bugs were a chocolate color, about the size of a match end and would bite you."[67] Besides risking infestation, the beds carried symbolic messages as the places where marriages were consummated, where children were conceived and born, where loved ones breathed their last. The spaces for loving and the beginnings and ends of life were treated with great care.

Only well-to-do landowners had much furniture other than beds. Myrtle Calvert Dodd recalled her family moving into the Attaway place in southern McLennan County as tenants and not having enough furniture to fill the house, which had been the landowner's home and had several rooms.[68] More affluent families bought furnishings, like Alma McKethan McBride's parents, who began married life with a handsome trousseau and bought their first furniture with their savings: an oak bedroom suite, a fancier walnut bedroom suite, three rocking chairs, and a dining-room table with six cane-bottom chairs. Her grandmother gave the newlyweds a wardrobe from home to round out their furnishings.[69]

Bernice and Pat Bostick had almost nothing left when her mother-in-law moved to town from the family farm in 1920, taking most of her possessions with her. As landowners, however, they had sufficient financial resources to be able to furnish their home themselves. "She took everything," Bernice Bostick Weir said. "Pat—I've forgotten what day of December she moved, but anyhow, he went to town and bought that chifforobe that's in there and this table and I've still got the library table upstairs. And he bought—we called them davenports then, you know, that they opened down and made a bed. And then he bought a stove. Maybe she left us the heater in the living room, and she left us a couple of beds. So we had a little to start out with."[70] With his own taste and on his own authority, Pat Bostick quickly made the decisions on the new purchases. He ensured that the furniture was of such quality that it remained intact for much of a century, with his widow still owning most of the pieces seventy years later. Some landowning families saved money for furniture for years. Jake and Mary Zotz married in 1905, but, according to Jake's detailed financial records, not until 1908 did they buy furniture and "veneer to beautify it."[71]

The quality of housewares varied with a family's socioeconomic status as well. Most young couples started housekeeping with a minimum of goods, often gifts from both sets of parents, who may not have had much to spare themselves. Bernice Bostick Weir recalled: "Oh, I got a few things. I got a towel or two. And of course, my parents gave me sheets and pillowcases and quilts, things like that, and Grandma did, too. So we had plenty of bedclothes." Etta Carroll recalled a similar situation from her marriage at the age of seventeen: "His daddy and stepmother gave us some things, and my folks gave us some things. They gave us pots and pans and things like that. They gave us some quilts, too. In other words, they started us out with the necessary things that it took to start keeping house with."[72]

Improvisation ruled the day in which housewares might serve multiple purposes. For people with cash to spend at the turn of the century, pack peddlers carried "fine lace and linen tablespreads, counterpanes, pillowshams."[73] For tenant farmers, house linens remained at a premium, as they were for Myrtle Calvert Dodd's mother: "For everyday tablecloth, it was oilcloth. You wiped it off. But she had a Sunday one that she had to wash and iron, that she kept put away. . . . And we may have had more than one then; I'm not sure. But didn't everybody have a napkin then 'cause you didn't have paper napkins. You know what she'd keep? Probably a towel, cuptowel or something kind of in her lap and if the little ones spilled something, she'd get up and wipe their faces or give it to them to wipe their hands and faces." Hester Calvert made dishtowels, cuptowels, and so on, "lots of times, out of feed sacks or—seems to me like she had bought some special material for cuptowels once or twice maybe. And towels was hard to come by, too, when we were all little. The little ones would all get to use the same; she'd use the same towel on them to dry them off. . . . Later on, when I'd get up a teen-ager, you could buy them. But you couldn't when I was right young; at least, we didn't. Some people may have been where they could."[74]

Having enough sheets for numerous beds could also prove difficult. Etta Carroll said, "Those days, we could buy feed sacks and they were unbleached muslin and we'd take and make part of our sheets and our pillowcases out of the feed sacks. Then later on, they started to making colored flowered feed sacks. . . . You could make the prettiest—make pillowcases, make sheets—that you ever have seen. All of our sheets used to have seams. We didn't have big sheets way back yonder."[75] Alice Caufield recalled resourceful women in her African American community making bedclothing from used material: "They bleached the cotton sacks, what you put cotton in. They would bleach them and sleep on them. You know it comes about this wide [three feet] and they'd sew it up on each side, so if you're going to make a sheet, you just unrip one side and hem the ends. And I know they have made sheets out of it and they have used it for tickings to fill pillows."[76]

Families saved feathers, especially from geese, for making pillows and feather beds and for sale. Lee Rice's mother kept geese and every six weeks picked the soft feathers from under their wings for feather beds.[77] As Emma Bourne recalled goose-picking day, the geese were penned the night before. The family kept a large barrel with a canvas cover especially for goose feathers. The daylong process began early, as family members sat in straight chairs near the barrel. Bourne recalled, "I learned to pick geese when quite young, and blistered my fingers many times." The picker would grab a goose, turn it on its back, hold it with one hand, and pick the down feathers off of it with the other. The picker next turned the goose over, picked its back, and let it go. Then she or he would sack the feathers in clean sacks, which were "placed in the sun each day until some one came along to buy them or mother made use of them. Mother made feather pillows and beds for all the children and sold feathers each year."[78]

Gathering the feathers carried special hazards, according to Dovie Carroll. He remembered helping his stepmother and suffering the consequences of handling geese: "They'd bite you. . . . Their teeth, they's thick, all right, but they're not over that long, but they're little, fine. And don't think they can't hurt you. Ooh. But you take one with young ones, them little goslings, I tell you, they'll eat you up if they've got those little goslings out and you get them around them. They'll slope them wings up and come in at you wide open, flopping them wings agin you and biting you. You've got to be pretty good to stand up to them."[79] Across the Blackland Prairie, women and their children stood up to angry geese to obtain their feathers for household use.

Dishes, pots and pans, and other kitchen goods were likewise in short supply. A Falls County minister's wife recalled visiting a home in the mid-1930s where "things were clean but very sparse." This particular family owned one knife, one glass, and one china plate, which they gave to their honored guest.[80] Some families, such as the Jumpers from Hunt County, fared better at harvest time than at other times of the year: "It made you feel good to walk to the wash stand on the porch and find a new washpan, after using one for two or three months with a hole in the bottom that had to be stopped with a wad of chewing gum or mud. It made you feel good to see a new dishpan, tea kettle or a new oil cloth tablecloth on the eating table. One thing we always got on the farm at the end of the harvest were double cotton blankets for every bed."[81] Bernice Bostick Weir remembered her days as a newlywed: "I think Grandma gave us some of her dishes when she moved to town, enough to get by on. My mother or my brothers gave me some silverware, and I just had skimpy affairs until I accumulated. You always had a dishpan; you had to have a dishpan and a drain pan. Grandma gave us a skillet when she moved to town and a bread [pan]—to cook bread on. And then one by one, I just accumulated."[82]

Myrtle Calvert Dodd could not remember exactly what her mother's everyday dishes were for their family of ten, "but they were not china, I'll guarantee you." She continued: "I'll tell you, the hardest part was keeping glasses for everybody. And you know, there wasn't any plastic or anything like that. You didn't buy jelly. I know my mother would choose kind of heavy ones when she did buy them. Buy them, I expect, by dozens or half-a-dozens." By the 1930s, families bought oatmeal partially because of the free dishes found inside the packages.[83] Socioeconomic factors strongly influenced the types of dishes in a Blacklands home, according to archaeologists. In the early twentieth century, some affluent families changed from plain ceramic ware to "more decorative styles," and by the 1920s, landowners were buying "lightly decorated and full matching sets of fine tableware . . . with considerable consistency." Those sets often featured white dishes with patterns of pink and red roses with green leaves. Most of this dinnerware probably was made in the United States and sold widely throughout the nation. Porcelain appeared only as treasured pieces protected from everyday use.[84] Women safeguarded their glassware as best they could; Refugia Sanchez, for example, carefully packed the family goods during their frequent moves around Bastrop County, wrapping the dishes in newspaper before they were loaded into the mule-drawn wagon for the trip to the next tenant farm. She also looked carefully after her cast-iron pots and pans.[85] Among migrant families, dishes and cooking utensils were limited to what they could transport with them as they followed the crops.[86]

The exterior finishes of homes in the Texas Blacklands also delineated the social classes of the occupants, as unpainted houses often outnumbered painted ones.[87] Alma McKethan McBride remembered that the community of Spring Valley had more painted houses, bigger barns, and better fences than her home community of Kukelbur because the Spring Valley soil was more fertile and its occupants more prosperous.[88] And Myrtle Calvert Dodd classified the various houses in which her family lived as tenants by the paint: The first, the Westbrook place, was not painted, but her favorite, the Stribling place, was: "It was pretty there. It was yellow with a little brown trim there at the Stribling place. And it was a gray house on the Chapman place. And he [Mr. Chapman] painted it. That was his job, to keep his rent property all up."[89]

By the twentieth century, most houses in the Blacklands had glass windows. In Ellis County, however, Dovie and Etta Carroll's first house, which consisted of one room open to the rafters, had but one wooden window when they moved in as newlyweds in 1921. During their second year, Dovie Carroll's father, who owned the house, put glass windows in for them.[90] The Almanza family, in McLennan County, lived in a house with canvas windows in the 1920s. Windows could be disadvantageous; sociologist Ruth Allen reported in the late 1920s visiting house after house in which the window panes were broken or missing and wet or cold weather came straight into the house.[91] The worst landlords appeared oblivious to the problem. Eddie Stimpson recalled overhearing conversations at church: "They ain't hardly got no window in they house and she said that they can't get that white man to put none in."[92]

Another feature that marked a Blacklands house was the presence or absence of screens on the windows, which kept out flies and malaria-carrying mosquitoes. A screen provided the first line of defense in keeping the house apart from the outdoors, and it was one that many of the poorest inhabitants lacked. In the 1920s in McLennan County, fewer than 10 percent of African Americans' rural houses were screened, while none of their Hill County counterparts had screens.[93] In his piercing novel *Farther Off from Heaven* (1977), William Humphrey portrays the difficulty of life without screens:

> The houses my father's parents were given to live in on the farms they sharecropped were seldom better than shacks, never as sound as the barn. Leaves from the mail-order catalogues papered the single walls and through the cracks in the boards the winter winds blew strong enough to make the coal-oil lamp smoke its chimney. In one that I remember, the floors of the two rooms were dirt—when it rained, mud. They never had window or door screens, and in the summertimes, when, even after the sun had set, the close little hut was blazing and breathless and the windows could not be closed, mosquitoes and moths came in clouds. The mosquitoes were malarial—both my grandfather and my father suffered chronically from fevers and chills, with occasional acute and devastating attacks—and so it was necessary to drape the beds with "bars."[94]

Etta Carroll recalled her life without screens with more humor: "We think back now—how we live now and how we lived then and we said, 'How did we do things then?' And we said, 'Well, I can remember when we didn't have a screen door, and at night, to have the air in the house, we'd lay a chair down in front of the door.' And I said, 'I don't why we done that; a dog could get over it as good as anything could.' Lay the chair down crossways and a dog or cat could get in there anytime they wanted to. We never thought anything about it. We didn't know what a screen door was." Dovie Carroll added: "The mos-

Board and batten tenant farmer's house in the midst of a cotton field, Ellis County, July 1937 (Photo by Dorothea Lange, courtesy of the Library of Congress, LC USF 34-17103-C).

quitoes was bad, 'cause they's raised on them creeks and things there, you see. And they didn't know back then what to use for them. So you'd just get maybe a coal-oil rag and wipe your hands at bedtime, your arms, something or another. That'd keep them off for a while."[95] While the Carrolls took the lack of screens in stride, Myrtle Calvert Dodd recalled vividly her mother's dismay when they moved into a tenant house without screens: "My mother just threw a fit when she saw that little house didn't have screens on it. . . . I can still remember when my mother said, 'Now listen, we're going to have screens. We can't live—my kids—with no screens.'" Her mother galvanized her father into action, and he quickly took some screens from an unoccupied house.[96] In efforts to battle flies and mosquitoes, some families kept their livestock at a distance from the house. They covered food whenever possible. Some people planted tansy at their doors to keep out the flies and ants, as well as a flowering plant known as "catch fly."[97] Because mosquitoes could not be routed, however, malaria remained at high levels, one more ailment that busy rural mothers had to dose.

Many houses either had no yard or one of hard, swept dirt, which turned to mud in wet weather. Mothers labored to keep members of their household from tracking in huge quantities of mud during rainy periods. Alice Owens Caufield recalled the tiny yard surrounded by cotton rows at their sharecropper's home in McLennan County: "We wasn't fenced in, and they would plant cotton to—just enough to leave you a yard to play in. I don't remember any grass. I don't remember anything but that black mud. When it gets on you, when you get to the door, there was always some kind of knife or something flat that you cleaned your shoes completely before you stepped in that house. You didn't step in the house with no wet feet, no muddy feet. You cleaned your shoes."[98] Gladys Everett, the wife of a Baptist minister, recalled visiting a family living in an old house "in the field," with no distinct road through the cotton.[99] Swept yards often appear in dry climates worldwide and have been commonly associated with West Africa and African Americans. In Central Texas, swept yards were found at the homes of black and white alike. Frank Locke remembered that at Bullhide, "because of the tendency of the fertile, black soil to stick to the feet, nearly all farm houses were built on the poorest soil on the ridges and hillsides where there was an outcropping of limestone shale. The yards of such locations were swept with a broom and became very hard and the limestone content glistened in the sun."[100] Women worked hard to maintain their swept yards. Millie Birks Stimpson and her children swept their yard every day with homemade brooms: "We kids would go out and pull broom weeds. Mother would twist and tie them together and make brooms."[101]

Many women also diligently cultivated landscaping plants, adding color and beauty to a monotonous, almost treeless landscape of cotton. Henry and Sarah Cooper's Navarro County board-and-batten homestead boasted ornamental lilies and a rock-lined walkway.[102] And in addition to her vegetable garden, Elisabeth Jupe Hennig of Tours worked in a large flower garden in front of the family home in the late evening.[103] Flowers such as bearded iris tolerated the prairie climate and multiplied without much water or cultivation. Families such as Mary Hanak Simcik's took a practical approach in using these hardy plants: "We had four o'clocks and morning glories and stuff like that on our farms—the only things that would grow without care."[104] Still others went to great pains to bring flowers into their lives, as an extension service employee pointed out in the 1930s: "In fields along the public roads there are unpainted weather beaten houses where cotton is planted so near to the house that it is possible to stand on the door step and touch the plants. About some of these houses there are discarded boxes and rusty tin cans with flowers growing in them. To grow them has taken water. The many loops of rope at the well or the long path to the creek tell a pathetic story of the labor cost for the short lived beauty of these flowers."[105] Flowers grew mainly close to the house. As Eddie Stimpson remembered, his mother "tried flowers along the yard fence but the horses and cows would eat them up so we moved back from the fence and made flower beds in each corner of the yard."[106]

The outbuildings for Central Texas farmhouses were simple and few. Almost every farm had a smokehouse, which served as storage for meat and also for canned goods and other foodstuffs. The smokehouses were generally placed close to the houses for convenience. Bernice Bostick Weir recalled that their first smokehouse was twelve feet square and "just a few feet from the back doorstep."[107] For migrant workers, smokehouses served a different purpose, as primary lodging facilities. In Hill County, for example, a Mexican family of two children and three adults lived in a smokehouse with no floor or windows. That family slept on cotton sacks, while others had mattresses fashioned of corn shucks.[108]

Despite the climate of the Blackland Prairie, given to violent spring storms, relatively few houses in the region had storm cellars, probably because of the slick clay soil, which tends to cave in easily.[109] One exception was the community of Cedar Hill, where about half of the houses had cellars. Archaeologists speculate that these cellars were built after a tornado struck the community in the late nineteenth century. Informants there indicated that many residents feared storms and "would take to the cellars at the first sign of a storm." One informant, whose parents apparently dreaded tornadoes, said that she was "less than twelve hours old when a storm struck. Her father carried her mother to the cellar and her grandfather carried her. She stated, 'I spent half my childhood in a storm cellar.'" Many of the storm cellars were simply dug out and shored up with railroad ties, with tin roofs covered with dirt. They were havens for snakes, and on at least one stormy occasion a Cedar Hill woman decided that she would rather face a tornado than snakes.[110]

Most people in rural Central Texas, as in the rest of the American South, lacked electricity until at least the late 1930s. While city dwellers in Texas enjoyed the convenience of electricity from the 1890s on, their rural counterparts made do with more basic lighting systems and appliances. The most common was the kerosene, or coal-oil, lamp. Keeping kerosene lamps cleaned and filled and the wicks trimmed was a constant task, often the job of children. As Bernice Weir remembered, lamps required care "real often if you didn't have that wick trimmed just right. If you had a wick and it wasn't trimmed just right, it would

Housekeeping and Clothing

smoke and one side of your chimney would be smoked."[111] Myrtle Calvert Dodd remembered: "If there was a smoky chimney at night, I got told about it. Had to clean those chimneys and fill them up. Trim the wicks. . . . And there's usually two or three of them, anyway. There'd be one where we sit and one in the kitchen and one in my father and mother's bedroom. And if we come in our room, I remember they'd bring it from the kitchen or wherever it wasn't in use. . . . When the wicks would get low and we'd forget to get them, why, that was the next thing when you went to town, be sure and get some wicks."[112] In 1930, 80 percent of the Anglo women and almost all of the African American and Mexican women interviewed by Ruth Allen still relied on kerosene lamps.[113] Households often had an insufficient supply of lamps for the number of members of the family. Families had to prioritize tasks so that those needing the lamps the most had the use of them. A mother's quilting or sewing, for example, might yield to children's schoolwork or a father's newspaper reading.

By World War I, a few Blacklands farms boasted systems that burned carbide. Edward Clark, a resident of the Boyce community in Ellis County, succinctly described a carbide system: "A container in the yard held the raw carbide and small pipes carried the gas to each room to a fixture in the ceiling very similar to electrical fixtures of today."[114] Hunt County resident Lee Rice added more to the description: "The carbide plant worked automatically, keeping a steady pressure of gas, which was piped into the building to overhead light fixtures. All one had to do was turn the gas on and light it with a match. It made a fairly bright light."[115]

Blacklands residents considered carbide lights to be a major improvement over kerosene lamps, as Bessie McRae recalled: "It was good light. It was wonderful. It was good, so soft for your eyes and everything."[116] Carbide systems nonetheless had major drawbacks. Myrtle Calvert Dodd remembered the carbide system on the Earle farm that her family farmed around World War I:

If I remember right, they were sort of like a candle. At our place, it hung down like this. And you had to light them. In the wintertime, it was good when your house was shut up. I know when that carbide'd get low, my father would go out to the shed and stir it up and it'd come on again. . . . But we usually cut ours off in the summer and just use them in the winter because you opened your house and your windows and your doors and it made a draft through there. It would make it flicker to where it didn't turn good lights and then even blow out. And you sure had to relight them, because you could smell that carbide.[117]

Another method of rural illumination consisted of battery-powered genera-
tors, frequently known as Delco systems. In the Bostick home, they had a "Ray-
O-Light. It was a light with a shade around it and a little bitty—oh, it was such
a fragile little sack in there. I don't know what that was for, but anyhow, if you
wasn't very, very particular, that would break. And then you'd have to go
several days without it and have to go and buy another one and put it in there
and everything."[118] Only the most affluent families could afford such a system,
for the estimated cost of the equipment in 1915 was more than three hundred
dollars.[119] In 1923, only 1 in 54 Texas homes had electric or acetylene lights, and
in Hill County, only 3 out of 458 did.

By 1927, most farms that received electric service from central power stations were those located close to towns, along highways, or close to "low-
voltage transmission lines" serving small towns. Again, only the more affluent
families were able to afford the connections that provided electrical service. A
contemporary study found that the average user of electricity was a landowner
with acreage double that of an average-size farm.[120] Lee Rice concluded, "The
electric plant as well as the carbide plant gave plenty trouble, and everyone was
glad when the R.E.A. came along."[121]

The Rural Electrification Administration did not come to the Blacklands
any too quickly, despite the promises of the REA bill's co-author, Blacklands
resident Congressman Sam Rayburn of Bonham.[122] As late as 1940, 75.8 percent of the rural homes in Bell County, for example, still had no electricity. For
tenant farmers, the proportion throughout the state remained quite low: 85.6
percent of white tenants and 97.7 percent of black tenants still had no electrification on the eve of World War II.[123] In cities, in contrast, almost 100 percent of
the occupants had access to electricity to make their lives more convenient.

Even more than the lack of electricity, the shortage of dependable, safe water
supplies made life difficult on the Blacklands, adjacent to the dry Great Plains.
Water shortages in the region have generally proven more critical than have
times of overflow. The rivers that cross the prairie, running southeasterly
toward the Gulf of Mexico—the Trinity, the Brazos, the Little River, the San
Gabriel, the Colorado—are usually small and unimpressive save for their occasional spells of deadly flooding.[124] Springs are rare in the region, and creeks or
streams not much more plentiful. Creeks are notoriously inconsistent water
sources, remaining shallow except in periods of heavy rain and frequently
drying up in the late summer, leaving only pools of water several hundred

Housekeeping and Clothing

yards apart in the creek beds.[125] Even when they flow, Blacklands creeks rarely have little to commend them; renowned Texas naturalist Roy Bedichek, who grew up in southern McLennan County, remembered the creeks of his boyhood as "all sluggish and slimy, often clogged with debris, tributaries of the Brazos, whose drowsy current . . . always reminds me of dirty dishwater."[126]

Instead of surface water, most Blacklands families depended on groundwater, which came only grudgingly, with no regional shallow aquifer to provide it. Early Anglo settlers dug wells in search of it, with the lucky ones finding flowing water twenty or thirty feet down.[127] In parts of Williamson County, however, one had to dig almost a hundred feet to find water. Deep wells, which in some cases had to be dug to depths of three thousand feet, were luxuries that few could afford.[128] Consequently, Blacklands families made do with the little water that they had, collecting rain in cisterns and hauling water long distances from creeks or shallow wells. Such water shortages led to both careful usage and the constant threat of typhoid from contaminated water sources.[129] Some Blacklands farms—possibly as many as one-third—lacked any water source at all, and those families had to depend upon shared wells and springs. Alice Owens Caufield grew up on a sharecropper's farm in McLennan County with no water source. She remembered her father hauling water from a windmill on a creek near the landlord's house, the equivalent of three or four city blocks away: "We had a slide, you know, like two-by-fours, made enough apart for maybe a couple of barrels to sit on it. And your horse would just pull the slide and you go get your barrels filled and you'd come on back home and you've got water."[130] The wealthiest households, on the other hand, had "multiple onsite water sources," sometimes having both a well and a cistern.[131] The amount of water available determined the ease of many household tasks, from washing dishes to bathing babies. A woman with easy access to water might pamper a vegetable garden longer into the summer season than a neighbor forced to rely on rainfall alone for her garden. Generous amounts of water made life much simpler.

For most families, water was scarce. In most locations, shallow wells, averaging anywhere from ten to fifty feet deep, were the most common sources of water.[132] Obtaining and hauling water from wells and cisterns was a major task in all Blacklands households. As one reformer commented, "Probably the heaviest work around the farm house is the carrying in of the water and the carrying out of the waste water."[133] Inez Folley paid the rest of her life for her work hauling water, which weighs eight pounds per gallon: "And we had to bring water from the tank to water the hogs. My brother was five years older than I, and we'd take a big tubful of water and I'd hold one handle and he'd hold the other and so I know that's why I had a weak back, is because I lifted too much, too hard a load, when I was young. My back was still growing."[134] Less than a third of Anglo families and only 2 percent of black families in one study had water "in the house or on the porch" in the 1920s.[135] In Dallas, Hill, and Navarro Counties, the average distance from the house to the well was almost thirty feet; some families had to go as far as three hundred feet, and observers estimated that "a much larger proportion" of African American families had to go long distances for water.[136] In southern McLennan County, the Locke family dug one well but abandoned it because its water was brackish; they then located the second well a hundred yards farther from the house.[137]

Drawing water from a well proved a challenge for many Blacklands women, the difficulty increasing with the depth of the well. A quarter of the African American families and almost half of the Anglo families used windlasses and pulleys to draw water from the wells.[138] The son of a Bell County tenant farmer remembered using a windlass and pulley to draw water from their well in a bucket four inches across and four feet long, which held three or four gallons of water, weighing between twenty-four and thirty-two pounds. Bernice Bostick Weir recalled that "Papa put a windlass on. Mama could draw water with a windlass so it'd be easier to draw that way."[139] Even with such conveniences, drawing water with a wooden bucket required much skill: "Dropping the bucket straight down did not always work as the bucket tended to float on the surface of the water; dropping it upside down was a more practical technique."[140] And water quality remained questionable. Frank Locke remembered that his family's dug well was open at the top, and rodents and snakes sometimes got into the supply.[141] Some families strained their water through a clean cloth to separate the impurities from the liquid.[142]

Cisterns—brick, concrete, or metal tanks for holding rainwater—were the other most common sources of water in the Blacklands, and in some areas they outnumbered wells.[143] Usually a cistern was located at the corner of the house, where a guttering system diverted the rainwater into the tank.[144] Keeping a cistern free of dirt and pests was difficult. Frank Locke remembered that their cistern, despite being covered with brick and concrete, attracted mosquitoes, and "the non-aerated water at times swarmed with wiggle tails."[145] The water supply in a cistern (and in many shallow wells) depended, of course, on the amount of rainfall, and water shortages were common in the Blacklands in July and August. Inez Folley remembered: "We had a cistern, a dug-in cistern, and when my daddy built it, he said, 'Now you can use a barrel a day because it holds 365 barrels.' But we always gave out in the summer and had to haul water to drink and to cook and to wash with." The Folley family brought water home in a tin tank on a wagon from the tank at the cotton gin in the nearby community of Nus or from a relative's well in the market community of Mart.[146] Some families were forced to buy water from their more fortunate acquaintances. Levi Steward recounted paying "two bits a tank" for water hauled five or six miles, and in Hunt County, water sold for prices ranging from a nickel to fifty cents a barrel.[147]

Another, less desirable form of water storage in the Blacklands was a device called a "tank." To create a tank, a farmer built an earthen dam across a small drainageway or ravine to hold water, then deepened and enlarged the basin to hold even more water.[148] Most of the time, families forswore drinking water from the tank, using it instead for laundry, bathing, and watering gardens, and saving the cleaner water from the cistern for drinking and cooking.[149] In the southern Blacklands, however, almost a third of the Mexican families hauled all of their water from "mud tanks," drinking and cooking with water from a source shared with mules, cows, and chickens.[150]

For the first quarter of the century, piped running water remained a comfort for the few. This exclusivity prompted Myrtle Calvert Dodd to remember the Earle place as "the best house that we lived in. . . . We even had running water."[151] By the end of the 1930s, the water situation had improved markedly for more affluent Blacklands families. For many years, agricultural reformers had, through lectures and pamphlets, stressed the necessity of indoor plumbing for rural homes, and those farm families who could afford to upgrade their facilities did so. When Bernice and Pat Bostick built their new home in 1938, they included piped-in water.[152] For the poor, water remained scarce. By 1940, only 16 percent of white tenants had running water in their houses, and fewer than 2 percent of black tenants had that convenience.[153]

Rural sanitation also continued to be difficult prior to World War II. With little attention paid to the disposal of human waste, waterborne typhoid fever was so common that it was considered "endemic" and frequently called "rural typhoid."[154] For most Blacklands houses, the outhouse, or privy, served as the primary location for human elimination. Despite the efforts of rural reformers, many farms had inadequate sanitation facilities.[155] On the Locke farm, the family had one privy, reserved for the women of the family; the men and boys relieved themselves outside.[156] Numerous surveys in the 1920s revealed the lack of sanitary privies. In Hill County, 20 percent of the white families and half of the black families surveyed had no privy facilities at all.[157]

The proper location of a privy warranted much discussion among farm families. State health department officials recommended that a privy be placed at least one hundred feet from the well to avoid contamination.[158] While this placement may have minimized infection, it virtually ensured that either the well or the privy would be inconvenient to the house. In Navarro and Dallas Counties, the average distance of privies from the houses was seventy feet, a long trek in wet or cold weather.[159] Often, families used their own criteria for establishing their privy sites, as Bernice Bostick Weir recalled about her parents:

> When we moved down on the creek, there wasn't any toilet. And so I don't know how long it was we lived there—we'd have to go out around in the bushes or a ditch or something. So Papa built a two-holer and one day he said, "Mammy!"—he always called Mama Mammy—he said, "Mammy, come out here and show me where you want this set." Well, the shop was out here and the woodpile and everything. Mama said, "Well, I think right back over here would be the best place." He said, "Well, hell, no, that's not where I want to put it." (laughs) So he put it across the ditch where he wanted to put it. There was a little ravine that ran down on the north side of our house which didn't belong to us. He put it on the ditch where it'd be easy to clean out.[160]

As Weir's father emphasized, proper care of a privy could be extremely important to a family's well-being. Some families sprinkled lime to speed decomposition.[161] Residents of the Richland Creek area cleaned their privies by shoveling out the back "once a month," "three or four times a year," or "just whenever it needed it."[162] Bernice Weir recalled, "Every so often, the back would be taken off and it'd be scraped out. We had to scrub the floor and the seat every once in a while to keep it clean with our wash water."[163]

By 1940, rural sanitation had improved in many quarters. Bernice and Pat Bostick built their new house with indoor plumbing and a septic tank. Ninety-seven percent of the Czech families surveyed in Bell County had toilet facilities in their homes by then.[164] Yet in many other Blackland Prairie locations, conditions remained primitive. For example, a landowner's daughter from Hopkins County recalled using her chamber pot as late as 1941, emptying it in the field, and rinsing it with a dipper of water at the well.[165] And among tenant farmers, only 4 percent of the Anglos and 0.5 percent of the African Americans had flush toilets by 1940.[166]

Another important aspect of sanitation in rural life was personal hygiene, which came at great inconvenience because of limited water supplies. For washing hands and faces, many families kept a washpan and towel by the back door. Bernice Bostick Weir remembered from her childhood, "Right here was a shelf built and it had an oak bucket with a dipper in it. We all drank out of the same dipper and a washpan; we all washed in the same washpan and dried on the same towel."[167]

Many families had washtubs in the kitchen. Water for bathing was brought indoors and heated on the stove during cold weather. In warmer weather, bathing might take place outside in a shed. Water was limited, and Geneva Kahlish of the Tours community remembered "two or three baths in the same water, with a little warm water added from the tea kettle before the next one took his turn."[168] A few houses had designated bathrooms. Myrtle Calvert Dodd recalled fondly the house on the Stribling place, where her father was a tenant: "It had a bathroom with a tin tub in it, you know, great big tin tub. And when we had running water, we used it. Have to heat a kettle, big kettle of warm water to warm it up with. And we had a little stove my father found somewhere. And you had to pump it and get it—when it got cold. Of course, they didn't heat it too often; maybe on Saturday. They would heat that bathroom and we'd all take a bath. Now, in the summer it was different. You could take a bath if the water wasn't short. . . . That's the last place we had a bathtub, too."[169]

Some families used homemade lye soap for washing their bodies and their hair, eschewing commercially produced cleaners. Inez Folley recalled that commercial shampoo made her hair "softer and smell better" than lye soap. The Folleys used mainly their homemade lye soap, however, because the commercial shampoo "wouldn't clean it any better."[170] Other families, such as the Calverts, eagerly used store-bought soap. Myrtle Calvert Dodd observed: "You know, I can't remember having to take a bath with any lye soap, but I've heard people say they did. Ever in my life, they usually found some somewhere that we kept for baths and face soaps. Some kind of bar soap. Of course, we lived close enough to Waco that they got it."[171] Like millions of other Americans, the Calvert family preferred the more pleasant commercially made soap, which required either cash or goods for barter, to the harsh lye soap, which they produced themselves. They favored the consumer world to that of home production.

Blacklands women avoided entry into the consumer world in most ways, however, and one of the primary areas of women's home production was sewing. A woman who sewed her family's clothing added many benefits to her family. Families that did not make clothes had to use meager resources for ready-made apparel. Alice Owens Caufield's mother died in 1912, and Caufield and her sister wore store-bought clothing until they learned to sew in high school. Shopping in Waco, they spent their small supplies of cash or bought on credit from merchants on the main street. The cost of ready-made clothing contrasted sharply with that of homemade apparel. Around World War I, for example, dresses for children cost at least sixty-nine cents, whereas gingham material cost only ten or twelve cents a yard.[172] By providing clothes for their men, their children, and themselves, women who sewed provided considerable savings of cash and contributed even further to the well-being of their families. The personal cost was inestimable, of course, with women spending long hours either "sewing on their fingers" or sitting at a sewing machine, many times squinting under an inadequate kerosene lamp. But sew they did, almost everything that their families wore. Many women actually enjoyed sewing, to a point; it was an exercise in creativity, which they rarely had other opportunities to express.

By the early twentieth century, few, if any, women in the Blacklands still wove cloth in the home; instead, they acquired fabric from peddlers or from dry goods stores, often bartering for cloth with eggs and butter. Seamstresses used materials commensurate with their families' economic circumstances, and clothing material marked financial status. In Hunt County, Pat McGee recalled assuming that her aunt Julia was from a "somewhat aristocratic background" because, among other things, "her clothes were other than homemade floursack cloth or Sears and Roebuck catalog-ordered."[173] As a prosperous landowner's wife, Alma McKethan McBride's mother fashioned her daughters' clothing from elegant materials like dotted swiss, lawn, and linen, with swiss lace, satin ribbon, and embroidery edging for trim.[174] Bernice Weir's husband made most of the trips into town for shopping, and she recounted her disappointment at his lack of discernment in buying material for their son's clothing: "And I told Pat one day when he's going to town—I said, 'Pat, buy me some little pink and white or blue and white checked gingham. I want to make Byron some rompers'—or a little dress. I guess I'd have made him a dress first. But anyhow, he came home with brown and white checks, and I just cried and cried and cried, and I said, 'Why didn't you get what I told you to get?' And he said, 'Well, they was without.' And I don't know whether they was without or whether he just went in and saw that check and said, 'I want some of that.'"[175]

Myrtle Calvert Dodd recalled her mother, the wife of a sharecropper, buying bolts of plain material and making clothing for the eight Calvert children: "She'd go in the fall and bring a whole lot and sew clear till Christmastime. . . . My sister was so close to me, she usually made us things at the same time, and lots of times nearly alike. . . . In the wintertime she would buy a bolt of what we called flannel cloth, and she made our slips and put sleeves in them and made us something to sleep in. Maybe it's all alike, but I remember she'd buy a whole bolt of it, have to make it up. Make our panties, you know."[176] Hester Calvert, making do for her large family, could ill afford to differentiate between the styles of clothing for her two stair-step daughters.

During the 1920s, clothing made from feed or flour sacks became common. For years, women had used the muslin from feed sacks for household use. Feed manufacturers, seeing an opportunity, began printing designs on their sacks. Printed cotton sacks turned up in uses from underwear to pajamas to everyday dresses and shirts.[177] Patterns were precious, shared among the women of the community. Myrtle Dodd remembered that her mother "usually had a pattern or made a pattern. And they swapped—different aunts and cousins would swap patterns."[178] Bernice Weir recalled the pattern for her lily quilt coming "from Mama's people."[179]

Some women sewed by hand, as Inez Adams Walker recalled of her young motherhood in the 1920s and early 1930s: "I had four girls. And before I was able to get my machine, I made them dresses on my hands. Get a needle and thread and made them on my hands."[180] But sewing machines were by far the most common appliances owned by Blacklands families, even among migrant families. The family's clothing supply was so crucial that it could not be neglected, and sewing machines expedited the process of clothing production immeasurably.[181] Families scraped together enough money to buy the machines that would help keep them clothed. Almost all machines were powered with a treadle, as electric machines in the region remained rare until the late 1930s (as did the supplies of electricity necessary to run them). Sewing machines could be procured in a number of ways. In some cases, the husband, perceiving the great value that a sewing machine could bring, made the purchase. Pat Bostick bought Bernice Bostick Weir's first machine from a peddler without her knowledge (but to her great delight). Inez Adams Walker's mother bought her own Singer sewing machine from a peddler with no input from her husband: "Mother would see about it herself. She knew more about it than he did."[182] Best of all, Lee Rice's mother won a new sewing machine in a drawing from Davidson's dry goods store in Greenville.[183]

Those who did not own sewing machines often had access to them. Hester Calvert borrowed her mother-in-law's machine "nearly every day before she got her own."[184] As Cheris Kramarae has pointed out, sharing sewing machines gave farm women chances to interact with each other.[185] Women sometimes sewed for others, for barter or for cash. Mary Hanak Simcik's sister took the family sewing machine with her when she married, and the family lacked the money to buy another one, so the sister made Simcik's clothing in trade: "I would do some work for her, and she would sew for me."[186] Bernice Weir loved to sew, and she made clothing for their young female cotton pickers for a dollar a dress in the 1930s. Josie Crenshaw traded with the chicken peddler and copied a pattern from the Sears catalog to make a gold linen dress for her neighbor, Martha Stone, to wear to the Juneteenth emancipation celebration in Greenville.[187] This service by the landowners' wives may have mitigated, temporarily at least, the racial and class boundaries between the white and African American women who shared a feminine enjoyment of clothing. Beulah Steward, who testified before the U.S. Senate Committee on Industrial Relations in 1914, had made "as high as $2 a day," working from morning until night sewing for "outsiders"—people who were not relatives—until creditors repossessed her sewing machine. The Steward family was living in the direst circumstances, squatting near Savoy, Fannin County, at the time of the Senate inquiry. Beulah Steward reflected on her poverty: "I never have got a dress ready-made for myself in my life since I have been a married woman."[188] Store-bought clothes were an indulgence very few farm families could afford.

Most Blacklands women sewed only for their own families, and numerous people recalled their mothers making virtually every stitch of the families' clothing, with the possible exceptions of men's dress shirts and the families' supplies of stiff denim overalls.[189] Most of the garments that these women fashioned were simple, and people had few changes of clothes. Women wore plain housedresses much of the time, and their husbands wore overalls. Tough economic times could make it difficult to obtain even the most common clothing: One Hill County renter told social workers that as a result of the drastic drop in cotton prices in 1920, "a lot of farmers round here haven't a cent in the world, and their wives and children are going without clothing enough to keep them warm."[190]

Keeping large, growing families of children clothed may have been the most difficult part of women's sewing duties. Babies wore homemade diapers and dresses until their first birthdays, but both Bernice Bostick Weir and Frank Locke, children of landowning families, recalled having distinct sets of clothing for various activities as children: Sunday, for church and special occasions; school clothes; "knock-about," worn to town and for casual visiting; work, usually denim, worsted, or gingham; and worn-out, which were saved for quilts or to give to tramps.[191] Mary Hanak Simcik, from the Czech tradition, added yet another category: "The best clothes went to church. The next was to dance."[192] Clothes received careful attention, as Myrtle Calvert Dodd said: "I had a certain dress to wear to school. I had to pull it off when I got home and have it ready. You didn't change every day then. Usually I had two or maybe sometimes more. After I got bigger I had more. But when I first started school I think maybe just two dresses. I'd wear one and then she'd wash it and have it ready for the next week and then you'd wear the other one and wash them that way. She did well to sew, I guess, and get that many ready."[193] The Calvert daughters were too close in age to hand down clothing as the Folley family did. Inez Folley recalled: "The oldest sister handed hers down to the next sister, and she handed them down to me, then I handed them down to the next one. I didn't get very many new dresses. I just got a different dress."[194]

Shoes were also very difficult to keep on hand in sufficient quantities for growing families. Adults wore shoes most of the time, but many children did not. Mary Ann Collier Campbell recalled that she and her siblings shed their shoes as soon as "the mesquite tree bloomed" and did not resume wearing shoes until "the onset of winter."[195] Shoemaking and leather tanning were skills that had long since disappeared in homes of the Blacklands, and families had to find funds to purchase shoes, which cost around $2.50 for a new pair in 1915.[196] The best way a mother could provide shoes for her children was to have access to cash or credit, with butter, eggs, or the like. The Folley children went barefooted until the arrival of cold weather; then, Inez Folley recalled, "My mother had to manage for us some shoes."[197] In Hill County, a tenant farmer's wife "had 'peddled' through three towns trying to buy second-hand shoes to fit her children so that they might enter school."[198] The Adams family of Milam County used the money that they earned picking cotton on farms other than their own to buy "winter groceries and shoes and things."[199]

The summer sun was a formidable foe in the Blackland Prairie. Just as dangerous, however, were the so-called "blue northers" that whistled south-ward down the Great Plains, dropping the temperature forty to sixty degrees in an hour and turning the usually mild climate of the Blacklands bitterly cold. Like women all across the nation, most Anglo and African American Black-lands women made quilts to ward off the cold.[200] Quilting was a skill handed down from older women to younger. Bea Strawn, from Lytton Springs in

Caldwell County, recalled her grandmother's coaching, saying, "No, Hon, you made too big a stitch here. Now take it out and make a little stitch."[201] For most women, quilting was an exercise not in fancywork but in utility: sewing two layers of cloth together with a cotton batt to make a warm bed covering. Never one to complain, Etta Carroll reminisced: "I never did like to quilt much but I quilted a lot. It is hard. It takes time to do it and do it right. You can't put one in like this morning and get it out this evening; you're going to have to take time to do it."[202] Myrtle Calvert Dodd recalled: "My mother forever in the summer made quilts. . . . She tried to get two. She just had to do it between meals." Hester Calvert quilted only during the day because the light was too dim at night.[203] She relied at times on her daughters' assistance with housework so that she could continue quilting or sewing with good light: "Sometimes the house wouldn't be as clean as she wanted it. Get in from school, she'd say, 'Now, I haven't swept the kitchen. Y'all go in there and do the dinner dishes and sweep the kitchen and be ready to make supper here before we know it,' because she'd be sewing or quilting."[204]

Many women used homegrown cotton for the quilt batts, learning to card cotton by hand to an exact thickness.[205] For the quilt tops they saved scraps of material from their sewing or bought new fabric; in the 1920s, the new printed feed sacks became a popular quilt material. Women who sewed for hire sometimes shared leftover material with relatives. African American women frequently made "britches" quilts, fashioned from worn-out men's pants. When asked if she had ever made a britches quilt, Matilda Brown from Manor, Travis County, replied: "Lord, child! That's the wrong question to be askin' me. You should say, how *many* britches quilts have I made. And then I'd say, I don't know. I'm eighty-two years old an' I done lost count!"[206]

For women like Hester Calvert and Matilda Brown, quilting was an activity carried out alone or with one's daughters; the women of the Carroll family quilted alone.[207] Social events related to quilt making waxed and waned in popularity throughout the early twentieth century. When Emma Bourne was a child at the turn of the century, women near the Red River "still had" quilting bees. Some women quilted while others prepared an elaborate dinner, which was followed by a dance.[208] African American women in the community of Robinson, McLennan County, held quilting parties before World War I, as Alice Owens Caufield recalled: "If they were going to have a quilting party, the women just got their whatever they had to have and went on over to that person's house. And the frames were set up and they quilted and they ate and had a good time." Most of the women in the community were members of the

Heroines of Jericho, an organization affiliated with the Prince Hall Masonic order, and the quilting parties often resembled lodge meetings.[209] Only twenty miles away from Robinson, Bernice Bostick Weir did not go to any quilting bees until her Anglo home demonstration club revived the practice in the late 1920s. Each woman pieced her own quilt and club members then helped with the quilting: "And then we got to quilting and we'd go from place to place and quilt. Living on the farm wasn't all dark and dreary and drudgery, because we had lots of pleasure."[210]

Quilts were utilitarian objects, but those women who had time to do so sometimes made their quilts into art, with elaborate pieced or appliquéd patterns and fancy stitching. Many of these fancier quilts from the early century still survive and have been featured in museum exhibits. Bernice Weir made numerous quilts: a star quilt, a Dutch doll, a grandma's fan.[211] Refugia Sanchez decorated her quilts with appliqués of stars and hearts.[212] In the Czech community of Tours, Mary Jupe Uptmor pieced between six and eight hundred tops. She did not enjoy quilting, and many of these tops were never turned into quilts. A landowner's wife who worked in the field "only in emergencies," Jupe bought her material in Waco, shopping carefully.[213]

Julia Savannah Beaty Florence, who lived near Mesquite, Dallas County, made an extraordinary quilt in 1911, three years before her death at age sixty-four. She pieced a crazy quilt from men's suiting samples, then embroidered the quilt with scenes from the Florence family history: "The china lamp her husband gave her that was cherished but never lit because she was so afraid of fire on the farm . . . her youngest son's pet javelina hog, 'Havie,' that terrorized the farm . . . a memorial block for her baby daughter Martha, dead of the 'summer complaint' before she was a year old and whose death caused Julia's hair to turn snow white at the age of twenty-two . . . a patch of flowers carefully watered daily when she threw out the dishwater . . . five-pointed Texas Lone Stars of every variety, even a Texas flag." Julia Florence, the creator of this elaborate family history, could neither read nor write.[214]

Etta Carroll made one or two quilts a year, but she also recycled old quilts into thick, heavy coverings known as comforters. She said,

If I had an old quilt that wore some I didn't want to throw away, I'd make a comforter out of it. I'd put the lining in the frame, then I'd lay this old quilt in there, and then I'd put the top on it. And then I'd pin it all around and I'd tack it; I didn't quilt it. Some comforters is quilted and some is tied. These were all tied, because I'd put old quilts in them. I'd wash the quilt and I'd get it good and clean and then I'd put it on top of my lining and put that down and then I'd put the top on it and then I'd go around and pin it all around, stretch it, and then take a needle and go about this far [four inches] apart and tack it.[215]

Quilts, made of used or leftover fabric to begin with, found even longer life in this way.

Some women did other kinds of handwork as well. Bernice Weir learned to crochet in her early teens, and Marie Vrba Hlavenka took her crochet bag with her "everywhere she went." Hlavenka made embroidered dresser scarves and runners to give as Christmas presents, and crepe paper flowers for the graves of relatives for All-Souls Day.[216] Also in the Tours community, the prolific Mary Jupe Uptmor crocheted doilies, runners, pillowcase edgings, and bedspreads for "every room." Her love for handwork provoked gossip in the community, as she hurried through her other work to have time for her sewing, quilting, and crocheting.[217] Mexican immigrant women worked together to crochet pillow covers and edgings for their sheets, which they then coated with heavy starch. Adelaida Torres Almanza remembered that even poor women could buy thread at three cents a ball, and she and her relatives decorated plain sheets when they could not afford other goods, adding crocheted borders to their sheets because they had no bedspreads. They also embroidered sheets and pillowcases, working by kerosene lamp to create their handiwork.[218] But for many women of all ethnic groups, the situation was as Hester Calvert's daughter flatly recalled of her mother: "She didn't have time."[219]

Making clothing and quilts was but one part of women's work; getting them clean was another—a hot, heavy chore most women dreaded. Without running water or any type of power assistance, laundry was an enormous task for most rural American women until World War II. Despite the difficulty, many families washed once a week during warm weather. Washing laundry for a family was not an easy job for one person. Many women relied on the assistance of their children, while Anglo women in particular hired African American women to do laundry for them.[220]

Most Blacklands families who butchered hogs made their own lye soap, which has two primary ingredients, lye and lard.[221] During the early twentieth century, families made drip lye from ashes. The family saved ashes from their fireplace and stove in a special hopper with a funnel on its bottom. Alice Owens

Caufield recalled her grandmother's lye-making technique: "Take wood ashes. They would be in a container; she'd pour water on them and stir it up and when it all settled, the water would be about the color of beer and that would be your lye."[222] The process made potassium hydroxide, which dried as lye. By the 1920s, however, ash hoppers had almost disappeared, and the majority of soap makers bought lye in cans.[223]

Soap cooking could take place immediately after hog killing or at a later time, depending on family preference. To make block soap, the soap maker cooked the lard and lye together in an iron pot over an open fire, "stirring and stirring and stirring so that it would get hard," then poured it into pans and let it harden and cut it into pieces for storage; some left it in a soft, jellylike form.[224] Mexican families made soap from the bones of hogs. Adelaida Torres Almanza remembered: "To make the soap from the hog's bones, they would get the bones and they would put them to boil with some old lye soap. They would also add pure lye to it. They would mix the bones with the lye, and after they were boiled they would form layers of grease. When these layers of grease had formed they would separate the layers one by one and from them they make the soap."[225] In addition to the homemade lye soap, families also used bluing in their laundry, purchased either from itinerant peddlers or in town.[226]

The source of water for laundry determined much about the washing procedure. Few families had access to creeks for laundry, and some used creek water only when their wells ran low in the summer.[227] Those who did their laundry on a creek bank expended great effort transporting the laundry to the wash site. Norma Miller Langford, who was born in 1914 and grew up near Quinlan, Hunt County, called wash day "a happy time for all of us, except Mama." Her father loaded the wash pot and washtubs into a mule-drawn wagon. Her mother packed up the dirty laundry and her five children, and the entire family rode a quarter of a mile to the pond. Her father unloaded the goods and left for field work. It was an all-day affair; her mother packed food for lunch and prepared it on a campfire for the entire family. "At the end of the day, the clothes all clean and dried, everything packed and loaded back on the wagon, everyone went home tired, even the kids. But still, supper had to be cooked, water drawed from a deep well, the livestock fed, cows milked, and finally, away after dark, bedtime. And no one fussed about going to bed."[228]

Most families did their laundry in the yards of their houses, using water from cisterns or wells. The laundry equipment usually consisted of two tubs, a wash pot, and a rub board. Fire under the wash pot heated the water. The white clothes were rubbed and boiled, while the prints were only rubbed. The clothes went through several tubs of rinse water. If the clothes were white, the last rinse was treated with bluing.[229] While children could assist with washing, their presence also contributed an element of danger to wash day. Eddie Stimpson recalled, "Everybody know of some kid, black or white, who got killed by falling in boiling wash pot."[230]

Washing schedules varied according to the mother's diligence and the amount of time available for household chores. Bernice Bostick Weir washed underclothes and bedclothes on Monday and the family's clothes on Friday. She laundered her babies' clothes every morning.[231] The Rice family washed every Monday.[232] Millie Birks Stimpson emphasized the need for clean undergarments: "Mother would not go or let anyone in the famley leave home without clean under ware, including Dad. If she had to wash our under clothes every night, she did."[233] Refugia Sanchez, who did no field work, washed every day. Frank Locke noticed a special fastidiousness about Mexican laborers. While most itinerant laborers "seldom" washed clothes, the Mexicans washed two or three times a week, immersing their garments in a shallow pool, flailing them with a stick, and spreading them on flat rocks to dry in the sun. As late as 1930, 41 percent of the Mexican women in the lower Blacklands did not own even a wash pot.[234]

Whenever an Anglo family could afford to, they hired a black or Mexican woman to do their laundry. Even tenant farmers sometimes availed themselves of the cheap labor of African American women, who left their own homes and chores to lighten the loads of their more affluent neighbors. In Collin County, for example, an unnamed black woman came out from the community of Allen once a week to do the Summers family laundry, bringing her son, Edwin, with her, and he played with the Summers children.[235] Frequently the wife of a farm laborer did laundry for the tenant farmer's wife, such as Ada Richardson, who washed for the Calvert family on the Chapman place near Hewitt. Richardson also brought her children with her, but they assisted her in tasks such as drawing water from the well. Wages for laundry work were low, and in the autumn black laundresses left those positions for better-paying cotton picking.[236] Alice Owens Caufield remembered her grandmother, Eliza Owens, washing clothes for their landlords, the Kersting family, around the time of World War I, and receiving fifty cents for a day's service over the washtubs and rub boards.[237] This type of employment was strictly segregated by race, and landlords' wives complained that the white wives of tenants and laborers would not do washing for hire.[238] Poor white women could have earned valuable cash had social mores not prohibited their taking in laundry. In segregated

Texas, almost no white woman would do work considered fit only for African Americans.

For more affluent Blacklands families, household help was accepted as a fact of life. Marguerite Thompson Westbrook, who married into one of the wealthiest rural families of McLennan and Falls Counties, later observed that in the 1920s, "You could have any number of Negroes, one to do the washing, one to do the cooking, one man to do the milking and the yard work."[239] Bernice Porter Bostick Weir grew up observing the African American woman who did most of her mother's laundry, and later as a wife she herself engaged the wives of their hired hands: "Well, I've always been real fortunate to have help in the house because we had that little one-room house there, and whoever lived in the house—usually blacks, you know—why, the woman would help me in the house." Weir paid her assistant, who helped her clean house and get the children off to school, in milk, butter, and eggs, and she also shared leftover food, such as cold biscuits, with her.[240]

Slowly, washing machines came into wider use after World War I. In 1930, only 4 percent of the white women and none of the black women interviewed in the lower Blacklands had washing machines. In Hill County, 15 percent of the white women had machines, possibly because of community restrictions against the labor of African Americans or Mexicans. Dovie and Etta Carroll acquired a gasoline-powered Maytag washing machine sometime in the early 1930s from the representative of a hardware store in Waxahachie who came to their house and convinced them to buy. The Carrolls mortgaged a hog and paid for the washing machine over a six-month period. Etta Carroll enjoyed her new acquisition despite its limited abilities: "You had to get your water hot and put it in the washing machine, and you had to wet your clothes and put it in there. Of course, that's a lot more help than rubbing them all right. But that little bit of help was a lot of help. . . . We thought we were really flying to get a washing machine. We never was used to one."[241]

Mechanical clothes dryers were unknown, and several areas of the house yard served as drying spots for laundry. In some places, clotheslines were common.[242] In Hunt County, Lee Rice's aunt had a clothesline made of barbed wire, and his cousin, Dora Holley, suffered severe injuries when she ran into it.[243] In other areas, such as the Richland Creek area of Navarro County, women more frequently hung wet laundry on bushes and fences.[244] Women sometimes put their towels and dishrags on berry bushes and broom weeds to dry, believing that the leaves would make their whites whiter.[245] In cold or wet weather, almost every surface in the house, or even in the smokehouse, might serve as makeshift clotheslines. Etta Carroll said, "If you'd catch a pretty day, you'd wash up everything, get everything clean that you could, and then if it turned off bad, you'd wash and have to hang them in the house somewhere, let it kind of dry. . . . I'd say you'd have clothes a-hanging on your chair and clothes a-hanging here to try to get them dry."[246]

Families washed selectively in bad weather, laundering perhaps only underwear or other small items. Inez Folley commented, "We had to pick the days to wash, too, because if it's raining you couldn't wash. In the spring of the year, when it rained so much, or in the winter, sometimes you'd have to go a good while before you could wash. You could wash by hand and hang it around the fire but you couldn't wash the sheets and something like that because it'd take too long for them to dry. So we'd have to pick a sunny day to wash in the wintertime."[247] For families with few changes of clothing, long waits between laundry often meant wearing soiled clothing day after day.

After the clothes were washed and dried came the chore of ironing. Many of the clothes that Blacklands people wore were made of cotton, which required ironing for a finished appearance. Most families ironed the day after wash day. The large majority of women did their ironing with flatirons, commonly called "sad irons," heated on stoves or in the fireplaces. Like woodstoves, flatirons required a special touch, a skill developed from childhood. They blackened and smoked from being heated in the fire, and had to be cleaned before use.[248] Families bought starch from peddlers or from merchants, and making liquid starch proved difficult, too. Mothers tried to share their knowledge with their daughters, giving them potentially valuable domestic training, but sometimes teaching gave way to expediency. Myrtle Calvert Dodd recalled: "I remember her [mother] trying to teach me to make starch, and that was a job. I would always either not make enough or get it too thick or something. We bought the starch and—I think it was old Faultless Starch then. . . . Sometimes she'd have to take over and do it over or thin it down or something."[249]

The use of flatirons, which required much stooping and lifting, worried agricultural reformers enormously. Charcoal and gasoline irons became available before 1910, and reformers began to push for their use, ignoring the fact that gasoline irons cost almost five times as much as flatirons.[250] In June 1917, Mrs. Nat P. Jackson, chief of the Rural Women's Division of the Texas Agricultural Extension Service, reported that in one community the extension worker had pointed out the need for gasoline irons. On a return trip, she said proudly, "We helped to conduct a regular lesson in which each member was to answer roll-call by naming her greatest convenience. From every member except three came promptly, 'My gasoline iron.' "[251] Bernice Weir commented, "I was so proud of my gasoline iron when I first got my gasoline iron. . . . I could heat it up and go to ironing and just stand there and iron. It wouldn't get cold on me. You didn't have to change out and everything. And I had so much ironing to do for the children, and I ironed Pat's overall and shirts and things that he wore in the field, too." Yet many women, like Etta Carroll, continued ironing with flatirons until around World War II. She was afraid of the complexity of the gasoline irons, which, according to Ruth Allen, were always "out of fix."[252]

Except for the most affluent few, women in the Blackland Prairie worked hard to provide clean, adequate shelter and clothing for their families. Their resources varied widely, and the labor, always difficult and time-consuming, was harshest for the poorest women. In their production of household goods and clothing, women contributed significantly to their families' comfort and circumvented expenditures of much-needed cash. At the end of the day, a farmwife might look around her house, whatever its quality: She might see the types of weatherproofing she had improvised. She might see household goods accumulated with great effort. She might see the clothing for her family, sewed, washed, and ironed by hand. A farm woman, no matter what her economic status, could take pride in these accomplishments, and possibly the poorest women were the proudest of all. Always, however, there would be something else on her mind. Breakfast would be just a few hours away, the first of two to five meals in a day, depending on the ethnicity of the family. Household chores done, a woman turned to the most recurrent of her jobs: feeding her family.

chapter *three*

Living at Home

Food Production and Preparation
in the Blackland Prairie

Bertha Blackwell, the wife of a Navarro County tenant farmer and the mother of nine children, was deadly serious about food, and she carefully shared her views with her seven daughters. Louise Blackwell Dillow recalled her mother's equation of wasting food with evil: "My first concept of sin was learned one cold winter evening as we children ate our supper huddled around the fireplace. I tossed a biscuit-half into the fire to watch it kindle and burn. Mother, in her quiet but persuasive way, admonished me that it was *a sin to waste food*."[1] Like many women in the Texas Blackland Prairie, Bertha Blackwell spent much of her time thinking about food and the lack thereof, and its preparation became one of the centerpieces of her life. Her daughters, to memorialize her, created a cookbook of her recipes.

With the exception of Joe Gray Taylor and Sam Bowers Hilliard, few southern historians have seriously looked at the role of food in the lives of farm people.[2] Previous studies have been those by anthropologists and folklorists, who consider carefully the meaning of food in society. They view meals as indicators of "deep-rooted sentiments and assumptions about oneself and the world one lives in."[3] To understand truly the lives of rural southern women, one must seriously and at some length consider food.

Food carried at least three levels of importance to women in the world of southern cotton growers during the four decades prior to World War II. The first was economic. Because the needs of the cotton crop held supreme importance, the most fundamental economic significance of food was as fuel for the field workers. Furthermore, the farm family's annual provisions made up a major part of the credit matrix around the crop-lien system. Families who could not grow their own fare were forced to buy supplies on credit, often at usurious interest rates, and their indebtedness continued year after year. The family that supplied much of its own sustenance was far better off than those who bought groceries on credit, with a much greater chance of climbing out of or remaining out of debt. Women who could devote their time and energy to growing victuals actively labored to subvert the crop-lien system.

The second area of note is the symbolic aspect of food and women's relationships to it. In growing food and preparing meals for their families, women carried out the traditional female function of feeding their mates and offspring—the highest manifestation of archetypal feminine nurturing and caring. The symbolism is strengthened by the fact that women actually have the capability to produce food from their own bodies in the form of breast milk.[4] Louise Blackwell Dillow remembered: "For Mama, preparing and serving food was synonymous with caring and nurturing."

A third realm of importance was as an arena of creativity and self-expression for women who often had few other outlets. Many women actually enjoyed cooking at least some of the time. Cooking also brought external satisfactions, for women won praise for their cooking as for few other activities. Dillow continued: "My father in particular ate with great gusto and was expansive in his praise of everything Mama cooked. 'Now that is what I call larrupin' good!' was his highest commendation."[5] A well-prepared meal could bring satisfaction from several directions: a woman had fed her family, and they had enjoyed it.

Providing adequate supplies of food for their families challenged many farm families, husbands and wives. Legendary southern cooking notwithstanding, the diet of most rural Blacklands people, like that in most of the South, rested on three parts: pork, cornmeal, and syrup. Joseph Martin Dawson, reared in Navarro County in a tenant-farming family just before the turn of the century, recalled: "Actually, we had little to eat. . . . We survived largely on home-cured bacon and cornbread."[6] Pork and corn had sustained American southerners since the early seventeenth century, when Native Americans introduced corn to hungry immigrants and both domestic and wild hogs appeared on early English American tables.[7] With the three-part diet, southerners formulated their own version of fat, carbohydrate, and sweetener that is found in many cultures worldwide.

With a diet based on three simple, high-calorie provisions, literal starvation was rare in the Blacklands, in contrast to the urban poor, who were forced to buy almost all of their foodstuffs.[8] But because most of the region's labor force spent its time in commercial agriculture, not subsistence farming, many families went hungry for parts of the year, a bitter irony for people living on the very rich Blacklands soil. Food supplies grew especially dear in late winter, when stores of canned goods and root vegetables were depleted, and during the summer, when money for purchased supplemental food supplies ran low before the cotton harvest. And while many poor people could depend on more prosperous neighbors to share their bounty, the supplies were inconsistent, and sharing was not at all systematic. People who bought rather than grew most of their food suffered; especially among tenants, observers found, the food was "almost uniformly bad," due partially to the "cupidity of dealers" who sold tenants near-rotten food of the lowest quality.[9] In 1920, shortly before the cotton harvest, one black Hill County woman reported that her family ate only twice a day: "We are trying to stretch as far as we can."[10]

The quality and amount of food available for meals usually depended on the family's economic status, which in turn rested largely on the tenancy status of the husband. Women worked diligently to provide meals from the means that they had. In the 1920s a white tenant farmer's wife confessed her frustration to Bernice Bostick Weir, the wife of a landowner in McLennan County. Weir remembered:

My neighbor across the road there said her husband lived from one January to the next. He'd pay up in the fall of the year and begin to get credit on January 1, buy their groceries. See, the store at Moody had everything: dry goods up at the front, groceries at the back, and stuff for the farm on one side of it. And of course, he always rented on the halves. . . . She [the neighbor] felt terrible about it. . . . And she said her stepmother used to tell her that she and her sister were so wasteful in cooking and everything. She [the stepmother] said, "Wasteful makes woeful wants." And she [the neighbor] said, "I really have seen it. . . ." We stopped there one afternoon when we were coming from town and he insisted we stay for supper—and she told me this afterwards. She had soup and cornbread, I believe it was, for supper. It was delicious soup and cornbread. And she said, "I never was so embarrassed in my life. That was every bit of the food that we had in the house to fix. I didn't have anything in the house to fix. I was so embarrassed because he asked you all to stay." And we stayed and ate.[11]

Weir, whose prosperous husband provided comfortably for his family, came away deeply impressed by both the woman's financial straits and her ability to produce a delicious meal from meager provisions. The husband, hiding his poverty, insisted on serving his well-to-do neighbors the last precious bits of food. But the wife refused to participate in the subterfuge, confiding their financial exigencies to Weir and complaining of her husband's inability to rise above sharecropper status and to keep cash for more than a month or two. She kept the confidence, however, until a later time, perhaps when the two women were alone together. Perhaps the fact that she had grown up in a more prosperous household enabled her to speak freely to Bernice Weir as a peer. The sharecropper's wife made do with what she had, but she was none too pleased about having to do so.

Like rural people in most societies, Blackland Prairie farm people of the early twentieth century observed a strict gender division in providing foodstuffs and preparing meals. Securing the three basic staples of almost all southern diets—pork, cornmeal, and syrup—was generally the initial responsibility of men, who were otherwise absorbed in growing the cash crop. They butchered the hogs, ground the grain, and cooked the syrup from sugarcane or sorghum. Grain milling and syrup cooking involved travel away from the farm and payment of either money or goods, both activities dominated by men. Women, relegated to the farm, were in turn responsible for creating meals from these rudimentary ingredients: two hot meals a day, usually for a large family, with leftovers for the evening meal. But perhaps to an even greater extent than monotonously cooking bacon and cornbread on a daily basis, women added variety to their families' diets. Attempting to augment their food supplies, those women who could do so grew vegetables, canned fruit, and raised chickens and cows, working to ensure plain but substantial, nutritious meals for their families.

Regardless of the family's social class, almost all meals were based on the three main ingredients. Corn served as the staple. Grown in the field and not in the garden, corn was the second-largest crop (after cotton) on almost every Blacklands farm, serving as feed for both the families and the livestock.[12] While corn products could be filling, by itself corn supplied incomplete protein and lacked amino acids.[13] Early in the summer, corn could be eaten fresh. For use the rest of the year, Blacklands families preserved it in a number of ways: dried, made into meal, or, as technology became available, canned.[14]

Most of the corn ended up as meal, which the majority of men processed off the farm. Dovie Carroll, who farmed in various locations around Ellis County for most of his life, took the family's corn to be milled in nearby Waxahachie, where he left part of the resulting cornmeal with the miller as payment for grinding.[15] The African American Adams children in Milam County assisted their father with shelling dried corn, which he then took to the community mill, as Inez Adams Walker remembered: "My daddy'd have us all shelling that corn off the cob. You shell it with your hand and he had—you could buy what they called a sheller. Shell a big sack and he'd take it to the mill and they'd grind it and have meal for a long time."[16] Some families ground only small amounts of corn at a time. Other families stored it in bulk, creating some difficulties, as Myrtle Dodd recalled: "My mother would keep things to store cornmeal in to keep the weevils out—cans, different things she could get ahold of, jars or anything. I can remember them being in cupboards or sitting on the shelf, trying to keep it."[17]

For many poor families, cornmeal was almost the only foodstuff available during lean months. Myrtle Calvert Dodd remembered very short food supplies in February and March, before the garden came in, as her parents struggled to feed their eight children and extended family: "We usually always had plenty of meal and flour, and my mother was good at making something out of that. When she'd fry cornbread patties for supper, she couldn't hardly make enough. We kids loved them. . . . And you can imagine, especially when my grandparents were there, trying to make cornbread patties for supper. It was a big job. . . . Of course, we would eat them—I guess she would have fried all night. She'd just put one big drop out of a spoon; be about like the palm of your hand. We had a big heavy skillet that was hard for me—she'd fill that full and then stack them and do it again. I don't know how she stood it in the summertime, to get stuff ready over that hot stove, but she did."[18]

Another use for dried corn was as hominy. The centuries-old process of making hominy was painstaking and labor-intensive, boiling the shelled corn in a wash pot with lye or ashes, then washing it multiple times until the husk "slipped" off each kernel, and finally cooking it.[19] Hominy might be eaten freshly cooked or canned. In only a few instances in Central Texas, farm people dried it again and made it into grits.[20]

The second staple of the Blacklands diet, as in much of the South, was syrup, sometimes generically called molasses, usually made from sorghum or ribbon cane. Syrup provided high energy and good taste.[21] Maggie Washington remembered raising cane as part of her never-ending chores: "There was always another field of cotton to be picked; another field of corn to be gathered; and another field of ribbon cane to be stripped."[22] Inez Adams Walker recalled that many of their African American neighbors in Milam County raised different types of cane: "Some of it was sugarcane to make syrup out of. They had a small cane that they planted and fed the horses and mules on some of that. And then they had a big cane called a ribbon cane, make syrup and stuff out of. Had a mill where he carried it and they made it."[23] Making syrup was a man's job, and the men of each household usually cooked a year's supply at a time. Syrup mills were scattered through the countryside, the fortunate few who owned the mills collecting part of their neighbors' yields as payment.[24] Other families bought syrup by the gallon, with the tin buckets serving many purposes after their initial use. Like cornmeal grinding, syrup making involved both off-farm activity and the exchange of goods or cash. Alice Owens Caufield, the daughter of an African American sharecropper, recalled: "I can remember there was always syrup. It was the lighter-weight syrup; it wasn't the black, black molasses. It was a middle weight, I guess. My daddy bought the syrup by the gallon. We could always have gallon tin buckets. We didn't grow ribbon cane out there where we were on the prairie."[25]

Once the syrup was brought home, its disbursement became the woman's prerogative. Families stored wooden barrels of syrup in their smokehouses and brought it into the house by the bucketful for use on biscuits or cornbread, and as sweetener.[26] Maggie Washington recalled: "We had two kinds of syrup, ribbon cane syrup and sorghum syrup. The ribbon cane syrup we used to eat mostly on Sundays. That was the special. The sorghum syrup, a much thicker, heavier syrup, we ate during the week. Poured real slow, real thick, and it was good."[27]

The third element of rural Blacklands provisions was pork, which supplied energy and complex proteins, providing balance for corn.[28] More than half of the families in the Blacklands kept hogs, and nearly every rural family depended on hogs as their main source of meat. Archaeological excavations at a tenant house in Navarro County revealed that the occupants of the house consumed five times more pork than beef.[29] In McLennan County, Myrtle Calvert Dodd commented: "We had lots of hog meat; we always had a storm house full of hog meat. I'd get so tired of it. Had lots of bacon and ham and sausage. And when the sausage were gone, why, then you did without." Among Czech families, pork was also the favored meat, appearing on tables as *veprova pecene* (roast pork) trimmed with *knedliky* (dumplings) or *zemaky s macku* (potatoes with gravy) and *zeli* (sauerkraut).[30] Mary Hanak Simcik, on the other side of McLennan County from the Calverts, echoed Myrtle Dodd's complaint: "In the winter we had pork and nothing but pork."[31]

Hogs required little care, living on scraps from the household or on what they could root out if woods were nearby.[32] To feed their hogs, most families kept a "slop barrel" by the back door, which held every kind of household refuse from surplus milk to table scraps to used dishwater. Stocking the slop barrel was part of the task of cleaning up after meals, a task almost always performed by women.[33]

Unlike beef or chicken, pork could be preserved relatively easily, and sometimes the supply of hog meat lasted from one year to the next. More often, however, the pork supply ran out months before the next hog killing, and the meatless time made people all the more eager for fresh pork. The few families without smokehouses salted down meat, which lasted at best until late spring.[34] When meat ran out, a family could buy more on credit, barter for it, or simply wait until the next hog-killing season to obtain more. Folklorist William Owens recalled the songs sung by an African American chain gang in Lamar County before World War I. To the tune of "The Crawdad Song," the members of the chain gang sang of meat shortages and the joy that accompanied hog-killing season:

> "What you gonna do when the meat gives out, honey?
> What you gonna do when the meat gives out, babe?
> What you gonna do when the meat gives out?"
> "Stand on the corner with my lips poked out,
> Honey baby mine."
>
> "What you gonna do when the meat comes in, honey?
> What you gonna do when the meat comes in, babe?
> What you gonna do when the meat comes in?"
> "Stand on the corner with a greasy chin,
> Honey baby mine."[35]

Scarce meat supplies caused trouble for many women trying to feed their families. A Hunt County resident told the story of a small boy's hunger for meat that created considerable embarrassment for his mother. She had been cooking greens without meat for seasoning, and the bitter greens had made her children ill. She "discussed the matter with a neighbor who had only one small piece of fat meat and loaned it to her to use with her greens that day." Her small son came in and gobbled down the borrowed meat. The beleaguered mother spanked him and sent him to the neighbors' with a note "explaining that she could not keep her word in returning the meat." As recompense, she offered a box of snuff that she had been saving for company.[36] In the early fall of 1920, perhaps two full months before the earliest hog-killing time, researchers in Hill County found that one-third of the white and one-half of the black families reported having no meat on the previous day.[37]

For a hired hand, raising a hog was a privilege extended by his employer for several years of reliable service, and almost half of the farm families in Texas owned no hogs in 1935.[38] Those families that did not keep hogs were forced to depend on others to share or sell meat to them. Landowning families sometimes butchered enough hogs so that they would have surpluses for tenants. The African American laborers who helped the Folley family with butchering received the hog's intestines, or chitterlings, as payment for their labors; presumably, that was their only access to fresh pork.[39] Such practices allowed more comfortably situated families to practice a rural form of noblesse oblige, offering poorer cuts of the hog to their neighbors who had no hogs.[40]

Accounts of hog-killing day number among the favorite stories of Blacklands people. The first of several annual hog killings took place when the first cold spell arrived that was likely to remain for several days, sometimes as early as November. Hog-killing day was often a community affair, when several families gathered and butchered enough meat for all of them. While some people recall hog-killing time as a carnival atmosphere, others remember only the huge amount of work involved. Inez Folley commented: "It wasn't fun at hog-killing time because you had too much work to do."[41]

The number of hogs killed on a day varied from family to family. Maggie Washington remembered that the number was determined by the amount of labor and storage space available: "You couldn't handle too many in a day. You see, you wouldn't kill more than you could handle in a day, because all that meat had to be processed, because if it piled up on you, you'd have no place to keep it."[42] A family also tried to gauge the number of hogs that they would need to carry them through the year, and the numbers differed, even among landowners. For example, the Jesse Carroll family in Ellis County usually killed seven hogs per year, one for each family member, while in Limestone County, the Folleys made do with five hogs for eleven people.[43]

People who did not own hogs tried to acquire meat for their families by assisting with the slaughter or presenting themselves at opportune times. Pat McGee, a Hunt County landowner's daughter, recalled that the ritual at hog-killing time lasted as late as 1940: "Sharecroppers, or any members of the community who could not afford to raise their own livestock, would happen to walk by or drive slowly by our farm. My father, or another of the men, would always call out to them and wave them back to where they worked. 'Abner,' they would begin, 'I've got more meat here than I can take care of today. Could you use some down at your house?' Although it was usually the parts of the hog or the cuts of meat that we did not favor anyway, it was gratefully received by the passersby."[44]

According to McGee's recollections, the sharecroppers expected the donations of meat, conveniently coming by when the meat was available. The owners attempted to soften the situation somewhat by thinly disguising the donations as taking something extra off their hands. Sharecroppers and tenant farmers, on the other hand, probably were pleased to receive the meat, if not delighted about having to solicit landowners' consideration to obtain their leftovers. And some landowners undoubtedly declined to share.

For all ethnic groups, gender roles were clearly delineated for hog killing both in terms of the allotted tasks and the physical space in which they occurred. The men and boys congregated outside in the cold, shooting the hogs or killing them with axes, bleeding, scraping, and finally butchering them. The work required the use of weapons, which usually excluded women, and it generally called for upper-body strength sufficient to move the hog carcass, suspend it, and cut it into serving-size portions.[45] Most often the women and girls remained inside, waiting for the meat and intestines with which to make sausage. Kate Peacock Jones wrote simply: "This sausage job was the girls job," and Mary Hanak Simcik remembered, "We all had to pitch in and work."[46] The waiting was hardly idle, however. The women cleared the kitchen table and scrubbed it with brushes and lye soap. Some families chose to make sausage casings out of flour sacks, which required forethought and preparation. Myrtle Calvert Dodd remembered: "We didn't care for the sausage that was put in the intestines, so Mother made sacks. You saved your flour sacks from one year to the other, so she would have flour sacks to tear up and make sausage sacks out of them."[47] Other families used the hog's intestines as sausage casings. The intestines were cleaned, their contents removed, washed inside out, and scraped before being stuffed with the ground meat and seasonings. Preparing the entrails could be unpleasant, as Inez Folley described: "It wasn't an easy job. And some people wouldn't want to do it because it's nasty, but you know, that was just part of a job." Mary Ann Collier Campbell observed that the adults always closely inspected the scraped intestines before stuffing them full of meat.[48]

Pat McGee recalled the procedure for the women and girls as "a long afternoon of labor at the kitchen table" as they ground some of the meat and seasoned and stirred the sausage mixtures in huge bowls. By the time all of the sausages were mixed and stuffed, she noted, "bits of fat would be everywhere and the table and kitchen floor quite slippery."[49]

The seasoning for sausage was a means of expressing personal taste in a world with few choices. The decisions occasioned heated debates among family members, and almost every rural Blacklands resident recalls the amount of sage that her or his family used in making sausage; other seasonings included red pepper, black pepper, and, occasionally, garlic.[50] Czech families made sausage called *klobasa*, and *jitrnice* (liver sausage) was considered a delicacy.[51] Mexican families called their sausage *chorizo*, and Luz Sanchez Hurtado recalled her mother making two kinds: American style, seasoned with oregano, and Mexican style, seasoned with garlic and peppers. Some women preserved sausage further by frying it in patties, packing it in crock jars, and covering it with melted hog lard: in Inez Folley's words, "put a layer of sausage and a layer of lard and a layer of sausage and a layer of lard in these big jars." This method kept sausage almost indefinitely, and the cooked meat could be heated quickly for a convenient meal.[52]

Other methods of preserving parts of the hog included making head cheese, commonly known as souse, a loaf made with the meat from the head in its own aspic; and mincemeat, with apples and raisins.[53] Mexican women cut their pork into chunks and fried it, adding their homegrown garlic and peppers to the meat as it cooked.[54] Some cooks resorted to their own special methods, such as one Fannin County woman who devised her own homemade sugar cure mixture for ham, consisting of brown sugar, saltpeter, red peppers, sage, and spices.[55]

After families finished butchering and completed sausage making, most of the rest of the pork was covered with salt, then cured in smokehouses.[56] Smoking meat could be a delicate procedure, as the teenage Mary Hanak Simcik found out when she and her sister-in-law neglected their duty. Simcik recalled, "They left the smoke to me; I had to watch it so it didn't get too hot.

But anyhow, we were supposed to smoke the meat; and we were playing cards together; (laughs) and we put—you know what kind of wood it is—resin, you know? And of course, we didn't pay any attention; and we put that under there all over the meat. It all tasted like resin. Boy, did we catch it that time!"[57] The young women's actions ruined an entire batch of smoked meat, and their families suffered the consequences.

Procedures such as these kept pork edible for an indefinite period of time, but sometimes decay ruined the best intentions. Women coped with rotting meat primarily by cutting the bad spots off, eager to use what they could and minimize waste. Myrtle Calvert Dodd remembered, "In the spring, it would begin to turn green around the edges; my mother would just trim all that off and cook that. She always cooked a piece in the beans or whatever vegetable you had."[58] And Vera Allen Malone, from an African American community on the other side of McLennan County, said, "Now, sometimes the hams would get blue, weevils or something in 'em, 'skippers' we used to call it. Old people called it 'skippers' [eggs of the skipper fly]. Now, when it got like that, they could cut it out and eat it; but even as a child, I never would eat it."[59]

Once the meat and sausage were put away, it was time to cook the hog fat in a wash pot, rendering it into the lard that was essential for the southern habit of frying food and for making biscuits, piecrusts, and other baked goods. Myrtle Dodd remembered: "Now, my mother was determined to have so many cans of hog lard so she wouldn't run out."[60] Etta Hardy Carroll described the procedure, which usually occurred the day after hog killing: "You had to cut [the hog fat] up and you'd put so much in a big wash pot with a little bit of water to start it off to start it to cooking so it wouldn't stick. And then after it started cooking, you had to stir it quite a bit. And then you'd cook it till your cracklings—until you cook all the grease out of it. And then after it got done, why, let it set a little while and you had a big strainer that you'd strain it through. We used a big cloth over a pan and strained it."[61]

Rendering lard was sometimes done by men, but more often by women. Bernice Weir remembered her strong-minded mother-in-law ordering seventeen-year-old Bernice to render lard: "When I married, Grandma Bostick had always been used to overseeing everything and all and when they went to kill hogs, she said, 'You better get out there and see about that lard and everything.' And I said, 'Why, I've never done that in my life. My daddy always did that, and I never did go out and do any of it.' So I never did take up that habit."[62] Robert Calvert helped his wife stir the lard, but Ada Richardson, their African American helper, assisted her with the storage: "We had special jars for the lard that we'd save from one year to another—crockery was what it was. If she didn't have enough of those, you know, she'd put it in anything she had. She didn't want it in too big a heavy a things because you had to have a space to set it in the kitchen. They put it in the smokehouse most of the time."[63] Other families stored lard in five- or ten-gallon cans.

Even with the families' best efforts, lard often turned rancid before the next hog killing, or the supplies ran out. When that happened, women might fry bacon, which was also running low, and use the grease in the place of lard. And in the Hewitt area of McLennan County, African American laborers used rancid grease given to them by white families such as the Calverts, who themselves were tenant farmers. Myrtle Calvert Dodd remembered, "I know it was hand to mouth with them. I know they used to come and, 'Mrs. Calvert, you got any old grease?' You know, she would save old grease for the woman that washed for us. It would get kind of rancid, but you know, she'd re-cook it and use it. And any cold bread—they begged. They begged. Just horrible."[64] The poorest Blacklands families demonstrated their deprivation by using grease already beginning to decompose, sometimes to the detriment of their families' health.

Rendered lard left a crisp residue of fried skin in the pot, known as cracklings. Some families discarded the cracklings, while others ate them plain or used them to make a favorite dish of crackling cornbread.[65] Mexican immigrants prized the cracklings, which they called *chicharrónes*.[66] Many families considered the fresh pork meat to be a rare treat, and they gladly indulged in a harvest-time feast. Family members had their favorite parts of the hog: the backbone, the tenderloin, ham, liver, and so on. The liver, melt (spleen), and heart, which spoiled easily, often went first (sometimes made into hash known as rashlets), followed by the spareribs, tongue, feet, and brain, often scrambled with eggs. Ham, shoulders, and sausage followed, and finally, by the late summer, only bacon was left, served with drippings on the side.[67] Little was wasted since Blacklands families made use of all parts of each hog; in the words of a popular saying, "all of a pig was useful but the squeal."[68]

Mexican families celebrated hog-killing time and holidays by making from the hog's head the delicacy known as tamales. Tamale making was labor-intensive, and the women of several households gathered to share the work and the bounty. Adelaida Torres Almanza recalled: "They would clean the head and they would make tamales out of the head . . . the whole night cooking tamales." First, she explained, the cooks boiled the whole hog's head, including eyes and brains, in a large pot of boiling water for a short time. Then they added the stock from the boiled head to the *masa harina*, a flour made of ground corn boiled with lime, to make a dough. Next, the cooks prepared cornshucks, which had been harvested carefully during the early summer so that they would be supple and unbroken, and saved until autumn. The cooks spread the corn shucks with dough and then a layer of cooked meat from the head, seasoned with chile peppers. They then folded the filling and dough carefully within the cornshuck and cooked the finished tamale in a large pot of rapidly boiling water. A batch of tamales might be shared with neighbors, or leftovers kept for a day or two.[69]

A diet based on pork and cornmeal, high in fat, protein, and carbohydrates, might keep a person alive, but, as reports throughout the South indicated, it would not necessarily keep one healthy.[70] For much of the year, rural Texas diets lacked essential vitamins. Pellagra, a niacin-deficiency disease that ravaged the South, was believed to be at epidemic proportions in the 1920s in the Lone Star State.[71] To supplement their diets, most people of the Blacklands, like other rural people in the United States, attempted to raise vegetables, fruit, and produce at home. Agricultural reformers urged them to "live at home" and to avoid buying food on credit from commissaries or village stores. In an economy that saw cash only in the fall, home production remained the only way that a family could ensure a variety of foodstuffs. As Dovie Carroll observed generally about the period before World War II, "Way back yonder, when them cotton prices dropped, you just wouldn't make much of a living. It'd sure be hard living. In other words, if you didn't raise your own living yourself back in those days, you wouldn't get by."[72] Almost all of the tasks involved in raising one's own living belonged to the women. Without their efforts in gardening and raising poultry and milk cows, people of the Blacklands would have suffered far more than they actually did.[73]

Economic situations often made difficult the ideal of "living at home." The initial purchase of livestock and garden seeds required financial resources beyond the reach of some families. Landlords often objected to their tenants using the land for raising foodstuffs—not to mention the profits that would be lost if tenants stopped buying groceries on credit. Caring for gardens and livestock required time as well. Consequently, those who could least afford it often bought the most groceries, at credit prices often double those of cash or trade, and therefore had little fresh food in their diet.[74] As cotton acreages increased throughout the early twentieth century, the amount of land devoted to other crops declined. Most of the land was consumed by cotton and corn, which fed not only humans but also the work stock. After World War I, one observer complained that "the cotton patch has, in varying degrees of course, encroached upon the pasture to such an extent that scarcely enough is left of it to support even a cow. In a similar way the orchards and the garden lots are diminishing."[75]

The poorest people suffered the most from the ever-spreading cultivation of cotton. Unable to establish orchards and gardens and to own dairy cows because of their frequent moves from farm to farm, and sometimes lacking even chickens, the poorest residents relied instead on store-bought food, often of inferior quality and at inflated prices.

In terms of food, families that were able to have a division of labor fared better than those that did not. The more time a woman spent at field work, the less time she could devote to the family's overall subsistence and maintenance. At a time when almost every meal had to be prepared from minimally processed foods, women participated in the market economy as field workers to the detriment of the short-term needs of the family. For more prosperous families, women's home production of foodstuffs represented the difference in a starvation diet and one that kept a family well fed with some variety throughout most of the year. For farm women, being able to devote themselves to their families' nutrition was a privilege afforded by their economic standing.

Predictably, home production varied with socioeconomic status and also by ethnicity. In the southern Blacklands, three-quarters of the Anglo women and a slight majority of the African American women kept gardens of some description. Among Mexicans, the participation rate fell to less than one-fourth.[76] Alice Owens Caufield, an African American whose father sharecropped in southern McLennan County, remembered that their family had no garden, and they either bought their vegetables on credit or relied on neighbors to share their produce with them.[77] For migrant families or those without gardens, potatoes or store-bought dried beans were sometimes the only vegetables available to them. A 1920 study found that in Hill County, two-thirds of migratory white families and one-third of black families reported eating only starchy vegetables the day before they were interviewed. Potatoes and beans would provide a reasonably healthy diet if supplemented with other foods, such as corn-meal and pork, that would make them sources of complete proteins.[78] But families without gardens lacked many vitamins from fruits and leafy vegetables.

For the fortunate majority, planning and overseeing the garden was usually the task of the wife and mother of the family. Often, the men of the household plowed the initial garden, and then the women decided what would be planted and where, as Myrtle Calvert Dodd remembered: "I remember my mother would say, 'We're going to plant this and plant that and plant the other thing.' Usually my mother bossed it, told what she wanted. If my father planted it, she would always say, 'Well, he planted too much of this or too much of that, or not enough of the other.'"[79]

Once the garden was planted, its care sometimes became the responsibility of the entire family under the mother's watchful eye. Bernice Bostick Weir remembered that when she was a young mother, she, her husband, and the children all worked in the garden: "Well, we all did, just a little bit at a time." Etta Carroll recalled that she and Dovie Carroll shared the gardening: "All the both of us done the chopping and the working in it."[80] Eddie Stimpson, conversely, observed that the gardens were the work of women and children alone: "No men I no of work the garden except to cover and dig the Irish potatoes with the team of mule and with a one man middle buster." Children were helpful, however, because they had "a growing hand."[81] Gardens were not always planted at convenient spots, and the trek from the house might be as long as half a mile.[82]

The vegetables in the garden tended to be simple spring crops, a welcome relief after the dreary sameness of winter food. Lou Thomas Folley always expressed eagerness for the first fruits of spring, according to her daughter: "My mother's ambition was to have fried chicken, fresh English peas or string-beans, and cabbage on Easter. Well, we always had the fried chicken and we always had the peas or beans, whichever we was going to have, but the cabbage sometimes weren't headed. But we had cabbage; she gathered the leaves off of the heads and cooked the leaves. So we always had cabbage and beans or peas and new potatoes and fried chicken on Easter."[83] Bernice Weir also remembered her mother's garden: "We always had green beans—she loved Kentucky Wonder beans. She always had a big row of carrots and just the usual run of a garden—peas and beans and potatoes and onions."[84] Mexican families, Adelaida Torres Almanza remembered, added peppers and garlic, common spices in the Mexican diet, to the standard garden fare. According to Luz Sanchez

Hurtado, the peppers were of three types: tiny, pungent chile peppers no bigger than the end of one's thumb; milder red peppers, six inches long; and jalapeños, green and loaded with fire.[85]

The poorest families, who could not plant foods that required the purchase of seeds such as peas and green beans, relied instead on items that could be started from the previous year's crop, such as potatoes, onions, and turnips.[86] The heavy clay Blacklands soil dictated some of the choices for food crops. Area farmers believed that the sweet potato, the vitamin-rich staple of many southern diets, rotted in the Central Texas clay. Myrtle Calvert Dodd recalled: "We didn't plant many sweet potatoes because they didn't do good in Hewitt. . . . But it seemed to me like there at Hewitt they never did plant watermelons or cantaloupes much because they didn't do any good. The ground was too black, heavy."[87] The Texas heat and the almost inevitable water shortages limited summer crops. Janie Kasberg Winkler, who cared deeply about her garden and spent "every spare moment" tending it, with her children hauled water from their tank, hitching their mules to a slide with a barrel on it. Some women utilized their leftover water from laundry and bathing to water their gardens.[88] But, as Bernice Weir observed, "It never lasted long, just through the springtime."[89]

A few families had winter gardens, with cabbage, collards, turnips (useful as much for the greens as for the turnips themselves), and onions. Greens and onions could be tied in bunches and hung in outbuildings for storage.[90] Myrtle Calvert Dodd recalled: "Now, I'll tell you one thing they usually had left in the garden was collards. I remember when my grandfather would come right after Christmas; he'd tell my mother, he'd say, 'Now, Hester, cook some of those collards. I'm tired of all that dressing and fancy stuff we have here at Christmas. Cook some of those collards today.' "[91]

Saving vegetables through the winter proved difficult. The few Blacklands residents with cellars placed root vegetables such as Irish potatoes, sweet potatoes, turnips, and onions there; others put them under the house and covered them with straw.[92] Myrtle Calvert Dodd remembered having "lots of Irish potatoes because they'd dig those and put them under the house. You had to get under there and get them in the winter. And they would sometimes freeze. And you know they're not good when they're thawed. That would worry my mother; if she thought it was going to turn real cold, she would take a bucketful and bring them in the house. Of course, we always ran out. After you could buy them, they did. But when I was real young, say, five or six years old [1910], I don't think you could buy them. They ran out. Probably when they went to

Waco they got them."[93] As one of the main sources of carbohydrates and vitamins, potatoes received great attention from farm families.

While the majority of Texans had access to vegetables, fresh fruits were amenities enjoyed by very few.[94] In 1935, less than 17 percent of Texas farms had orchards.[95] Although peaches, plums, and pears grew readily in the Blacklands, orchards required several years to mature and bear fruit after planting. Planting an orchard meant that a family intended to stay in one location for a long period, and a big orchard was considered a definite sign of prosperity.[96] For a tenant family, an orchard was a special attraction, a lucky draw with the selection of a farm. Even with little control over the situation, tenant farmers noticed the availability of fruit trees. Lee Rice recalled: "We had a large orchard at Bethel. One day, [his sisters] Maudie, Ruth and I were throwing and wasting peaches. Maudie said she had heard that when you wasted fruit you wouldn't have any the next year. The next year we lived on the Cassel place and we did not have a fruit tree on the place."[97] Myrtle Calvert Dodd remembered that her mother depended partially on wild supplies and rejoiced when she had access to fruit trees: "Some of the places, we didn't have any. But usually there was a few plum trees. When we lived at Eddy that year, we had a big peach orchard, but the peaches—the freeze got them. We didn't have very many. But if we had one peach tree and plum tree, they were always so glad."[98]

Prosperous landowning families planted large orchards. Particularly before canning was readily available, the fruit had to be used quickly, and sometimes their bounty was more than one family could consume alone. At those times, landowners might share their harvests with tenants and relatives, as Bernice and Pat Bostick did: "Pat put in an orchard down here. We had a hundred trees, and you never saw such a peach crop in your life. And so—of course, we couldn't use near all of them, and everybody else's peaches made just like ours did. You couldn't sell them, hardly. I know one of my neighbors that was over here a long time ago, said, 'We'll never forget the tub of peaches that you brought us.' And I didn't even remember us ever bringing them a tub of peaches."[99] Etta and Dovie Carroll depended on his landowning parents for their supplies of peaches, and Myrtle Calvert Dodd recalled: "Usually we had neighbors or friends that would have a big [orchard] and when peaches come on, you know, they shared. You had to use them up quickly."[100]

Not all neighbors shared, however, and memories of selfishness stung, staying in families' collective memories for generations. Lee Rice recalled his mother being accused as a girl of stealing peaches by their wealthy Hunt County neighbor.[101] And those who gave sometimes did so grudgingly, as Bessie Winniford McRae admitted: "We had a big orchard. We had lots of fruit, and we never thought about selling it. They'd come there and bring great big boxes—wooden boxes like these you ship dry goods in. We kids would have to get out and help them pick the fruit. They'd shake them off the trees. Of course, we didn't say anything before them; we'd gripe to one another. 'Well, it looks like it's enough to give them the peaches without having to get out and help gather them.'"[102]

During the early part of the twentieth century, few families, regardless of their economic status, had access to home-preserved fruits and vegetables out of season. Although the process of preserving food through canning had been recognized for almost a century, few families had the proper equipment to preserve food successfully. Bernice Weir remembered that in her childhood her family had fresh vegetables and fruits while they were in season and then no more until the following year despite her mother's efforts: "Peaches was about all we had, you know, and sometimes she'd cook peaches—put the sugar in them and cook peaches and things like that. But we used more dried fruits then."[103] Getting enough surplus produce to save some for the winter proved problematic for Myrtle Dodd's mother with her eight children. Dodd recalled: "She didn't can many vegetables. We ate them all as they—she might have enough green beans to can a few, but it was hard because you didn't have a canner then. It seemed to me like that she very rarely ever canned anything out of the garden like they did later. We ate them all, fresh."[104]

Some families dried fruit on the tin roofs of buildings "leeward to the outhouse."[105] Drying was a simple process that required only a sunny rooftop, a vigilant eye, and patience. Vera Allen Malone remembered, "Before they started much canning, they would cut it and then put it out on top of the smokehouse and let it dry. And then when you'd take that in, you'd wash it— you know, when you got ready to use it—and that took care of a lot of the fruit."[106] In Dallas County, farm families dried peaches, pears, and plums on rooftops under layers of cheesecloth to shield them from insects and birds. The fruit had to be taken in at night to protect it from the dew and turned and placed in the sun again the next day for a period of about two weeks. Dried fruit appeared frequently in cobblers or in pies fried in lard.[107]

As canning equipment became more common after World War I, many women began devoting as much time as they could to preserving fruits and vegetables, a process that required long hours in the kitchen during the hot time of the year. Having a large supply of canned goods required forethought and careful planning. A forward-looking mother would plant her garden with an eye to the next winter's needs, and she would begin gathering jars and lids well ahead of the harvest. Making preserves took time, and it required fresh produce. Because of these demands, the most affluent families preserved the most food. In Ruth Allen's 1930 study, 61 percent of Anglo-American farm women who did no field work put up preserves; among black women, the percentage fell to only 21 percent, and fewer than 3 percent of the Mexican women preserved any food.[108] Storage space also limited the amount of food that women could save. A landowner's wife with a storm cellar and smokehouse had far more space than did a tenant's wife crowded into a two-room house without a spare inch.

For those who saved fruit, one of the most common methods available was jelly making in open kettles, which most families owned in some form. As a tenant farmer's wife, Hester Calvert rarely had access to fruit cultivated on their own farm; instead, she preserved those that grew wild in Central Texas, such as dewberries, plums, and mustang grapes. Her daughter remembered: "It seems like she had a pan that would cook up five or six jars. You had to have a pan to cook it in. . . . And the fencerow—I can just see it now—that had so many grapes on it. I hated picking them, too. They were sticky, I guess. The leaves were kind of sticky. They'd be on the fence and you'd have to watch out for it, the briers down underneath; had to watch out. Sand burs, too, at one place."[109] Women seeking to maximize all resources took advantage of wild supply regardless of their financial situation. Landowners' wives made jellies from wild mustang grapes, but they also had the option of growing grapes and other berries suitable for jelly.[110] Their jelly making could be more purposive and less dependent on luck.

Women also preserved food with vinegar, making pickles from peaches, cucumbers, or beets, especially, in crock jars, and processing cabbage with salt into sauerkraut.[111] They relied on time-tested recipes, as Inez Folley recalled: "I remember one year we put up eighty-seven half-gallons of cucumber pickles. Nobody could make any better pickles than my mother could. She knew just what ingredients: one, two, three: one cup of sugar, two cups of vinegar, and three cups of water. And we made our own pickles and own beets. We grew the beets and the cucumbers."[112]

In the first two decades of the century, a few women canned fruits and vegetables with the water-bath method, preparing foods in glass jars in simple open kettles. Inez Adams Walker remembered her mother's technique and her knowledge before World War I: "Had big pots where she'd cook it. She'd know about how long to cook it. And put it in them jars hot and seal it up."[113] Many fruits and vegetables preserved reasonably well in glass jars, but some, most notably corn, soon went bad.[114]

Shortly before World War I, pressure cookers began appearing in some areas of the Blacklands, bringing much more consistent results with metal cans or the older-style glass jars.[115] Agents of the newly created home demonstration clubs, the women's branch of the Agricultural Extension Service of the U.S. Department of Agriculture, realized the potential of canning for preserving food. They began with the youngest farm residents, who were often most open to new ideas. Female agents organized rural girls into "Tomato Clubs," in which the girls grew plots of tomatoes and learned to can them.[116] In May 1917, the Texas legislature agreed to fund "canning demonstration agents" to spread the technology among rural women.[117] With enthusiastic encouragement from home demonstration agents, women began slowly adopting the new method of canning, with results that changed the eating habits of middle- and upper-income farm families.

Landowners' wives such as Bernice Weir quickly adopted the new preservation techniques. "We didn't have anything that way until—oh, it must have been in '26 or '27," Weir remembered.

> There was a woman that moved into the community here and she said she didn't see why we couldn't all get together and have a home demonstration. And we'd have the agent out of Waco to come down once a month and then was when we began to buy—seemed to me like somebody had canners to rent and everything. And Pat went and bought us a twenty-five-quart pressure cooker and we could—we first canned in—well, I think we killed a calf first and canned it in those tin cans. And then we got to raising bigger gardens and canning stuff in glass jars. And we had a storm house; we never did go in it. Pat took a bridge plank and put a shelf across that storm house and when I'd can vegetables and things we'd take it down there.[118]

The new canning techniques and equipment provided a venue in which women shared their resources. Pressure cookers cost money, and most Blacklands families could not afford them at first. Near Winnsboro, Odena Glover Bannan's mother had the only pressure cooker in the neighborhood. Other families in the neighborhood provided all the vegetables and half the jars; Mrs. Glover provided half of the jars, did all the canning, and took half of the canned vegetables as her share.[119] In the African American community around Robinson, McLennan County, Gillie Harkey shared her canner with the women around her, as Alice Owens Caufield remembered: "We would carry the corn and Mrs. Gillie and the older ladies would cut the corn. And you'd carry your corn and whatever else was needed, and your cans, and they had the container that you put the corn in and it was cooked. Then when they put the top on it, they had a machine that sealed it. I can remember, Mrs. Gillie was just a person who was open to do things like that."[120]

Extension Service agents also urged the creation of community canning plants. Cooperative canning work began in 1918, when the service established seventy-seven plants throughout the state and combined orders for equipment and cans. Farm women brought their own produce and canned it on a toll basis—a set amount of canned food in return for the use of the equipment.[121] Many of these early community canning plants were in the county-seat towns and thus inaccessible to most farm women, but they were a beginning.[122] Using a community canner involved travel from the farm but may have been acceptable because transportation was improving dramatically and women were becoming more mobile at this point. Wives and mothers at the canning plants, moreover, were almost always only in the company of other women.

Tenants' and sharecroppers' wives acquired pressure cookers as they could. Etta and Dovie Carroll carefully discussed the potential that having their own pressure cooker presented. The rewards seemed so great that in the late 1920s, when they took out their annual loan to make their crop and pay their choppers and pickers, they made the loan large enough to purchase an eighteen-quart canner and a sealer from a local hardware store at a cost of twenty-five to thirty dollars, plus interest. With these new machines, Etta Carroll could process six quart jars or fourteen tin cans at a time. One of her favorite projects was preserving plums and berries with which to make fresh jelly during the winter. She eventually became proficient at the difficult task of preserving meat, proudly canning beef, chicken, and chili.[123]

By the 1930s, pressure cookers had spread throughout the middle and upper levels of Blacklands Anglo society.[124] When the crops were ripe, entire families had to move quickly to ensure that they were put up before they spoiled. Alma Stewart Hale discussed the complexity of corn canning: "When we canned corn we were organized. We'd can corn about a hundred cans per day. We had pressure cookers. Papa and maybe two of the boys would go to the field to pull the corn. Another one would cut the ends off and shuck it. Then somebody else would come along and silk it. Somebody else would cut it off the cob. Then somebody else would cook it and put it in the cans. And then somebody sealed. In other words, we all had jobs."[125]

In some households, the women alone worked to get the harvest put up. Gladys Everett remembered accompanying her evangelist husband to a church revival during corn-canning time. The woman in whose home they were staying left her canning duties to go to the church service but returned to long hours of intensive labor. Everett remembered: "We left it—went to church and returned to finish up. The next day was Sunday. We quickly changed clothes and got busy. The ears of corn were shucked, silks cleaned off and ends trimmed. We took a sharp knife, held the ear upright, cut off the grains in a pan and then scraped the juice or milk out of what was left on the cob. It was cooked slightly, put in jars or cans and pressure cooked in the big canner on the wood or kerosene stove at a certain temperature for so long. At 2:30 A.M. we finished up. The men and kids had slept through it all."[126]

So important were canned goods in the domestic economy that they sometimes took the place of cash. Bessie McRae recalled: "Oh, we canned lots of stuff, and in those days we paid the preacher a lot with stuff like that—meats, hams, and canned stuff. He didn't have a set salary. We just gave him—I can remember my mother canning fruit and setting aside every tenth jar. She tithed on it."[127] The canned goods became McRae's mother's way of giving what she could to her church. But, like almost all other foodstuffs in the Blacklands, the stores of treasured canned goods frequently ran out before the next supply came in. Etta Carroll commented, "You just canned until you thought you had enough and sometimes you run out and sometimes you didn't have enough to can. If the crop was short, why, you just canned till you didn't have anything to can." And when the Folley family ran out of their homemade canned goods, they sold eggs to buy other supplies of food at the community store.[128]

Even with community canning centers, however, poorer women often had little food to preserve or could not leave the fields long enough to devote long hours over a canning kettle or pressure cooker. Ruth Allen found in the late 1920s that only 21 percent of the African American women whom she surveyed preserved any food at all, and only a handful put up fifty quarts or more. Mexican women were able to save even less; fewer than 3 percent preserved food, and only 2 out of 269 had more than fifty quarts of home-canned food. Anglo women either canned nothing at all (49.7 percent), or they preserved a great deal; almost a quarter of the women in Allen's survey preserved more than fifty quarts of food.[129] Women with access to canning equipment and the time to do it could make dramatic improvements in their families' diets. But those who lacked the resources had few options through the 1930s.

Many Blackland Prairie families went for long periods of time with pork as their only meat. An additional source of high-quality protein that many people had, regardless of their financial status, were chickens. Small, inexpensive, easy to feed, and highly portable, chickens fit into even the poorest family's lifestyle, providing eggs and meat for home consumption and, for those who had surpluses, eggs and live poultry for cash sales or trade. In Hill County in the 1920s, almost 100 percent of the white families and 80 percent of the African American families raised at least some chickens; Ruth Allen found farther south that among Mexican women, who were unlikely to have gardens or cows, 71 percent managed to tend chickens.[130] Like hogs, keeping chickens was a privilege for hired laborers, as Etta Carroll remembered: "A lot of times they would have maybe a few chickens because the house would be far enough back in the field where it wouldn't bother us."[131] Their care almost always fell to the women of the family.

Gathering the eggs was a major responsibility in tending chickens, a daily task most of the year. It was a job sometimes easily accomplished by children. Inez Folley said, "I have gathered eggs every day for months and months after months." Gathering eggs might also prove difficult, as Myrtle Calvert Dodd recalled: "You know, hens are funny. There'll be a few of them stay in there but they like to get out and go to the barn and hide in the hay lofts and underneath the feeding troughs. I can remember when the hens used to steal nests up there and they'd be close and I can remember my father putting me on top of a ladder and saying, 'Now, get those eggs there over in that corner.' It was too close for him to get in. Put me on top of the ladder and reach in there and get the eggs. I wanted to be sure the hen wasn't there. They'd steal nests out on the fencerows if there were weeds, too." Children's small arms and hands might reach the eggs easily, but little people also might have unpleasant encounters with the "protective instincts of the setting hens."[132] Mexican immigrant families did not let the lack of chicken houses stop them from maintaining chickens; Adelaida Torres Almanza remembered that her first home in America had "a big old tree" that served as a roost "full of chickens," while the Sanchez family had special boxes in the open for chicken nests.[133]

Even though the chickens sometimes refused to use them, their houses required careful maintenance every few months, when the aroma became overwhelming. First, the cleaners raked and scraped the floor down to a hard dirt surface, then carried tubs of droppings and feathers out to the garden for fertilizer. They next cleaned out the nests and took the old straw to the pasture and burned it to get rid of mites and insect eggs. The final step entailed gathering fresh straw for new nests and dusting the entire henhouse with London purple, a commercially made arsenic poison, to get rid of the rest of the mites and insects.[134] Other problems could affect chickens as well. R. W. Williams remembered that chickens were occasionally afflicted with "the sore head," a disease that could kill entire flocks. His father read in *Farm and Ranch*, a weekly newspaper from Dallas, how to make a solution that cured this affliction by dipping the chickens' heads in it. As a child, Williams helped his mother "many a time" with this job.[135]

Still, chickens were easy to feed and water. Texas naturalist Roy Bedichek wrote nostalgically about the strong taste of chickens fattened on army worms from the cotton patch, while Myrtle Dodd remembered watering chickens with leftover bathwater: "And when the water got short, you know what they did? They dipped it out of the bathtub and put it in the chicken troughs to drink. Didn't waste it. It just ran out from a pipe across the back of the yard into what we called the chicken yard. And the chickens would be glad to have it."[136] Some more meticulous families, disdaining the taste of army worms and other unpleasant sources of food, penned their chickens before slaughtering them. Maggie Langham Washington, the daughter of black sharecroppers in Navarro County, commented that her family was more particular than most: "We were, I thought, very progressive. I now often wonder every time I go to eat a piece of chicken, Now, has this chicken really been put up and fed and cleaned out thoroughly? before eating it. Because that's the way we did it. We would catch several chickens off the yard, put them into a coop, and feed them. That's cleaning out all the impurities, you know, that they get just running wild."[137]

Chickens provided two important sources of food: eggs and meat. For many families, neither was in supply year-round. Myrtle Calvert Dodd remembered vividly the scarcity of eggs in her McLennan County home: "We didn't always have them, because the chickens wouldn't lay in the wintertime much."[138] The difficulty of the shortages remained with Dodd eighty years later; she commented, "You know, after I was grown I dreamed one time about getting in a hen nest after eggs and me telling my mother there wasn't any in there and they was wanting some so bad. Yes, I dreamed she was standing wanting eggs so bad and I couldn't find any." When eggs were in short supply, her mother hoarded them for bread making or Christmas baking. "I can remember when we got short of eggs; most of the time it'd be January and February," Dodd commented. "When they started their spring laying we'd be so thrilled—run out of their ears then, you know. Mama would boil them and stuff them and fry them and any way in the world to get rid of them because you couldn't keep them very long." Extremely high in protein, eggs served as a superior meat substitute during lean times. Dodd added: "She'd boil them and put a little bacon grease in them and a little salt and pepper and mash up the yellow, you know. We liked those, too. If you're short of meat, that's a good thing to have for lunch. And even sometimes when we had hog meat we ate those instead—us kids would—instead of the meat."[139] Female chickens were rarely separated from the roosters, and Louise Blackwell Dillow recalled with great distaste the surprise of breaking open fertilized eggs: "Experience taught one to crack the eggs into a separate bowl—not directly into a pot full of other ingredients."[140]

Chickens often had to be rationed as sources of meat, for a family that ate its last chicken would immediately find itself with neither eggs nor meat. Myrtle Dodd continued: "My mother couldn't wait till an old hen would go to setting after Christmas so we'd have early fryers. Set 'em, you know, watch 'em, take care of them. They just killed the roosters most of the time to eat. But in the wintertime, we'd have a baked hen once in a while. Just have to have some meat or something; we'd get so tired of—that would be, most of the time, on Sunday that she would bake a hen." Some families reserved chickens only for Sunday dinner, with the best pieces from the breast reserved for the father and perhaps a visiting minister.[141]

Preparing a chicken for cooking involved, first, killing it on the night before the intended meal if the weather were cool enough or on the day of the meal if the weather were warm. Dodd remembered as a young girl getting chickens ready for cooking: "Scald it and take your feathers off. And if it had pinfeathers on it, I hated that, getting those off. And my mama didn't like it if you didn't get them off. Give you a knife to kind of scrape them off around the neck and places where they were short, you know. It didn't take too long. But she always cut it up."[142] If the chicken were fried, very frugal families cooked even the feet and head (with brains left in, gouging out the eyes and cutting off the beak), discarding only the tail.[143]

In addition to providing eggs and meat, chickens, guinea hens, and turkeys also became the sources of other valuable items. In an economy that brought in money from harvest only once a year, many women sold eggs and chickens, as well as butter, as sources of cash, occasionally for their own personal use but more often for the use of their families. Sometimes women, rather than obtaining cash, instead bartered their poultry for other goods.[144] As historian Joan Jensen has remarked, most income produced by women required little capital investment and likewise accumulated little capital; the goal of women's household production, Jensen observed, was "to make ends meet."[145]

Prior to the arrival of the automobile, farm women rarely left their homes for trips into town. At a time when women seldom encountered the public marketplace directly, the marketplace came to their private space in the form of peddlers. Itinerant chicken peddlers traveled back roads with all sorts of goods, from buttons to spices to cotton ducking for cotton picking sacks, accepting poultry products as payment for their goods. Usually they came at regular intervals, once every week or two, in wagons or, later, automobiles with chicken-wire coops on them. In McLennan County, the peddlers would buy almost anything—fryers, hens, old roosters, guineas, ducks—except turkeys and geese, making it possible for women to cull their flocks by getting rid of old, unprofitable stock.[146] The prices that the peddlers paid the sellers depended on the freshness of the eggs and the health of the chickens.[147] Troy Crenshaw recalled his mother's careful bookkeeping: "She kept her little peddler's notebooks of I-owe-you's and you-owe-me's in the shallow top drawer with the fresh eggs in her kitchen cupboard."[148]

With improved roads, the market for poultry expanded into nearby towns as merchants and private customers bought produce from farm people. Sometimes women began entering the commercial arena by peddling their chickens on their own; often, however, their husbands accompanied them. Mexican women played a private role in the chicken market; in the Sanchez family, for example, the wife raised the chickens but the husband sold them in town.[149] Selling poultry and eggs could be a challenge and not altogether pleasant. Lee Rice remembered the difficulties that his parents faced in Greenville: One customer, a Mrs. Rosenthal, "never would pay the first asking price of fryers. Mama and Papa had to haggle with her. When they priced the fryers at twenty-five cents each she would try to buy them for twenty cents each."[150]

As the market increased due to improved transportation and growing urban populations, some Blacklands women expanded their chicken production. By the 1930s, the majority of women had at least fifty chickens, and a quarter of them had more than one hundred.[151] Bernice Bostick Weir began her operation modestly: "Back then they didn't have [wedding] showers, but different people would give you things. Some had given me some eggs to set and some one or two had given me a hen or two, and Grandma gave me some hens when she moved to Moody. . . . I don't remember just how many I had—six or eight, though. And of course, a hen could set on fifteen eggs easily, and it wasn't long until we had quite a bunch of chickens." By the mid-1930s, the Bosticks had bought a hundred-egg incubator, run with kerosene, which they kept in their storm shelter.[152] Mary Zotz of northern McLennan County kept careful accounting of her sales; around 1910, she sold as many as twenty-two dozen eggs at a time, at fifteen cents a dozen. She also made $9.35 that year by selling thirty-one hens at eight and a half cents a pound in Waco.[153]

Yet, like almost everything else in farm life, the chicken market could prove disappointing. A 1920 study of farm women in the western and northern United States revealed that, while 81 percent of the women in the sample cared for chickens, with flocks averaging ninety chickens, only 22 percent had poultry money and only 16 percent had egg money.[154] In their antiphonal style of dialogue developed during seventy years of marriage, Etta and Dovie Carroll remembered difficulties selling eggs. "We've seen the time that you could bring eggs to town and couldn't even hardly sell them," Mrs. Carroll commented.

"I've seen the time you'd bring them to town and couldn't get a dime a dozen for them and have to take them back. A lot of times, why, I'd throw them away," her husband added.

"Cook them for the chickens or the dogs," Mrs. Carroll continued.

"They's just so cheap and they had so many," Mr. Carroll concluded.[155]

Families continued to depend on chickens for cash despite the quirks of the market, and some expanded their poultry flocks to include turkeys. Before World War I, Bernice Bostick Weir's mother raised "a big bunch of turkeys" to sell each fall.[156] Turkey raising was extremely labor-intensive and required much skill, which women mastered. Robert Calvert found out just how difficult turkeys were in the spring of 1905. His daughter, Myrtle Calvert Dodd, recalled:

We always had turkeys, too, up until, oh, I was grown. My mother, that was her project, to get the turkey money, was how we'd have Christmas money—to sell turkeys. They still laugh about—when I was born, it was in May. And Mama had some turkey to come off with little turkeys, and you know, you put a little meat grease on top of their head to keep lice off. And my mother couldn't get out and do it, had my father to do it, and every one of them died. And my uncles just laughed so, said Papa had the idea, if a little bit did good, a lot would do more good, and he put too much on there and they died. He lost a whole setting of little turkeys. They laughed about that as long as most of them lived, about Bob greasing the turkeys.

Adelaida Almanza remembered the travails of one of her relatives who attempted to raise turkeys: "She had to spend her whole day taking care of them because turkeys are restless and they wouldn't stop picking at each other. Turkeys are a lot of trouble. You have to take care of them and make sure that they come back home whenever they get out because they can never remember the way back home." When the owners managed to get the turkeys to survive to the autumn holiday season, they sold the birds alive in nearby market centers.[157] The profits wrought with painstaking care brought money for families to spend for Christmas.

Another type of livestock that women tended were their families' few cows. A family that kept only one cow could have milk and butter at least part of the time. Having more than one cow helped ensure that the family would have a steady supply of milk, with a minimum of one animal producing when the others went dry.[158] Many families, however, did without. Cow ownership usually carried definite messages about a family's ethnicity and social class. In Ruth Allen's study, 81.4 percent of Anglo women kept at least one cow, while only 43.8 percent of black women and 22.3 percent of Mexican women did.[159]

For sharecroppers and tenants, the lack of cow ownership had several causes. One reason was poverty; it cost money to buy a cow. Some landowners forbade their tenants enough space for a pasture. Families who moved frequently could find relocating a cow cumbersome. The decision could be made for the family, or they might exercise a choice in keeping their cow population low. Alice Owens Caufield remembered her father limiting the family to only one cow as a way to maintain a cash balance in the family: "My daddy never did keep but one cow at a time. And she would have a calf, and he would always sell it to be sure to have some money, maybe get his children something to wear."[160]

Comfortable farmers tended to regard the lack of cows as a choice made by their less-affluent neighbors. Although they looked down on those families with no cows, they recall giving away dairy products regularly. Bernice Bostick Weir commented on the tenant families around their home: "Some of them

Food Production and Preparation

never milked a cow or anything. I gave milk and butter—or milk, especially, to several of my neighbors. . . . People that rented lots of times just—I don't know why they didn't have cows. I don't know whether it was because they—on account of moving, or why. But so many of them didn't have cows."[161] In Navarro County, Bertha Blackwell, herself the wife of a tenant farmer, frowned upon their neighbors who were "too trifling" to tend cows. Some of those neighbors sent their children to the Blackwell farm each day for buckets of skim milk, possibly the leftovers from butter making. The Blackwells themselves drank whole milk.[162] Etta Carroll, also a tenant farmer's wife, recalled offering their laborers pastureland: "We let them have their own cow if they would want one, because we always had a pasture—but they didn't ever want a cow much. You could get milk for a nickel a gallon and a lot of times we'd just give them milk along."[163]

All neighbors did not give away milk, however, and it was not always readily available for purchase. Bernice Weir gave away milk to white neighbors, but she required work from Narcissus Bean, an African American whose husband worked as a laborer on the Bostick farm. Bean received milk, butter, eggs, and leftover food in exchange for tending the Bostick children and cleaning.[164] Bean was fortunate to have access to dairy products. A Texas economist observed in 1922, "Good milk is relatively hard to buy in many localities."[165] Outside observers concluded that milk was not as plentiful to all residents, as more prosperous farmers believed.

For even the relatively well-off families that did own cows, dairy products were easily spoiled and difficult to store in the days before commercial refrigeration. Women used time-tested methods of refrigeration to keep food as best they could. The Owens family lacked any refrigeration on their sharecropper's farm, and they used an old method of evaporation cooling for their milk, storing milk "in one of those white crock" jars. "And that same kind of [flour] sack that you covered it with," said Alice Owens Caufield. "They had a way where they could just tie that towel around that part [the neck]; they wouldn't have to have no extra string. It's just like maybe four knots in it or like we take a scarf and fix it in a triangle, you know; you can tie it around here so it won't slip off, and that kept out all the flies."[166] Some families kept milk and butter cool by putting it in their water sources: a cistern, spring, or well. Wells could prove particularly tricky: if the milk or butter spilled, the well might have to be drawn dry and cleaned and the walls scrubbed.[167]

The simplest indoor device for ensuring the freshness of perishable items was an evaporative cooler. As Gladys Everett described it, "The four metal posts held four shelves with the rims turned up. The bottom one was filled with water and milk jars and such set on it and the others, except the top one. A piece of clean or new cotton sacking was stretched tightly around the outside with the bottom resting in the water. It was pinned together at the front with clothes pins. The cloth absorbed the water thus keeping the food cool."[168]

Although coolers worked fairly well, they required careful maintenance by the housewife. Bernice Weir recalled: "You put a cloth around it and that water keeps that towel wet and oh, it can sure get stinky if you don't change it pretty often. It just gets slick or something. The pan will get slick; you've got to wash the pan and then wash your cooler cloth—that's what we called it—cooler cloth, 'cause that's all it was used for. But it kept the milk and everything good. And then we had a box that I slid in underneath the bottom of the pan because that bottom sat on little legs. And I kept my eggs in that there. And so it was used for eggs and the milk and butter inside."[169]

"If Mama got busy and let the cloths get dry, everybody fussed because it wouldn't be cool," Myrtle Dodd remembered. "But she'd draw water in the middle of the afternoon and put on and let it go down those cloths. And if the wind was blowing, it kept pretty cool."[170]

Commercially manufactured iceboxes, which had separate compartments for ice to cool the food, were considered significant improvements over coolers.[171] Iceboxes came into fairly common use throughout the Blacklands in the 1930s. Mechanical refrigerators remained rare.[172] Bernice Bostick Weir recalled her kerosene refrigerator as a big improvement over her icebox: "We had much more room in it. It was big. And it had two or three trays in it, and the freezing unit was up at the top."[173]

Necessity often prevailed in times before refrigeration, and Blacklands families used spoiled milk as well as fresh. Soured, thickened milk, known as clabber, frequently appeared on Blacklands tables. Bernice Weir acquired a taste for clabber as a newlywed: "Pat loved clabber with sugar on it. Oh, and I thought that was the awfullest thing I ever saw or heard of because I sure didn't have anything like that at home. And I said, 'Well, when we have children, they're not going to do that.' But I kept tasting and tasting, so I learned to love clabber with sugar on it. So don't say what you're going to do and what you're not a-going to do, because you sure have to eat your words."[174]

Clabber also sometimes became cottage cheese, an excellent source of protein that nutritionally complemented cornmeal.[175] The cheese maker heated the clabbered milk to just below the boiling point, strained it, placed it in a cloth bag, and hung it outside or over the sink, where it could drip. The remaining whey dripped out of the bag, leaving a solid mass of curd.[176] Mexican women took the processing a step further. Some kneaded the curd in the flat stone known as a *metate* to remove the whey, and then molded it in a wooden mold. Others mixed the curd with hot peppers and dried it in the sun.[177] Czech Catholic families transformed the cottage cheese into cooked cheese as well, a homemade meat substitute for Friday fasting. "If you want a limburger cheese, you let it rot, like they say," Mary Hanak Simcik recalled. "You put soda in it. Soda and cream and you leave it about two hours, and the soda would kind of dissolve the cheese and then cook it, and then it would keep good. . . . And then of course you put it in a crock—you don't put it in aluminum or anything like that—never. You put it in an earthenware crock, you know, and you put salt in it. And if you want the smearcase, that's limburger cheese, you know, you put the caraway seed in it and let it rot—I mean ferment. And I remember it could smell to high heaven, you know, when it's ripening."[178] Cottage cheese was the only type of cheese produced in Central Texas, and it was used only at home. Cheddar and other hard cheeses, so much a part of farm diets in the northern United States, came only store-bought.

Making fresh milk into butter was a frequent task among Central Texas farm women, bringing a source of high energy and some vitamins to their families.[179] Some families made butter every day, others as seldom as twice a week.[180] Churning was tedious, and many women required their children to assist with the process, for it required no skill or physical strength—"just patience." Children might recite nursery rhymes in time with the dasher to keep themselves amused.[181] "My mother hated it," Myrtle Calvert Dodd commented. "Nobody liked to churn. My sister Thelma used to read and churn and if Grandma's there, she'd say, 'Thelma, you're just slowing down. You've got to keep paying attention. Just get busy and churn. Get through with it!' "[182] Bertha Blackwell, with nine children, often did her own churning; her daughter speculated that it was a way to get off of her feet and have "some thinking time to herself."[183]

The skill passed from generation to generation, whether the young women wanted to learn or not. Bernice Bostick Weir recalled her mother teaching her to let milk "just barely clabber," then skimming the cream off with a little bit of clabber. Weir's mother had a crock churn with a wooden dasher; later Weir and many other women had glass barrel churns with cranks, which hurried the process. After the butter "came," or separated from the liquid, it had to be worked and molded, according to Weir: "I had a wooden butter mold, and it held a pound. It was supposed to hold a pound if you just smooth it off even with the top, but I always kind of let mine come up a little bit more so I'd be sure and have a pound. It was a little square one. Just plain. And my daddy made me a butter paddle out of cedar. He whittled it out with a knife and he made it round and then put the handle onto it. You have to work the milk out—you keep a-working it; you put a little salt in it, you know, to keep it fresh and everything."[184]

Hot weather without refrigeration made butter making especially difficult, and some families did not even attempt it in the summer, giving the cream to their pigs instead.[185] The availability of ice made butter making a little simpler. Inez Adams Walker recalled that her father bought ice to help with butter making: "My daddy always had a barn with cotton seeds in it, and they'd wrap that ice up and bury them, and that's the way they saved it for a long time. Wrap it up, maybe, in some kind of sack or something."[186]

Selling butter was another important way in which women brought in cash or goods for their families. Many had regular butter customers in town and sold the remainder to local stores.[187] As a teenager, Alice Owens Caufield relied upon a network of family friends in African American sections of Waco to buy goods from her and her sister, Peaches: "We used to sell the butter, the buttermilk, and we'd sell eggs to our friends that we knew here in Waco. So my daddy was a very friendly, talkative person and a widow[er], and all of them widow women were going to buy stuff. (laughs) We didn't have to go ask some strange person. And they would always do that, because they always said, 'We're going to help out Howard's girls.'"[188]

Women developed their regular clientele on the quality of their product. Avon Rice recalled delivering his mother's butter in Greenville:

When my brother Oswald and I were small boys, about nine, ten, and eleven years of age, Mama molded butter to be sold to customers in Greenville. Mama's butter mold had two stars in it, which showed on top of each pound of butter. Oswald (Dub.) and I would take turns going to families that bought butter from us each week. We took the extra pounds of butter to the Naud Burnett grocery store, corner of Johnson and Washington streets. Mr. Mack was the clerk in the store. He would take all the butter we had left from our regular customers. Mama's trade-mark for the finest country butter was the two stars, on top. People knew her for this fine product, the *two stars*.[189]

Like Mrs. Rice, many Blacklands women cared deeply about the quality of their butter. Their reputations depended upon a premium product, and they prided themselves on producing excellence. Lou Thomas Folley carefully guarded her name as the producer of sweet-tasting, fresh butter. Her daughter recalled: "Whenever it rained in the spring of the year, the grass would grow, you know, and the cows would eat this grass. And the butter was just real yellow. And she was selling her butter at a grocery here in Mart, and she brought some butter to him, and he said, 'Mrs. Folley, my customers wants to ask you, will you please not put so much coloring in that butter.' And she told him, 'Well, say, you'll have to talk to the cows because I don't put it.' She never bought any coloring in her life to put in butter until World War II, when we had to use margarine."[190] Mrs. Folley put her word against the grocer's, who was working on behalf of his town-dwelling customers.

Excellence in butter making was one way for a woman to be known and to gain standing in her community. To verify the origin of her product, Bernice Weir used personalized butter papers:

I had butter papers printed with my name on it. . . . I'd buy a box—oh, I guess it'd weigh a pound or more—of butter papers and then I took them to a printer. We always had a little paper up here at Moody and had my name and everything. How come me to do that—when I'd have a surplus, I'd sell it to the grocery store in Moody, and I found out that this woman went in and told them that she wanted a pound of my butter and I knew my butter wasn't up there. And they sold her somebody else's butter. So then I had my butter papers printed so they'd know that they got my butter. And they bragged on the pound that they got, and I was proud of that. But what if it had of been a bad pound of butter? I would have gotten a bad name instead of a good name. And I didn't have too much to sell to the store because I had the other customers.[191]

Women's production of butter and egg money broadened their families' choices for other foods. Bernice Weir commented, "It just helped us buy groceries and things because living on the farm, you don't have a paycheck every week or every month. So with my butter and eggs and milk, it always—we always had a little bit of money in the sugar jar."[192] Myrtle Calvert Dodd's father took his wife's butter to Waco and made discretionary purchases through barter or with cash: "He'd go maybe twice a week then, you know. And then's when you got things—he'd find things coming in that we didn't normally have. You got more potatoes, maybe, and rice and raisins and apples and stuff like that if you were there when it all came in."[193] In the case of the Calverts and many other farm families, the father had the pleasure or the responsibility of choosing what to take home from the butter money. Inez Folley's mother sometimes bought beef with her egg money and occasionally used the funds for other special needs: "I can remember my—one of my best friends was getting married, and I wanted to give her a wedding present and so my mother gathered up the eggs and I went to town and sold the eggs and took the money and bought her a towel for her wedding present."[194]

In Collin County, Millie Birks Stimpson traded eggs and chickens to buy her family an occasional steak or roast.[195] Because families depended heavily on dairy products for their own consumption and as a source of cash, they rarely killed their cows to eat. The Carroll family, for instance, butchered a calf only once a year.[196] Beef spoiled quickly, so a family that butchered a cow (usually a calf) often shared it with relatives or neighbors.[197] Among Czech and German farmers, sharing was systematized through organizations called beef clubs. Once a week a member family contributed a calf, and all the other member families received parts of it, knowing that their turn to provide the calf would come around eventually.[198] In other communities, little organized sharing existed.

Because beef spoiled easily, preserving it required ingenuity. Mary Hanak Simcik remembered: "Meat would last from Saturday until about Tuesday. They put it in a bucket—stuffed it in a bucket and covered it. . . . And they lowered it into the cistern, right above the water, just kind of in the water."[199] In Milam County, enterprising German farmers sold beef to their black neighbors, as Inez Adams Walker recalled: "Those Germans, every weekend, they'd go out and they'd kill a beef and they'd come around peddling it. And maybe Mama'd buy a big roast for dinner Sunday. And we didn't have no Frigidaire, but she'd take a big clean flour sack and put—when it's fresh, it don't spoil so, and she'd hang it up on the porch to get air."[200] The Sanchez family dried their beef; Refugia Sanchez cut it in pieces, put it outside covered with paper to keep flies away, and brought it in at night; after the meat dried completely, the family stored it in sacks.[201] The development of canning systems made possible the longer-term preservation of meat. After Dovie and Etta Carroll bought their pressure cooker, they butchered calves and canned the meat for future use. Fresh beef, however, remained a rarity, available only at the most special times.[202]

No matter how hard they tried to "live at home," almost all Blacklands families purchased some food from local merchants and peddlers. Because of their lack of gardens, chickens, cows, and other means of raising their own food, African American and Mexican families were most likely to obtain food from other sources. Wage laborers in particular produced relatively little food at home.[203] Even for those who raised most of their food, the most common purchases included coffee, sugar, salt, and wheat flour, sometimes as much as two hundred pounds at a time. Many Czech families also bought dried fish, usually herring.[204]

Before the automobile, women traveled the distances to town only seldom. Peddlers for regional and national companies such as McNess, Jewel T, Rawleigh, and Watkins sold goods from farm to farm, and they were often the only vendors with whom women traded directly. Louise Dillow remembered the wonders that the McNess man brought to their Navarro County farms, touting his wares "in perfect rhythm with melodious incantation":

> "Almond, Lemon and Vanilla extract;
> Black pepper, Red pepper, Chili pepper, Cloves;
> Ginger, Nutmeg, Cinnamon, Allspice;
> Liniment, Shampoo, Toilet soap, Toothpaste;
> Brushes, Combs, Brilliantine, Fly spray."[205]

Women bartered poultry, butter, vegetables, and fruit to obtain these wares, and many depended upon the peddlers' merchandise. Bernice Weir remembered buying products for her own household from the same companies that had supplied her mother's kitchen: "We always had Watkins vanilla, you know; we didn't think there was anything else but Watkins vanilla."[206] By bartering with peddlers, women were able to exercise some choices in their household goods. Otherwise, they depended on the males traveling to town to make their purchases for them.

Cash with which to pay for groceries was scant among farm families. Dovie and Etta Carroll bought flour and other staples at the general store in Waxahachie at harvest time, paying in advance for a year's supply but picking the goods up only as they needed them. If their family's harvest was not fruitful, the Waxahachie merchant carried a balance for the Carrolls until the next harvest, charging no interest—an exception to the high interest charged elsewhere in the Blackland Prairie. The same merchant furnished credit to the Carrolls' hired hands.[207]

No matter how often family members made trips to the store, goods from town held special allure for the shoppers and their families who waited at home. Myrtle Calvert Dodd's father went alone to Waco on shopping expeditions, but the entire family enjoyed his return:

> And there was Geyser Ice House where he could get ice, you know, later on [after World War I]. And my father would carry a cotton sack to wrap that ice in. It melted some coming home, but he'd get home enough that we would have sometimes ice cream on Saturday night. And, oh, that was a thrill, too. Bury it in the cotton seed. . . . After I got bigger, they began to get some canned goods, and that would always thrill my mother, to have some canned goods, have some different things that were canned, especially canned peaches, because you'd run out, you know. And tomatoes, too. I was about five or six years old when we still lived at Eddy and my father found some canned tomatoes and brought them home and we put sugar on them—the kids. They didn't. We did. They salted theirs. But I remember we'd have a day or two when he'd come to town.[208]

Through gardens, poultry and dairy production, and the purchase of staple goods, women of the Blacklands acquired food for their families. After bringing the food into the kitchen, many women spent much of their time each day preparing meals for their sizable families. Some women enjoyed cooking, turning it into a creative exercise. For others, it was pure drudgery, something to be gotten through two or three times a day. Regardless of their feelings, women faithfully prepared meal after meal for their families.

Most women cooked on woodstoves, a carefully learned skill in which timing was crucial. "The first time Grandma went off to visit after we got married, it took me an hour to cook breakfast," Bernice Weir recalled. "I just didn't know how to manage or what to do first or what to do next or anything." But she learned, and her life soon became a round of preparing meals in succession: "And I'd have breakfast ready. . . . And then there was all those dishes to wash. And right then you got to think about what we're going to have at twelve o'clock, whether we're going to have red beans or white beans or what. And at the garden time, you've got to go to the garden and gather what's in the garden and come back. . . . And then by the time I got dinner ready, it was time to eat again."[209]

The physical circumstances of a woman's household greatly affected her ability to perform her daily duties. In food preparation, for example, the type of stove that a family owned could either complicate or make easier the job of cooking for a large group. By the beginning of the twentieth century, most (but perhaps not all) Blacklands families had abandoned open-hearth cooking for stoves made of cast iron.[210] The majority of women in the Blacklands cooked on woodstoves until the Second World War. As they changed farms, tenants had a particular difficulty in getting the stove to fit the new house. Myrtle Calvert Dodd recalled: "Sometimes you have to get another one if it didn't fit in the chimney or the location. I've seen that happen. When we moved to Hewitt, I know that was the case. We got a bigger stove."[211]

Woodstoves varied greatly in size and quality, with the size of the top limiting the amount of food that could be cooked. The size of the firebox dictated the frequency with which wood would have to be replaced. Other accessories that eased cooking were warming closets, which kept cooked dishes heated, and reservoirs for hot water. Men often acquired stoves, as they did other household goods. Bernice Bostick Weir spoke fondly of her mother's blue enamel range, which her father bought when her parents moved onto their own farm about 1905, and which she used in her own home after her parents moved to town in the 1920s: "Papa bought her the prettiest great big blue range. It was blue porcelain, and it had a warming closet up above and a fifteen-gallon reservoir on the side so we always had hot water because there was fire in that oven from morning till noon. You could cook wood or coal; the grate turned, you see, and it turned one way for wood and then up this way for coal. But we never—because we had plenty of wood down there."[212] Weir's mother numbered among the fortunate women whose husbands were inclined to provide high-quality goods with which they could do their daily chores.

Woodstoves required a steady supply of fuel, which was difficult to come by on the treeless open prairie. Pecan and oak trees suitable for firewood grew primarily along small waterways, few and far between. Men bore the responsibility for leaving the farm and acquiring wood. Like the Hunt County families who purchased wood in the Sulphur River bottoms, the Calvert family got their supply not from their own farm at Hewitt but from the Bosque River area, buying several loads and carting it several miles to the farm.[213] In Ellis County, Dovie Carroll went "away back over yonder" to cut a winter's supply of firewood: "We'd leave before daylight, and by the time we got over there to cut that wood and got back, it'd be maybe 9 or 9:30 at night."[214] Black farm laborers in McLennan County, with no money to purchase wood, picked up sticks, decayed trees, and other wooden odds and ends for firewood.

Keeping stove wood cut was a chore shouldered mostly by men and boys but sometimes by women and girls as well. Inez Folley said: "We had a saw that we sawed and cut it and that was—the saw—two people had to pull the saw, you see. And I've chopped wood and I've sawed and I've done a little bit of everything; my mother did, too. You can't explain it if you've never done it. It's backbreaking."[215] Women and girls also assisted by picking up wood chips and carrying the stove wood from the yard into the house.[216]

Gradually kerosene-burning oil stoves began to appear in Blacklands homes. By 1923, 17.9 percent of white families in Hill County had oil stoves. The Calvert and Rice families bought kerosene stoves in the early 1920s despite their tenant-farmer status. Enough families thought the advantages of an oil stove important enough to spend extra money when acquiring a new stove, regardless of the increased need to keep a supply of kerosene bought with cash or through bartering.[217] Bessie McRae had less fond memories of the kerosene stove, compared to gas: "You could smell that coal oil fumes. I imagine I could taste it. I don't know whether I could or not, but you could smell the fumes of the coal oil and all. . . . That was the messiest stuff to clean up after. It would smoke up your vessels." Inez Folley also complained of the taste of kerosene in food, but said that oil stoves were better than chopping wood.[218] By 1940, 36.8 percent of white tenants in Texas and 7.5 percent of black tenants cooked on kerosene stoves. Throughout the state, only the most privileged few had gas or electric stoves.[219]

Stoves provided both warmth and means of food preparation, but sometimes they caused destruction as well. Repeatedly, Blacklands residents told of house fires, usually started from the kitchen stove. Lois Lacy Lewis, from western Hunt County, recalled their house fire of November 1914: "That big house that I was telling you about caught fire one dry, fall morning and caught from the roof because we had a woodstove and they thought that a spark from the morning fire, the stove pipe, caught the roof."[220] Lee Rice's tenant house caught fire twice within one week from the wood-burning heater. On the first occasion, the family fought the fire by the women drawing water from the cistern and handing buckets of water to the men on the roof; the second time, the parents had gone to town and the children succeeded in dousing the flames.[221]

The Calvert family lost almost all of its possessions in a disastrous 1923 fire caused by an oil stove. Myrtle Calvert Dodd remembered:

My mother—it was Saturday afternoon, and she had laid down to take a nap. My younger sister, Nadine, was roaming around through the house and she woke her up and said, "The house is afire, Mama! In the kitchen! The stove's afire!" And Mama said it was going up the wall, back of the stove. Now, they think—there was a burner—you know, you raised your burners up—wasn't turned off good someway. Don't know who did it or anything about it. Probably to one side because—my mother said she had found them sometimes where they wasn't entirely out, wasn't turned low. We kind of think Nadine was probably the one that heated some water to wash her hair. She was eight or nine years old, ten, and didn't put it out good. Maybe water boiled over on it or something. But she was the one that saw it.

Of course, Mama and them went to getting it out at the front, but there wasn't anybody there. The boys were baling hay. One of the neighbors stopped and helped them. They got out a few things, and that's just all. They got out Papa's trunk that they had when they married, you know. Got that out. There was a few of the better things in that. But the boys were back in the middle room, and all their clothes were there. And there was a closet there. Not one thing was gotten out of it. There's a few quilts Mama got out.

Despite the danger of oil stoves, Hester Calvert regretted going back to a woodstove: "Mama was sick about having to go back to the stove. She'd gotten used to cooking on that oil stove. My father said, 'We're not going to have another one of those to burn the house down.'"[222] While the wife was willing to risk fire again to gain the convenience of an oil stove, the husband was not, and his will, as almost always in the family, prevailed.

Women, especially mothers, did almost all of the cooking in Blacklands families. Many enlisted the help of their daughters and sometimes young sons. Little girls playing house imitated their mothers before they began cooking in earnest. Bernice Weir reminisced: "After my girls got big enough to play, they just played up a storm all the time, and there was lots of poke salad and it'd have red berries. They knew not to eat those or anything, but you know, they played with those and made red water and everything else. They sure did play house a lot. . . . I don't think they ever had a real set of little-girl dishes or anything—just whatever they could get to hold mud pies, that's what they played with."[223] Some daughters became their mothers' assistants because of mitigating circumstances. Deenie Blackwell Carver, for example, could not do farmwork because of a hip injury she sustained when she jumped off a barn roof. She "learned to cook at Mama's apron strings," becoming her mother's "first assistant in the kitchen," skilled at cooking and child care.[224] White women eschewed African American help in cooking. Myrtle Calvert Dodd's mother had definite ideas about the ways in which blacks could be employed on the McLennan County farms on which the Calverts were tenants: "Ooh, goodness, Mama wouldn't have had a meal that a black around us cooked; no way in the world. . . . She just wouldn't think they'd be clean or know how. That was her idea of it. She didn't mind them washing and ironing and scrubbing and things like that, but as far as cooking, now, that was just out of the question."[225]

Women relied on basic, typically southern methods of cooking: frying, boiling, or roasting meat; frying eggs; and frying, boiling, or baking Irish and sweet potatoes. Green vegetables were usually boiled for a minimum of thirty minutes (frequently much longer), seasoned with pieces of fat pork.[226]

Bread, especially cornbread and biscuits, was the mainstay of rural diets. Cornbread was such a ubiquitous part of the Blacklands diet that it passes almost without comment in people's recollections. Cornbread could be made cheaply from cornmeal, baking powder, salt, and water, or it could be enriched with a combination of buttermilk, baking soda, eggs, white flour, or sugar. Widely adaptable, cornbread was the most economical of foods. Young people complained about the monotony of cornbread day in and day out. It was scorned as poor people's food, never to appear in the school lunch of a status-minded young person.[227] Most black and Anglo families ate cornbread at least once and often twice a day. Cornbread spoiled quickly, and women often cooked fresh batches with each meal.[228]

Among Mexican families, tortillas, round unleavened bread made from corn or wheat flour, served as the staple.[229] Tortilla making was a skill passed carefully from mother to daughter. Cayetana Martinez Navarro, who earned her living for almost seventy years by making and selling tortillas in the United

States, learned as a tiny child in Mexico City to make tortillas from her mother. She recalled that her mother hit her on the backs of her hands, forcing her to cup her palms in the way for best shaping tortillas: "And then the second tortilla I made was round."[230] Tortillas could be made from store-bought flour or the more traditional ground corn. Preparing corn for tortillas was a slow process, which included boiling corn kernels with lime water and grinding the cooked corn in a stone bowl known as a *metate* with a stone pestle called a *mano*. The cooking and grinding resulted in a dough, *masa*, which the tortilla maker then shaped into round, flat balls indented on the bottom. Most Mexican women used a *comal*, a smooth, flat or saucer-shaped iron sheet, to cook the tortillas. The cook patted and smoothed one dough ball into a flattened round, then greased the *comal* and put the tortilla on it. As the tortilla on the *comal* cooked, she flattened the next tortilla. She covered the cooked tortillas with a cloth to keep them warm. The procedure was repeated dozens of times, until the cook had enough tortillas for a meal. Many Mexican women prepared fresh tortillas three times a day or more; others prepared enough in the morning for the entire day.[231]

Biscuits and cornbread for the majority, and tortillas for the Mexican minority, made up the bulk of many Blacklands meals. In the early part of the century, so-called light bread made with yeast was a rare treat for most families; the difficulty of keeping yeast and the time consumed in making yeast bread put it beyond the capability of all but a few.[232] As transportation and refrigeration improved, yeast bread became more readily available in the early part of the twentieth century. At first, families might buy loaves of yeast bread on their weekly trips into town, as Robert Calvert did, according to his daughter: "My father would go on a Saturday to Waco and he'd always bring back two or three loaves of bread. I could just make out my meal on light bread and butter."[233] By World War I, Hester Calvert began making yeast bread at home: "But I was a great big teen-ager before she started the light bread and they began to get the yeast, you know. And she'd make it a day or two, as long as it would last."[234]

Eventually, some Blacklands women baked yeast bread on a regular basis, a real accomplishment in a woodstove. "I learned that you had to get it sort of hot before you put your bread in," Myrtle Dodd remembered. "You wanted your fire to burn a while before you did that—get it hot. You didn't want to put it in an oven that hadn't heated up much because it would cook before it rose, my mother said. And you had to hurry to get it all cooked because you know your fire died down."[235]

Food Production and Preparation

Yeast bread eventually became such an important food that women who worked in the fields sometimes managed to find time to make it. In Tours, McLennan County, Agnes Straten Kasberg, who led her children in chopping and picking their family's crop, baked bread almost daily. She started the dough early in the morning before going to the field; then her daughter, Rosie, going home at eleven to prepare dinner, kneaded and baked the dough before going back into the fields.[236]

Meals were usually family affairs, a ritual coming together of the group. Many families had regular seating orders in their dining areas, and the father traditionally sat at the head of the table.[237] This arrangement was not always the most efficient, and Bernice Porter Bostick Weir remembered the inconvenience of the dining-room arrangement in her parents' home:

> The dining room area was—oh, I guess it was fourteen foot long and everything, 'cause we had a table with benches on each side, you know, and we children sat on the benches. Papa sat at the head of the table. My sister and I have laughed so many times—Mama never did manage her footsteps or her work to make it easy. Papa sat at the head of the table— the kitchen's back here behind him—and she'd go plumb down here to the end; she'd fix our coffee and put cream and sugar in it for each one, you know, and everything you ever saw. We have laughed so many times and wondered why didn't Mama sit at that end and let Papa go down there?[238]

Mrs. Porter traveled many extra steps because of the rigidity of dining arrangements.

Meals often began with prayers, as Eddie Stimpson commented: "We never sit down at the table one by one. We sit down together and eat together and not before prayer and thank God for the food."[239] Babies ate along with their families, eating soft adult food. Etta Carroll reminisced: "We never did buy baby food. We would make cream gravy and different things and creamed potatoes, and if we had green beans we'd mash everything up where it would be soft for them to eat. We didn't know what buying baby food was at that time."[240] Louise Blackwell Dillow recalled that by the end of a meal, the baby of the family would be in the lap of an older sibling, who buttered her bread, cut up her vegetables, and "ma[de] over her generally."[241] With the help of older children, mothers of large families could manage to have a meal with some semblance of peace and order.

Because of the time and work involved, most meals were utilitarian: the goal, feeding a family three times a day. Some women enjoyed cooking, however, and they availed themselves of special occasions to show their talents. The Rice family of Hunt County, for example, had elaborate Sunday meals despite their tenant-farmer status, sometimes cooking for as many as thirty people. Rice's mother stayed home from church, and when her family returned, she had the round dining table set with a white tablecloth, reserved for Sundays only, and covered with food: a six-layer cake or two (chocolate and coconut); a peach or berry cobbler; a green grape pie; a large baked ham and a large pan of dressing or four fryers; stewed Irish potatoes; half a gallon of canned green beans; a dozen large baked sweet potatoes; a pan of cornbread; a pan of biscuits; a pound of butter; and a quart of wild plum jelly. Her son commented, "Mama never did complain."[242] Perhaps she enjoyed the ritual, tiring and expensive though it was.

Women also cooked in competition with one another, particularly for shared food experiences where one woman's cooking would be put next to another's. Novelist William Humphrey described the rivalry around cemetery-working day:

Knowing that one of these Saturdays would be graveyard working day, the women had cooked each Friday for weeks in possible readiness, and among those in our family there was keen emulation. There were whole baked hams and roast joints of beef, fried chicken, cold turkey, fried squirrels. There were great crocks of potato salad and macaroni salad and chowchow; brandied fruits, and pies of every sort: chocolate, pecan, lemon meringue, coconut custard, banana, sweet potato, peach, berry cobblers—each the best of its kind, the product of that one of your aunts known for that dish, and you had to have a little of each for fear of offending any one of them. You were allowed to pass up only the things your own mother had brought.[243]

Such joint efforts were undoubtedly welcomed by some and dreaded by others. Gladys Everett may have reflected the feelings of many women regarding these shared suppers. She remarked about the monthly church workers meeting supper: "The ladies were glad when their turn to fix and serve the meal was over. Each one cooked their assigned food at home and brought it to the church. This was work and worry as to whether there would be enough food."[244] Women who worried about feeding their own families may not have enjoyed feeding others.

Many Blacklands families ate the hearty breakfasts commonly associated with the South, suitable for energizing field workers. Depending on the availability of other foods, families might have bacon, sausage, ham, fried chicken, milk gravy, grits or oatmeal, eggs occasionally, syrup, hoecakes, and coffee. More affluent families also might have Irish or sweet potatoes, and jellies and preserves to go with their biscuits.[245]

Regardless of their social standing, almost all Anglo and black families ate biscuits at breakfast. During much of the year women rose before the other members of their families to have biscuits ready for those who would be in the fields by first light. Lou Folley made more than three dozen biscuits each morning for her large brood.[246] At age ninety, Bernice Weir still remembered her mother's biscuit-making technique: "She always used buttermilk to make her biscuits and that requires a pinch of soda and two pinches of baking powder and about a tablespoon full of lard. And then about a cup and a half of milk—that would make about fifteen or eighteen biscuits, you see. She rolled them and cut them with a cutter."[247]

As was typical throughout the South, the primary meal of the day came at noon, and Blacklands families uniformly called this meal "dinner." Bernice Weir recalled dinners as a child in her comfortable Bell County family: a different kind of meat from breakfast, blackeyed peas, beans, and potatoes stewed, mashed, or fried.[248] Myrtle Calvert Dodd remembered fried potatoes as a special luxury, "because you got out of potatoes if you fried them all up. Once in a while she'd fry some big pans of potatoes and we'd be so thrilled."[249] And in the Carroll home, as in others, many chickens that were alive at daybreak found their way to the noontime table, slaughtered, feathers picked off, pinfeathers singed off, butchered, and cooked. Etta Carroll recalled her timing for chicken: "It's according to how we were to cook it. If we were going to fry it, I'd start it early, get it done by dinner. But if we's going to have chicken and dumplings, I'd maybe cook the chicken up early and then when I fixed my dumplings and then have them hot for dinner."[250] The *obed* (dinners) among Czech families relied on *polevka* (soup) as their daily fare. Mary Hanak Simcik commented that chicken or beef noodle soup "was kind of a basic of all the dinners everywhere. . . . We had some 365 times a year; and if it was Leap Year, we had it 366 times. Dinner without soup was unthinkable."[251] Czech families considered excellent noodle making to be an accomplishment, and rolled-out egg noodles spread on a table or draped over the backs of chairs to dry were a common sight in Czech homes. Czechs also enjoyed liver dumpling soup and various kinds of *gulas* (stews).[252]

At chopping and picking time, women contributed heavily to the effort by cooking for work crews. This task appears to have been less widespread than that of women who cooked for threshing crews in the Midwest, probably because in the Midwest women did not assist with the physical harvesting, but women in the Blacklands did participate in this way.[253] Bernice Weir remembered preparing scrambled eggs, fried Irish or sweet potatoes, as well as "whatever kind of meat I had or bacon or something like that" for three or four hired workers as well as for members of her family.[254]

During these periods of intense labor, the presence or absence of a woman who was not working in the fields created significant variations in a family's dinners. Maggie Langham Washington's mother played an active role in the fields, and she relied on young Maggie to feed the family. Maggie was expected to have a dinner consisting of greens, potatoes, and cornbread on the table precisely at twelve: "I can just see myself now, standing at the well—it was just there at the back porch—drawing enough water to wash these greens, you see, and get them cooked by twelve o'clock, with no gritty taste. And by all means, don't forget to put those potatoes in the oven so they can bake in time to be done for twelve o'clock. Get them out of the way of the cornbread you're to cook. All farmers, everybody that worked on the farm, around five minutes to twelve laid their farming aside and came home to eat, you see. And then, five minutes to one, they started on their way back to the fields."[255] If the family were working close to the house and the mother or another cook were not working in the fields, the noon meal for the workers could be elaborate. Bessie McRae recalled: "Oh, it would be fried chicken, boiled ham, and beans, squash, and a big peach cobbler right in the middle of the table. . . . Oh, we had good food. I can remember as a kid coming in from the field, Momma would have dinner on the table. Oh, it was a beautiful picture. She always cooked what she knew we were crazy about."[256] The Collier family always welcomed the sight of the white pillow that their mother threw on top of the roof to signal her family to stop for their midday meal.[257]

The Calvert family ate dried beans, purchased for the purpose, for dinner during cotton picking season. "My daddy'd say they'd stay with you," Myrtle Dodd commented.[258] J. B. Coltharp's mother brought snacks to the field at midmorning: "sausage, brown beans, biscuits, bacon, cookies, light bread rolls."[259] Other field workers wanted little to eat in the hot summer sun. William Owens recalled feeling too feverish from the sun to eat much at noon, preferring to drink only iced tea.[260] Letha Jumper of Hunt County concurred: "If we could get a good glass of ice tea for dinner and supper, very little food mattered."[261]

Others, who might have liked elaborate meals, had neither the time nor the food for heavy noontime dinners. Mary Hanak Simcik recalled using cooked pork stored in jars with lard for quickly prepared dinners: "In the summertime a lot of times we rushed in from the field maybe fifteen till twelve; at twelve o'clock we had dinner on the table. In other words, dig out that thing, put it in the skillet, because it was thin then, you know. Put it in the skillet and warm it up and maybe open a jar of pickles or something like that, and we had dinner. When we were busy in the field, we didn't have time to do much cooking."[262] Adelaida Torres Almanza would leave her family at their tasks and return to the house to cook fresh tortillas for their noontime meal: "I had my *metate*, and I would leave everything ready in the morning before I would go to work in the fields. And I would work in the fields, and then when it was 11:30 I would come back and then I would make tortillas." She reflected on the effort involved: "But I was very young and I could do all those things."[263]

Laborers hired to do chopping and picking ate much simpler meals through necessity, because most could not return home for hot dinners. William Owens recalled African American pickers "sitting on their sacks, eating in the broiling sun."[264] Migrant workers who camped out near their workplaces sometimes fared better at noon than those who came out to work from town. They sometimes brought one woman along to serve as their cook, often an older women whose best days of picking were behind her. These women prepared simple, starchy meals that gave workers energy: cornbread, biscuits, navy or butter beans seasoned with bacon grease, cabbage, bacon, or potatoes.[265] Mexican workers frequently ate leftover tortillas for their midday meals. Luz Sanchez Hurtado recalled their typical midday meal of beans mixed with chile peppers and wrapped in a flour tortilla.[266]

By the late 1930s, some workers who came to the farms from town brought store-bought meals with them: pork and beans, crackers, cheese, Vienna sausages, light bread, and bologna.[267] The contrast between meals of the farm families and the hired workers was obvious to all. Bernice Weir's mother-in-law cooked dinners for her son's family as they worked out in the fields, but not for the seven cotton pickers living in a one-room house nearby. Weir recalled, "Every time we'd come up the hill, they'd say, 'Ooh, your something to eat smells so good!' They could smell our dinner; Grandma'd cook fried chicken and maybe boil beans and potatoes and things like that. And they smelled so good."[268]

The evening meal, generally known as supper, was usually simpler than the midday dinner. Women rarely fixed entirely new hot meals at night. Instead, supper might consist of leftovers from dinner, sometimes with fresh biscuits, or cornbread crumbled in milk.[269] Mary Shumate of Rains County remembered a favorite evening meal consisting of hominy, baked sweet potatoes, and milk.[270] Myrtle Calvert Dodd's mother frequently made bean soup or potato soup for her family as well: "It wasn't a big fancy dinner. Never. Now, if we had—in the spring when we had lettuce out of the garden and radishes and onions, my mother would make a salad to go with those beans or potatoes. And we'd have sweet potatoes if you could get them in the winter. But where we lived, they didn't grow much. And if we heard they were going to be at the store, my father would get some."[271]

Farm laborers, who had not eaten much at midday, might have heavier suppers. Among Mexican migrants, supper was the only hot meal of the day. On the Locke place in McLennan County, the workers camped under trees and cooked over open fires. They made tortillas, using a large rock, smooth on one side, instead of a metal *comal*. They put the rock on a bed of hot coals with hot coals also placed on top. When the rock was hot enough, they raked the coals off the top, dusted the rock, and then greased it with a rag or bacon rind and cooked the tortillas.[272]

In addition to cooking entire meals repeatedly, women made accompaniments for their plain fare. When there was meat for a meal, gravy made of fresh meat drippings, flour, and milk, poured over biscuits, could make the meal seem more ample.[273] Some women served unadorned, clear bacon grease as a condiment or over biscuits, while others made bacon-grease gravy with just a dash of sweet milk.[274] Pot likker, the liquid left at the bottom of the pot after cooking greens, also dressed up plain cornbread.[275] The Calvert family acquired hot peppers from relatives and made pepper sauce by pouring vinegar over the peppers and letting the combination stand for a while.[276] Bernice Weir's family made the southern condiment known as "chow-chow—tomatoes and onions and all of that ground up together and you put vinegar and peppers and things in it and cook it and then jar it up, you see; anything with vinegar in it usually keeps good that way."[277]

The beverages that went with such meals were simple, consisting of coffee, milk, and sometimes iced tea. Coffee was fairly common, and young girls learned early in life to parch green coffee beans in a slow oven or a large skillet on top of the stove.[278] Families bought coffee from local stores or from peddlers, and both men and women drank it.[279] Before refrigeration, iced tea was reserved for special occasions, and perhaps only then at harvest time, when families had enough cash to purchase tea.[280] "I guess I was about eight or ten years old [1913 or 1915] when I had the first tea, iced tea," Myrtle Calvert Dodd remembered. "If you could get ice, you'd have iced tea. But you didn't get ice maybe on just the weekend."[281] Aubrey Garrett, born in 1907 in the Clifton community in Hopkins County, recalled, "We did not have iced tea at home. In fact, I was nearly grown in size before I ever tasted tea, and it was worse than medicine."[282] Lemonade was another occasional rare treat, depending on the availability of lemons at the local store. Where fresh, cool well water was available, lemonade remained the drink of choice for many.[283] For special occasions, Mexican families made a foamy drink from commercially produced Mexican chocolate; as Adelaida Torres Almanza commented, "With some big pieces of bread and a pitcher of chocolate, now we are talking."[284] African American families gathered a "tea weed" in the pastures and fields to make "wild tea," which served both as a beverage and a medicine. Vanilla flavoring mixed with water also served as a beverage.[285]

Moravians produced stronger types of drinks. These Czech immigrants were noted for their wine making, using wild grapes, dewberries, and blackberries. Katherine Schneider Berger, for example, brewed wine in a crock. Beer making was also a common skill; Berger fermented beer, bottled it, and capped it.[286] Anglo families tended toward abstinence from alcohol, at least in public, and Anglo women were seldom involved in brewing strong drink.

Women also prepared sweets for their families. They began with their teething babies, as Etta Carroll said: "Then if they wanted something to eat, that's the reason we made teacakes. They were kind of hard and they could eat on that teacake along. And it didn't get all over everything."[287] Louise Blackwell Dillow observed that desserts were likely to be fruit cobbler or pudding during the week and a cake or pie on Sunday. Cobblers and puddings stretched, she remarked, to fit an indeterminate number of diners.[288] Hester Calvert was especially careful to keep treats for her children in the house at times of heavy field work: "When we were working, she'd have them ready. Usually if we were picking cotton or hoeing cotton she had something sweet every time for lunch because we thought that gave us energy. And it did, I guess."[289] Bernice Weir kept sweets on hand for her children's school lunches, baking on Fridays.[290] Czech families baked recipes from Moravia, especially pastries: *kolaches*, circular tarts with sweet toppings of fruit or poppy seed; *buchta*, dough baked in a square pan with fruit filling; apple strudel; and Czech cookies.[291] Mexican women made *pan dulce*, or sweet bread, leavened with yeast, a process that often took all day. Their families loved the treats; Adelaida Almanza commented, "I would make leavened bread, and it would turn out so good, but my kids wouldn't leave a bit of it!"[292]

Most of the food prepared on Blacklands cotton farms remained very plain. Starchy, simple foods provided the energy for long days spent both in the fields and in the house. By working diligently to keep food on the table, farm women fulfilled the most basic needs of their families. Those who could afford to do so concentrated substantial amounts of their energies on feeding their families as well as on keeping their houses. But for many Blacklands women, cooking and keeping house were but part of their overall duties. These women performed field labor along with their domestic duties. How they balanced the two demanding endeavors is the subject of the next chapter.

chapter *four*

Making a Hand

Women's Labor in the Fields

For more than a century, cotton ruled the South, its needs shaping daily life in all of the areas where it grew. From the early nineteenth century until the 1940s, methods of cultivating cotton changed very little, always demanding much from those working in its service. Before mechanization, cotton growing was a labor-intensive task. Particularly at chopping time, in late spring and early summer, and at picking time, from late summer to late fall or early winter, cotton farms required large labor forces. Well-to-do landowners and tenants who could afford to do so hired crews to assist their own families. Those unable to employ help often used the labor of every available kinsperson, young and old, male and female. Whether they were hired by strangers or neighbors, or worked only for their own families, women played a critical part in the production of cotton on the Texas Blackland Prairie.

Within the tenant system, women had extremely limited autonomy. The husband almost always negotiated the work contract. The amount of equipment that a family owned consigned them to sharecropper or tenant-farmer status. With the work contract came the location of the farm and the expectation that the entire family would be committed to making the crop. The men usually led the workforces into the fields, deciding when they would begin work and who would perform which tasks, and determining when enough work had been done to conclude the day.[1] Women's roles remained largely contingent upon the actions of men, but their part in the agricultural labor cannot be dismissed.

The subject of women doing field work generated considerable emotional response in the Blackland Prairie before World War II. The statistics clearly illustrate the reality: the majority of adult women of all ethnic groups performed at least some type of field labor every year, providing a significant portion of the labor force. Reformers, both male and female, spoke loudly against prevailing conditions, however. Farm women themselves voiced considerable ambivalence about field work, both as an idea and as a practice. On an abstract level, many people in the Blacklands believed in the separation of gendered spheres, reinforced at times with the ideal of the southern lady, and including all of the ideology of the cult of true womanhood. Mrs. Vina Cochran of Farmersville, Collin County, put the argument into simplest terms in a letter to the *Semi-Weekly Farm News* in 1910: "I believe God made man to till the soil and woman to care for the house."[2] On a pragmatic level, reformers and many farm women alike believed that if a woman handled her household responsibilities in a suitable manner, she had no time for field work. A woman who attempted to combine the two, they said, risked injury to her own health and decreased the quality of her family's life. The rising expectations for cleanliness in a household argued against women's participation in the cash crop.

From an ideological standpoint, the arguments against women's outdoor work mirrored many of those used elsewhere in the late nineteenth and early twentieth centuries to delineate separate labor spaces for men and women. In rural Texas during the early twentieth century, the expectations for the proper behavior by women—the southern lady, as it were—were still present, a relic of the antebellum South. The southern lady was an upper- and middle-class construct, and antebellum yeoman women had not always adhered closely to its prescriptions. But, as Elizabeth Fox-Genovese points out, in areas dominated by slave culture, yeomen could not forge "alternate gender conventions," and the hegemonic ideals of the slave-owning class controlled the yeomanry.[3] The Blackland Prairie, originally settled by yeomen from the Upper South, became the home of émigrés from the Lower South after the Civil War. The gender and class conventions of the Lower South persisted throughout the rural Blacklands at least until World War II, for, as Anne Firor Scott has observed, many of the changes in southern ladyhood that affected the South in the early twentieth century were confined to the towns and cities.[4] Buttressed by this ideology, many women from upper-class, landowning families performed less work in the fields and frowned upon those who did. Fifty years after the New Deal, when a landowner's daughter from Navarro County was asked about picking cotton, she drew herself up to her full height, glared, and vehemently declared, "I *never* picked cotton!"[5] She still felt strongly the need to differentiate herself from poorer women who had worked in the fields.

Clearly, aspirations to ladyhood had strong class overtones, with definite ties to the economic power of the husband. Lula James of Forreston, Ellis County, recognized her privileged status when she commented, "I do not have to work in the field now. My husband does not want me to."[6] James's husband had risen to an economic status where he could choose not to have his wife do field work. No one ever made a checklist of exactly what made one a lady or put one beyond the pale, however. One school of thought argued that ladyhood was based on what one *was*, not what one *did*. A true lady, this school declared, would rise to any occasion and do what was necessary to help her family but would still maintain certain qualities that marked her as a woman of refinement and breeding. The aptly named "Happy Belle" from McLennan County wrote to *Farm and Ranch* in 1910: "My father died when I was small and I had to work for a living. I will tell you what I have done in life, and I am still a lady, thank God. I have plowed and hoed and built fences and have done almost everything on a farm a man has done. . . . I worked everywhere, and I am still a lady. If a girl is going to be anything, she will be it anywhere you put her."[7] For "Happy Belle," meeting the needs of her family was more important than maintaining someone else's cultural ideal.

Many Blacklands residents, however, lacked "Happy Belle's" easy self-confidence and were especially uncomfortable with the labor of Anglo women in cotton. In 1911, when a meeting of an incipient renters' union in Waco presented its grievances to the public, the complaints included "the conditions . . . forcing the landless farmer to live in miserable shacks and keeping women and children in the fields to such an extent as to be exceedingly detrimental to the mental and physical well being of our people and a menace to the homes and social institutions of our state."[8] While the primary complaints were economic, the breaching of gender taboos greatly concerned agricultural protesters. To these critics and to many others, extensive work of women in agriculture was extremely undesirable. Women—at least white women—were supposed to remain in the house as much as possible.[9]

Possibly because of such public outcry, Anglo women sometimes hid the fact that they did field work. In the late 1930s, for example, anthropologist

Oscar Lewis observed in his study of Bell County: "Among the old-line Americans it is considered degrading for a woman to do this type of work. . . . It is not uncommon for old-line American women to work in the fields, but in conversation they will not readily admit to picking cotton, and it is a point of pride with a husband to be able to say that his wife does no heavy work on the farm. This discrepancy between theory and practice is, in part, a result of the carrying over of old southern mores based on plentiful Negro labor supply to a new environment characterized by labor shortage."[10]

Such theoretical niceties were confined only to Anglo women, as women of German, Czech, African American, and Mexican heritage freely admitted doing field work.[11] An incident in the community of Tours, McLennan County, demonstrates the perceived importance of women's work among the Czechs. Alois Rauschhuber interviewed with Ignatz Damhues, a wealthy landowner, about renting one of Damhues's farms. When Damhues found out that Rauschhuber was married to a "city girl," the daughter of a Tours merchant and not a farmer, he quickly ended the interview, saying, "She will be no good on the farm."[12]

Anglo women who worked in the fields were aware of the social taboos that they were breaking, but at least some willingly crossed the line. Frances Freeman of Falls County disputed the shame of women's field work, writing, "Move over sisters, please, and give me a seat by the sisters who help their Johns in the field. I do, and do not think it is a disgrace."[13] Judging by Freeman's choice of words, apparently many of her peers did believe that women's field work was a disgrace and therefore something of which to be ashamed. Women such as Freeman, however, seem to have seen their abilities to combine house- and field work as strengths, and they either ignored their critics or constructed their own version of a gender ideal.

Some male farmers refused to acknowledge publicly the necessity of female labor in the fields. In a study of Hill County, 502 fathers were asked, "Could you farm without the aid of the mother in the field?" Of that number, only 44.6 percent said no. The higher his economic status, the more likely a man was to declare himself free of his wife's labor. Of white men, 37 percent of owners, 44 percent of renters, and 46 percent of sharecroppers said they needed the field labor of their wives. More black men admitted need: only sharecroppers answered the question, and 56 percent of them said their wives' work was indispensable. These numbers, particularly for black sharecroppers, fall far below the actual numbers of women in the field. Perhaps pride kept men from divulging how badly they needed their wives' assistance. Or perhaps the statistics reveal the socioeconomic necessities for women's work: The poorer the farmer, the more he relied upon the work of his wife in the field.[14]

Social conventions notwithstanding, women worked in the cotton fields of the Blackland Prairie, as several studies conducted between 1920 and 1940 illustrate. A 1920 U.S. Children's Bureau investigation found that 61.4 percent of all white women in its Hill County sample did field work, and 99 percent of all black women in that study worked with the cotton. Sociologist Ruth Allen discovered that in the lower Blacklands, 46.2 percent of the white women, 86.5 percent of the African American women, and 56.5 percent of the Mexican women with whom she spoke worked in the fields.[15] No statistics exist to distinguish the number of German and Czech women who performed field work from their Anglo-American counterparts, but one observer commented that such labor was "much more customary" for "wives of Negroes and foreign-born than for native white women."[16] The European immigrants worked steadily with the crop even though their families owned land in much greater proportion than did their Anglo neighbors. A much higher percentage of Blackland Prairie women did field work than did their counterparts in the western and northern United States, of whom only 24 percent "helped" in the field.[17]

A strong correlation existed between tenure status and the likelihood of a woman's performing field work. In Allen's study, 36.0 percent of women from white landowning families did field work. Among white tenants, 57.2 percent went to the field, and 44.7 percent of women in the families of white farm laborers did so as well.[18] A higher proportion of white landowners' wives (58.5 percent) worked outside in Hill County than in the lower Blacklands, but in their sample more tenants' wives also did—63.4 percent.[19]

Among African Americans, the correlation of land tenure to farm labor by women remained strong and further demonstrated the importance of race in determining a woman's lot as worker. Two-thirds of women in black landowning families worked in cotton: 65.5 percent in Allen's study and 66.6 percent in the Hill County study. For African American women in tenant-farming families, field labor was the rule rather than the exception; the two studies showed 89.8 and 100 percent of these women working outside the home. For black women in the families of farm laborers, Allen documented 90 percent of them in the cotton patch, while the Hill County sample showed a complete 100 percent participation.[20]

Information about Mexican women's field labor is limited to the southern Blacklands, for the investigators in Hill County interviewed no Mexican women. In the lower Blacklands, Mexican women represented only the tenant, sharecropper, and laborer classes, because Allen discovered no Mexican landowners in the area. The Mexican women's participation was roughly equivalent to that of Anglo women and much lower than that of blacks. Of the Mexican women whom Allen located on tenant farms, 56 percent worked in the fields, and 59 percent of the women in farm laborers' families did field work.[21] First in Bastrop County and then in McLennan County, Luz Sanchez Hurtado recalled no Mexican adult females doing field work: "It was just the men."[22] Among Mexicans, gender constraints evidently weighed more heavily than economic necessity.

The length of time that women worked in the fields varied widely from family to family. The wider the variety of tasks that they performed, the longer they stayed in the cotton patch each year. Women who worked less than three months per year usually participated only in cotton picking. Those working three to six months a year generally spent time chopping as well as picking. And those who worked more than six months each year most likely were involved with every step of the cotton crop, from the initial plowing of the land in February or March to the final stalk cutting in December or January.

Ethnicity played a major role in determining the number of weeks or months that a woman might labor in the cotton field. As Table 4 shows, white women worked in the fields far less than did African American women, with Mexican women falling in the middle.

Clearly, black women carried heavier loads of field work than did either Anglo or Mexican women, continuing the legacy of slavery well into the twentieth century. But even Anglo and Mexican women in the Blackland Prairie labored for longer periods than did their counterparts elsewhere in the United States, who worked an average of 6.7 weeks per year.[23]

Individual cases further complicate the search for a definitive set of variables for detecting patterns of women's field work. Because of their numerous obligations and duties, mothers of growing families sometimes worked only sporadically in the cotton fields, struggling to keep housework and child care in balance with the outdoor demands of the cotton crop. Only a third of the women in Hill County who performed field work had any assistance with housework, usually in the person of an older relative or young daughter. (The ability to keep a relative out of the fields for housework varied with social class: 50 percent of white landowners, 32.2 percent of the white renters, 30.4 percent

Women's Labor in the Fields

TABLE 4. Months of Field Work Women Performed Per Year, by Ethnic Group

	Less than 3	3–6	More than 6
Whites			
Lower Blackland[a]	46.1%	39.9%	14.0%
Hill County[b]	39.8	42.4	12.0
Blacks			
Lower Blackland	12.9	38.9	48.2
Hill County	20.9	34.8	39.5
Mexicans			
Lower Blackland	22.3	58.0	29.5

Sources: Allen, *Labor of Women*, 134, 191, 231; Matthews and Dart, *Welfare of Children*, 45.
[a]Lower Blackland = Bastrop, Travis, Caldwell, Williamson, and Burnet Counties. Figures are from a 1928–30 study.
[b]Figures are from a 1920 study.

of the white croppers, and only 18.9 percent of black croppers had help.[24]) One observer commented that during harvest time, "Often married women, with housework to do, hurry out after breakfast, pick a few sackfuls, hurry back to cook dinner, and then in the afternoon come back to pick more."[25]

In Ellis County, sharecropper's wife Etta Carroll considered herself a casual laborer, recalling: "I helped some. I never did just go to the field and make a hand all the time, but I'd go to the field and help out as I needed to be. [Other women] done some, just like I did." Her husband, Dovie Carroll, added: "They done some, all right. They worked in the fields, too, some. People back in those days just didn't have the money to hire everything done. They had to either do it theirself or do without because money back in those days was something else."[26] Bernice Bostick Weir, a member of a landowning family, remembered picking a little bit and putting the cotton that she gathered into her husband's sack.[27] Every moment of labor helped, however brief, and even women who did not pick consistently made valuable contributions to the harvesting effort.

The majority of women in the Blackland Prairie spent fewer than six months a year in the field, suggesting that most of their field work involved chopping and picking cotton. Women confirmed this by describing their specific tasks. In the 1920 study of Hill County (see Table 5), researchers found that 89 percent of the white women who did field work picked cotton, while 95 percent of their black neighbors did so. More than 69 percent of the white women and 81 percent of the black women hoed and chopped cotton. The congruence between the months of field work and the reports of work performed is less clear

TABLE 5. Percentage of Women Performing Farming Tasks,
by Ethnic Group, in Hill County, 1920

Task	Whites	Blacks
Picking cotton	89	95
Hoeing and chopping	69	81
Plowing, harrowing, and planting	11	7
Cultivating	12	2

Source: Matthews and Dart, *Welfare of Children*, 44.

for other tasks. Of the white women, 11 percent reported plowing, harrowing, and planting, and 12 percent reported cultivating. But only 7 percent of the black women reported plowing, and only 2 percent reported cultivating—far below the percentage of black women who worked more than six months per year.[28] These statistics may reflect the number of black women working for wages, in which they chopped and picked for farms besides their own. They continued working as long as their services were needed, whereas women working on their own farms could stop when their own families' jobs were complete. Also, women seldom plowed and cultivated for wages, for these tasks went quickly enough that a family usually could take care of its own field labor.

Many mothers, even those married to landowners, worked nearly full-time in the fields during chopping and picking times. At times women took the roles of lead workers in the place of their husbands, brothers, or sons. Sometimes female lead workers freed the men to perform wage work elsewhere. In the Czech community of Tours, for example, Clara Wolf Schroeder raised the crops while her husband, William, worked with cattle and on road crews. Marie Vrba Hlavenka and her children brought in the family's cotton every year while her husband worked at the gin.[29] In other instances women replaced their invalid or dead husbands. Lou Thomas Folley, with an incapacitated husband, worked alongside her ten children on their Limestone County farm. In Tours, Annie Uptmor Willenborg gained special recognition first as overseer on her parents' farm and then as the lead worker on the farm that she and her husband owned after their marriage in 1912. As lead worker, Willenborg set the pace for the others, moving one frazzled laborer to declare that he had never before worked so hard in his life. Her husband, Joe Willenborg, died in 1928, and Annie, with her eight children, continued to farm their land successfully.[30] Many other widows and their children supported themselves, albeit meagerly, with the proceeds from family labor.[31]

The subject of women's double duty in the house and fields greatly concerned rural reformers, who realized that farmwives had limits on their time, energy, and health. The Children's Bureau study of Hill County discussed with mothers how they balanced their house and outdoor obligations. One Anglo woman said she went to the fields with the rest of her family, rushing through housework while "the feeding was being done." Another white woman, who had no clock, said she got up about four o'clock and went to the field as soon as her morning chores were done; except for an hour and a half at noon, she worked until sundown. After that, she still had to prepare supper and finish her daily housework. Researchers found that black women worked longer hours in the fields but spent less time on housework.[32] Another study of Hill County, conducted in 1925 at the behest of the National Child Labor Committee, found that white women worked an average of eight hours per day in the fields, while black women averaged nine hours.[33]

Ruth Allen found that in the lower Blacklands, three-quarters of the white women worked between seven and nine hours a day in the cotton patch.[34] The breathless heat of the Texas summers often dictated the work day. In the White Rock community of Hunt County, Ruth St. Clair recalled going to the field at four in the morning to avoid some of the heat, then working until dinner with a one- to two-hour break when the sun was at its zenith, and working again until dark.[35] Add to these days in the fields the chores of cooking and doing laundry for a family, and the days stretched long indeed for Blackland Prairie women. Even when they were not doing field work, women worked long days, often rising before the rest of the family to cook breakfast and sometimes working in the house after others had retired.[36]

Women with small children were, ironically, more likely to do field work than those with older offspring. As the children grew older, they could take their mothers' places as field laborers, the family labor system responding to the family life cycle.[37] Hester Calvert, for example, seldom worked in the fields but was able to stay indoors and prepare meals for her sharecropper husband and eight children, who worked outside as soon as they were big enough. Alma McKethan McBride, from a prosperous landowning family in McLennan County, observed that her father and three brothers performed most of the field work with an "occasional assist from my second sister and me." During harvest, the McKethans hired extra labor when they could, but when hands were scarce, everyone in the family except the mother went to the fields.[38] Daughters, then, served as their mothers' replacements.

Combining care for small children with field work challenged rural women. As many as two-thirds of mothers, including those who came from town to chop and pick, took their little ones to the fields with them, "either giving them what care they could themselves or delegating the responsibility to older children."[39] Mothers who were chopping sometimes tied their children to nearby cotton stalks to keep them from wandering away.[40] During cotton picking season, two methods of on-site child care prevailed. One, useful only in caring for small infants, was to lay the baby on the end of its mother's cotton sack and pull it along as she went down the rows. Mothers devised numerous ways to care for babies on cotton sacks. Rosie Filer Berger used two cotton sacks for this purpose; when the baby fell asleep, she slipped out from under the band of that sack and picked up another so that the baby could nap in peace.[41] Millie Birks Stimpson "stomped a holler" in the cotton in her sack to nestle the baby. She sometimes pulled her newborn daughter and her two-year-old at the same time: "Ruth were big enough to walk but would get tired." Pulling two small children added twenty pounds or more to the weight of the cotton sack.[42] The other method was to leave children in the shade of the cotton wagons, with small ones on pallets and toddlers perhaps tethered to wagon wheels. Slightly older children walked alongside their mothers, helping with the picking.[43]

Depending on the family situation, mothers sometimes delegated care of their youngest children. Older children or other relatives might remain at the house and supervise infants and toddlers, with mixed results. When Elsie Hoelscher was assigned to watch her baby brother, Robert, she placed him in a big tub of water to protect him from centipedes and tarantulas.[44] Maggie Langham Washington began caring for her baby sister when she was little more than a baby herself. Their mother, Leta Taylor Langham, was the wife of a sharecropper and African Methodist Episcopal minister, who matched her husband stride for stride, taking off only Saturday mornings to catch up with household chores. Mrs. Langham depended on young Maggie to take care of the younger children while she worked in the fields. Maggie Washington recalled, "She worked side by side with Daddy until he started in the ministry, and then she carried on the work on the farm. I didn't do much farm work when we lived in the country because I had to take care of the smaller children. You see, when I was six years old, I was keeping house like a woman. I had the babies to care for, the food to cook, clothes to wash and iron the hard way." While Mrs. Langham delegated most of the tasks to Maggie, there were some that she could not: "My mother would come home and cool her breast off, breast feed the baby, and eat."[45] Clearly, the female members of the Langham family, as elsewhere, pulled together to keep the household going despite the mother's heavy load of field work.

Cotton demanded close attention for most of the year, with the growing season usually extending from March until November. The first step in putting in a new cotton crop was disposing of the stalks from the previous year, cutting them with a mule-drawn stalk cutter and sometimes raking or burning them.[46] In almost all cases, men or boys performed the stalk cutting, using both machinery and livestock, which were in most cases taboo to women. Dovie Carroll, a longtime Ellis County tenant farmer, commented, "Well, back in those days, they said, 'Well, it's a man's job.' "[47]

Preparing the land for planting—plowing the land into furrows and build-ing up beds to receive the cotton seeds—was the next task. Raised beds allowed for maximum drainage, and the soil warmed more quickly.[48] Plowing was not an uncommon task for women, but it carried a significant social stigma, especially among Anglo-Americans. At least one out of ten Anglo women plowed, and yet this continued to be considered men's work; people referred to "plowing just like a man." Sociologist Ruth Allen found that even Anglo women who chopped and picked for long periods of time referred to cultivat-ing and plowing as "men's work." She observed that women were reluctant to give her information about the amount of plowing and cultivating that they performed, for they were "rather ashamed of having to do" those tasks. "The woman who plows seems to feel, and others feel, that she has lost something real but indefinable," Allen wrote.[49] Popular cultural expressions strengthened these views. In the sentimental 1929 novel *Can't Get a Red Bird*, Johnny, age eleven, has to shoulder the field work when his father falls ill with consump-tion and his older brother has left home: " 'It's your bad luck that you're the only boy left, Johnny,' said Pa. 'The girls can help you chop and pick when the time comes, but your sisters can't plough. And I haven't got any money to hire it done. You'll have to be the man of the family, now, Johnny, and do a man's work.' " Clearly, for the novelist Dorothy Scarborough, as for others, girls plowing was simply not an option.[50]

A portion of the stigma came from the widespread belief that working with mules was unsuitable for women, partly because of mules' widely reputed flatulence. Other lines of reasoning asserted that women were not physically strong enough to handle the plow or that mules were too dangerous for women. Dorothy Woods Moore, whose family sharecropped near the Scatter- branch community in Hunt County, picked and chopped but was not allowed to plow because her father said that girls were not strong enough. She re- marked that she never understood the distinction because picking was such heavy work.[51] Whether they knew the reasoning behind the taboo or not, many families of Anglo women avoided putting their women at the plow whenever possible. Some African American and Mexican families also ob- served social constraints on women plowing. Alice Owens Caufield recalled that neither she nor her sister ever plowed, nor did they know any women who did in the African American and German farms around Robinson, McLennan County: "They were using mules, and the mules pulled the plow, the middle buster. No woman was going to be struggling. That wasn't her job. Men did that. Women didn't have nothing to do with the stock. Her place was in the home."[52]

A female might plow especially if too few males were available to perform the work. In the Folley family, the father was too feeble to plow, and the older brothers left to farm on their own. Under these circumstances, young Inez Folley plowed along with her brothers, despite her poor eyesight: "Well, when I was working in the field, I plowed. And my rows of cotton was thisaway [makes jagged motion] because I couldn't see well. My brother and I took turns—he'd go the first row and I'd go the second row, the third row and the fourth row, you see. I had every other row. So whenever we got ready to plow, he gave me my crooked rows, and I had to follow the crooked row rather than go down straight."[53] For families such as the Folleys, need rather than social conventions dictated the work of the female members. Czech, German, and African Ameri- can women also took the expedient route rather than the socially accept- able one, with some limitations; Mary Elizabeth Jupe reported one widowed mother who could not plow because she was pregnant with twins.[54]

After farm families "busted" and bedded the land, it was time for planting. In the Blacklands, farmers planted their cotton crops around the first of April, two weeks after the average date of the last killing frost.[55] By hand or with mechanical planters, they dropped the fuzzy cotton seeds, about a quarter of an inch long, into the open furrow and covered them with a harrow. Lillian Jane Alford recalled using a walking planter in Bell County around World War I: "It starts in spring, the planting does. And I helped plant cotton with a walking planter." Her brothers, however, used a more technologically ad- vanced mule-drawn riding planter: "The boys, some of them, they planted the cotton mostly with the riding planter. You see, that planter, you put the seed in the container and just drive along, and that drops from there. And then it covers up. It has little plows at the back that covers that all up, you see. Makes a beautiful little row."[56] Alford, like many women, was prohibited from using technology.

If the spring rains were sufficient, the seeds sprouted quickly, sending up small shoots each with two round leaves in three to seven days.[57] About two weeks after the cotton came up, the long rounds of cultivating and hoeing began, activities in which women participated fully. The first cultivating was followed by the first chopping. With special hoes, choppers thinned the young cotton plants and destroyed the weeds that inevitably appeared. The desired outcome was clumps of three or four cotton plants, with three to four feet left between the bunches in the rich Blacklands soil. Chopping was a labor-intensive task; working from sunup until sundown, the strongest worker could cover only one-half to one acre a day under average conditions.[58] The labor for chopping commonly came from one of four possible sources: hands hired in a nearby town and brought to the farm exclusively for chopping, migrant workers passing through the region at chopping time, neighbors who worked their own land and finished early enough to hire out to others, and the farm family itself. Anglo families were most likely to hire the labor, taking a chance, as one observer commented, "between high costs and high farm prices." Czech, German, African American, and Mexican families depended almost exclusively on family labor.[59]

In her 1931 study, Ruth Allen found that almost three-quarters of Anglo women who worked in the fields chopped only for their families, as did a comparable 73 percent of the Mexican women. Many fewer African American women (52.5 percent) chopped only for their families. Another group worked for their own families until their crops were chopped out or laid by; then they went to work for others, often neighbors. This group included 19 percent of the Anglo women who did field work, 6 percent of the Mexican women, and 38 percent of the African American women.[60] In the Tours community, for example, the families of Arnold and Agnes Straten Kasberg and George and Clara Wachsman Schneider each worked through their own land quickly so that they could hire out to neighbors.[61] The labor of young people also proved important in bringing in cash. In Red River County, for instance, Kate Peacock Jones declared that "most children would work away from home any time they could."[62]

African Americans formed the core of the choppers brought from nearby towns, coming in sizable groups that could chop an entire large farm in one or two days.[63] Dovie Carroll recalled driving into "colored town" in Waxahachie, picking up choppers, whom he paid seventy cents to one dollar a day in the 1920s. He arrived at four A.M. to gather the choppers, who would be "ready and waiting with a lunch," and took them back into town at night. He recalled that "women's the same as men" as choppers, bringing their children with them. They worked equally as hard and as quickly, and employers expressed no preference for male hands. Asked about using Mexican choppers, Carroll responded, "They didn't know what that was back in those days."[64] But fifty miles south, in Limestone County, during the same time period, Robert Sharpless hired a crew of Mexican choppers—men, women, and children—with his teenage daughter, Frances, serving as an interpreter and his young sons sharpening hoes at the ends of the rows.[65] The use of Mexican labor became increasingly common, especially in the lower Blackland Prairie, as immigration from Mexico continued throughout the first third of the twentieth century.

Frequently Blackland Prairie farm families worked alongside hired labor in chopping. Etta Carroll boasted of her ability as a chopper: "We hauled nigras out of town to do our chopping. So one day I said, 'I'll do the chopping.'

"Dovie said, 'No, let me chop today and you plow. It'll be easier on you.'

"Well, I plowed one round, and I went up there, and I said, 'You just have the plow; I'll just take the hoe.'

"But the niggers didn't like for me to chop with them. I could chop so much faster than they could. I can chop left-handed or right-handed, either one.

"And they said, 'I don't like for her to chop with us. She just runs off and leaves us.' "[66]

As an employer, Etta Carroll may have set an unreasonable pace for the hired choppers. She may have been exceptionally skilled, but certainly her incentive to clear the land quickly may also have been greater. And hired choppers who could look forward only to another farm to chop may have exerted themselves less to sustain the labor over the long haul of summer.

Because chopping required the use of very sharp, dangerous hoes, children generally did not take up that task until they were about ten years old.[67] Myrtle Calvert Dodd, who began chopping at age thirteen, remembered, "My father sharpened [the hoes] every morning. We had to be careful—don't hit your feet. But after we got up bigger, we chopped in shoes. We had some old shoes we chopped in."[68] In the hard-pressed Folley family, Inez began chopping at age eight. She received a spanking after leaving excessively large skips between the cotton plants, thinking in her child's mind that the less cotton that grew, the less she would have to pick the next fall.[69] The Stimpson family expected less of their children, using a cooperative method: "If we were in the field chopping cotton, if one got a clean row and one got a bad row, you help out."[70]

Chopping served as a first line of defense against weeds in the days before chemically treated agriculture. Weeds grew luxuriously in wet weather, thriving in the warm, humid days of late spring. Tullia Hall Ischy remembered the hardship of chopping the Blacklands then: "Lots of times we'd get out there when it was too muddy. We'd chop a while and then we'd take a piece of metal—maybe an old knife—and have to clean our hoes off every so often. It just wouldn't chop anymore. It'd stick in the mud."[71] A chopper had to work diligently to stay ahead of the weeds, which if left unchecked would rob much-needed nutrients and moisture from the young cotton plants.

Johnson grass was by far the most pernicious intruder into the cotton crop, and it proved a formidable foe, with large roots and rhizomes that survived winter frosts.[72] Bernice Bostick Weir, as a prosperous landowner's wife, never chopped herself, but she remembered the wife of a tenant, Mattie Jones, and her struggle with the weed: "This field out here was in cultivation then and we had it in cotton. Pat [Weir's husband] said something about they had better get out there and get that Johnson grass out of the cotton. And so Mattie said, 'Oh, that'll be like taking candy away from a baby.' And then it rained, and then that Johnson grass grew, and she said, 'Oh, no. I take that back. If candy is that hard to get away from a baby, I don't want them to have any!'"[73] Perhaps impressed by the tenant wife's bravado (or maybe defiance), Weir long recalled Mattie Jones's overconfidence in her ability to root out the stubborn Johnson grass. The tenant, she implied, should have listened to the wisdom of the landowner.

No matter whose land one was working, chopping cotton was hard work. Texas folklorist William Owens remembered the monotony and the difficulty: "A hoeing rhythm had to be set, not fast like killing snakes—the hoer burned out too soon—but slow and steady, a pace that could be kept till the sun was down and dark coming on, broken only when it was necessary to lift the head long enough to stare down the row ahead at green leaves in shimmering sunlight. One row done, another waited, rows down a long hill to a creek and back up again."[74]

The Owens family lightened their work a little by singing in the fields. One of the songs reflected the philosophy behind the music:

> Whistle and hoe, sing as you go
> Shorten the rows with the songs you know.[75]

African Americans sustained themselves by singing hymns. Eddie Stimpson remembered the trials in Collin County and the inspiration, led by the women:

> And one of the beautiful sound in the heat of the day whin the blister bust in your hand from chopping and blood running from your hand where the tough Johnson grass blade have cut your hand, back hurting from bending, foot hurting from standing, clothes sweaty and sticky, then a tear began to roll from your eyes, some body would raise up, pull the bonnet off, wipe the tear and sweat, look at the sun beaming down at about 100 degree and say, Lord help me make it the rest of this day, and start to hum mum mum mum, then every body brake out with a humming song, like "Nobody Knows the Trouble I See," "Swang Low Sweet Chariot," "I'm Going Home on the Morning Train," and "I've Got a Home Over in Glory, Just Wait and See." These type of song would be like cool breeze blowing in your face, dry up the sweat and tear, rough up the hand. Seem like the hoe get sharp, strength get in your back, feet get happy, grass get tender and you could see the cotton sticking up through the grass. . . . Then all of a sudden some one would say, "Thank you Jesus. I've made this day."[76]

Working together, farm families plowed, or cultivated, the cotton again after the first chopping. Keeping the soil turned conserved moisture, slowed down the growth of weeds, and aerated the soil. Workers might chop the cotton again, then cultivate it as many as five more times between May and July.[77] Because of the fertility of the Blackland Prairie, farmers spent little time fertilizing, and for many years, they put very little insecticide on their crops, even during boll weevil infestation.[78]

By the first of June, the cotton began to "square," or put on buds. The four-petaled cotton bloom opened white in the morning, darkening to yellow, pink, red, and then mauve as the day went by. On the second day, the dark mauve blossom dropped off, leaving a tiny cotton boll in its place. Blooming continued right through the first frost, with new blossoms appearing on the same plant beside mature bolls.[79]

As June drew to a close, families began to think hopefully about "laying-by time," when cultivation stopped and everyone waited for the cotton to ripen. The Carroll family strove to have its crop laid by before the Fourth of July, when they usually attended a gala at Getzendaner Park in Waxahachie. Dovie Carroll recalled his father setting goals for himself and his older sisters: "A lot of times we'd be out in the field chopping cotton, me and my dad and the girls. We's there maybe a couple of weeks, though, before the Fourth, and then we'd say, 'Papa, you going to take us to the picnic the Fourth?' He'd say, 'Well, if we get through chopping cotton and laid by, I'll take you. If we don't, well, we'll chop cotton.' But we'd generally try to get through—work like everything and try to get through."[80] Laying-by was the time for religious revivals and for storing up energy for the long picking season to come.

Throughout August, the egg-shaped cotton bolls were swelling and beginning to burst open, a process that would continue unevenly until frost. As they opened, the casings, called burs, hardened, the ends forming sharp points. Each bur contained three to five locks of cotton.[81] Just as the Texas summer heat was reaching its awful extremes, picking commenced, sometimes lasting until the new year.

Women began their preparations for picking well ahead of time, and even women who never went to the fields made crucial contributions to the family's effort. They started their harvest work by fashioning picking sacks for hired pickers as well as for family members, and by patching sacks from previous years.[82] Josie Henderson Crenshaw began far in advance by bartering with the chicken peddler for cotton ducking cloth in the off-season, before demand made ducking prices rise.[83] Seamstresses made new sacks of cotton ducking, with the final products about thirty inches wide and as long as twelve feet, with shoulder straps and sometimes rings or loops on the bottoms to facilitate the weighing process. Myrtle Calvert Dodd recalled that each of the Calvert children had her or his own cotton sack: "My mother made them, too. And she used to dread when time come to make all those cotton sacks." For children's sacks, Dodd recalled, "They'd kind of measure you. So it had to hit the ground and drag the back part of it on the ground. It seemed like she put about three [yards] in mine when I started."[84]

Etta Carroll discussed the procedure for measuring a cotton sack: "Well, we bought the material—ducking. And then they'd say, 'How many yards you need?' And I'd say, 'Well, I want a three-yard sack.' Well, you'd buy double that and then enough for the strap to come over the shoulder. You'd buy about seven yards to make a three-yard sack. And then you'd fold it up this way [lengthwise] and then you'd sew up the side seam. Then you'd hem it; you made your strap and sewed it on."[85] Dragging the sacks on the ground eventually wore them out, and some women put extra cloth on the bottoms for reinforcement. Others spent their dinner breaks reversing the straps on worn-out sacks.[86]

Pulling the cotton sacks, pickers could either stoop or crawl as they plucked the cotton from plants waist-high or shorter. Those who chose to crawl tried to give their knees some protection from the sun-baked ground. Pickers with cash or credit bought rigid leather kneepads lined with felt. But most relied on the family seamstress to create kneepads, fashioned of various forms of cotton: layers of ducking sewed together, ducking stuffed with cotton, or even old quilts sewed together, tied about the knees with cotton strings.[87]

Family seamstresses also provided much of the clothing for field workers. The clothing worn for field work had little variety: usually plain dresses for Anglo and black women, and sometimes skirts and blouses for Mexican women.[88] Field work was the only venue in which women were allowed to wear men's clothing, strongly symbolizing the crossing of gender lines to perform men's work. Girls and women sometimes wore overalls or pants, just like their male cohorts, but found the cross-dressing anything but liberating. Myrtle Dodd commented, "What I hated was when we went to the field we had to wear overalls like the boys had, with suspenders. . . . And I didn't go and try them on. And if they's too long, Mother took them up. Usually, she did, but the suspenders were adjustable anyway. . . . We'd be so glad to get out of them when we got home. I can remember getting out of mine when I was just going to be home an hour, hour and a half. . . . They's hot."[89]

Inez Folley's mother recycled old materials to provide more traditional clothing for her daughter for field work: "My mother made the [cotton picking] sacks. She bought the ducking and made the sacks. When they'd wear out, she'd use those sacks—I had a chopping-cotton dress and a picking-cotton dress, and they were made out of the ducking of the sacks that had worn out. They took the good part of the sacks and made me a dress out of it. It had butterfly sleeves; it was just a slip-on; it was just a common, plain dress, but that was the style at that time. [The ducking] wasn't stiff any more because it had been washed so many times."[90]

Women's attire also included garments to protect them from the burning sun, from their tools, and from the cotton itself. Almost every female field worker wore a deep cotton bonnet to shield her face and neck. Some Anglo women tried to avoid sunburn, which would darken their skins and mark them unmistakably as women who did field work. Lillian Jane Alford remembered that her mother made bonnets with long tails down the backs for her daughters, reflecting her racial prejudices in her desire to shield her daughters from the sun: "I'm dark colored, dark complected anyway. And I can hear her say, 'Honey, come and get your bonnet on. You're gonna be just like a little Mexican.' "[91] For other Anglo women and for many African American women, the bonnets served less for vanity than for comfort. Inez Folley described a bonnet that could protect its wearer from heat or cold: "The bonnet that I wore to the field was different from the one that I wore to church or around the house. They were called slit bonnets. And the way it was fixed, you put stuff in that slit to make it nice and warm in the wintertime and to sweat with in the summertime where it'd keep your head cool."[92]

Etta Carroll recalled the gloves that she wore at chopping time: "Back in those days, you just used plain old cotton gloves; that's about all you ever saw then. That hoe handle—if you didn't, it would blister the hand. But it made our hands hurt. And I have blistered my fingers even with the glove on."[93] For picking, women often wore fingerless gloves, sometimes made of cotton ducking, that covered the backs and palms but left the fingers free to snatch the cotton at optimum speed.[94]

With the cotton sacks made and the kneepads securely in place, cotton picking began. Only in prosperous families were young daughters exempted from picking, and the mothers who did not actually pick cotton remained heavily involved in the process. Children, girls as well as boys, began picking almost as soon as they could walk, sometimes using flour sacks as miniature picking sacks.[95] Inez Folley recalled: "I followed my mother to the fields. . . . We had a job. I picked cotton. I picked little piles of cotton and she'd come along and pick it up, you know." Folley got her own sack when she was about ten years old.[96] In Hunt County, the 2 November 1917 issue of the *Wolfe City Sun* noted the prowess of two-year-old Theo Clark, who picked three pounds of cotton in an afternoon. The newspaper reported, "Mrs. Clark is quite elated at the industry displayed by her young son and wonders if the record can be beat." The excited Mrs. Clark apparently expressed no ambivalence about seeing her two-year-old at work in the cotton patch.[97] Parents often expected young children to work carefully as well as quickly. Margaruite Pitcock received whippings when she left more ripe cotton on the stalk than her father thought was correct.[98] Disability or old age did not keep most Blacklands residents from picking cotton, either. Cass Nation grew up picking, along with her mother and five brothers and sisters, "for anyone who needed help" in western Hunt County. She told the story of her brother Paul, who was blind and picked cotton with the rest of the family by feeling his way up and down the cotton stalks. Kathryn Peacock Jones recalled picking for her uncle with her three sisters and their ninety-three-year-old grandfather in 1914. "He [the grandfather] didn't work fast but very steady," she said, and brought in very clean cotton.[99]

By the time that a young woman in the Blacklands married, more often than not she had been working in both the house and the field for five to ten years. Many young women made the transition from daughters to wives as important agricultural laborers. Ray Summers, from Collin County, told the story of his mother-in-law's abrupt shift at the turn of the century: "Mrs. [Mary Hollie Hayes] Hilger, Jester's mother, said that she picked cotton in her father's field one day, got married that night, and picked in her husband's field the next day. All she did was change her cotton sack from one field to another when she got married."[100] In changing her marital status, Hilger switched the beneficiary of her labor, as her work became part of that of her marriage family rather than her birth family. In both cases, however, the authority over the fields lay not with the young bride but with the two important males in her life. Like other women, she had little time to adjust to the transition. The tasks were the same no matter whose field one picked in.

In Hunt County, R. W. Williams and his seventeen-year-old fiancée eloped with her mother literally pursuing their buggy in September 1911. They drove to Greenville and were married in the county courthouse. After this dramatic beginning, however, the realities of life on a cotton farm immediately took over. Williams wrote in his newspaper column thirty-nine years later: "Perhaps we would have taken our honeymoon away from home but I hadn't gotten out any cotton and didn't have any money so I got E. E. O'Neal to let me have 12 yards of ducking 'till I could get out a bale of cotton and we spent our honeymoon picking our first bale."[101] According to Williams, many young men timed their marriages at cotton picking season deliberately: "June is now the month for weddings, but September was the time when I was a boy. . . . The boys usually got married about the first so their new brides could make their sacks and get ready to spend their honeymoons picking cotton."[102] Czechs preferred to marry in January so that the young couple could move immediately onto a farm of their own for the following year.[103] Young women may have acceded to such arrangements because they simply expected little else. Most had grown up on cotton farms, and they knew that the crops took precedence. For some daughters, the work became harder after they became wives. Inez Adams Walker commented, "I picked more cotton after I married than I did when I was on the farm."[104]

The cardinal rule that governed picking in Central Texas prior to World War II was that the cotton had to be picked, not pulled: the locks of cotton removed from the bur, with as little trash as possible.[105] "Used to be, every boll of cotton was picked by hand," Tullia Ischy commented. "And what I mean, it was picked; it wasn't pulled. You had to pick every bit of it out of the burs. I hated to pull them old burs 'cause they hurt your hands. Even if you had on some gloves, they'd stick you anyhow. When they open up, there's a little point on every one of those at the edge of the burs."[106] The burs were every cotton picker's nemesis, as J. B. Coltharp remembered: "The cotton could be wet with a chilly dew, which could wet your clothes, but worst of all it softened your fingers so the sharp point on the cotton burs pricked your fingers until they might bleed, but you kept on picking. In a little while the sun might come up and drive the dew away, then the bur points would get sharper, but you kept on picking."[107]

"Keep on picking" may have been the second most important rule of a cotton worker. Rain could endanger a family's income, for dampened, mud-spattered cotton brought lower prices on the market than bright, clean, dry cotton.[108] With this realization, farm families tried to gather their harvests quickly. Myrtle Calvert Dodd commented, "We'd come up and see a cloud and he'd [her father] think it's going to rain. And the fields would be so white and he'd say, 'Let's get so much done today because it may rain,' and you know it never did pick as good after it rained. When it picked so good was when it was first open—be fluffy and white. Then it would kind of draw up after it rains, you know, and be dirty. We'd try to get it all out before that happened."[109] Another time for extra effort came at the end of the day, according to Letha Jumper: "About an hour before sundown, everyone would weigh up. He [her father] would ask, 'Say, Sister, how much do we lack on the bale?' Sometimes, we would have to go back to the field and pick another weighing to finish it out so that Dad could leave by daybreak to be one of the first in line at the gin."[110]

Many people remember picking cotton as something akin to torture. Historian Eugene Hollon, recalling his childhood, said, "The actual picking season lasted only six or eight weeks in the summer and early fall, but it seemed like it went on forever."[111] The merciless heat of Texas in the late summer, with temperatures averaging close to one hundred degrees, accounted for part of the tribulation.[112] In Hunt County, Oscar Adams's "personal recollections of cotton picking embrace the memory of an enormous, treeless, sun-blistered field with plants either too short or tall for comfortable harvest."[113] Yet picking sometimes lasted well beyond early autumn. Cotton ripened unevenly, with mature bolls and new blossoms on each stalk at the same time. Each field had to be gone over at least twice, often three times, and picking sometimes went on until Christmastime or even later. The final picking, or scrapping, pulled the last valuable bits of cotton from poorly developed bolls on the plants. Inez Folley remembered: "You had to go over a whole acre, nearly, to get a sackful. . . . And you didn't get as much for bollies—that's what it's called. You didn't get as much for bollies as you did cotton. . . . [It was] the way you wound up your cotton crop."[114] Picking in the chill proved to be just as bad or worse than in the heat, as cold, stiff fingers fumbled about the plants.[115]

And the work itself strained the body. A pound of seed cotton (the lint with the seeds still attached) required one to two hundred bolls, and a good picker could average 250 pounds per day. Sustaining the quick work of picking over a twelve- to fourteen-hour period resulted in sore backs and knees as the pickers stooped or crawled along the rows.[116] Sunburn also created a problem for those pickers who had previously been shielded from the sun. Patent-medicine salve or fresh dairy cream provided some relief from burned, cracking skin.[117]

Pests, too, made picking laborious and unpleasant. "I remember one fall, the worms came," recalled Myrtle Dodd. "Just eat up all the leaves off the cotton. We hated to pick. They'd get on you, you know, little crawly green ones. And my mother always fixed us a little morning lunch and the afternoon, too, you know. Maybe tea cakes in the afternoon. And I remember, we said, 'We can't eat them. There's just worms everywhere.' Get in your hair if you wouldn't be careful."[118] Other pickers complained of caterpillars, spiders, chiggers, and ticks.[119]

A substantial portion of the Blackland Prairie cotton crop was picked, just as it was chopped, by African American labor from nearby towns or distant regions.[120] Some of these workers stayed in their own homes in town at night, coming to the rural areas each morning, while others camped on farms in tents, shacks, or smokehouses.[121] Inez Adams Walker remembered: "People running the farm would hire us and come get us. And if it wasn't too far, maybe they'd come get you every morning or either they had little houses you

Women's Labor in the Fields

could live in through the week and then go home on Sunday and go to church and everything."[122] A male family head might contract his entire family's labor. Julia Hardeman grew up in Hunt County, one of nine children whose mother died when she was "too young to remember." She and her brothers and sisters worked alongside their father, harvesting cotton:

> My daddy would carry us early fall when the cotton opened. . . . We'd go along about the first week in September, and he'd keep us until—maybe he'd contract to gather a crop for a farmer, and it'd take us to about the middle of November. We wouldn't really get going to school just like we should till, say, after Christmas.
>
> Some folks taken it like, you know, enjoyed it like that. Of course, as I said, I like to work. But I was serious. When we went to work, we went to work. This is the way our father trained us and taught us. . . . But ordinarily Papa would have a contract with a certain farmer. . . . The connections are the family—maybe our brothers and their wives and whatnot, you know. But we just didn't socialize. Now, some colored people and some people get together that time of year and socialize. Go out together and live together and all like that. But we didn't. We didn't.

Instead, they went back to their own home at night.[123]

Black pickers faced an irony in the region: the white farmers needed their labor, but the farmers also distrusted African Americans and blatantly discriminated against them. Anglo laborers compared their own work with that of their African American counterparts. William Owens, unused to picking, found himself lagging behind "even the Negroes," and a white companion told him, " 'You've got to snatch fast to keep ahead of them niggers.' "[124] An Anglo Hunt County resident recalled that African American families were brought in to help with the harvest and then were told to leave as soon as the cotton was gathered.[125]

The system of hiring additional laborers, most of whom had little or no formal education, brought ample opportunities for exploitation. Many pickers complained particularly about being cheated in the recorded amount of cotton that they picked.[126] On the other hand, Julia Hardeman characterized the white people that her family worked for as "kind." Bernice Weir presented both sides of the story in her recollections of employers. Her husband, she said, treated his employees fairly, but others did not: "Of course, we worked lots of blacks over there, and one year we had two teen-age girls that lived in the little one-room house down there. And they picked cotton and they could neither read nor write and they didn't remember how much they picked that day or anything. But Pat always—we always paid them for every bit—we never cheated them out of anything." When asked if other people cheated their pickers, Weir reluctantly admitted, "Well, sometimes they did."[127] D. Y. McDaniel observed that pickers liked his father because he treated them equitably: "They wanted to come up to Granger and work for 'Mr. Claude' and he never mistreated them; he paid them what he owed them; he had no commissary."[128] Workers aware of the credit system preferred to work for employers who did not require them to buy groceries at a commissary with prices set by the farm owner. Unsuspecting pickers often found themselves at the mercy of their employers' ethical decisions on how they would treat their workers.

African American workers who came out from town were not by definition transient workers, for they usually found employment close to their hometowns. Had they wanted to become transient laborers, their race and the limitations on their means of transportation would have greatly reduced their choices of destinations. The true transient labor force, instead, consisted primarily of white and Mexican families who traveled the countryside, following the crops. During the early part of the twentieth century, Anglos dominated this work. Bernice Weir recalled that during her childhood on Elm Creek in Bell County,

> We'd have to have cotton pickers to come through and pick cotton. They was usually transient people that was traveling and would camp out. We didn't have any Mexicans and just a few blacks. But we did have some white people that was transient that way, that had their wagons and teams. Just go from place to place. [They camped out] down close to the creek under trees, and they'd get their water out of the creek. There'd be plenty of wood they could pick up to cook with and everything. They cooked on a campfire. It'd be families. There'd just usually be a family to a wagon and maybe they'd be a couple of wagons. They usually went in couples that way.[129]

Frank Locke recalled that his father used migratory Mexican labor only once in a ten-year period around the turn of the century.[130] In the northeastern Blacklands, away from the busiest highways and out of the main migration stream, Mexican labor remained scarce; in Hunt County in the 1920s, farmers hired "mainly Negroes and transient whites." In Hill County, one hundred miles south, at the same time, half of the eighty-one families who came to pick cotton were African American, seven were Mexican, one was German, and the remainder were native-born whites.[131]

Over time, Mexican labor became increasingly common in the Blackland Prairie, particularly in the southern end. Mexicans helped pick the Texas cotton crops as early as 1885, but not until the upheavals of the Mexican Revolution of 1910 did they become numerous, thousands of Mexican people fleeing northward.[132] Better wages in the United States also drew the Mexicans. For picking cotton, a family could earn up to five dollars a day in 1910 in Collin County, compared to twelve and a half cents apiece in Jalisco. In 1923, workers earned three dollars a day each, opposed to fifty cents in Mexico.[133] As migrant workers, Mexican families traveled together in groups, usually under the direction of one male, known as the *jefe* or *patron*. The *jefe* made all the work agreements and accepted payment for the group, disbursing the funds to his workers. Often he was the only person in the group who spoke English.[134]

Blacklands cotton pickers of all ethnic groups were legendary for their high levels of productivity. An 1896 U.S. government study reported that nine-year-old girls sometimes picked two hundred pounds of cotton a day, while first-class pickers averaged more than five hundred pounds per day.[135] Blues singer Huddie Ledbetter (Leadbelly) sang of a husband-and-wife team that could pick a bale of cotton in a day:

> Me an' my wife can
> Pick a bale o' cotton
> Me an' my wife
> Can pick a bale a day.[136]

Leadbelly exaggerated, of course; it took 1,500 to 1,600 pounds of cotton with its seeds still in (known as seed cotton) to make one 500-pound bale of ginned cotton, far beyond the combined abilities of even the best pickers.[137] As the song reveals, many women of the Blacklands prided themselves on their abilities to perform the job well, in defiance of the culture that frowned on their work. Czech immigrant Frances Podsednik recalled, "I worked hard. I picked five hundred pounds of cotton a day, not pulled, picked. I was so strong. I could swing a sack of 150 pounds on my shoulder like nothing. I was strong."[138]

Women sometimes actively tried to best each other at picking, even in the status-conscious Anglo culture. Families knew who their best cotton pickers were, and although there were no tangible rewards, there may have been some recognition. Women who were lead workers had to pace themselves carefully, for they could not afford to burn the other pickers out. Marguerite Cooper, whose greatest daily picking weight was 315 pounds, commented: "It was something if a girl could pick five hundred. And they tried, just a lot of them."[139] Inez Folley remembered her mother as "a good cotton picker. My greatest delight was trying to beat her picking cotton, but I never did. She could always—we'd go to the scales to weigh the cotton, she'd always have two or three or four pounds more than I did, and I just picked myself to death, I thought, trying to beat her. But I never did. One time, I was able to pick over two hundred pounds of cotton, and she could pick two hundred pounds without even thinking about getting tired. She was just used to working. She was a strong woman."[140]

Julia Hardeman boasted of her ability to pick 475 or 500 pounds a day: "I was a good cotton picker. . . . I mean what I say. . . . I'd drag about a hundred. I mean about seventy-five and around eighty. Yes. Yes. I was pretty strong. . . . I could pick as much as I could pull, almost."[141] But Alice Owens Caufield confessed that she and other family members picked badly:

> Poor cotton picker. I can remember when my daddy would say, 'We're going to take [so many days] to pick a bale of cotton, and we're going to see, can we get five hundred pounds today.' Well, my daddy was a poor cotton picker, too, 'cause if he got 250, I think he was doing pretty good. And if we could just get a hundred—cotton picking was always hard for me. I just couldn't snatch it out of the bolls. But whatever we got, under a hundred or what, if we could go out that morning and pick fifty pounds each, my daddy was grateful for us doing that much. I can remember how tall cotton has grown—as tall as we were, almost, when you could stand up and pick some of it. I never could stoop if it's low. And I would always take too much time pulling it out of the bolls and picking all the little specks off.[142]

Slow cotton pickers worked as long as excellent pickers, but they gained only small rewards for their efforts.

Pickers gathered at the cotton wagon parked nearby in the field. When a picker's sack was filled with fifty to seventy pounds of cotton, she or he trudged over to the wagon to have it weighed, straining back muscles to pull and lift the weight.[143] Often, the landowner's or tenant farmer's wife or teenage daughter weighed the cotton and kept accounts on the pickers. Women with some education in arithmetic proved particularly suitable as weighers, and they

Landowner's daughter weighing cotton, Kaufman County, August 1936 (Photo by Arthur Rothstein, courtesy of the Library of Congress, LC USF-34-5190-D).

constantly battled the workers about the accuracy of their figures. Inez Adams Walker recalled weighing cotton as a young teenager on her father's tenant farm: "I kept the books. I stayed at the scale so when somebody come up, I weighed their cotton and kept the books." She recalled being "pretty good" at arithmetic: "Just common figures—I was good at them."[144]

"After Dovie and I married, and I think it was the next year, I done the weighing," Etta Carroll remembered.

You know, you had these long scales, and . . . that pea[145] had to balance just so. And a lot of times, if you let them do the weighing, they'd call it one thing and they wouldn't have that much cotton. So I did the weighing. But most of the time they wouldn't. The main reason was, back in those days, it was before you'd know how much to put on there for a bale of cotton. Just one weighing, you see, they could keep up with all of it. We had a book, and we had each picker's name in that book. And we put that weight under each name. Then when time to settle up the last of the week, why, we added that up and told them how much they had and how much money they'd get. I done the weighing every year.[146]

Bernice Bostick Weir concurred with Etta Carroll's need for caution in weighing:

> I didn't keep books like they do now. I had their names here, you know, and name here and name here and name here. When they'd weigh, I'd put their weight down. You know, Mexicans are the worst people in the world about when they empty their cotton sacks not emptying all of it. You had to watch that. . . . And so I'd let them weigh their own but I'd stand back there and watch them and I'd put down what they weighed. . . . If somebody threw their sack off and it looked like it had a hump in it, I went and examined it. If it had cotton in it, I made them shake it out and throw it back up on the wagon.[147]

The sight of young farm women arguing with or reprimanding cotton pickers must have been a provocative one, as the weigher exerted the authority of her position over other adults.

Wages earned for picking cotton varied with the availability of labor. The more pickers that were available, the lower the wages offered. In the mid- to late 1920s, wages in the Blackland Prairie varied from $1.25 to $3.00 per hundredweight, but during the Great Depression they dropped as low as thirty-five cents per hundredweight.[148] A good picker earned wages comparable to those available in town and much superior to those earned from doing laundry. And cotton picking was one domain in which women's wages equaled those of men. One's pay depended on the amount of cotton one picked, not on one's sex. Work in town was usually steady, however, compared to the seasonality of picking, and could not always be easily postponed or jettisoned. While picking might bring in a good infusion of cash, the work lasted only briefly and then the season ended for another year.

Some Blacklands women, particularly unmarried young women, picked cotton on an individual basis to earn "pin money" for personal expenditures. Inez Adams Walker remembered scrapping cotton for pocket change: "In late fall, people had done picked—went over the fields and picked cotton; there'd be a lot of cotton still they left out there. Me and my sisters would go out on weekends and pick and make our own money."[149] Others, working only in family groups, brought in significant amounts of their families' income, earning little money to call their own. Instead, their work mingled, indistinguishable, with that of other family members through a family wage, and they received no special credit for their efforts in making the crop. Julia Hardeman recalled that her father controlled the earnings of his entire family, doling funds out to those who had earned them: "Our father was over it [the family money]. He was the one, you see. He'd collect the money, but he was always good and kind enough to give us a percentage to spend."[150] This lack of remuneration appalled reformers such as sociologist Ruth Allen, who declared that only through the exploitation of women's labor could the cotton industry continue to produce a profit. But the family wage may have helped justify women's labor in the eyes of society. Work done on behalf of one's family was more acceptable than work performed for oneself.[151]

Once the cotton locks left a woman's hands, she virtually lost control over them. When the weigher calculated that the cotton wagon held enough to make a bale, a designated person, almost always a male, began the trip to the gin. Women were generally relegated to waiting at home while the cotton was ginned, compressed, classed, and sold, and the men returned home with money.[152]

"The gin was just strictly a man's world," commented Etta Carroll. "Now, maybe there'd be some woman going through the weighing, but the bookkeepers maybe sometime would be women and sometime would be men. But not very many women worked as bookkeepers even at the gin in those times."[153] If a family were lucky, the ginned cotton brought a price that would enable them to pay their creditors and receive some hard-earned cash with which to buy a few luxuries as well as necessities. Most of the time, women depended on their men to provide them with a share of the harvest income, having little say over the money that they had helped earn.

Many Blackland Prairie families ended the harvest season the same way they had begun it: in debt and in want. It may have taken an entire family to make a cotton crop, but the living that cotton provided in the Blacklands and elsewhere hardly sustained most families. They lived skimpily, waiting until they could start again the next season. Lacking other options, they tried to muster some optimism and always hoped for better times the next year. The better times seldom came in the early twentieth century. Little changed in methods of cotton cultivation before World War II, and rural people began leaving the country for the nearby towns and cities.

chapter *five*

Life Beyond the Farm

Women and Their Communities

Farm women in the Blackland Prairie lived within small, intense circles, concentrating on home, family, and the status of the cotton crop. Most did not live in complete isolation, however. They communicated with neighbors by personal visits and telephone, and some heard or read of the world far beyond them. Women enjoyed community gatherings with their families. They shared work and troubles, caring for the sick, the newly born, and the dead. Above all, women shared their beliefs in Christianity, and many participated in churches and their related organizations.

The small circles of women's lives were usually segregated by race and ethnicity. Eastern Europeans living in Texas formed their own enclaves, keeping alive their own customs, much to the chagrin of their disapproving Anglo neighbors. Mexicans and African Americans sometimes created their own communities as well, but perhaps because few of them were able to buy land, many were scattered among groups of whites, who usually shunned them completely. Census records reveal this isolation graphically: page after page recorded only white families, and often only one black family appeared amid twenty or thirty white families. Isolated African American families had to work actively to maintain any semblance of community, with churches and schools sometimes significant distances away. Small areas of concentrated African American population created vital communities of kin and neighbors, with churches and schools.[1] In southeastern Navarro County, for example, the Langhams were surrounded by family despite their sharecropping status. So enveloped by her people was Maggie Langham Washington that she had "no real contact" with white people until she moved to Waco as an adolescent.[2] For Mexicans, who had no access to land of their own, creating community proved even more difficult, but occasionally enclaves arose. In northwestern Ellis County, the road between Soap Creek and Mountain Creek outside the village of St. Paul became known to permanent local residents as "Greasy Row" around World War I because of its large numbers of Mexican occupants.[3]

In the days of muddy roads, neighbors often relied on each other for communication and recreation, either in gender-divided groups or in family units. Many houses on the fertile prairie were no more than one-quarter to one-half mile apart, and the dense population fostered close communication.[4] Sociologists in the 1920s found that almost all farm people in the Blacklands visited with their neighbors, but only with those from the same ethnic group.[5] Many families created tight social networks, as discussed in Chapter 1, sharing ties of kinship as well as ethnicity, and they maintained those networks with regular contact.[6] In Hunt County in 1920, thirteen families out of one hundred reported visiting neighbors and relatives daily, while forty saw others on at least a weekly basis.[7] Many times, the tasks of keeping in touch with distant relatives fell to women.[8]

While the majority of families spent time visiting with others, some Blacklands residents remained isolated on their farms. Farm owners tended to bond with their landowning neighbors more than tenant farmers or sharecroppers did, for, compared to the more transient nonowners, they had long periods of acquaintance built up. For those people who did not indulge in visiting, life could be lonely indeed. Some Travis County residents, finding themselves isolated among established family groups, grumbled, "Our neighborhood is not neighborly. Only kin folk visit."[9] Children's Bureau sociologists reported that many mothers in Hill County complained of the loneliness of country life. In a probable worst-case scenario, one woman responded to the question of what she did when not working by saying, "I jes' sets 'round the house and gets up and walks 'round the yard and looks at the chickens."[10] A tenant or sharecropping woman, separated from her birth family, without means of transportation or a telephone, could find herself very much alone amid the hard work of the farm.

Visiting was very casual, rarely following formal plans. Most often, Blacklands residents simply dropped in on their neighbors. Frank Locke recalled the invitation, "Y'all come," encouraging everyone in the household to drop by. "Neighbors within walking distance visited, impromptu, at any time during the week," Locke commented.[11] T. R. Rampy remembered that his mother often packed up her children to visit the Jackson family, which lived "200 yards distant."[12] The visits would be limited by time and space, since someone in the family would usually have to return home in time to care for the livestock.

Bernice Bostick Weir remembered her social life as a young wife and mother around 1920. She and her husband passed time with neighbors who, like they, had small children. Although the women might visit separately while the men played games, they did not leave their homes without their husbands.

> We didn't go places then through the week or anything, but if it rained where they couldn't get in the fields and work, Pat loved any kind of a game. It didn't make any difference what it was, but back then it was mostly dominoes. This family that lived over here—Lilburn was already married, and he had a child when we married. And they didn't have a car, but we could see them coming a-walking down this road here—this was a dirt road then—with their diaper bag and everything. And they'd come spend the night; the menfolks would play dominoes. And the Patrick that Pat went in the service with—they lived over this-away from us, and we could see them come walking up through the lower pasture with their baby and a diaper bag. And sometimes both of them would be there, so we always had a good time.[13]

The primary connections were between the men, but the wives apparently welcomed the chance to socialize. They gathered at the home of the Bosticks, who owned their land.

Another occasion for socializing was Sunday dinner, a time for women to show off their cooking abilities, as discussed in Chapter 3. Inez Folley remembered that her mother, despite a heavy load of field work, "cooked a big dinner; we had friends that we'd take turns about. We'd eat at their house one Sunday; they'd eat at our house one Sunday. . . . They lived on a farm about a mile or two away."[14] Czech women, too, traded cooking Sunday dinner for relatives or friends.[15] On Sundays, Czech families also indulged in the ritual of the coffee klatsch (which they called by its German name) at four in the afternoon, bringing out pies, cakes, and coffee for all, whether they had been guests at midday dinner or not.[16] Families with access to ice made ice cream a Sunday specialty.[17] By trading off the preparation of large meals, women practiced economies of scale and ensured for themselves an eventual Sunday with a meal cooked by someone else.

Longer-term visiting also occurred, especially during the winter or at laying-by time, when field work was less demanding. Guests might stay all day or all month. As Frank Locke commented, friends and relatives from outside the neighborhood would ask to come and spend the day: " 'Spending the day' meant just that, for Sunday visitors came in the morning and left 'just in time to get home and attend to things afore dark.' "[18] Emma Bourne remembered, "We thought it the proper thing for a wagon load of people or whole families to drive up late Saturday evening to spend the night and the next day. Sometimes we had them for several days at the visit."[19] Geneva Berry Robinson recalled her mother "looking forward" to having large groups of kinspeople visit. But unquestionably women bore most of the responsibility for cooking for such crowds and finding bedding for them if necessary.[20] Perhaps they looked forward to their turns as guests.

Some Blackland Prairie residents gathered in groups for candy-making parties and other popular types of inexpensive amusements such as picnics or "socials." Many families reported "singings," where neighbors gathered to spend evenings together. As discussed in Chapter 1, singings were prime opportunities for young people to find mates, but they also created entertainment for neighbors of all ages. Invitations came by word of mouth or by penny postcards.[21] Myrtle Calvert Dodd explained, "We usually had neighborhood singing. . . . And you know, once in a while they would hear a song or somebody would have the sheet music—Like 'When You and I Were Young, Maggie.' I remember they sang that and different things. 'Beautiful Ohio'—I remember they sang that. . . . [Around Hewitt] they had quartet that sang real good, the Taylors." As Dodd remembered, neighbors also took turns hosting parties, providing lemonade and cookies for their company.[22]

Alice Owens Caufield remembered the conviviality of the black residents of Robinson, McLennan County: "There's always one house open that—who's going to say come on." Social activities centered around suppers for all ages at neighbors' houses, according to Caufield: "Suppers were usually outdoors. All the children would entertain and tell jokes and we used to have some folks that could tell good jokes and their lies wouldn't be too long or they might—some of the men would love to tell something about their hunting and their dogs and all the courting girls would be in one group and all those that wasn't courting didn't allow you close to 'em."[23]

Despite the stern admonitions of Protestant ministers, the majority of the people in the Blackland Prairie amused themselves with community dances.[24] In black and Anglo groups, dances during the early part of the century usually took place in homes and were called house dances. Participants cleared one or two rooms of furniture and sprinkled cornmeal on the floors to make a better sliding surface. These dances, distinct from courting rituals, were family affairs, with children running about until they fell asleep, exhausted, in adjoining bedrooms.[25] Dancers moved to the sound of fiddles and French harps that played such melodies as "Over the Wave," "After the Ball Is Over," "I Dreamt I Dwelt in Marble Halls," "Flow Gently, Sweet Afton," "Drink to Me Only with Thine Eyes," and "I Was Seeing Nellie Home."[26]

For Germans and Czechs, dancing was their principal social outlet. Weddings, as discussed in Chapter 1, almost always culminated in dances at the brides' homes. Dances also took place at halls specifically built for that purpose. The tiny village of Tours, for example, sported two dance halls. Residents of Tours seeking the pleasure of the bigger city could go to Germania Hall in the nearby town of West, touted "as German as Germany itself."[27] Among Mexican immigrants in the lower Blackland Prairie, dances were also the most common form of group entertainment.[28] These immigrant groups followed the teachings of the Roman Catholic Church, which had no moral qualms against dancing.

With options for transportation limited by poor roads, women in the Blackland Prairie sometimes remained at home for months at a time. During those periods, many of them relied on mail and the telephone to stay in touch with the outside world. Rural free delivery of mail arrived in much of the Blackland Prairie around 1902.[29] With RFD, women could receive communications from distant family members and get publications that brought news of the world beyond their immediate vicinity. T. R. Rampy recalled that rural free delivery reached his family in Bell County in 1903. The family looked forward to receiving its weekly newspaper by RFD, which his mother read aloud in the evenings to his father, who could neither read nor write.[30]

The senior Rampy's plight was not uncommon in rural Texas in the early twentieth century. While the illiteracy rate in Texas overall in the 1920s stood at 3 percent for whites and 17.8 percent for blacks, a study of Hill County found higher rates among women: 4.4 percent of white women and 19.6 percent of black women.[31] Among migrant families, who had extremely limited access to formal education, the illiteracy rates were highest of all: of seven Mexican families, in only one family could the mother read, and in four, neither parent was literate. In 11 percent of both black and white migrant families, neither parent could read.[32]

TABLE 6. Literacy Rates for Women under Age Forty-Five in Four
Blacklands Counties, by Ethnic Group, 1900 and 1910

	Whites		Blacks		White and Black, Combined	
	Can read	Can write	Can read	Can write	Can read	Can write
1900						
Ellis	97%	92%	66%	62%	87%	82%
Hunt	95	94	68	64	86	84
McLennan	96	95	74	68	89	86
Williamson	98	98	72	68	89	88
1910						
Ellis	97	97	74	74	89	89
Hunt	96	94	84	78	92	89
McLennan	91	88	88	84	90	87
Williamson	99	97	74	72	91	89

Sources: *Twelfth Census of the U.S.*, 1900; *Thirteenth Census of the U.S.*, 1910.
Note: N=100 white women and 50 black women for each county.

Table 6 reveals the percentages of women in the Blackland Prairie under the age of forty-five who could read or write. The literacy rate was considerably higher among white women than among black, reflecting the greater availability of education for rural whites. African Americans, often isolated on the prairies, had to travel farther to reach fewer schools with poorer facilities. As transportation improved, however, the likelihood of a young woman going to school increased, and so did the numbers of women able to read and write.

The horizons of literate rural women broadened with mail delivery and books. Ruth Allen found that almost 84 percent of the white women in her study received either a magazine or a daily newspaper.[33] A survey of Hunt County in the early 1930s revealed that the average farm family in the county subscribed to two magazines.[34] Opportunities were considerably fewer for African American women, however, as fewer than a quarter of Allen's sample received any sort of magazine.[35] Daily newspapers ranged from the *Dallas Morning News* to smaller papers such as the *Waxahachie Daily Light*, which came to farm homes every day through the mail.[36] Small papers appeared weekly in market towns throughout the Blacklands.[37] In 1930, Hunt County alone supported ten newspapers, and Williamson County had six.[38] Newspapers also reached out to members of ethnic communities. In the early part of the century, for example, the *Taylor Journal* and the *West News* regularly had Czech-language sections, and Mexican immigrants perused issues of *La Prensa*, a Spanish-language newspaper published in San Antonio.[39]

Men read Dallas-published periodicals such as *Farm and Ranch* and *Holland's Magazine*. Women also read these publications, as well as the *Semi-Weekly Farm News*, with its weekly women's pages tucked between pages of articles on farm practices. The women's pages, completely concerned with domestic affairs, typically featured recipes, home remedies, household tips, and letters from readers. Ruth Allen reported that the magazine most popular with women was the aptly named *Comfort*, "filled in the main with extravagantly ideal stories of innocence and youth, of love and hate, of vengeance and reward. . . . Love is still beautiful and triumphs over evil and opposition."[40] Etta Carroll recalled *Comfort*: "It had a little bit of everything that would help you; it'd have recipes and tell you about different things and stories. And I took that for a long time."[41] Only a handful of farm women subscribed to such prevalent American urban periodicals as *Better Homes and Gardens*, *Ladies' Home Journal*, or *Woman's Home Companion*.[42]

With little cash, Blacklands families had minimal resources with which to buy books, and families' libraries were sometimes limited to a Bible only. Some families included a dictionary, textbooks for the children, or a farmers' almanac in their holdings. White women owned many more books than did black or Mexican women, with more than 90 percent of them having at least one book besides the Bible, and 3 percent owning more than one hundred books. Two-thirds of black women and 89.2 percent of the Mexican women in the lower Blacklands owned no books except possibly a Bible, but 2 of 207 black women in the study possessed more than fifty books.[43]

Only a few women had access to a lending library. Of the fifteen public libraries in the Blacklands in 1939, all except one (in Italy, Ellis County) were located in the county seats, and those were reserved for white patrons only.[44] Some rural schools had libraries for their students, and occasionally wealthy families allowed their poorer neighbors to use their personal libraries. Myrtle Calvert Dodd, who read "everything that I could get my hands on," borrowed books from Dr. Hallie Earle, the first female physician in Waco, whose wealthy family had owned land at Hewitt since before the Civil War. Hallie Earle singled out young Myrtle, lending her "mostly novels or books with a lot of poems in them, as well as I can remember. And some history books; I liked history. She had those, too."[45] In Penelope, Hill County, the village doctor also loaned out books from his library, determined to uplift his unfortunate neighbors. His daughter, Lavonia Jenkins Barnes, commented that her parents "decided they weren't teaching these Czech children to learn to read, so my father and mother put in a circulating library, in our house of all places; and my sister and I were the librarians." Her parents bought sets of "the classics and they would come in and suggest what they thought the children should read, and what their parents should read."[46] Magazines and newspapers, along with a limited number of books, gave rural women an outlet to the world.

Only a small number of rural women in the Blacklands had access to radios before World War II, but its impact on those few was significant.[47] Roomsful of people gathered to listen to broadcasts.[48] Lois Lewis recalled, "When the radio came along, that was our entertainment. . . . We just lived by that radio because we got interested in all the programs."[49] Farm families received national programming over the radio, broadcast over powerful fifty-thousand-watt stations located in the major Texas cities.[50] Several people mentioned "Ma Perkins" as their favorite radio show, enjoying events in the life of Ma Perkins, the owner of a lumberyard in the mythic village of Rushville Center, "a woman who managed to travel widely, mend broken hearts, and counsel her family and loved ones."[51] Rural people enjoyed hearing tales of an independent woman who saw the world but still maintained close ties with her kin. Local stations produced programming to attract special audiences; for example, station KTEM in Temple began the "Czech Melody Hour" in 1936.[52] By 1940, even small county-seat towns boasted low-power radio stations, and the numbers of families with radios had risen significantly.[53] For the few rural people able to listen to them, radio could push back their horizons.[54]

For many years, the primary means of communication between farm families was word of mouth. The Blackwell family relied on traveling salesmen to bring news of the world outside. The drummer for the McNess company, they recalled, "brought word of marriages, new babies, and deaths from throughout the county, as well as pertinent weather information such as which farms back down the road had had rain showers, which farms had been hit by hailstones, and the flood stage of Chambers Creek (which was a vital bit of information for those of us living on the other side of the creek from Corsicana)."[55] Fathers going to town to buy groceries or sell farm products brought back the news as well.

The telephone increasingly kept families, neighbors, and friends in touch with one another. Landowning families acquired telephones as early as 1900.

By 1924, almost two-thirds of white families in Hill County had telephones, as did 53 percent in the lower Blacklands. In the late 1920s, people of color in the region still lacked service, however, with only 2 of 207 black women and 4 of 269 Mexican women having telephones.[56] A family that did not move and had equally stable neighbors was the most likely to have telephone service, for they could share the expense of building a party line. Tenants moving frequently from farm to farm sometimes found themselves with telephone service and sometimes without. Myrtle Calvert Dodd remembered: "We didn't have a telephone in the last place that we lived in Hewitt so long because you had to build your own private line." Those without their own telephones depended on neighbors and family to share their telephone service. Dodd recalled, "Our good neighbors, the Warrens, had one and we used that for emergency. My father used to tell him, 'I'll pay part of yours every month.' "[57] By World War II, most rural areas of Texas had at least limited access to telephone service, but some farms would remain without service until the 1960s.[58]

In Hunt County, Troy Crenshaw's family shared a party line with eight other families, with nine possible combinations of long and short rings delineating each family's calls. Crenshaw reflected, "Cumbersome as it was, this early telephone service added a whole new dimension to everybody's life."[59] Telephone calls announced all types of activities, from national events such as the end of World War I to the first hog killing of the season. A woman with telephone access could contact whom she wanted, when she wanted (assuming the line was available), and not have to wait on word of mouth to carry the area news. She could call the doctor for a sick child or a neighbor to borrow sugar or thread. And muddy roads no longer meant complete isolation.[60] Staying in touch had a price, however, and telephones became yet another item that required the expenditure of cash, broadening the gap between the comfortable and the poor.

Despite full schedules of housework combined with field work, most women in the Blacklands managed to maintain contact with people outside of their immediate families. Many of the activities in which women engaged outside of their farms actually extended the nurturing tasks of wives and mothers. As making a home was a crucial part of a woman's duties, so was helping others outside the immediate household. When the Calvert family's tenant house near Hewitt burned in the 1920s along with nearly all of their material goods, their neighbors quickly rallied to their aid, sharing their own meager possessions. Myrtle Calvert Dodd recalled: "Neighbors gave us mattresses, and we bought two. A couple of rockers in there and maybe a little table. . . . And different ones—just until we could get things together. And the missionary society had a shower and we got some dishes and cooking things."[61] The Calverts sharecropped and moved fairly often, but their landowning neighbors assisted them despite the class differences.

Caring for the sick carried great importance for people for whom a physician's services came dearly. For some, the assistance came on an informal basis, with individuals volunteering their time independently. Inez Folley remembered: "Whenever anyone got sick, well, instead of hiring a nurse—they couldn't afford to hire a nurse; well, the women go over and help them to nurse. My mother could come out there at midnight, maybe, to go sit up with someone that was real sick. And that's the way they did on the farms; they just helped one another."[62] Women tired from caring for their own families nonetheless missed nights of sleep tending the sick.

A kind-hearted and brave neighbor tenderly nursed the Carroll family during a scarlet fever infection that took the life of their second son, Stacy Lee, in 1927. Etta Carroll and all three of their sons caught the fever, and Dovie Carroll tried his best to cope with the infectious disease that prevented others from coming in the house, and to run the farm at the same time. He remembered: "Rocked on there for three or four or five days and I'd done went about as far as I could go. She [the neighbor] come up there one day; I told her, 'This is quarantine.' She said, 'I can't help it if it is. I'm coming in.' And she did." Etta Carroll commented, "She done everything," and Dovie Carroll added: "She'd do anything: cook, sweep the floor, anything else."[63] Eventually, Dovie Carroll's father helped with the farmwork and Etta Carroll recovered to the point that she could care for her sons with the help of a nurse from town. But it was the assistance of the unnamed neighbor, risking her own health, that came at a critical time and greatly helped the young family in need.

Church groups organized relief efforts on a more formal basis. Around Robinson, McLennan County, Alice Owens Caufield recalled that the black women's Masonic auxiliary, the Heroines of Jericho, provided strong community leadership, especially supporting the needy: "Back in those days, when we didn't have all this insurance, you always had some money in the treasury. Anybody takes sick, you had—so much money was already allocated to go to certain people. Then there's the good members; they supplied you with whatever your needs were—food. If a sick person, they sat up with you; the women took care of the washing and all that sort of thing. They stuck with you when you need them most."[64]

When the ministrations of neighbors failed, communities joined to grieve for the dead. According to Aubrey Garrett, born in 1907 near the Clifton community in Hopkins County, funerals in that area usually involved most members of the community. The tasks divided clearly by gender. He recalled, "The deaths in the community were immediately made known to every family and the neighbors and friends. . . . The neighbors and friends took care of the dead and prepared them for the burial. The women would meet and prepare a shroud. Sometimes they already had their burial arrangements made and complete, but most of the time they didn't. The women would meet and sew and fix the corpse ready to be buried. Some who were carpenters would make the coffin and other things that were necessary."[65] Women extended themselves and their sewing skills to prepare properly their dead. The work had to be done quickly, because little embalming was available, and most funerals and burials took place within a day or two of death.[66] A serious illness and death had an impact on an entire community, as neighbors inconvenienced themselves to care for the sick and dying.

A proper burial carried great meaning for most Blacklands residents. In the German-Czech community of Tours, Katherine Schneider Berger attended many mothers and newborn infants after her marriage in 1910. Around the time of World War I, she was working at the nearby Peterson home when their baby died shortly after its birth. As historian Mary Elizabeth Jupe tells it, "Mrs. Peterson did not have a pretty dress for the baby so Katherine went home and found Catherine's [her oldest daughter, born in 1911] baptismal robe with all its ribbons and lace and dressed the little Peterson girl for the funeral."[67] The wife of a renter, Berger had probably worked diligently to attain a fancy christening gown for her own firstborn, yet she willingly gave it up to serve as a less fortunate baby's shroud.

In another German community, Walburg, Williamson County, a neighbor supplied caskets lined inside and out with black cloth for those unfortunates who died without families to bury them.[68] Cecil Mae Jenkins, the wife of a Hill County doctor, lent her assistance to local funerals by tacking together pieces of carded cotton between two layers of pastel-colored silk that would protect the casket from the dirt being shoveled onto it. Her daughter recalled, "She would make this long thing—that she called a casket cover because the dirt was very black and she felt as if it lessened the terrible shock and trauma of having to put your people under this black soil if you had something to go between the soil and the casket." Jenkins also provided funeral sprays of asparagus fern and ribbon.[69]

The tradition of "sitting up with" the dead came to the Blackland Prairie with immigrants from the southern United States. The body remained in the home, perhaps resting on a cooling board, with silver on the eyes and a cloth tied around the jaw. Aubrey Garrett remembered that men sat up with the bodies of men, and women sat up with the bodies of women, a final gesture toward the social mores that divided the sexes.[70] This practice remained in place well into the 1940s, when Bernice Bostick Weir's daughter Bonnie Nell died in an automobile accident and the family laid out her body in its Liberty Hill home.[71] Through community participation in funerals, rural Blacklands people showed their respect for the dead and their continuing support for the living.

Death was omnipresent in the Blackland Prairie, a visitor to almost every household. The death of a loved one occasioned expressions of the one value that united almost every person in the region: the beliefs of the Christian religion. Women of rural Texas considered themselves spiritually tested on numerous occasions. As Eddie Stimpson recalled, "I can remember those old sister saying, Child, it not easy to go through what I went through this past week and not lose your religion."[72]

Most women in the Blacklands succeeded in keeping their religion. In the rural South, religion played multiple roles. Sunday was for most farm families the only day without field work, as they followed with relief the biblical injunctions against working on the Sabbath.[73] On an external level, religious organizations structured much of the social life in rural areas and also provided a means of reinforcing community discipline and morality. Women constituted the majority of church members in every denomination, sometimes outnumbering the men by a ratio of three to two.[74] On a deeper level, churches served as the conduit for worship and for spirituality. For many women, belief in Christianity became the centerpiece of the religious faith that gave them strength and comfort in trying times.

Many families attended church gatherings regularly, particularly Sunday school and Sunday morning worship services. Inez Folley commented, "That was one thing about the rural countries; that was one place that they always went because, you know, they didn't get to go very much, and so they could go to church."[75] Protestant churches were scattered throughout the rural Blackland Prairie at roughly five-mile intervals. With some effort, most people could be within reach of church services at least part of the year.[76]

Sociologist Ruth Allen found that 90 percent of the white and black women

African American church on the open prairie, Ellis County, June 1937 (Photo by Dorothea Lange, courtesy of the Library of Congress, LC USF 34-17445-E).

that she interviewed had attended church in the past year, and 35 percent of the white women and 23 percent of the black women went to church once a week. Those who had not gone to church cited the difficulty of attending, not a lack of desire, as the reason.[77] Most often, muddy roads prevented traveling the several miles to church.[78] Family responsibilities also sometimes rendered churchgoing difficult for some women, as Myrtle Calvert Dodd recalled, "And always a little one or two that you didn't take much to church then."[79] Etta Carroll commented, on the other hand, that she and her husband together took their babies to church: "When we had a family we still went to Sunday school and church. Some people say you can't take a child to church, but that's altogether different. We took ours to Sunday school and church ever since they was little bitty things. When you bring one up in the church, they know how to act in church."[80]

The most active church members also attended prayer meeting on Wednesdays, according to Eddie Stimpson: "Most all the farm community would be there at church on Sundays and Wednesdays." He commented: "On Wednesday night you go to pray meeting. You pray, sing, and fill up on the Holy Spirit so it will last until Sunday."[81]

For Roman Catholics, opportunities for formal worship were not as great, with few rural Catholic churches in the region. Despite scarcities, however, three-quarters of the Mexican women whom Ruth Allen interviewed had attended church within the past year.[82] Some immigrants went to great lengths to attend church, as Adelaida Torres Almanza recalled. Her family traveled twenty miles in a borrowed wagon to attend Sunday services at the Spanish-language Catholic church in Waco, the county seat and largest city in a two-hundred-mile radius. She remembered: "Mr. Nostorio, who owned the farm, would let us borrow the mules so we could come to church, and we could only do it once a week because the mules would be used for all the work during the week. So, we couldn't come to church within the week. Mr. Nostorio would also think that it was not fair for the mules to work all week and for them to be also working on Sundays, so there were times when we couldn't come to church at all because we couldn't use the mules." The Almanzas sacrificed financially for the church, picking extra cotton for cash to give as offering. Adelaida Almanza endured the trip to town in the wagon while she was still recovering from childbirth, as she and her husband made sure that their six children were baptized into the faith as newborns: "We both liked it that way better. We thought it was better to baptize them at an early age. There would be families that would wait one, two, or three years. But we liked to do it not even a month after they were born."[83] Women whose husbands, such as Dovie Carroll and Juan Almanza, were active in family religion may have fared better than those who bore the sole responsibility for getting the family to church. Two sets of hands simply made the logistics easier, and the husband's cooperation made the venture a partnership.

Religious practices in the home supplemented and sometimes substituted for participation in community worship. Many women kept religious practices in their homes through Bible reading, prayer, and song. Scripture carried great meaning for many, and, as mentioned above, often families who owned no other books possessed a Bible.[84] "A number" of the women with whom Ruth Allen spoke reported that they spent several hours a week reading the Bible, and some spent two or three hours each day doing so.[85] Even those who could not read memorized long passages of Scripture. Alice Owens Caufield remembered the scriptural knowledge of her grandmother, Eliza Owens, who had been born a slave and never learned to read: "My grandmother had a deep faith in God because she recited scriptures from the Bible all the time. So you don't have to read to know. There are many ways of learning, and she had that kind of learning ability. She could recite scriptures better than I can read them because they had meanings."[86] Her illiteracy did not keep Eliza Owens from learning the Bible, and countless other women drew similar knowledge and comfort from their Scripture.

Many women in the Blacklands considered Scripture the ultimate authority in rearing children. Parents who knew the Bible by heart used verses to discipline their children, according to Myrtle Calvert Dodd: "In Sunday school we learned the commandments and the Beatitudes and all that. And we got 'em said to us if there's anything they thought was amiss; they knew 'em. They'd say 'em to you."[87] Alice Caufield's grandmother followed similar tactics in disciplining her small charges: "And then after she would recite one, she would always have a parable, I might say, or an illustration to go along with what she was saying. At home, whatever you're doing, whatever discussion anybody came up or whatever that she disapproved—she always had a Scripture that'd tell you the right way to go. At any time—just general knowledge, God-given knowledge."[88]

Regular religious practices pervaded rural homes. Mothers taught their children to pray at mealtime and bedtime, believing, as Etta Carroll did, "If it hadn't been for the Lord, we wouldn't have this food."[89] Millie Birks Stimpson led her children in regular devotionals at home without the assistance of her husband. Her son wrote, "Famleys read the Bible together every night before bed time and then have prayer. At our house every body would get on their knees, except Dad who was respectful but might be rolling a cigerette."[90] Many Roman Catholic families in the Blacklands had home altars and held worship services that usually included reciting the rosary, particularly on holy days when farmwork precluded a trip into town to church.[91] The discipline of the liturgical calendar also created a daily awareness of religion for Roman Catholics. During Lent, the season of penitence preceding Easter, the Hanak family allowed themselves only one meal per day, eating plain bread for breakfast, a full meal at noon, and bread and milk for supper. They also fasted during

Advent, the time of anticipation before Christmas. No weddings or dances took place during Lent or Advent.[92] Fortunately, the times of heaviest field work fell in between those two periods of penitence, so that field laborers could eat hearty meals during chopping and picking times without breaking religious taboos.

A large majority of rural Blacklands residents, both black and white, belonged to some variety of either the Baptist or the Methodist Church, and evangelical Christianity dominated religious belief in the region.[93] After the Baptists and Methodists, the next most common white churches in the Blackland Prairie were the Disciples of Christ and the Church of Christ, which developed from the same root and split around 1900. These congregations often stood aloof from the Baptist-Methodist hegemony in the region. Members of the Church of Christ especially believed strongly in certain methods and procedures aimed at "restoring" the church to its basis in the New Testament, and their belief in the absolute correctness of their doctrines and the absolute wrongness of everyone else's isolated them from their neighbors.[94] Emma Bourne experienced this coolness firsthand when she and her sister Mattie married members of the Church of Christ. She complained: "People everywhere were prejudiced against the Church and called its members Campbellites."[95] In Williamson County, with its sizable European immigrant population, numerous Lutheran churches held services in German and Swedish.[96] Almost 90 percent of African Americans in rural McLennan County were Baptist or Methodist, with a handful of "Colored Presbyterians" and Church of God in Christ members.[97] Rural Catholic churches were clustered near the Czech and German settlements in Falls, Williamson, McLennan, and Ellis Counties.[98]

For Anglo Baptists and Methodists and members of ethnic Lutheran and Roman Catholic churches, religious homogeneity sometimes alleviated some of the social strains created by the tenant system. Recalling life near the community of Nash, Ellis County, where tenants lived amid landowners, Etta Carroll declared, "Everybody went to church. We nearly—everybody belonged to the same church out there," adding, "We used to not hear of all these kind of churches that they have now."[99] By "everybody," Mrs. Carroll meant "all the white people," for churches were strictly segregated by race. Inez Adams Walker recalled going to Beall's Chapel Baptist Church in northeast Milam

County, whose congregation was composed only of African Americans, in a "little old lumber building" that doubled as the racially segregated elementary school.[100]

Within ethnic groups, the unifying effect of the church helped smooth social relations at times, as landowners and tenants met on an ostensibly even footing in worship. Belonging to a church gave tenants and sharecroppers a sense of membership in the communities where they lived, however temporarily. Members of the congregation worked hard to maintain their buildings; as Gladys Everett, a minister's wife, said, "Many wanted better for the Lord's house than what they had at home. Most of them were land renters and moved often. They couldn't afford much house repair."[101] Unable to improve their own houses, members concentrated community efforts on their church buildings. Church membership also provided a common experience and a shared source of strength for workers. Eddie Stimpson remembered women congregated at the cotton wagons bidding each other farewell at the end of the picking day: "Last word would be, I'll be praying for you all. Some body say, Me too. We'll see you Sunday at church if the Lord willing and the creek don't rise."[102] Intercessory prayer may have given women a sense of agency. By praying for others, they were performing an action that would have a positive effect on people's lives.

In communities such as Tours, McLennan County, and Westphalia, Falls County, home to Czechoslovakian and German settlers, the Roman Catholic churches flourished, influencing parishioners' lives on a daily basis.[103] Many of the Catholic churches sponsored parochial schools, which reinforced the importance of religion, culture, and language in the home. Mary Hanak Simcik recalled going to communion every morning before class: "In those days we couldn't eat anything from midnight on [before receiving the Eucharist]. And I would walk three and a half miles to school. Three and a half miles! And I'd walk without breakfast to be in church at 7:30 to go to Mass and Holy Communion."[104] The sacred and secular often blended seamlessly in such communities.

Many of the dominant Anglo Baptist and Methodist church members shared similar beliefs and in many locations also shared buildings in what were known as half-time churches. A Baptist, Etta Carroll characterized the distinctions as ones of practice rather than belief: "Really, I can't tell the difference in the two churches. Of course, they do have a little bit different in their belief; they have things in Methodist church, reading and different things, that we don't have in the Baptist church. They believe in sprinkling, and Baptists believes in baptizing. I never saw that much difference in them."[105]

Despite the similarities, Baptist and Methodists knew clearly the denominations to which they belonged. Denominational affiliation was frequently a matter of family tradition. Deciding which church to join usually was not a difficult decision, according to Inez Folley: "Well, they usually did what their parents were. Sometimes when they grew up a Baptist but would marry a Methodist, then they'd decide themselves what—and sometimes the mother carried the girls to the Baptist church and the daddy carry the boys to the Methodist church. And then when they got old enough to decide which one they wanted to be, you know, they'd join that particular church. But my mother and daddy were both Baptist, so we didn't have to have that decision." For serious Christians, membership became a matter of conscience and not of merely following the family. Inez Folley observed, "When I first started going, it was because my mother was Baptist, but that wasn't the reason I became a Baptist. I realized why I was Baptist. It's in the Bible, tells you what to do. And I knew I was a sinner; I joined the church."[106]

Blackland Prairie women exercised powerful religious influences over their children. Within the formal structures of the church, however, the power of Anglo women was severely limited. Only men could be pastors, deacons, or elders. Sunday school classes were usually divided by sex.[107] In Protestant churches, the power of the minister might be limited because of his mobility. Methodist ministers transferred at the will of the governing conference, and Baptist ministers were often young men constantly in search of greener pastures. Roman Catholic priests, with greater centralized authority than their Protestant counterparts, had significant power over the lives of their members. In Tours, for example, the priest requisitioned each family's annual contribution to the church "according to his own judgment."[108] And a local priest's stern warning may have saved the life of Mary Hanak Simcik's mother in 1907. Simcik's father died from typhoid, which her mother then contracted. Simcik recalled,

> She didn't eat for six weeks. She like to have starved to death. She wanted to follow my daddy until—in those days, a priest was almost like a god. And so somebody told Father Felnar that my mother just didn't want to live, that she wanted to die, and she was starving to death because she didn't have an appetite. And so he came out to the house and talked to her like a dutch uncle and said, "You've got to live; you've got these three

children to raise; you can't just lay down and die." And you know, she just took it to heart, and she started eating and she didn't die until 1932.[109]

In African American congregations, women's authority was far greater than that of their Anglo counterparts. Women preached and served in leadership roles, a practice dating from slavery.[110] In the African American Baptist church that Eddie Stimpson grew up in, a Sister Riddle preached regularly, "in her long black robe (sometime white robe on special occasion) and big white handkerchief throwed over her shoulder for wiping sweat." She preceded her sermons with singing her favorite songs such as "I'm Going to Lay Down My Burden" and "Down by the Riverside." If a male preacher went on too long, the women in the congregation could quiet him down: "Some sister start humming and the people start singing till they sing that preacher down."[111] African American women also attended the services more faithfully than men, both on Sunday, when men would "dress up and go to church and stand around out side talking, and most would nevver come in church," and on Wednesday, when "men could not be there due to ther work schedule, especial during harvest time."[112]

Churches structured the cultural life of rural women through their organizations: for Anglo Baptists, the Woman's Missionary Union (WMU); for Lutherans, Ladies Aid; for Methodists, Ladies Society; and for Roman Catholics, assorted sodalities, or lay societies for religious and charitable purposes.[113] These groups could play significant roles in women's lives; 12 percent of the women in a Hunt County survey cited church work as their "chief interest in life."[114] In many churches, any woman with the inclination could join a church society. In the Methodist Church, whose members were often of higher social standing than members of the Baptist Church, requirements for membership reflected the Methodists' relative affluence. In Perry, Falls County, a woman over age eighteen living a moral life could join the Ladies Society of the Salem Methodist Church if she could pay twenty-five cents at the time of her admission and ten cents a month thereafter.[115] The demand for a cash deposit probably excluded many women from the sisterhood in Perry.

Most women's church groups spent their time in good works, often for needy people far away from their communities. Helping others at distant locales gave women a wider perspective on the needs of the world. At Perry, for example, the women of Salem Methodist Church gave $125 and four boxes of food to the poor in "war-torn Europe" during World War I, and also sent funds to a Methodist orphanage in Missouri.[116] Inez Folley remembered that her WMU group raised money specifically for Baptist missions: "They would have a supper and take that money and send it to WMU for missions. We did all types of mission work." The WMU assisted with missions both in and out of the United States.

Women's religious societies also met needs within Texas, but still far away from home, with goods rather than money. The Woman's Missionary Unions supported an orphanage in Dallas, a hundred miles away, with homemade items, according to Inez Folley: "And we gave Buckner's Orphans Home a shower of eggs around Easter time. And we also gave them tea cakes in the fall of the year. . . . The WMU quilted quilts for orphans' homes, Baptist orphans' homes—Buckner's, and also they had one at San Antonio. And we quilted quilts for that and always sent them some clothes. They'd send us a list of things and we'd always manage to get those socks and underwear and so forth for the orphans' home. And we always did that at a certain time of the year. But our time came, why, we always came across and did what we's supposed to do."[117] Gladys Everett told of the women of Friendship Baptist Church who could not afford to send sheets and pillowcases but made "many nice white feed sack dish towels for Central Texas Baptist Sanitarium," a denominational hospital in Waco. They also gave eggs to the sanitarium and to the Buckner's home.[118] Lutheran churches engaged in similar activities, including quilting parties as fund-raisers.[119] Occasionally the women's church groups in a community worked together, as when the Baptist women of Limestone County made cookies for the Methodist Children's Home in Waco.[120] African American women actively supported the work of white social agencies, giving food to the Buckner's home in Dallas, according to Eddie Stimpson: "Remember, there were no money during the Depression, but you don't all way have to have money to help some one or take a can of food to the give away food bank at church for Buckner's Orphans Home."[121] In some African American churches, the Heroines of Jericho held quasi-religious status, assuming the duties of a missionary society. They held rituals in rural churches on Palm Sunday, wearing white dresses with red cords and gold crowns, in addition to caring for the sick, feeding the hungry, and disciplining the children of their home communities.[122] Rural women for the most part eschewed the formal groups that meant so much to urban women, such as women's clubs and suffrage organizations, but they made time for their church work.

Training young people blended social and educational aspects of rural churches. While the groups ostensibly taught means of salvation, young people were most interested in one another. Social functions generally blurred any

Women and Their Communities

fine points of theology separating Protestant denominations. Myrtle Dodd discussed her membership in the Epworth League at the Hewitt Methodist Church: "Everybody went; that's the social thing. We had Epworth League, they called it then, and over at the Baptist church they had BYPU. And we had the church at our church one Sunday and the Baptist the next and everybody went to the Baptist church and everybody come to the Methodist when we had those."[123] These groups provided simple entertainments, led by adults in the community. In Limestone County, Inez Folley led a Baptist Young People's Union, or BYPU, group: "I had a little group on Sunday night—BYPU, we called it then. And I had the little ones and the big ones, too. And we'd choose sides and I'd mix 'em up and they'd sing against one another and so we had a lot of fun doing that." Leaders of the BYPU also instituted "sword drills," exercises in which young contestants raced one another to find given Scripture passages in their Bibles, and put on programs for other churches.[124] Lutheran churches sponsored similar youth groups called Luther's League and Walther League.[125] These groups served multiple functions, providing entertainment and giving the young people of the community the opportunity to scrutinize potential future mates. The groups also emphasized substantial training in reading and memorizing Scripture.

For all of their members, Blacklands churches supplied moral teachings that reflected concerns over modernizing society. A 1904 directory of the Methodist-Episcopal church in Ellis County included directives for members who wished to "continue to evidence their desire of salvation" by avoiding a lengthy list of evils, including cursing. They desired to keep the Sabbath as a day free from field work by prohibiting "profaning of the day of the Lord, either by doing ordinary work therein, or by buying or selling." They allowed only for medicinal use of alcohol, forbidding "drunkenness, or drinking spiritous liquors, unless in case of necessity." A significant part of the prohibitions covered financial matters, seemingly aimed at the heart of the farm tenure system. Both greedy landlords and careless tenants could feel guilty when being admonished against "the buying or selling goods that have not paid the duty; The giving or taking things on usury, i.e. unlawful interest . . . The putting on of old or costly apparel . . . Softness or needless self-indulgence; Laying up treasures on earth; Borrowing without a probability of paying, or taking up goods without a probability of paying for them."[126] Fair financial dealings would ensure continued grace for the Methodists around Waxahachie.

Two of the most divisive subjects in rural Texas were the Baptist and Methodist prohibitions of alcohol consumption and social dancing, which set them at odds with their Lutheran and Roman Catholic neighbors. The open use of alcohol polarized the people of the Blacklands. Many of the Protestant church-goers leaned to the prohibitionist side in their views, while those of the Lutheran and Roman Catholic faiths were more likely to tolerate alcohol use.[127] Most people admitted knowing someone who drank, but many Anglo men kept their public imbibing of alcohol to a minimum. Frank Locke recalled that in the eyes of the Bullhide community, alcohol consumption was limited to men only, and then only on special occasions.[128] Drinking alcohol was much more commonly accepted in Roman Catholic communities, especially among German and Czech immigrants. Even in these groups, however, only the men drank publicly. Mary Hanak Simcik recalled, "It was usually men. Why, you wouldn't see a woman going to a saloon, for anything in the world." Women, she said, drank a little, "but it was just not common for women to drink."[129] Some, like Annie Uptmor Schneider, indulged in "strong homemade wine."[130]

While the boundaries were rigidly set for alcohol consumption, dancing was far more ambiguous, especially for active young people. Evangelical Protestants had frowned on dancing for more than two centuries, and twentieth-century Baptists and Methodists continued the taboo.[131] George Wehrwein commented that in Travis County, "Dancing is a moral question with many of the people. Very often they not only answered that they did not dance, but added that they objected to it." Native-born whites and blacks especially disapproved of dancing, while Mexican- and German-born respondents had no qualms about it.[132] Protestant church members, both black and white, danced only at the risk of being disciplined by their congregations.

Churches forbade dancing because of its sensuality, the embrace of two members of the opposite sex, to instrumental music. Ring games, discussed in Chapter 1, were performed to only singing voices, and they were acceptable to even the strictest congregations. Folklorist William Owens observed, "A church member would not be called before the church for joining in play-party games."[133]

Opposition to dancing began at home as parents vigorously impressed the prohibition upon their children. Alma Stewart Hale remembered her mother's strong admonitions, based not on moral suasion but on her father's position in the Baptist church: "Oh, you can't dance. You can't do that. Your dad's a deacon. No, you don't go to dances, no sir, because your daddy's a deacon."[134] More subtly, folklorist William Owens's mother often sang "The Wicked Daughter" to her children when trying to persuade them to join the church.

Women and Their Communities

The song tells the story of a proud young woman who "went to parties, both to dance and play," saying that she would change her ways when she got old. The pretty young woman took sick and died in torment from her evil habits.[135]

Myrtle Calvert Dodd, from a devout Methodist family, remembered, "Of course, then, they didn't believe in dancing. Oh, it was horrible if you had a dance around Hewitt. And some of the older ones would slip and go. . . . Didn't ever dance. Can't till this day. My husband didn't either; his mother was just like mine. Just thought you'd sure go to the bad place if you went to dances."[136] As George Wehrwein noted, the taboo extended into African American families. Alice Owens Caufield's father shamed her for her love of dancing: "I know I'd come from church and turn on the Victrola and I'm going to dance, and I'd just walked away from the church, and my daddy would come in and say, 'You don't have a religion. You don't have no religion acting that way.' "[137]

Churches strongly enforced rules against dancing. According to Ray Summers, who later became a Baptist minister, around 1925, three college-age women were brought before the church conference of the Allen Baptist Church in Collin County, "and the church withdrew fellowship from them. . . . All of them confessed: Yes, they had danced. They had not felt that they were doing wrong in dancing."[138] Decades after the fact, Emma Bourne regretted that her deeply felt religious conversion had eliminated a source of innocent pleasure from her life: "I believe square dances we had were the most harmless and enjoyable entertainments that anyone could ever indulge in. Yet, preachers of those days preached against them just as they do many harmless entertainments of today. If one joined the church, it was against the rules of the church to dance, hence I joined at the age of thirteen, and have never danced since. My dancing career was short lived, but I enjoyed what little I did dance."[139]

While dancing was forbidden, sacred music was encouraged for the people of the Blacklands. Opinions differed widely on proper worshipful music, and the split between the Church of Christ and the Disciples of Christ had been precipitated by a fundamental disagreement over the use of instrumental music. Most Blacklands churches had choral music regardless of whether they had instruments. Inez Folley and her mother labored intensively on their farm, but they set aside the time to participate in their church's formal music program: "I grew up singing in the choir. . . . My mother had a beautiful alto voice. She had a friend that had a pretty soprano, and they sang duets together. We practiced on Wednesday night after prayer meeting, and we made time to go to prayer meeting."[140] Lutheran churches especially emphasized music as well, with large rural churches sponsoring a variety of choral and instrumental activities. Several Lutheran congregations supported two or three choirs of various age groups as well as brass bands and other musicians.[141]

At the Shepton Baptist Church, Eddie Stimpson remembered women leading the congregational singing: "Some sister begins singing a song. The spirit may move some one to start clapping ther hand and stomping ther feet. It won't be long whin the feeling would fill the church." The spirited, vigorous singing provided an important release, according to Stimpson: "Some one would say, I've sweat all the week in that field for that white man. Now I'm going to enjoy God Day. After sweating all week and blister in hand and feet, this one day I'm free to sing. I can clap my hand because I happy. I can stomp my feet because I glad. I can shout because I feel alive and don't have to worrie bout no body stopping me. This let all the last week burden out. I don't have to think bout famley problum. I don't have to worrie bout that bad field of cotton. And I don't have to worrie bout no body telling me what to do." The singing brought solace: "Some time you could leave after service and some one would say, I can go home and face the trouble now. God have lifted all my burden. I ain't gonner let the kid worrie me. I ain't gonner bother about my husband running around. And I show ain't gonner let that white man cotton field get me down." The effect could last for days: "All that week you could hear some one say, Child we sure did have good service Sunday. I can still feel it in my bones."[142] The comfort brought by music extended beyond the church. According to her son, Millie Birks Stimpson sang hymns at home to help her cope: "She use to sing all the time around the house, especial whin she was tired or worried about something. Songs like 'Just a Closer Walk With Thee,' 'Jesus Keep Me Near the Cross,' 'I'm Going to Lay Down My Burden,' and 'Down By the Riverside.'"[143]

Singing schools and community singings also brought sacred music to the countryside. Shaped-note, or sacred harp, music appeared early in the Blackland Prairie, and the form remained strong throughout eastern Texas in the early twentieth century.[144] Other forms of gospel singing were also popular. Lois Lewis recalled:

In those days they called it, I guess, sacred music singing or Stamps singing. Did you ever hear of that? A family named S-T-A-M-P, or Stamps, created a rhythmic type, religious type songs. They still sang a lot as bass, alto, tenor, you know; it makes harmony. And you play it all over the piano, that sort of thing. There was an awful lot of singings. And they had singing schools, and people would attend. We had those at Lane, and we'd go to those schools. They would teach you the fundamentals of music there with that type of singing. . . . And it remains to be known by a higher power how good that was, how much good you got out of it.[145]

Social and religious purposes also blended at the annual revival or camp meeting, typically one of the highlights of the year for most Protestants. Also called protracted meetings, revivals were relics of the frontier religions that had quickly found their way into Texas from the southeastern United States. During the early twentieth century these occasions were often bona fide camp meetings in which participants camped on the church grounds for up to two weeks and heard special preaching services, but most such events had shrunk to a week by World War I. The annual revival meeting had a simple purpose, according to Bernice Weir: "Why do you go to a revival? To get revived! That's what a revival is for, is to revive the church people, to strengthen them to make them get out and work."[146] Over the years, the purpose and elements of revivals in the Blackland Prairie stayed much the same. Evangelical Protestant congregations most often held their meetings during laying-by time, in July and August. Each congregation had its own gathering; for example, the community of Floyd, Hunt County, had local Methodist, Baptist, and Christian churches, all of which annually held summer meetings.[147] Inez Folley recalled that in western Limestone County, everyone went to other denominations' meetings each summer: "The first revival was Baptist, and the second revival was Methodist; the third revival was Church of Christ. And we attended all of them. And we lived close enough to Kirk to where we could go to their revivals. And they just had two; they just had a Baptist and Methodist."[148] At least in some locations, blacks and whites attended each others' revivals as well.[149] After the arrival of automobiles, larger revival meetings in county seats attracted participants from across the county.

Revival meetings in the Blacklands were almost always well attended; as Hazel Riley commented, the preaching and music attracted even those who were not interested in salvation: "The people, having lived out on farms all year, were starved for music and drama. They came in droves. Those who were not religiously inclined went for association and entertainment, and most of the time they were not disappointed."[150] Even people who could not attend regular Sunday services often made special efforts to get to nighttime revival meetings.[151]

The mainstay of the revival was the spellbinding visiting evangelist, a male guest preacher who stayed in church members' homes and enjoyed special meals as honored company.[152] Dovie Carroll characterized the evangelists that he heard: "A lot of them, you needed cotton in your ears. Yeah, they preached back in those days. They preached that Bible. And man, you could hear them for half a mile down the road." Etta Carroll added, "When they read their Scripture and their text, why, they started preaching. And they preached. Seems to me they preached more about the saving grace of God than they do now. Their messages were—as we'd call them, more down-to-earth messages that you could understand."[153] In a more cynical vein, newspaperman C. W. Goff reported on a Reverend Culpepper holding a meeting in Greenville at which "the county towns and outlying precincts are well represented." According to Goff, the preacher "arraigned and denounced" the sinful practices and customs of modern society: "He is scathing, almost lurid, in summing up the evils and lowering of public morals through subjective as well as objective influence of the movie show, mixed bathing in one-piece suits, dancing, card-playing, forty-two, the divorce evil, and the flippant regard of the sanctity of the marriage vow."[154]

The attitudes of journalists and other skeptics notwithstanding, many rural people found revival meetings compelling and became official members of their respective churches during revivals. They were usually baptized shortly thereafter. Emma Bourne joined the church at Old Bethel as a teenager: "I confessed and accepted Christ as my personal Savior. . . . I have counted that step I took that day to be the most important step of my life, one that I have never regretted and one I have tried to live up to as best as I knew how."[155] Baptisms soon followed, often in nearby creeks or even cattle tanks.[156] In the African American community outside of Plano in Collin County, baptisms occurred only once a year. The baptism followed dinner on the grounds and was accompanied by women standing on the creek banks singing.[157] Public redemption played an important role in the spiritual lives of Blackland Prairie communities as new believers confessed themselves to be sinners in need of Jesus' help. Some recent converts quickly reverted to their old, "unsaved" ways, but others remained faithful to the accepted teachings of Christianity for the rest of their lives.

For many women in rural Texas, Christianity gave them strength. They

Women and Their Communities

believed in life after death as a result of the death and resurrection of Jesus Christ. They strived to follow Christ's teachings as they interpreted them, and they prayed to God the Father for daily help. A lifelong Christian and professing Southern Baptist, Etta Carroll believed in intercessory prayer, as did many of her coreligionists: "If we didn't have faith to pray and the Lord answer our prayers, what would this world be? Because he made this earth and he made everything on the earth. And that's what I can't understand, why some people can think that there isn't a Jesus when, if you read your Bible, you know there is a Lord. Because everything that's made, he made it. . . . You don't do anything by yourself. You have to have help, and if you ask the Lord to help you, he might help you in a way that you don't understand, but he's there to help if you will ask. He's not going to do it unless you ask."[158] To more critical eyes, religion helped believers passively accept their lots in life. Ruth Allen found a woman with nine children living in one room with eight other people, who stated, "The Blessed Book says whatever the Lord sends, you must be content with." Allen commented disapprovingly, "If ever a group needed a doctrine of passive acceptance and contentment, that group of women on the Texas tenant farm does."[159]

Many women relied on religious faith to assist them in personal family crises. As discussed in Chapter 1, Anglo women invoked the will of God in justifying the deaths of their children and counted on seeing them in the afterlife.[160] African American women also depended on their faith in God to sustain them through larger social problems, including the intractable racism of the early twentieth century. Alice Owens Caufield attended the St. Paul Baptist Church in the village of Robinson before moving her membership to the Second Baptist Church in Waco. She recalled the supplications at prayer meetings: "I've heard some folks back there express to God the trouble and the tribulations that they were going through, begging God to change the situation, never call a man's name; never called your president or anybody's name; always to God to change the circumstances that we might survive; same prayer I pray today—to guide and protect me, pray for healing, pray for forgiveness of sin. Those were the kind of prayers: Forgiveness of sin. For livelihood. For guidance and protection. To move the evils. Pray for leadership—a man with Christian belief to head the government." Caufield's belief in God's special plan sustained her:

I understood God was always close to you or to me. When I felt friendless, when I felt like I wasn't being treated right, I felt like there's a better day.

Because God has that. It's already in the plan. Like if you're struggling to do right and to learn right from wrong, that God is always in the plan. And that—why be afraid when God is going to protect? I've always felt like that, even today. My trust is in my God, whom I believe will be with me now and until the breath is gone. But as I'm in this world, then as a child and all my growing up and all the struggles that I have had dealing with people and their opinions, dealing with racism and taking it coolly and never saying too much. See, there's no hate. We believe that we're all God's children; he's got 'em in many colors, in many lands, born to one blood.[161]

Others in the African American community also responded to racial discrimination and violence with religious faith. Caufield declared: "This is trouble and sorrow and sending you to your knees to pray to God for deliverance of all these evils. This is where the spirit can move to fight hate within yourself until we overcome—trying to overcome the suffering that we've suffered, the push-backs, the nonpays, the slave. Whatever they wanted to give you, you took it and said thank you, thank you on the outside and maybe hurting on the inside." Supplications to God could be general, as in praying for strength, or specific, as in asking for limited care. In Caufield's church in Waco, the pleas in prayer meeting included protection against lynching, which terrorized the Waco community in the early twentieth century: "You had to pray for protection from one place to another. Protection—protection against the evil who have committed such sins."[162]

Many African Americans in the Blackland Prairie relied on their God to see them through the toughest times. Eddie Stimpson stated forthrightly, "You think, these days of the push button world, How in the world did they make it? I can tell you how they made it. First thing they did at night, they read the Bible and pray. The next morning the first thing they did whin ther feet hit the floor, they went on ther knees and thank God for another day and say, Lord help me make it through this day."[163]

If evangelical Christianity kept Blackland Prairie farm women resigned to their fates, other elements of the culture showed them different ways to live. Technological developments in the early twentieth century greatly expanded the horizons of Blackland Prairie farm families. For half a century after the Civil War, most rural communities remained relatively isolated, forcing residents to develop networks of reciprocity and to devise homegrown entertainments.

The telephone, radio, and rural mail delivery fostered the end of rural isolation in Texas and elsewhere.

The greatest changes in the rural Blacklands before World War II, however, came as the result of the mass production of the automobile and the subsequent development of improved roads. Once farm people could reach towns and villages with ease, they did so frequently and in great numbers. The focus of the culture shifted from clusters of individual farms to nearby market centers. The next chapter depicts the increasing urbanization of the Blackland Prairie in the 1920s and 1930s, spurred by the New Deal and capped by World War II.

chapter *six*

Staying or Going

Urbanization and the Depopulation of the Rural Blackland Prairie

Our children live in the city
And they rest upon our shoulders
They never want the rain to fall
Or the weather to turn colder
—Nanci Griffith, "Trouble in the Fields"

Between 1901 and 1918, Annie and Robert Sharpless brought five daughters and three sons into the world on the various farms that they sharecropped in McLennan and Limestone Counties. By 1940, only the eldest daughter still lived on a farm, and even she would leave in a very few years. The various paths that the Sharpless daughters took away from rural life illustrate the choices that many women in the Blacklands made during the first half of the twentieth century as they physically left rural life behind them.

Ethna, born in 1901 and soon known as "Big Sister," was the only Sharpless daughter who married a farmer, uniting with Jim Dromgoole in 1923. The newlyweds first moved to his father's farm near Watt, Limestone County, and then tried farming on the shares in Rockwall County for a year. They soon returned, with their own young daughter, to Limestone County, where they sharecropped until Jim Dromgoole's death in 1942.

Exa, born in 1905, never liked school, and she stopped attending at age eleven, becoming her mother's helper and taking in sewing for neighboring families. In 1926, at age twenty-one, she moved to Waco, twenty miles from her parents' tenant farm near Prairie Hill. At first Exa worked as a companion to an elderly relative of Jim Dromgoole, then took a job as a salesclerk at Sanger Brothers Department Store in Waco. Through an acquaintance in the all-female rooming house where she lived near downtown, Exa met her husband-to-be, Davis Hill, the son of a well-established Waco family. They married in 1928, and for the next forty years Exa was an exemplary, affluent city housewife.

Mae was born in 1907 and entered adolescence with cornflower blue eyes, silver-blond hair, and a rebellious streak. She ran away from the farm in 1924 and her whereabouts remained unknown to her family for three years. During her estrangement, she moved to Dallas, eighty miles north, and went to work in a millinery factory. By the time she was reunited with her parents in 1927, Mae had married the factory owner, a Jewish Polish immigrant named Morris Rosen, and had set up housekeeping in a fashionable North Dallas neighborhood.

Frances, born in 1908, was by many accounts the liveliest and most charming of the sisters. She "set her mind to it," according to her younger brother, and became the first member of her family to graduate from high school. In 1927 she entered nurse's training at a Waco hospital and upon graduation accepted a job at a Fort Worth hospital. There she met Ewell Hunt, a young physician intern from Lubbock, in faraway West Texas, and after their marriage accompanied him to his hometown, where they lived elegantly on his income as a surgeon.

The youngest daughter, Dorothy, born in 1916, also finished high school and soon moved to Lubbock at Frances's urging. Bookish and unworldly, she completed a bachelor's degree in history at Texas Technological College, taught school for a while, then went into nurse's training. She married a Lubbock dentist, J. M. O'Rear, and became a housewife the rest of her life.[1]

The four daughters who left the farm all did so as young, single women, meeting their urban-dwelling husbands only after they arrived in the cities. Each headed for a sizable metropolitan area, not settling for anything smaller than the regional market centers. The cities, apparently, held more opportunity and more allure for these young women than did lives on the farm. Except for the independent-minded Mae, they formed a network that assisted each other: Ethna providing a contact for Exa's first job, Frances moving to Waco the year after Exa, and Dorothy following Frances to Lubbock. With some sisterly help, each made her own way until she met and settled down with a man of means and began rearing her one or two children. None of them ever returned to the farm except on visits. Like thousands of their contemporaries across the South, the four younger Sharpless women purposefully established lives vastly different from that of their mother, with her eight babies and succession of rundown Blackland Prairie farmhouses.

Urbanization of rural southerners such as the Sharpless sisters began gradually. Technological changes, including telephones and radios, enabled people to be in touch with the world outside their farms. As roads became more passable through the prairie, rural people became even more aware of the opportunities in nearby towns, and they wanted more of the perceived excitement of town life.

Railroads remained a common means of traveling distances from the farm, and rural people took the train for occasional ventures to big cities. Some Hunt County families used trains for everyday marketing trips, as Lois Lewis commented: "Mostly we as children never came to town in the wagon very much; we had a buggy and horse. I'm talking about before I married during the 1910s–1919. We'd drive over here with a horse and buggy and catch a train to go to Greenville or catch a train to go to Dallas. That was our way of getting out."[2] In McLennan County, with one of the largest market centers in the Blacklands, the Missouri, Kansas, and Texas Railroad (known as the Katy) connected passengers from Lorena with other nearby small towns, and especially with Waco, the county seat.[3] Even as tenant farmers, the Calvert family regularly took the train to Waco, fifteen miles away: "You know, we never were so far from Waco . . . because we rode the train from Eddy to Waco and back the same day," Myrtle Dodd recalled. "And that's where I came to get my school supplies. How thrilling it was to ride that train after dark when we got back. But you know, we managed to go enough to get most everything like that."[4] Electric railways, or interurban lines, also sprang up between the largest towns, stopping to board and drop off passengers at smaller towns along the way.[5] Mary Hanak Simcik reported that her family traveled very little but did take the interurban line for the twenty-mile journey between West and Waco: "As far as I went was to Waco. . . . When we got to the Cotton Palace, that was, oh, boy!"[6]

By far, the greatest change in rural life in the early twentieth century was the advent of the automobile, and the accompanying road improvements. For many decades, rural people had depended upon horses, donkeys, and mules for transportation, either riding the animals or hitching them to wagons or buggies. Mules moved slowly, and the addition of a horse expedited transportation. Mary Ann Collier Campbell remembered when her father bought the beautiful brown mare that she and her siblings named "Lady": "It was a big event for us. We could now go to Mooreville (3 miles) rather quickly and bring home miscellaneous items my mother used to prepare meals."[7] Young women sometimes rode horseback for several miles to visit friends and neighbors. Bessie McRae even raced the family's gray horse: "We used to get out, unbeknownst to my mother and daddy, and we'd run races on Sunday evening because that horse wouldn't let anything pass it. . . . Momma would say every once in a while, she'd say, 'Bessie, I'm just afraid for you to ride. That horse is high-spirited.' I would say, 'Momma, he's just as calm as he can be.' And, of course, he was, until somebody would try to pass him."[8] Some women drove wagons and buggies at times. These vehicles, however, were generally considered the property of the men.[9] Horses and mules had significant limitations to their use. A living animal could travel only so far, and if the animal were used behind a plow as well as for transportation, family travel needs often yielded to the exigencies of the farm.[10]

For many decades, poor road conditions kept many Blackland Prairie residents sequestered in their immediate neighborhoods; they moved about in bad weather only with great difficulty. Dirt roads often turned into mud roads, becoming impassable even on foot for as long as a month at a time during wet weather.[11] During "mule days," as Dovie Carroll called them, trips to town were infrequent, sometimes as seldom as three or four times a year, and often only the man of the household went.[12] Men alone gained the experience and the knowledge that a trip to town brought. Myrtle Dodd observed about her father: "He was like all the other men; you'd go to the store and get all the news."[13] Women remained isolated in the private worlds of their farm, along with children and hired hands.[14]

The introduction of the Model T Ford in 1908 made cars accessible to and practical for many Americans, and rural families slowly began to acquire them according to their means. Despite the relative poverty of people in the rural Blackland Prairie, many families somehow scraped together enough money to buy cars.[15]

By and large, the car became the province of the men in the family; as Etta Carroll observed, "There wasn't a lot of women that drove way back yonder."[16] Ruth Allen noted that rural women were less likely to drive than their urban counterparts, despite the obvious utility of the skill for countrywomen.[17] But many rural women in the Blacklands, like Bernice Bostick Weir, learned to drive as young women after World War I. Even though neither her mother-in-law nor her mother drove, Weir learned to operate a car "right after Pat and I married. He said . . . it was essential that I drove. I could go get things if he broke plows or anything; I could go get parts for him and do things to help him out. . . . I don't remember having any trouble learning to drive."[18] Being able to transport herself gave Weir greater freedom than her neighbors who had to depend on their men to take them places. For some young women, cars became extensions of the horses and mules on which they had relied. Alice Owens Caufield drove her family's horse and buggy to Waco to school for several years before learning to operate the second-hand Buick that her father acquired. At age sixteen or so, Caufield drove the car "to Waco to somebody's house and back home." She alone among her female peers had this adventure: "I was always brave, like boys."[19]

Women realized what the automobile could do to increase their mobility, and those who could not drive themselves encouraged their daughters. Mary Ann Collier Campbell's mother could not drive their Model A Ford, so she "let" her nine-year-old daughter chauffeur her four miles across the field to the neighbor's house. When small Inez could not reach the brake pedal, her mother "quietly told her just run into a tree that was in the Blackburns' front yard." They enjoyed an afternoon of visiting and "cruising through the fields," and Inez used the same method of stopping when they returned home, with a tree "between the house and barn." The clarity of this memory indicates that perhaps this happened only once in the Collier family.[20] Muddy roads remained problems in some areas, particularly on the lanes leading to individual farms.[21] But by World War II, many counties had paved or graveled state roads, and some had paved federal roads as well.[22] Never before had rural people moved about with such facility.

Most rural residents used their newfound mobility to increase the number of their trips to nearby towns. The "towns" to which rural Blackland Prairie residents traveled formed a continuum of size and urbanity. Rural people often identified first with a community built around a church or school, such as the Liberty Hill community, where Bernice Bostick Weir moved in 1919. The Bosticks distinguished Liberty Hill as their home. They attended church there, and their oldest son began school there. But they went to Moody, four miles away, for many of their material needs, with Pat Bostick often leaving Bernice at the farm while he made the trip. Moody was a country town by any definition, with an economy that catered to the needs of the farmers, with stores, gins, and banks. No one would mistake Moody for a metropolitan center, even in its most prosperous years before 1930. But life in Moody little resembled that on the farms. Moody had electricity and running water, a high school, an assortment of churches—features that Liberty Hill lacked before World War II. More than in a farming community, life in Moody resembled that of the larger town of Temple, the third type of community with which the Bosticks interacted. Temple in 1920 was similar to many county-seat towns in the Blackland Prairie. It had a population of 11,000 (slightly larger than most county seats), with many types of services available, including two hospitals. And at the widest point in the Bosticks' circle was the small city of Waco, with a population of 38,500 in 1920. Families and courting couples might go there once a year for special events. In Waco, those with the financial means could buy oranges or ice year-round, see live vaudeville acts, go to the Texas Cotton Palace extravaganzas, or ride a streetcar. Waco seemed very exotic to residents of communities such as Liberty Hill. But even Moody offered many opportunities for excitement and material goods that the farms did not.[23]

The automobile greatly changed the ways in which rural people related to the market centers near them. Going to town on the weekends became the goal of almost every Blackland Prairie family after the arrival of the automobile. Myrtle Calvert Dodd recalled the transition around World War I:

Oh, we went once a week later on. By the time I was in teen-ages, we—we didn't go every time, but my father went. And Mother—on Saturday, that was my job to help us girls get the house cleaned up and maybe iron or work and have clothes ready for church and they went to town and got groceries and shopping. My mother would make a list then, just like she did, of what all she had to have. I know sometimes it'd be thread and it'd be all kinds of things that she'd have to have. . . . Up by then, she went to town nearly every time my father went. But when my brother was little and she [her sister] was little, she didn't go. He had to do all the buying.[24]

The Carroll family illustrates the changes brought about by easy access to Waxahachie. Dovie Carroll recalled: "Way back there when I was a kid, great big kid, on the average about three times a year is all I'd get to come to town. All children—they didn't come to town every Saturday, for no means." His father came to town once a week in the wagon to buy groceries, leaving his wife and children back at the farm. Dovie Carroll's stepmother came to town "very seldom," her world limited to the community of Nash and the South Prong Baptist Church. Etta Carroll commented on the changing times: "And by the time Dovie and I married, why, we'd come to town every Saturday. The children always come to town with us. . . . We would come to town on Saturday evening and get a place to park on the square and maybe we'd sit in the car for the longest just to see people passing by. We'd get our groceries and come back home."[25]

With improved transportation, women began participating in such activities as first-Monday trades days.[26] On the first Monday of each month, farmers from all parts of the county came into the county seat to trade livestock and other goods.[27] The first-Monday traders were primarily men, but women and children went along with pleasure.[28] William Owens recounted Mondays in Paris, the county seat of Lamar County, and his work at Kress's, part of a national chain of dime stores:

[Monday] could last from seven to eleven. There were always people waiting for the store to open, country people who had come in with a wagon load of firewood or with eggs and butter in the back of a buggy— women in ankle-length dresses, some of them in starched sunbonnets, the men in duckings and wide-brimmed hats. The doors open, they moved slowly down the aisles, fingering the goods on the counters, spending their money carefully, talking in low voices. . . . The square was crowded with country people who, their buying done, had nothing to do but stand around and look and talk till it was time to hitch up and go home again. Some crowded around the hamburger stand; others bought a dime's worth of cheese and crackers at Pete Humphries', watching the clerk whack off a piece of cheese and dig into a barrel for a handful of crackers.[29]

As countrywomen began coming to town in increasing numbers, townswomen reacted in some areas to make their visits more comfortable. As early as 1901, townswomen's clubs began establishing so-called rest rooms near the squares of market towns. These rest rooms were places where farm women and their children could sit for a while and get something cool to drink or eat lunch.[30] Typical of such efforts was that of the Waxahachie Shakespeare Club, which was founded in 1897 as a study club but like many women's literary clubs of the Progressive Era soon branched into social causes. In 1902, as the club's "first civic efforts," they leased a cottage near the town square for their rest room.[31] Women in other Texas cities followed suit, including the Gainesville XLI Club in 1911 and the Dallas Federation of Women's Clubs and the Rural Welfare Association in 1915.[32] These facilities provided club women a means of joining rural reform efforts, and rural women gained comfortable places to pause, in spite of the overly solicitous attitudes that urban club women sometimes exhibited.

Even with cars in their families, however, rural women still traveled to town less often than their men. Ruth Allen found in the late 1920s that of 546 white women, 296 (54.2 percent) reported going to town once a week; 156 (28.5 percent) went once a month; and 94 (17.2 percent) reported going less than once a month. She reported that "some few women said they went to town only once a year, in the fall when ready money income from the cotton crop is used to buy clothes for the children to start to school." The Mexican women whom Allen interviewed especially remained homebound, as 47 percent had not gone to town at all in the preceding year, while 10 percent more had gone only once or twice. Allen observed that Mexican women were apparently not able to enjoy themselves in town as others could. Speaking little or no English, they could visit only with small groups of friends, and their husbands did not allow them to shop. Allen commented: "The attitude of the men seemed in general to be that of the man who stated that his wife was 'too foolish to spend money.' "[33]

Blacks, Allen observed, often had limited access to cars, and their trips to town consequently were irregular. "The car is quite often of unknown genre and very untrustworthy, but it does furnish a means of getting to town on Saturday afternoon," she wrote. Those without cars relied on neighbors or relatives to take them to town, as automobile traffic on the road made riding in buggies too dangerous and wagons seemed unbearably slow. If a black woman without a car lived among other blacks, she could easily walk to stores or church, but if she lived in a community of whites or Mexicans, "she was very much isolated from outside contacts, especially if she lived 'off the road.' "[34] Some rural employers made sure that their African American hired hands were able to make it to town; Etta Carroll said, "Maybe they [the hired hands] didn't have no way of going, so you'd have to see that they could get to town and get what they needed on the weekend."[35]

When the trips became less time-consuming, rural families eagerly embraced the opportunities to partake of the delights of the bigger settlements. Town was a place where children found special goodies like soda pop and their parents bought groceries and visited.[36] Lois Lewis remembered Saturdays in Celeste, Hunt County: "Everybody came to town on Saturday afternoon and Saturday night. The streets were full of people, visiting, and buying the groceries. Maybe they'd go on into Greenville and come back by. There was a lot of social contacts made. There was usually a lot of the times there was something going on up there on the square, like a carnival, or during the Charleston craze, they had Charleston dances and contests. And local people took part in those. When you say local that would be the town and community."[37] During harvest time, when cash flowed most freely, going to town became even more fun, according to William Owens: "Saturday night there was time to go to Brookston, to walk along the line of stores on a boardwalk, to lay down a nickel for a red and white peppermint stick or some chewing wax."[38] Sunday mornings found most people back in their neighborhoods, at home or in church.

For the majority of people in the region, town beckoned with many temptations, not the least of which was entertainment. Some of it was free, like the popular outdoor medicine shows that historian Eugene Hollon remembered from his boyhood:

There was always something going on in the square each Saturday afternoon or evening when most country people came to town. One of the attractions that never failed to draw an audience was the traveling medicine show. The self appointed "professor" or "doctor" would arrive the day before, mix up a batch of miracle medicine in a tub and then bottle and label it. He usually started with a ventriloquist or song and dance act to draw a crowd. After warming up the audience he explained how he had acquired a secret formula from some old Indian to cure cancer, heart condition, arthritis, headaches and especially female sickness. The spiel invariably followed the same line: the medicine that he was prepared to offer at give-away prices would soon be in all the local drug stores for two dollars a bottle. But as special advertising he would sell to a limited number of people two bottles for only one dollar. The routine as well as the product were pure hokum but it invariably worked for the con artist then as well as for politicians today.[39]

Traveling circuses and shows came to small towns, often at laying-by time or after harvest. Lucille Mora Perkins remembered the circus in the village of Ben Franklin:

My father never missed a time that there was something around that he didn't take us to see. Even Molly Bailey's show. That was a show that always came, tent show, that came to the different communities; and we could get to see things that were brilliant. Those ladies with all sparkling clothes, you know. They walked the tightrope. And we could live from one year to the next thinking about it, talking about it. They had some animals. They had some dogs. I believe they had bears, yes, baby bears.

They had a big, black bear that was trained. They had a parade. The parade went from Ben Franklin, from town, what we called town, to the school, which was about a mile and a half. Then they would circle around and go back and then to their grounds.[40]

Alice Owens Caufield remembered the Ringling Brothers circus in Waco with equal enthusiasm. She loved sitting high in the big tent, watching the glamorous goings-on. Further, she recalled, the circus in Waco was not segregated, and black people could sit wherever they chose.[41] Circuses provided glimpses of an exotic world far beyond the farm.

Another, more highbrow, form of entertainment, chautauqua shows came to small towns on a circuit, usually sponsored by local businessmen, and flourished in the Blackland Prairie from 1900 until the 1920s.[42] Chautauqua shows, named for the town in upstate New York where they began, provided summertime traveling educational programs for small towns in the early twentieth century.[43] Lois Lewis remembered the chautauqua in Celeste. She reminisced: "They would bring lecturers and musicians, things like that. . . . I was going with one of the fellows out there at Lane and I wanted to come in here to hear a speaker on James Whitcomb Riley. . . . And he read in dialect, like Riley was written in. But this little young fellow that was my date didn't enjoy it a bit. He twisted and turned. He probably had worked all day in the field and he was tired."[44] In Waxahachie, Ellis County, in 1912, the chautauqua ran for an entire week, featuring local speakers and musical groups along with speeches by such imported dignitaries as the governor of Missouri and a "judge from Denver" and recitals by two singers formerly with the Metropolitan Opera. On the final night, a Saturday, a crowd of four thousand heard the Royal Italian Guards Band.[45] Those attending the chautauqua enjoyed worldwide perspectives on those nights.

Technological innovation shifted entertainment from human performances to recorded ones with the arrival of moving pictures. Towns as small as Cumby, Hunt County, had "picture shows" by 1908, and the larger towns of Commerce and Greenville, the county seat, had three theaters each. The people of Hunt County had ample opportunity to sample the glamorous world of the motion picture.[46] Alice Owens Caufield recalled vividly the experience of going to segregated movie theaters in Waco.[47] Mexican immigrants, too, enjoyed movies, as cities as small as Waco featured Spanish-language films.[48] Motion pictures featured landscapes of faraway places, widening the horizons of all who saw them.

Because going to moving-picture shows was part of the premarital court-ing ritual, Ruth Allen observed, unmarried women represented most of those who responded positively to her questions, and it was probable that married women went to shows "very little if at all."[49] Etta Carroll confirmed this premise, saying, "We didn't go to many picture shows. I don't know; we just never did go much."[50] The broad perspectives offered by movies, then, were limited to those with the mobility to go see them. Those who already had relatively wide perspectives had them broadened even further with movies, while those of narrow vision became even further constricted without a cinema screen.

One annual special event that proliferated in the period before the Great Depression was the fair, an event that was ostensibly attended by "most of the rural population."[51] While county fairs have been sentimentally regarded as gala days for rural people, George Wehrwein found in southern Travis County that fewer than 10 percent of the farmers, black and white, that he interviewed had attended even one fair during the past year, 1919.[52] Many rural people's experiences may have resembled that of Lee Rice, who, on one occasion while he was picking cotton and unable to leave the field, saw a parachutist drop from a balloon as part of the county fair. The faraway vision of the parachutist was as close as Rice came to the fair that year. The needs of the cotton crop, as always, prevailed over all other activities.[53]

Small communities sponsored their own small fairs, but most county fairs were organized and supported first by town businesspeople and later by local chambers of commerce.[54] The events and exhibits of county fairs clearly re-flected the booster spirit that prevailed in the urban United States before the Great Depression, catering to the interests of townspeople or the most finan-cially stable farmers. After paying admission, fair patrons could buy cold drinks, peanuts, and hamburgers from vendors. Elaborate agricultural, textile, and culinary exhibits showcased the best products of affluent farmers and their wives as well as those of women from town. In Hunt County in 1911, for example, women competed for prizes in such fancywork categories as white embroidery, colored embroidery, tatting, and battenburg, a type of cut-work lace—endeavors far beyond the realm of possibility for farm tenants' wives struggling merely to clothe their children. The 1914 Hunt County fair featured a Better Babies Exhibit sponsored by the U.S. Children's Bureau and Hunt County Fair Association to promote good infant and child care. Nurses and physicians gave advice, and one hundred mothers entered their children in a contest to find the healthiest child in Hunt County.[55] Again, this contest was hardly designed for the rural poor subsisting on cornmeal and fatback.

As fairs centralized, they became even more elaborate.[56] In 1925, the Ellis County Fair booked nine "high-class vaudeville acts" that were en route to the State Fair of Texas in Dallas.[57] In 1937, the Ellis County Fair featured a week's worth of activities.[58] Women of that county competed for numerous culinary prizes for canning and jelly making. The art and textile division featured prizes for such handwork as embroidered luncheon cloths, crocheted bedspreads, smocked children's dresses, silk infants' caps, and silk hooked mats. Numerous competitions were open only to members of home demonstration clubs.[59] Fairs continued to discriminate against the rural poor.

One of the most elaborate fairs in the region was the famous Texas Cotton Palace, a two-week extravaganza held every October in Waco between 1910 and 1930.[60] The entrance to the Cotton Palace grounds reflected the urban prosperity brought by the cotton economy: an archway constructed of hundreds of cotton bales supported a figure of King Cotton, holding cotton bolls in one hand and the globe in the other.[61]

The Cotton Palace was really two events: an agricultural fair in which rural residents could participate and a flamboyant social affair for the elite of Waco. Many people who grew up in the radius of Waco attended the Cotton Palace. Myrtle Calvert Dodd came to the Cotton Palace annually: "Then's when I was a kid, say eight or nine years old. Then's when I'd run and play and eat sweet stuff. . . . My mother used to, too. We all come—spent the day. Every year."[62] As a young adult, Dodd watched the Cotton Palace social events, as the common folk were allowed in to view the local royalty in their velvet and ermine raiment. Bernice Weir attended occasionally as a young woman but not after her marriage: "Oh, I thought it was wonderful. . . . Of course, I had my boyfriends, and we took in all the rides and just wandered around and looked at everything. Of course, we had to eat a little bit along as we went, you know. . . . I would go—I'd be in Waco and stay with friends. I'd go up on the train and come back on the train, if they were not down here for me to go home with them."[63] Elizabeth Estes remembered the midway with its high Ferris wheel and "rolly-coaster": "I was terrified of both of them. The millstream was more my dish, a dark place where you floated down in a wooden boat and saw a little scene on the side occasionally."[64]

Others could not or did not attend the Cotton Palace. Alice Owens Caufield remembered as a child going to her Aunt Emma's house, which abutted the Cotton Palace grounds, and watching through the fence. She recalled: "We never went on the inside of that park, but when the Indians had their dance, we would always go to that crack and look in. And I learned how to do the Indian dance then." An African American, Caufield did not know why she never went inside the grounds but surmised that it was a matter of race rather than economics.[65] Fairs, which were ostensibly rural harvest celebrations, ironically drew rural people away from their farms to show them the wonders of town life.

Greater access to events such as county-seat markets, traveling entertainment, and centralized exhibitions profoundly changed the culture of the Blackland Prairie. One of the first victims of the shift was the community store, with its limited stock selection. Instead of buying at the store nearest their houses, country people began buying their goods in the county seat or other nearby population centers, where they could have more choices and sometimes pay lower prices. Myrtle Calvert Dodd watched how easy trips to Waco affected the little community of Hewitt in the mid-1920s: "It hurt that little store. Wasn't near as big—and the bank, too. The bank went out. See, they had a bank and a doctor's office. And it all went out before I graduated from high school. It all went out. It was all gone."[66] George Wehrwein found that by 1920 farmers in Travis County had begun bypassing visits to villages such as Manchaca, Elroy, and Creedmore, since they made twice as many trips to Austin, the county seat, instead. The farmers reportedly were finding the village "too small" to hold their interest.[67] As people's perspectives widened, their need for stimulation also increased.

The patterns of social interaction changed, also, as home visiting, neighborhood gatherings, and parties declined when families sought their fun outside their immediate communities. Ruth Allen observed that by the late 1920s "in community after community questions concerning the existence of social gatherings such as the 'singing' and the 'play party' were answered in the negative. The reason seems to be self-evident; the material of which such gatherings are made has gone from the country. Unmarried young people are not found in great numbers in the rural homes."[68] Not only were rural people spending more time in town, they were moving there to live in greatly increasing numbers. Pushed by the lack of economic opportunity in the country and pulled by the increased chances in town, people were packing up and moving away.

The residents of the Texas Blackland Prairie who moved to the cities did so for both personal reasons and causes related to national economic and political trends. Some families with children sought the superior educations that they believed town schools could offer.[69] Some people moved to town because of changes in their family situations. For example, Bernice Weir's mother-in-law went to the community of Moody when her son brought his new bride home, and Weir's parents relocated to Temple as they aged and her father was no longer able physically to farm.[70] Widowed and divorced women sometimes found themselves unable to make crops, even with the work of their children, and went to town to try other means of supporting themselves and their families.[71]

Young people formed the bulk of the immigrants to town.[72] The most important reasons that single young people moved to town undoubtedly were, on the negative side, the poverty engendered by cotton farming and, on a positive note, the optimistic hope that their lives would improve if they moved to town.

Young women came by the thousands to the cities because their families could not afford to feed and house any unmarried adult, even one as young as seventeen, who was capable of earning her own way. One farmer's daughter who had moved to Austin reported, "Daddy couldn't support me any longer. I had to work."[73] William Owens's brother, Monroe, and his wife, Mae, decided to quit their Lamar County tenant farm in the early 1920s, believing that they would fare better away from rural life: "When the crops were laid by, or when they were gathered, he wanted to move to town and get a job carpentering. Times were getting hard on the farm; a tenant farmer didn't have a chance, no matter how many hours a day he and his family worked. People were moving to town, working shorter hours, drawing better pay, sending their children to school instead of the cotton patch."[74] Monroe and Mae Owens were sure that people in town lived better than they did.

Alice Owens Caufield's family moved to Waco in 1921. More than seventy years later, she eloquently expressed her disdain for farm life and the life she had known as the daughter of a black sharecropper:

Everything was on a move. This is after World War I. Mobility—everybody was going where they could make a better living than what they'd already done. Folks were leaving the farm. Because they hadn't been prosperous. Everything had been going to the man who owned the farm. Like I'm saying, my dad went up back to the big house, the barn, where all the stock was. Like this German—he had mules and mules, you know, to plow the land—many teams, cows, and sheep. So the [tenant] farmers were going back up there taking care of those duties. Well, where's his income? And then if he rented land, say he's got forty acres he's got to take care of. Well, whatever percent commission that he was going to receive, and when the cotton is sold and do all the checking up, he's barely got enough money to buy winter clothes. Because this [landowning] farmer says, "Well, you know, during all the season I furnished you with so much money to survive on." So at the end of the year you don't have enough to do what you would like to do if you just farmed here. And a lot of the farmers—tenant farmers or whatever kind of farmer you want—whatever you were—I'm talking about those who lived on them big farms—they moved away. Now, a lot of black folks who owned their own farms, they didn't hurry away. Some of those old folks are still on their farms today. But their children went to the cities where they could—you see, they've always had schools in the communities, and these children would learn in school that they're not going to stay out on that farm. I said, "I wouldn't farm any more for nothing; I wouldn't." I still mean it. Because there was no—all hard work, no income to get what you'd like to have. Who wouldn't leave?[75]

Making a living seemed easier in the city, without the physical labor and monotony of farm life. J. B. Coltharp admitted that as a farm youth he saw other people's lives "through rose colored glasses," presuming that townspeople had easier times than he had. But he added that life on a cotton farm truly was difficult: "When you hoe goose grass from the cotton for hours and hours with the hot Texas sun beaming down, pick 400 pounds of cotton from dawn to dark, ride a plow pulled by 6 horses from sun to sun, gather corn by the wagon load, and then hand scoop it into the barn, when you do all these things or combinations of them for days and days and weeks and weeks, you can acquire supreme motivation to get away from what becomes detestable drudgery."[76]

In addition to the initiative of the young people, the U.S. government also encouraged rural-to-urban migration in the 1930s, as New Deal land policies spurred landlords to turn tenants off the land and World War II revolutionized the American economy and provided plentiful urban jobs. The effects of the Agricultural Adjustment Administration became noticeable immediately in the Blackland Prairie. Landowners, under the provisions of the AAA, often held back farmland for themselves, and many dismissed their tenants. Sometimes they refused to carry the tenants on credit any longer but hired them

TABLE 7. Change in Numbers of Tenants and Farm Owners in
Four Blacklands Counties, 1930 and 1940

Numbers of Tenants	1930	1940
Ellis	4,682	2,435
Hunt	4,238	2,765
McLennan	4,752	2,518
Williamson	3,461	2,385
Numbers of Owners	1930	1940
Ellis	1,100	1,111
Hunt	1,196	1,267
McLennan	1,514	1,540
Williamson	1,227	1,297

Sources: *Fifteenth Census of the U.S.*, 1930; *Sixteenth Census of the U.S.*, 1940.

instead as wage laborers. Between 1930 and 1940, the number of farm tenants in Ellis and McLennan Counties dropped by almost half, and in Hunt and Williamson Counties by more than one-third. The number of farm owners in these counties, conversely, remained stable and in some locations even rose slightly.[77] The overall rural population of the Blackland Prairie dropped during the decade by more than 13 percent, the greatest percentage of any area in Texas.[78] (See Table 7.) In addition, during the 1930s, an estimated twenty thousand Texas families were displaced by tractors from their cotton farms as capital-intensive agriculture arrived in the region, and a significant number of those lived on the Blackland Prairie.[79]

More optimistically, young people in particular viewed the city as the land of opportunity. With improved transportation and communications, rural people grew more and more sensitive to the disparities between their own lives and those of the city dwellers, who were enjoying unprecedented prosperity and buying power in the 1920s. Myrtle Calvert Dodd remembered her awareness of her tenant-farming family's poverty: "I didn't have things that I'd hear about. You know, I read the paper and read books, the [things] that they had. Of course, we all had the idea of going to town and having better things, and that's what most of us did."[80]

Popular culture, too, denigrated rural life. Dodd remembered stereotypical characters in her high school plays: "I remember Marvin Trice always had the old country boy part. . . . Well, you know, just like country people—they'd always talk real ignorant. And I remember he had an old floppy straw hat he wore. The scene opened one time with him sitting on a bale of hay and he was regretting certain things, you know, and he didn't—couldn't go to see his girl and I just don't remember how it all was, but I remember that. And they had two or three like that that he was in—different ones. . . . But he could really play that part: (mimicking) 'Paw, just so-and-so.' "[81] Rural people may have recognized the irony of rural schoolboys portraying "hicks," but the culture told them that country people were inferior unsophisticates. Many may have believed the message.

Life in the city simply had become more convenient, as town dwellers had easier access to labor-saving devices such as the electricity and running water that remained scarce in the Texas countryside until after World War II.[82] Many young people believed, furthermore, that life in town would hold more excitement for them. Madeline Jaffe, a University of Texas graduate student in sociology, in 1931 surveyed the unskilled labor of young women who had migrated from outlying areas into Austin. She found numerous young women in Austin who had come to the capital city to escape "the monotony of life on a farm." Many of these young women expressed hope that the town would be a better place to find a husband than the farm.[83] When Alice Owens Caufield moved to Waco for the first time as a fourteen-year-old, she loved the new opportunities for socializing: "Well, you know city life is different than what it is in the rural. You were closer to people and you'd talk with more people, and you became interested in other people and they became interested in your welfare."[84]

Older women who stayed behind in the country gloried in the supposed advancements of their younger relatives in town. Sociologist Ruth Allen found that mothers often encouraged their daughters to escape the farm: "While the 'old folks' do not wish to leave the farm, they take a distinct vicarious pleasure in the different lives which their children lead. Many women answered that they had no electric iron but 'the daughter in town uses one all the time.' " Allen reported that many farm women expressed pride that their daughters had found "relief from the drudgery of housework" and that their daughters had their own paychecks. She found that the older women had "a keen but rather questioning sympathy with [the younger women's] lack of desire to marry and settle down."[85] Bernice Bostick Weir, who married at age seventeen without finishing high school, "thought it was wonderful" that both of her daughters planned to have jobs. Bonnie Nell Bostick attended college away from home before dying in a traffic accident. June Bostick finished business school and worked for the Rural Electrification Administration.[86]

TABLE 8. Population Growth of Towns in Four
Blacklands Counties, 1900–1940

	1900	1910	1920	1930	1940
Ellis total population	50,059	53,629	55,700	53,936	47,733
Waxahachie	4,295	6,205	7,958	8,042	8,655
Ennis	4,919	5,669	7,224	7,069	7,087
Midlothian	832	868	1,298	1,168	1,027
Total urban population	10,046	12,742	16,480	16,279	16,769
Percent of population urban	20.0%	23.7%	29.5%	30.1%	35.1%
Hunt total population	47,295	48,116	50,350	49,016	48,793
Commerce	1,800	2,818	3,842	4,267	4,699
Greenville	6,860	8,850	12,384	12,407	13,995
Total urban population	8,660	11,668	16,226	16,674	18,694
Percent of population urban	18.3%	24.2%	32.2%	34.0%	38.3%
McLennan total population	59,772	73,250	82,921	98,682	101,898
Waco	20,686	26,425	38,500	52,848	55,982
Mart	300	2,939	3,105	2,853	2,856
McGregor	1,435	1,864	2,081	2,041	2,062
Total urban population	22,421	31,228	43,686	57,742	60,900
Percent of population urban	37.5%	37.6%	52.6%	58.5%	59.7%
Williamson total population	38,072	42,228	42,934	44,146	41,698
Taylor	4,211	5,314	5,965	7,463	7,875
Georgetown	2,790	3,096	2,871	3,583	3,682
Total urban population	7,001	8,410	8,836	11,046	11,557
Percent of population urban	18.3%	19.9%	20.5%	25.0%	27.7%

Source: *Texas Almanac* (1992–93).

Their mother did not lament the fact that her daughters' lives followed paths divergent from hers.

Some migrants moved to market centers in their home counties, and the populations of small towns throughout the region grew significantly between 1900 and 1940, as Table 8 demonstrates. Even more dramatically, the larger cities of Central Texas grew at astonishing rates throughout the first half of the twentieth century, fueled by rural immigrants. Austin's population almost

TABLE 9. Population Growth of Major Blacklands Cities, 1900–1940

	1900	1910	1920	1930	1940
Austin	22,258	29,860	34,876	53,120	87,930
Dallas	42,638	92,104	158,976	260,475	294,734
San Antonio	53,321	96,614	161,379	231,542	253,854
Waco	20,686	26,425	38,500	52,848	55,982

Source: *Texas Almanac* (1992–93).

quadrupled between 1900 and 1940, while that of Dallas increased sixfold, to almost 300,000 people. San Antonio jumped from 53,000 in 1900 to 253,000 in 1940.[87] The rural population dropped in absolute numbers as well as in percentages relative to the towns. By 1940 the Blackland Prairie was well into its transformation from a densely populated agricultural region into a depopulated farmland interrupted by several of Texas's largest cities.[88] (See Table 9).

Prior to World War II, minimally educated rural people who needed or wanted to move to town had various options available to them. Some found work in the region's slowly growing factories, for, like much of the rest of the South, the Blackland Prairie developed industries in the early twentieth century. The region's civic boosters attempted to catch onto the cotton-mill mania that erupted across the South, believing that textile mills would be a boon to the region, and they eagerly sought to have such facilities in their villages.[89] Between 1901 and 1910, at least fourteen Blacklands towns sprouted textile mills.[90] About half of the people who worked in the mills were women and girls.[91]

Cotton mills hardly proved to be the blessing that their promoters anticipated, and Texas farm people resisted the industrial imperative. By 1908, the manager of the Itasca Manufacturing Company, in Hill County, was complaining that "parties raised on the farm are hard to hold at the mill and those raised in the mills do not take to the farm." In West, McLennan County, all of the operatives at the Brazos Valley Cotton Mill were fired after a 1907 strike.[92] An ill-fated cotton mill in Celeste, Hunt County, cost $60,000 in 1901, when its poorly informed managers bought outdated, overpriced equipment. Storms twice blew down parts of the mill, and finally, a Mr. Carver of Farmersville bought the Celeste mill building for $10,000 and built barns out of the material.[93]

The Waxahachie Cotton Mill, in Ellis County, lasted longer than many others, surviving into the 1930s. An unnamed former operative recalled his days in the mill as less than desirable: "Myself, like most of the other employees, were from small farms and badly in need of a way to make a living. Conditions were bad. Pay was poor. A man with a family just lived from one small payday to another. Cotton Mill Village, as many of the local residents called it, was a cluster of small houses, two and three rooms at most. Rent was deducted from your pay each week. Actually 'cotton millers' were held in low esteem by most Waxahachie residents. I was real glad when the thing finally went broke."[94]

Not only did cotton mills fail to provide desirable employment for Texans, they also misfired as users of the local cotton crop. Despite the wild expectations of developers, Texas cotton mills never used more than 3 percent of the state's annual cotton harvest, and the fabrics manufactured were usually "low grade" ducks and coarse osnaburgs. Texans grew intimately acquainted with the colonial practice of shipping the cotton out to have its value added elsewhere and, ironically, having to buy cloth made of cotton.[95] Clearly, textile mills provided little opportunity for rural people wanting to leave the farm.

Another option that brought some chances to male Blacklands residents came in the oil patch, but many who took this path had to travel hundreds of miles from home to take advantage of the cycles of boom and bust that appeared in several parts of Texas in the first half of the century. A few areas of the Blackland Prairie enjoyed significant oil deposits, most notably the Corsicana Oil Field in Navarro County, developed in 1894; the Mexia Oil Field, Limestone County, which spouted in 1921; and the Luling Oil Field, Caldwell County, discovered in 1922.[96] But oil production in the Blackland Prairie paled in comparison to that of the rich East Texas fields and those farther west, and many of those seeking their fortunes in the oil patch left the region entirely. Rural women followed their men who left in search of employment. For example, Gertie Carroll, the daughter of an Ellis County landowner, married an electrician, and they struck out westward for the oil fields at Breckenridge, Stephens County, in the early 1920s. Her brother, Dovie Carroll, and his wife, Etta Carroll, joined them in 1923 with the intention of Dovie's working as an electrician's helper. When Dovie developed appendicitis shortly after their arrival, however, he returned home to Ellis County and farming.[97] Ten years later, Lee Rice helped his sister, Ruth, move south to Conroe, Montgomery County, where her husband, Raymond, was working on an oil lease, the 250-

mile trip from Greenville to Conroe taking twelve hours in Ruth's Chevrolet pulling a trailer.[98] Farm people of the Blackland Prairie could not stay close to home and take advantage of these fleeting opportunities.

With most oil fields and new refinery facilities far away, the oil that instead held the most sway in the Blackland Prairie was cottonseed oil. Towns across the Blackland Prairie supported innumerable cotton gins, cotton compresses, and cottonseed oil mills, which provided seasonal off-farm employment for men.[99] Young women moving to town might find work in manufacturing, such as the textile mills or the few factories such as the Taylor Bedding Company, which made mattresses from Williamson County cotton. In larger cities, the chances for unskilled work varied widely and included a growing array of service industries. Madeline Jaffe determined that young white women could find employment in the state capital, with its 1930 population of 53,120, in various places: state institutions and agencies, the telephone exchange, local mercantile establishments, chain variety stores, laundries, hotels and cafes, beauty parlors, canning factories, or binderies. Black women could get jobs only in laundries, domestic service, and sometimes in hotels as "scrub women or chamber maids," while Mexican women could gain employment in a canning factory, domestic service, laundries, and occasionally as seamstresses in mercantile establishments. The supply of countrywomen seeking work became so great that the local telephone service began requiring each applicant to have a high school diploma and a year of residence in Austin.[100] In McLennan County, farm women also found unskilled jobs in Waco, with its population of 52,848. In the 1930s, four young women from Tours rode into Waco together each day, one employed as a babysitter and housekeeper, one working at a local furniture store, and two employed in a sewing factory.[101]

Ironically, many immigrants to the city continued to earn significant parts of their income from working seasonally as cotton choppers and especially as pickers. The Langham family moved to Waco in 1928 so that the father could pursue his calling as an African Methodist Episcopal minister. The family existed on what the father's congregation could give and the meager wages that their mother earned as a laundress. Both parents and their seven children worked each fall picking cotton. Maggie Langham Washington recalled that both the lien holder on their house and the neighborhood grocer "carried" the family from harvest to harvest, when the family could pay off its accumulated debt with their cash wages: "If we made under a hundred dollars a week during the fall, that was a bad week. So that money was used to catch up so much on the house notes and pay Mr. Gilliam, the groceryman."[102] Despite their urbanization, the Langhams and thousands of others needed to supplement their incomes through traditional rural means.

Each family member who left the farm could tell of the wonders of urban life and smooth the ways for those who came after them, as the Sharpless sisters did. Increasing the possibilities for others who wished to follow, those who came back to the farm on visits would "broaden the horizon of the group and open vistas of things" that could be had.[103] Once a family member left home, she often developed into a different person, shedding her old rural appearance and taking on new urban values. According to novelist William Humphrey, living in town even made urban people physically dissimilar to their rural relatives. He likened the urbanization process to "evolution in action," commenting that rural grandparents "presented a picture of wild flowers, more like weeds than flowers, stubborn, tenacious, tough," compared to their city-bred grandchildren, "a domesticated seedling of the same species, shade-grown and delicate."[104] The changes might be positive or negative, but surely families living on the farm noticed the differences in their young, newly urbanized members.

Many families formed a chain migration, where one member would smooth the way for others. Gladys Everett remembered two sisters who displeased their father by joining the Baptist church. " 'Daddy will make us leave home but with Jesus our Savior, we can bear it,' she said. . . . They told their parents what they had done and the next morning while the parents were caring for the cows and chickens they took their bundle of clothes and left home. They couldn't take the father's wrath." The sisters caught a ride to Temple, where their sister lived, and found jobs. Having a sister in an urban area provided the young women with a means of escaping their harsh father.[105]

Lillian Alford's brother persuaded her to join his family in Dallas in 1927, when she was nineteen: "My oldest brother was in Dallas. And he called and he said he wanted me to come up to Dallas. He said, 'I want you to come up here,' and said, 'get you a job and go to work.' And he said, 'I would just love for you to come.' I took a few of my clothes. And I thought, 'I'll only stay a week or so and then I'll come back.' And I went up there and I never did go back—only to visit." As in many other families, Alford's sister-in-law assisted her in finding employment in the growing service economy, which badly needed abundant labor: "His wife worked there. It was a huge cleaning plant. They put me to work without anything. I didn't know one end from the other. But I walked in and it didn't take me long." Alford quickly made her specialty of blocking hand-knit sweaters, which were "all the rage." A rural immigrant could make her way by learning to serve urban fads.[106]

Preparations for World War II brought even further change to rural Texas, as war-related employment drew away many people who had remained on the farm throughout the Great Depression. In the Blackland Prairie, as elsewhere, people headed for jobs in lucrative wartime industries as the direct effects of the "national defense program" became apparent as early as June 1940.[107] Bernice Weir commented on the dispersal of the residents of the Liberty Hill community as the war came on: "The two houses that was on the Bostick land, they're both gone. Pat's sister moved to Waco, and of course his brother and his wife moved to Moody, you see, and done away with their house. . . . You see, when the war came on, up here at McGregor, there was—they called it the Bluebonnet Ordnance, and that's where they were making explosive things and bombs and everything. And they were trying to get in closer to their work and all. Quit farming and went—because that was a monthly income."[108]

Increasing urbanization significantly decreased population in some rural areas, affecting rural social institutions. School consolidations began in the 1920s, ostensibly not because of falling enrollments but because of the opportunities afforded by larger schools newly accessible by improved roads.[109] In 1925, the Texas legislature passed a law enabling county boards of education to annex contiguous school districts without their consent and providing for the closures of any schools in which attendance fell below twenty students. As a result of these new laws, throughout Texas small schools folded into larger, more distant ones.[110]

Predictably, school consolidation in the Blacklands, as elsewhere, met with mixed reactions. School reformers zealously promoted consolidation as the solution to all problems in rural education, while rural people and educators resisted the loss of local autonomy and the inconvenience of sending children long distances on buses.[111] Longtime Hunt County schoolteacher Lucille Turley believed that rural schools in one's own community were better than consolidated schools: "Because you understand the situation. The people have their own interests on their own levels, their own friends, and their own businesses. When you pull them away, it's just like throwing them out into space without any particular interest."[112] Bernice Bostick Weir recalled the shock of the consolidation of the Liberty Hill school, where her son had just begun first grade in 1926: "I guess we didn't realize the meaning of it." Reflecting back more than sixty-five years, Weir called consolidation "a blessing in disguise, because after the children got out of the seventh grade up here, you see, it was kind of hard for them to go to school in other places. And by being consolidated and the school running the bus, why, then they could go until they graduated in the same school." Weir concluded that the children received more instruction in consolidated schools: "He had a longer lesson period of time over there, and there wasn't as many in the room and the teachers had more time to put in with their children than they did up here."[113] Despite the benefits of consolidated schools, rural communities lost much of their identity when they lost their schools.

In the 1920s, rural churches in Texas faced a great challenge as the automobile made possible members' attendance at any churches they chose, not merely those they could reach easily. Contemporary pastors disagreed over the effects of the automobile on church attendance. Some said that it distracted their congregations, while others said that it made attendance easier. Many wrung their hands over a perceived decline of the rural church.[114] A rural Roman Catholic priest told Ruth Allen that local people were still attending church faithfully in the late 1920s, but that church was playing a smaller role in their lives. He fretted that his parishioners were "spending their substance on gasoline and pleasures which would be unattainable without a car."[115]

If Texas church records can be trusted, however, the ministers' fears were unfounded, at least in the short term. In Hunt County, for example, membership in Southern Baptist churches, whose followers accounted for one-fifth of the county's population, rose by one-third between 1924 and 1944, and the number of rural churches in Hunt County increased from thirty-eight to forty-two even as the county's population declined slightly. While many Baptist churches declined and ceased to exist during that period, others sprang up with remarkable facility. Too, the gains made by Baptists may have been at the expense of other churches, for, as a Methodist pastor in Bell County told anthropologist Oscar Lewis, "the Baptists are spreading like Johnson grass."[116] But the members stayed faithful in other rural Protestant churches. Despite the departure of people from the land, the rural church as a social institution remained strong throughout the Great Depression.[117]

By World War II, however, numerous small churches were experiencing severe losses of members. In the late 1930s, Gladys Everett's husband served as pastor for two small Southern Baptist churches that were feeling the effects of urbanization, as were many others. The Valley View Church, in southern McLennan County, had a small membership "due to aging farmers having to turn their farming over to men, with heavy machinery, who lived in town." And in Perry, Falls County, "the school had been consolidated and many young families had moved away. Many of the older people were unable to attend any longer so the church suffered greatly."[118] The withering of the churches represented a decline in the most important institution of the countryside.

Urbanization also brought great changes to the social lives of rural communities. As seen above, improved roads spurred many farm folk to seek their pleasures in town rather than among each other. Ruth Allen observed that community amusements were dying out as young people left. Allen found one community with only two young women and three boys, and by expanding her survey found only three more unmarried young women.[119]

The feelings of rural people leaving the farm varied widely. Myrtle Calvert Dodd and her sister, Lillian, attended Southwest Texas State Teachers College in San Marcos. Lillian sorrowfully left behind a boyfriend in their village of Hewitt, and her older sister observed, "It was good she did." Dodd believed that Lillian's marriage to a Houston oilman was far better than a liaison with a McLennan County farm boy. Dodd's parents eventually left farming and moved to Waco, and Dodd remembered her mother's excitement: "When they bought their home over on Reuter and moved to town . . . she was thrilled. She was just ready to move to town. . . . She had a cousin just a few blocks from her that was real close, and they visited and she could walk to the little store and do things like that that was good for her."[120] After more than thirty years as a tenant farmer's wife, Hester Calvert welcomed city life.

Others who left for the city fared poorly. In his memoirs, William Owens recalled many examples of rural people's struggles in the cold, impersonal world that was Dallas in the 1920s. Working in a warehouse, Owens lived in a four-room house with his cousin, who was employed in a dress factory, her husband, who was engaged as a policeman, and their two boarders, who were laundresses. He described his housemates as "country people in town, working at the jobs they could get, living from payday to payday with no hope of anything better." They depended on each other, friends and relatives from Lamar County. Later, working for the Salvation Army, Owens met a couple from Navarro County who were almost starving in Dallas. Without a trade, the husband found, he could earn but little, and he longed to return to the country. Owens reported the husband's frustration: "'Dang it,' he said, 'I cain't make a living in town. It's hand to mouth all the time, and they ain't nobody around here any better off, after no telling how many years of trying it. If I'd a knowed what it is like before I come, they couldn't a drug me here. They can say what they like against the country, but it's good enough for me.' "[121] This urban immigrant, at least, thought that he would be better off returning to rural life.

African American women found that city life often had its own peculiar problems. Many found employment only as domestic servants. Alice Owens Caufield, herself a former domestic worker, remembered the religious faith that sustained many of the black women working for white families:

> Everybody went to church because we all have struggled working here in the city. There were so many women who worked in what we called servant. You know, the old-style houses in Waco always had the big house and then they have a servant room. Well, those women who came out of those serving rooms were just like fire, they were so full of the spirit. We're speaking of believing in Christ and leaning on Christ with the strength that you've got to have to do that day's work out there for them white folk. Women who had struggled. And a lot of the women who wasn't in the serving room who lived, maybe, in rented homes or—some of them had homes, but they got these children to raise, and they got to go out there and work for Miss Ann and take everybody's foolishness, and the white woman might disapprove. And what happens, they take it 'cause they've got to feed those young ones; they've got to survive whatever way. So we have carried the weight of disapproval and whatever you were told to do on your shoulders because you must work. I'm talking about women, you see. Women had to work.[122]

The harsh reality of rural life gave way to the harsh reality of city life.

Sometimes the glamour of the city shone only briefly, and country people sang about the dangers of city life. Dallas, with its thriving nightlife, proved to be both attractive and bewildering. African American immigrants to the city altered the lyrics of the blues song, "The Midnight Special," to reflect the jeopardy of the city:

> If you ever go to Dallas
> You better do right;
> You better not gamble
> And you better not fight.[123]

Another favorite song, "Deep Ellum Blues," depicted the false glitter of Dallas's famous district of nightclubs and bars:

> When you go down on Deep Ellum
> Keep your money in your pants
> Cause the women in Deep Ellum
> They don't give a man a chance
> Oh, sweet mama, daddy's got them Deep Ellum Blues
> Oh, sweet mama, daddy's got them Deep Ellum Blues
>
> When you go down on Deep Ellum
> Keep your money in your shoes
> Cause the women in Deep Ellum
> Got them Deep Ellum blues
> Oh, sweet mama, daddy's got them Deep Ellum Blues
> Oh, sweet mama, daddy's got them Deep Ellum Blues.[124]

A country boy in Deep Ellum might easily be parted from his money, resulting in the Deep Ellum blues. Women might have the Deep Ellum blues for a variety of reasons, among which might be the fear of the country girl swayed by the confusing big city.

In moving from the farm to the city, the change came most easily for the young, who were free and flexible and often unsentimental about the land that they left. For many older women, the adjustment to the city proved difficult. Bernice Bostick Weir's parents moved to Temple in 1922, their children already having left the family land. Weir speculated that her mother found it "right smart of an adjustment . . . because she didn't have her cows and chickens and turkeys and things like that. But they were both getting up in years, you see, and I guess it was the best for them."[125] Many older parents followed their children to the city, wanting to be close to them in their old age. Sophie Dulock's husband divided their farmland among their four children, and the parents moved to Waco to be near their daughters, who were nurses at the local Roman Catholic hospital. Sophie Dulock missed her relatives and friends terribly, keenly regretted the move, and died within three years after moving to Waco.[126]

After separating from her third husband, William Owens's mother took hard her adjustment to Paris, the county seat of Lamar County. Her son wrote: "My mother arrived in Paris not long after her forty-fifth birthday, a country woman, shy, afraid to raise her voice, afraid of not being able to get used to town ways. She worried that she was overweight and that all her clothes were homemade and looked country." She went infrequently to church, spoke only when spoken to, and kept clear of her town neighbors, afraid that she would "be laughed at for the kind of clothes she had to hang on the line." In Paris, according to Owens, his mother "was like herself again only when my grandmother or Aunt Niece came from Novice for a visit, when there were hours of quiet talk of old times in the country, of quiet complaint about the do-nothing life she had in town, not even a garden or chickens to take up her time or help out."[127] After all of the Owens children moved to Dallas, their mother followed them there, and that adjustment proved even more daunting for her: "She was glad to have us together and to do for us, but she kept longing to go back to Pin Hook. She scoured the floors and cooked, read the Bible and the *Daily Times-Herald*, but she rarely left the house, either to talk with neighbor women or to go to the corner grocery." Increasingly, Owens's mother withdrew into her own house, afraid of the city and all of its unknown elements.[128] She resented being shut up in three rooms without crops or livestock for which to care, longing to return to her productive ways as a farm woman.

Adjusting to life in the city proved more difficult for some rural people than others. Despite the problems, most who moved to the cities stayed there, and others continued to follow them. Before 1930, the migration had been gradual but steady. After 1930, the numbers of farm people leaving their rural homes rose abruptly and continued to climb throughout the 1940s. In the twentieth century, as Pete Daniel has articulated well, a three-hundred-year-old rural tradition abruptly crumbled under the impetus of depression, war, federal agricultural policy, and technological change.[129]

For many residents of the Texas Blackland Prairie, the New Deal and World War II brought to a close a way of life that had dealt poverty and despair to many who suffered under the iniquities of the crop-lien system. Yet the old ways had not been without their satisfactions. Wresting a living from the rich black clay soil had challenged many farmers, working by the rhythms of nature rather than those of a factory whistle. Williamson County native Charles Hairston, writing in 1948, commented that many of his neighbors never wanted to see cotton again. For others, however, the white staple still held a sentimental attraction: "For most of us in Williamson, feeling for the fleecy stuff is one with our feeling for the women who bore us and the men who brought home the victuals and their daddies and mothers before them. It's as one with the smell of the 'fresh-broke' dirt behind the planter opener with the fuzzy seeds kicking out in sight and just a second before the covering shovels gently fold them with exactly three inches of good Williamson dirt."[130]

For Blacklands women, the end of small cotton farms meant dramatic changes after years of drudgery, of toting water and chopping kindling while city women turned faucets and flipped switches to achieve the same ends. For some, moving to town meant that they could concentrate on keeping house exclusively without also having to work in the fields. Others continued to put in double shifts, working outside the home for wages and also doing house-work. For many women, urbanization ended their days as the primary pro-viders of food for their families, as they entered the world of the American consumer and bought rather than grew their families' foodstuffs. Women who stayed on the farm became less integral to the overall farming process, as many withdrew from the fields with increased mechanization. They, too, took on consuming rather than producing roles.

Few former farm people wax nostalgic about the old days. No one misses the near-starvation, the shacks, the rags that sometimes passed for clothing. Etta and Dovie Carroll finally moved into Waxahachie following World War II, after more than thirty years of tenant farming. Realizing the need for financial security, Etta Carroll took a job in a sewing factory. She understood intellec-tually the advantages of town life: "Farming, you don't make—when you're in town and you have a job, you know what you're going to make and you know what you can spend. And when you're living on a farm, you're working and thinking you're going to make—it's just a gamble. And it's just easier if a person can live in town and has a good job." But Etta Carroll remains a country-woman at heart. She recalled with satisfaction her years as a farmwife: "We worked hard, but we were used to it. And it didn't seem like—that you were putting in more time—and I guess you were. And I think that back in those days we were just as happy with our lives then as we are now.... I'd just as soon live in the country.... You had more freedom in the country. You could get up and do what you wanted to do. And when you're in town, you do what the other person wants you to do."[131] Etta Carroll chooses not to remember the harsh imperatives of the owners whose land they tilled. For seventy years, she has strived to put a pleasant face on her family's rural work. But she also realizes that city life brings benefits as well as losses. When the people of the Texas Blackland Prairie shook the dark mud off their feet and headed to Waco, Dallas, Austin, and points beyond, they left behind a way of life that had challenged them, body and spirit, virtually every day. So daunting were these challenges that few mourn their passing.

notes

Preface

1. Weir interview number 1, Institute for Oral History, Baylor University, Waco, Tex. (hereafter IOH).

2. Grundy, "Alabama Landmarks," 6.

3. Dillow and Carver, *Mrs. Blackwell's Heart-of-Texas Cookbook*, xix.

4. Aptheker, *Tapestries of Life*, 44.

5. Marks, "Context of Personal Narratives," 39.

6. Broughton, "Women's Autobiography," 77.

7. Smith, "Autobiographical Manifesto," 192.

8. For a discussion of the importance of privately published autobiographies, see Healey, "Privately Published Autobiographies by Texans," 497–510.

9. Spacks, "Selves in Hiding," 112.

10. Ibid.

11. Billson and Smith, "Lillian Hellman and the Strategy of the 'Other,'" 163.

12. Other historians have also used oral history to document the lives of rural women. See *The Oral History Review* 17, no. 2 (Fall 1989), a special issue entitled "Oral History and Rural Women in the United States," edited by Nancy Grey Osterud with the assistance of Lu Ann Jones.

13. Sommer, "'Not Just a Personal Story,'" 111.

14. Some of the most provocative discussions on this subject appear in Gluck and Patai, *Women's Words*.

15. For an example of this loose structure, see Osterud, "Land, Identity, and Agency," 75.

16. Hampsten, "Considering More than a Single Reader," 130.

17. Marks, "Context of Personal Narratives," 40.

18. For excellent discussions on the role of the researcher as interpreter of the spoken word, see Borland, "'That's Not What I Said,'" 63–76, and Lawless, "'I Was Afraid Someone Like You,'" 302–14.

19. Marks, "Context of Personal Narratives," 40.

20. Pittenger, "World of Difference," 47.

21. Shostak, "'What the Wind Won't Take Away,'" 239.

22. Bateson, *Composing a Life*, 181, 213.

23. Aptheker, *Tapestries of Life*, 44.

24. Mercier, "Women's Role in Montana Agriculture," 51.

25. Flynt, *Poor but Proud*, ix.

26. Steedman, *Landscape for a Good Woman*, 107.

27. Kniffen, "On Corner-Timbering," 1, quoted in Toelken, "Folklore and Reality."

28. Brooks, *Maud Martha*, 2.

Introduction

1. Lula Kathryn Peacock Jones, *Recollections*, 4–5.

2. Gray, *History of Agriculture*, 77.

3. White, *Ar'n't I a Woman?* 66–67, 120–21; Ramey, "From Seamstress to Field Hand."

4. McCurry, *Masters of Small Worlds*, 62, 72, 74, 78, 79, 80, 81–82.

5. Jacqueline Jones, *Labor of Love, Labor of Sorrow*, 79; Saville, *Work of Reconstruction*, 130–31, 133–34, 140.

6. Within the Blackland Prairie, I have chosen four counties out of a possible thirty to examine statistically. These four counties range over a distance of 200 miles, and none of them borders on any of the other three. The northernmost, Hunt County, is 100 percent Blacklands soil. Culturally, it is the most homogeneous and, in the 1990s, most rural of the four counties. It lies fifty miles northeast of Dallas and thirty miles south of the Texas-Oklahoma border. Approximately fifty miles south of Hunt County, just below Dallas, Ellis County is also entirely within the Blackland Prairie. In the early twentieth century, Ellis County was primarily the home of black and Anglo-American Texans, although numerous Czech immigrants and their descendants made their homes near Ennis, in the eastern part of the county. For most of the early twentieth century, Ellis County was the most productive of all Texas counties in cotton output. McLennan County, eighty miles south of Ellis County and near the center of the Blacklands, differed from the other three counties because of its significant urban population. The McLennan County seat, Waco, had a population of 38,500 in 1925, and Waco's economy depended heavily on cotton production and related industries, such as compressing and shipping. The nearness to an urban center created significant differences between McLennan County rural women's experiences and those of their comparatively more isolated counterparts in other counties. McLennan County also contrasted with the other counties because it encompassed the northernmost part of the Brazos River Valley, which offered a different version of the cotton culture with its bottomland plantations. Because the Brazos Valley forms a different physiographic and cultural region from the prairies, its farms were not included in this investigation. Another sixty miles south, and one hundred miles north of where the Blacklands taper to an end near San Antonio, is Williamson County. With the Blackland Prairie growing more and more narrow in its southern reaches, Williamson County lies half in the Blacklands and half in the less productive Grand Prairie. So rich were the Williamson County Blacklands soils, however—and so heavily concentrated in cotton—that the county raised as much cotton in 1925 as most other Texas counties whose soils were entirely in the Blackland Prairie. Williamson County was by far the most ethnically diverse of the four counties before World War II, with significant German, Czech, and Mexican immigrant communities in addition to Anglo-American and relatively small African American populations. This study considers only the Blacklands half of the county. The

position of each county within the Blackland Prairie made differences in the local cultures, but overall economic and cultural patterns prevailed throughout the region, making it possible for one to make general statements about the Blacklands with some surety.

7. Gabbard and Rea, *Cotton Production in Texas*, 5; *Texas Almanac* (1925), 222; Bennett, Burke, and Lounsbury, *Soil Survey of Ellis County*, 8; Morgan, *Fieldcrops for the Cotton-Belt*, 76–77.

8. Jensen, *Loosening the Bonds*; Jensen, *Promise to the Land*; Fink, *Open Country, Iowa*; Deutsch, *No Separate Refuge*; Fink, *Agrarian Women*; Glenda Riley, *Female Frontier*; Osterud, *Bonds of Community*; Neth, *Preserving the Family Farm*.

9. Strong-Boag, "Pulling in Double Harness," 32–52.

10. Matthews and Dart, *Welfare of Children*, 47.

11. Elbert, "Women and Farming," 245, 251; Adams, "Resistance to 'Modernity,'" 89. Excellent studies of poor urban women's endeavors on behalf on their families are Bradbury, *Working Families*, and Ross, *Love and Toil*.

12. Agee and Evans, *Let Us Now Praise Famous Men*.

13. Sanders, *Farm Ownership and Tenancy*, 5.

14. Ibid., 4.

15. Kirby, *Rural Worlds Lost*, 140.

16. Peteet, *Farming Credit in Texas*, 51, 62; Locke, *Action on Bullhide Creek*, 63; Templin and Marshall, *Soil Survey of Hunt County*, 8; Cauley, "Agricultural Land Tenure in Texas," 140.

17. Fuller, "Occupations of the Mexican-Born Population of Texas," 140.

18. Sanders, *Farm Ownership and Tenancy*, 48–49.

19. Crenshaw, *Texas Blackland Heritage*, 47; Rampy, *Choice and Chance*, 12, 15.

20. Sanders, *Farm Ownership and Tenancy*, 49; Motheral, *Types of Farm Tenancy in Texas*, 25.

21. Lee Rice, telephone conversation with author, 23 October 1992.

22. Rice, "Some Highlights in the Life of Lee Rice, Part 1," Rice Papers, Archives, James Gee Library, Texas A&M University, Commerce (hereafter Archives, Gee Library).

23. Bateson, *Composing a Life*, 231.

24. Sanders, *Farm Ownership and Tenancy*, 12; Peteet, *Farming Credit in Texas*, 58.

25. For a concise account of the dangers to the tenants, see Johnson, Embree, and Alexander, *Collapse of Cotton Tenancy*, 6–33.

26. Hunt County, Texas, tax rolls, 1900 and 1910. I am deeply indebted to Kyle Wilkison for sharing his samples and statistics with me. See Wilkison, "End of Independence."

27. Locke, *Action on Bullhide Creek*, 5–6.

28. Wehrwein, "Social Life in Southern Travis County," 504.

29. Leonard, "Economic Aspects of the Tenant Problem," 121.

30. Sanders, *Farm Ownership and Tenancy*, 44.

31. Lula Kathryn Peacock Jones, *Recollections*, 66–67.

32. Newcomb, *Indians of Texas*, 133, 135, 140, 247, 253–56; Wallace and Hoebel, *Comanche*, 287; Moore and Shafer, *Archeological Test Excavations at 41WM21 in Granger Reservoir*, 9, 13.

33. Amsbury, "Spanish and French Nonsettlement of the Blacklands," 128–29; Chipman, *Spanish Texas*, 147–56.

34. Jordan, "Imprint of the Upper and Lower South," 677; Jordan, "Population Origins in Texas, 1850," 87, 91.

35. Newcomb, *Indians of Texas*, 354; Neighbours, "Indian Exodus," 80–97.

36. Newcomb, *Indians of Texas*, 344–47, 350–51, 360–62; Calvert and De León, *History of Texas*, 108.

37. Campbell and Lowe, *Wealth and Power in Antebellum Texas*, 141. In Ellis County, 1,104 slaves were 21.1 percent of the total population of 5,230; in Hunt, 577 slaves out of a total population of 6,630, for 8.7 percent; McLennan, 38.66 percent with a slave population of 2,395 out of a total of 3,799; and in Williamson, 891 slaves were 19.6 percent of the total population, 4,529. Only McLennan County had any "free colored," with nine freedpeople. See U.S. Department of the Interior, *Population of the United States*, 473, 475, 477, 479, 481, 483.

38. Figures for Blackland slaveholding are compiled from Campbell, *Empire for Slavery*, 264–66. It is not possible to break out figures for black/white population ratios for only the Blackland Prairie sections of the counties in the study.

39. Kerr, "Migration into Texas," 189, 190, 193.

40. *Texas Almanac* (1928), 63–64; Matthews and Dart, *Welfare of Children*, 3.

41. Machann and Mendl, *Krásná Amerika*, 19.

42. Ibid., 19–20.

43. Sparkman, *Souvenir of Historic Ellis County*, [6]; Machann and Mendl, *Krásná Amerika*, 20; Jordan, *Texas*, 86.

44. Almanza interview number 2, IOH.

45. Reisler, *By the Sweat of Their Brow*, 5, 14–16.

46. *Texas Almanac* (1928), 63–64.

47. Calvert and De León, *History of Texas*, 245.

48. Bateson, *Composing a Life*, 13.

49. Jehlen, "Archimedes and the Paradox of Feminist Criticism," 581–82.

Chapter One

1. Fox-Genovese, "Between Individualism and Community," 36.

2. Simcik, *Oral Memoirs*, 17, The Texas Collection, Baylor University, Waco, Tex. (hereafter Texas Collection).

3. Caufield interview number 4, IOH.

4. Locke, *Action on Bullhide Creek*, 92, 104–5.

5. Owens, *Season of Weathering*, 241–45.

6. Owens, *Texas Folk Songs*, 211, 297.

7. Ibid., 218–19.

8. Bourne, *Pioneer Farmer's Daughter*, 188–89.

9. Osterud, *Bonds of Community*, 94–95.

10. Perkins interview, 2–3, Archives, Gee Library.

11. Locke, *Action on Bullhide Creek*, 114.

12. Weir interview number 1, IOH.

13. Rothman, *Hands and Hearts*, 294. See also Scharff, *Taking the Wheel*, 138–41.

14. Dodd interview number 3, IOH.

15. Simcik, *Oral Memoirs*, 30, Texas Collection.

16. Machann and Mendl, *Krásná Amerika*, 145.

17. Weir interview number 3, IOH; Locke, *Action on Bullhide Creek*, 99, 124.

18. Locke, *Action on Bullhide Creek*, 123.

19. Dodd interview number 2, IOH.

20. Caufield interview number 3, IOH.

21. Crenshaw, *Texas Blackland Heritage*, 77.

22. Locke, *Action on Bullhide Creek*, 125.

23. Crenshaw, *Texas Blackland Heritage*, 11, 13.

24. Simcik, *Oral Memoirs*, 82, Texas Collection.

25. Locke, *Action on Bullhide Creek*, 58.

26. James Conrad, "Grisly Tales Part of Yesterday's Headlines," *Commerce Journal*, 22 June 1988.

27. Barr, *Black Texans*, 136.

28. For a detailed analysis of the Washington lynching, see SoRelle, " 'The Waco Horror,' " 517–36.

29. R. W. Williams, "Backward Glances," *Wolfe City Sun*, 22 January 1951.

30. Carroll interview number 1, IOH.

31. Bourne, *Pioneer Farmer's Daughter*, 180.

32. Wehrwein, "Social Life in Southern Travis County," 498.

33. Almanza interview number 1, IOH.

34. Personal conversation with Inez Adams Walker, 23 October 1992.

35. Stimpson, *My Remembers*, 36–38. The University of North Texas Press has chosen to retain Stimpson's original spelling and prose.

36. Willis interview, IOH.

37. R. W. Williams, "Backward Glances," *Wolfe City Sun*, 4 June 1948.

38. Owens, *Texas Folk Songs*, 144–45.

39. Lula Kathryn Peacock Jones, *Recollections*, 64.

40. Bourne, *Pioneer Farmer's Daughter*, 216; McRae interview, 19, Archives, Gee Library; Clara Jones, *Pillars of Faith*, [95]; Dodd interview number 4, IOH.

41. Carroll interview number 1, IOH.

42. Weir interview number 2, IOH.

43. Numerous wedding photographs appear in Jupe, *History of Tours*.

44. Jupe, *History of Tours*, 442–43, 444, 699, 711; Machann and Mendl, *Krásná Amerika*, 147, 162.

45. Pazdral, "Czech Folklore in Texas," 33.

46. Folklorist William Owens recorded near Rosebud, Falls County, a song entitled "Zasovu," or "A Song Sung at a Wedding," with similar gender roles, in which the groom sings to the new wife: "Yesterday you were Mother's, but today you are my wife" (Owens, *Tell Me a Story*, 213–15).

47. Stimpson, *My Remembers*, 38–39.

48. Locke, *Action on Bullhide Creek*, 114.

49. Jupe, *History of Tours*, 443, 598–99.

50. Jurney and Moir, *Historic Buildings*, 205–6; Spain, *Gendered Spaces*, 22.

51. Ischy interview number 2, A. Frank Smith Jr. Library Center, Southwestern University, Georgetown, Tex.

52. Locke, *Action on Bullhide Creek*, 61; Rampy, *Choice and Chance*, 4; Dodd interview number 1, IOH. It is not possible to estimate the number of young men living independently of their parents.

53. Lula Kathryn Peacock Jones, *Recollections*, 4–5.

54. Weir interviews 1 and 2, IOH.

55. Information on the Bostick family genealogy is from McGinnes and Potter, *They Found the Blacklands*, 36.

56. Jupe, *History of Tours*, 480–81.

57. Ibid., 732.

58. Carroll interview number 2, IOH.

59. For an overview of the anthropological literature on rural women, isolation, and autonomy, see White, "Female Slaves," 63–64.

60. Clara Jones, *Pillars of Faith*, 13.

61. Folley interview number 1, IOH.

62. Carroll interview number 2, IOH.

63. Fink, *Agrarian Women*, 9, 10.

64. Sachs, "Women's Work in the U.S.," 131–39, quoted in Elbert, "Farmer Takes a Wife," 174.

65. Jensen, " 'I've Worked, I'm Not Afraid of Work,' " 231–32.

66. The legacy of Latin American patriarchy also affected the lower Blacklands. Rosalinda Gonzalez declares that families from Mexico brought "feudal patriarchal attitudes" with them, "perpetuated by such mechanisms as the family labor contract, the family wage paid to the male head of the family for the agricultural labor of women, and the isolation of Mexican peon families in labor camps. . . . Thus monopoly capitalism, in practice, not only fostered sexism but encouraged the retention of feudal patriarchal attitudes in Mexican communities in the United States" (Gonzalez, "Chicanas and Mexican Immigrant Families," 72).

67. Joan Cashin finds that in the Old Southwest, men almost always decided to migrate without consulting their wives (Cashin, *Family Venture*, 44–49).

68. Vaughan, *Cotton Renter's Son*, 142.

69. Jameson, "Women as Workers," 149–54.

70. Locke, *Action on Bullhide Creek*, 2, 147, 149.

71. Dodd interviews 1 and 4, IOH.

72. Weir interview number 3, IOH.

73. Weir interview number 2, IOH.

74. Carroll interview number 6, IOH.

75. Machann and Mendl, *Krásná Amerika*, 76–78.

76. Pitcock, "Voices of Experience."

77. Weir interview number 2, IOH.

78. Cloud, "Farm Women and the Structural Transformation of Agriculture," 292; James Tull Richardson, "Social Changes in Hunt County," 30.

79. Leonard, "Economic Aspects of the Tenant Problem," 114.

80. Allen, *Labor of Women*, 31–32; Jerome Kearby Bentley, *Spring and Autumn*, 29. The counties designated as "lower Blackland" in Ruth Allen's study are Bastrop, Caldwell, Travis, and Williamson. Allen's study also included Burnet County, which lies to the west of the Balcones Escarpment and is not on the Blackland Prairie. Allen considered the inclusion of Burnet County to be a mistake in her research design. Its physiography differed significantly from the other counties; it had a substantially smaller population than its neighbors to the east and had fewer than 500 Mexican or African American residents. Allen's total sample of

664 Anglo women included only "about 50" from Burnet County (7.5 percent), while her total sample of 293 Mexican women included 10 from Burnet County (3.4 percent) (Allen, *Labor of Women*, 22).

81. D'Emilio and Friedman, *Intimate Matters*, 173–74.

82. May, *Barren in the Promised Land*, 63. Statistics from specific parts of the Blackland Prairie are congruent with the overall averages for the region. In the late 1920s, white women in the lower Blacklands had an average of 3.69 living children, while African American women averaged 4.8 and Mexican women 4.35. While most women had five children or fewer, almost 3 percent of the white women, more than 14 percent of the African American women, and more than 4 percent of the Mexican women had eleven or more children. Tenancy status as well as ethnicity apparently had an impact on family size. The average number of children in lower Blacklands tenant-farming families was slightly larger than that of landowners, white landowners having an average 3.27 children and tenants an average of 3.74. In Ellis County, tenant families had an average of 6 living children per family. As late as 1940, white tenant families statewide had an average of 3.96 children, and black families had 3.76 (Allen, *Labor of Women*, 68, 177, 213; Leonard, "Economic Aspects of the Tenant Problem," 113–14; Brophy, "Black Texan," 74).

Contemporary observers had little difficulty correlating tenancy with greater numbers of children. William Leonard observed in 1921, "The relation of the size of the family to the tenant problem is a very intimate one. For it is quite universally the opinion that landlords prefer large families on their farms." He contrasted the income of two families, one with small children and one with older ones, to demonstrate the importance of children as labor (Leonard, "Economic Aspects of the Tenant Problem," 114).

83. Crenshaw, *Texas Blackland Heritage*, 18.

84. Ibid., 78.

85. Weir interview number 2, IOH.

86. Folley interview number 3, IOH.

87. Dillow and Carver, *Mrs. Blackwell's Heart-of-Texas Cookbook*, xxii.

88. Navarro interview number 2, IOH. For a discussion of lack of information for young women in the early twentieth century, see D'Emilio and Freedman, *Intimate Matters*, 176–77.

89. Graham, *No Name on the Bullet*, 5.

90. Dodd interview number 1, IOH.

91. Hazel Beauton Riley, *Washing on the Line*, 1.

92. Estes, *Oral Memoirs*, 38, Texas Collection.

93. Bateson, *Composing a Life*, 164.

94. James Tull Richardson, "Social Changes in Hunt County," 21; Allen, *Labor of Women*, 177.

95. Folley interview number 3, IOH.

96. Texas kept no mortality statistics until the 1930s, but across the United States maternal mortality gradually declined from 26.7 deaths per 100,000 population in 1900 to 12.8 deaths per 100,000 in 1930 and 6.7 in 1940 (U.S. Department of Commerce and Labor, Bureau of the Census, *Mortality Statistics, 1900 to 1904*, lxx; and U.S. Department of Commerce, Bureau of the Census, *Mortality Statistics, 1910*, 21; *Mortality Statistics, 1920*, 17; *Mortality Statistics, 1930*, 13; and *Vital Statistics of the United States, 1940*, 390, 469).

97. Weir interview number 2, IOH.

98. Dodd interview number 2, IOH.

99. Gibbons, *Child Labor among the Cotton Growers of Texas*, 51; Allen, *Labor of Women*, 64–65.

100. Personal conversation with Inez Adams Walker, 30 October 1992.

101. Allen, *Labor of Women*, 66, 178, 214; Stimpson, *My Remembers*, 5.

102. Folley interview number 3, IOH.

103. Jupe, *History of Tours*, 626.

104. Almanza interview number 2, IOH.

105. Hazel Beauton Riley, *Washing on the Line*, 2.

106. Allen, *Labor of Women*, 178.

107. Barnes, *Oral Memoirs*, 12, Texas Collection.

108. Westbrook, *Oral Memoirs*, 35, Texas Collection.

109. Carroll interview number 2, IOH.

110. Rampy, *Choice and Chance*, 7.

111. Weir interview number 2, IOH.

112. Allen, *Labor of Women*, 65, 141, 188, 198–99.

113. Garnett, *Some Socially Significant Rural Conditions*, 9.

114. *Semi-Weekly Farm News*, 8 February 1910, 7.

115. Ibid., 15 March 1910, 7.

116. Weir interview number 4, IOH.

117. Carroll interviews 4 and 5, IOH.

118. Weir interview number 1, IOH.

119. Crenshaw, *Texas Blackland Heritage*, 83.

120. Weir interview number 2, IOH.

121. Dodd interview number 1, IOH.

122. Dillow and Carver, *Mrs. Blackwell's Heart-of-Texas Cookbook*, xvii.

123. Dodd interview number 2, IOH; Rice, "Recollections of Other Highlights in My Life," Rice Papers, Archives, Gee Library.

124. Stimpson, *My Remembers*, 66–67.

125. Weir interview number 2, IOH.

126. Sowell, *Girl Named Laura*, 44; Dodd interview number 1, IOH.

127. Dillow and Carver, *Mrs. Blackwell's Heart-of-Texas Cookbook*, 14.

128. Carroll interviews 4 and 5, IOH.

129. Stimpson, *My Remembers*, 32–33; Caufield interviews 1 and 6, IOH.

130. Collins, "Shifting the Center," 55–56, and Shaw, "Mothering under Slavery in the Antebellum South," 253.

131. Personal conversation with Inez Adams Walker, 28 October 1992.

132. Dodd interview number 3 and Carroll interview number 4, IOH; Locke, *Action on Bullhide Creek*, 180; Sowell, *Girl Named Laura*, 45; Caufield interview number 4, IOH; Campbell, "Country Life in Mooreville Texas," Texas Collection.

133. Dodd interview number 3, IOH.

134. Locke, *Action on Bullhide Creek*, 179; Dodd interview number 3 and Weir interview number 2, IOH; Sowell, *Girl Named Laura*, 45; Stimpson, *My Remembers*, 56.

135. Bourne, *Pioneer Farmer's Daughter*, 169; Carroll interview number 4, IOH; R. W. Williams, "Backward Glances," *Wolfe City Sun*, 18 March 1949.

136. Dorothy Scarborough, *Can't Get a Red Bird*, 59; Joseph Abner Hill, *Autobiographical*

Notes, 6; Jerome Kearby Bentley, *Spring and Autumn*, 21; Norma Miller Langford, "Daughter of Early Settlers Recalls Life in Quinlan," *Tawakoni News*, 4 July 1991, 17; Campbell, "Country Life in Mooreville Texas," 5, Texas Collection.

137. Hurtado interview number 2, IOH; Stimpson, *My Remembers*, 57.

138. Folley interview number 3, Weir interview number 2, and Carroll interview number 4, IOH; Jupe, *History of Tours*, 804; Sowell, *Girl Named Laura*, 45; Locke, *Action on Bullhide Creek*, 42; Almanza interview number 2, IOH; Stimpson, *My Remembers*, 55.

139. Caufield interview number 4 and Dodd interview number 3, IOH.

140. Locke, *Action on Bullhide Creek*, 177.

141. Lula Kathryn Peacock Jones, *Recollections*, 44.

142. Graham, *No Name on the Bullet*, 8–10.

143. Jurney and Moir, *Historic Buildings*, 205–6.

144. Bourne, *Pioneer Farmer's Daughter*, 35.

145. Carroll interviews 1 and 2, IOH.

146. Allen, *Labor of Women*, 37.

147. Weir interview number 1, IOH.

148. Jupe, *History of Tours*, 693.

149. Allen, *Labor of Women*, 178–79, 214–15.

150. Hardeman interview, 3, Archives, Gee Library.

151. Carroll interview number 1, IOH.

152. McKay, "Race, Gender, and Cultural Context," 185.

153. Dodd interview number 1, IOH.

154. Clara Jones, *Pillars of Faith*, [12, 13]. See also Jupe, *History of Tours*, 565, 608, 676, 748, 763, 781, 804; Humphrey, *Ordways*, 103, 108–9.

155. Jupe, *History of Tours*, 748. See also Dodd interview number 2, IOH.

156. Dodd interview number 2, IOH.

157. Allen, *Labor of Women*, 174, 210–11.

158. Jupe, *History of Tours*, 619, 631, 760.

159. Allen, *Labor of Women*, 39, 175, 209.

160. Gibbons, *Child Labor among the Cotton Growers of Texas*, 18; Wilkison, "End of Independence," 85.

161. Folley interviews 1 and 3, IOH.

162. James Conrad, "Lone Oak Woman Showed Unique Courage," *Commerce Journal*, 11 March 1987. For a description of bluejohn, see Dillow and Carver, *Mrs. Blackwell's Heart-of-Texas Cookbook*, 56.

163. Personal conversation with Inez Adams Walker, 23 October 1992.

164. "The Madison Maxwell Taylor Monroe Clan," C. G. Butler, Hunt County History Vertical File, Archives, Gee Library.

165. Everett, *Among the Salt*, 91–92.

166. Crenshaw, *Texas Blackland Heritage*, 48.

167. Stimpson, *My Remembers*, 21, 55, 128–29, 131, 134.

168. James Conrad, "Turn-Of-Century Headlines Full Of Mayhem," *Greenville Herald-Banner*, 22 January 1991.

169. *Gunn v. Gunn*, Bell County District Court, October 1919, and *Texas v. Gunn* (no. 9460), Bell County District Court, February 1921, Gunn Family Papers, Texas Collection.

170. Ibid.

171. *Gunn v. Gunn*, Bell County District Court, October 1920, Gunn Family Papers, Texas Collection.

172. Garnett, *Some Socially Significant Rural Conditions*, 13.

173. Allen, *Labor of Women*, 38, 174, 211–12.

174. Jupe, *History of Tours*, 546.

175. Weir interview number 1, IOH.

176. Dodd interview number 4, IOH.

177. Carroll interview number 6, IOH.

178. Carroll interview number 7, IOH.

179. Jupe, *History of Tours*, 482, 624, 629, 756.

180. Graham, *No Name on the Bullet*, 6, 18, 19.

181. Jupe, *History of Tours*, 734.

182. Podsednik interview, 11, Texas Collection.

183. Malone, *Oral Memoirs*, 3, Texas Collection.

184. Jupe, *History of Tours*, 779.

185. Ibid., 729.

186. Carroll interview number 4, IOH; Lula Kathryn Peacock Jones, *Recollections*, 10–11.

187. Burnett interview, 30, Archives, Gee Library.

188. Britton, "Notes on the Authors and the Stories," 327. Britton's story, "Infections," is loosely based on her great-grandmother's torment (see *Common Bonds*, 222–27).

189. Dodd interview number 4, IOH.

190. Ibid.

191. Crenshaw, *Texas Blackland Heritage*, 17–19.

192. Burnett interview, 35, 26–27, Archives, Gee Library.

Chapter Two

1. Lomax and Lomax, *Negro Folk Songs as Sung by Lead Belly*, 184–87.

2. Grier, *Culture and Comfort*, 3–5.

3. Most of the farmhouses in the Blackland Prairie were built before 1900. Twentieth-century families would have had little of the autonomy or creative experience designing their own houses described by Sally McMurry in *Families and Farmhouses*. See Moir and Jurney, *Pioneer Settlers*, 75, 80, 83, 89, 95, 100, 101, 102, 105, 106, 107, 113, 118, 121, 123, 126, 130, 132, 133, 139, 142, 144, 146, and Jurney, Lebo, and Green, *Historic Farming*, 44, 63, 73, 97, 101, 129, 147, 153, 160, 176, 189.

4. Jacqueline Jones, *Labor of Love, Labor of Sorrow*, 12.

5. A Blackland Prairie farmhouse fits the description of a "gendered space" described by Daphne Spain. While women might enter into the work of the farm, the men almost never participated in any form of housework. By segregating women into a separate work space, Spain argues, men deprive women of necessary knowledge of the world outside the home. See Spain, *Gendered Spaces*, 3.

6. For a discussion of expectations of cleanliness, see Hoy, *Chasing Dirt*, especially chs. 5 and 6.

7. Dodd interview number 2, IOH.

8. Stimpson, *My Remembers*, 150.

9. Jordan, *Texas*, 185–87.

10. Jurney and Moir, *Historic Buildings*, 45–46. Blackland Prairie houses were much smaller than those found in the North and West by Florence Ward in 1920; in her sample, the average farmhouse had seven rooms (Ward, "Farm Woman's Problems," 441).

11. Jurney and Moir, *Historic Buildings*, 7, 11, 12, 18; Jurney, Lebo, and Green, *Historic Farming*, 227.

12. Caufield interview number 2, IOH.

13. Weir interview number 1, IOH; Jurney and Moir, *Historic Buildings*, 148.

14. Jurney and Moir, *Historic Buildings*, 13–17, 45. In 1920, social workers in Hill County found that 27 percent of the white families in their survey lived in houses with single walls, "rough, unpainted, upright boards with weather strips over the cracks" (Matthews and Dart, *Welfare of Children*, 38).

15. Matthews and Dart, *Welfare of Children*, 38; Locke, *Action on Bullhide Creek*, 168.

16. The average value of a sharecropper's house in the Blackland Prairie was $532, compared with $731 for a share tenant's and $1,532 for an owner-operator's (Sanders, *Farm Ownership and Tenancy*, 50).

17. Templin and Marshall, *Soil Survey of Hunt County*, 8. For a general discussion, see Wehrwein, "Housing Conditions among Tenant Farmers," 41–45.

18. Gordon, "Negro in McLennan County," 73.

19. Cotton, *History of Negroes of Limestone County*, 32.

20. *Studies in Farm Tenancy in Texas*, 101.

21. Stimpson, *My Remembers*, 28.

22. Lula Kathryn Peacock Jones, *Recollections*, 65–66.

23. Hatch, *Oral Memoirs*, 17; Westbrook, *Oral Memoirs*, 26; McLennan County tax records, 1909, Texas Collection.

24. Estes, *Oral Memoirs*, 11, Texas Collection.

25. Weir interview number 4, IOH.

26. Stimpson, *My Remembers*, 24–25.

27. Allen, *Labor of Women*, 179–80, 216–17. See also Crenshaw, *Texas Blackland Heritage*, 47.

28. Jurney and Moir, *Historic Buildings*, 20. Of thirty-two farmsteads investigated at the Richland site, six were always occupied by landowners; six were first occupied by landowners and then by tenants; seventeen were always tenant-occupied; and three were always occupied by day laborers (Moir and Jurney, *Pioneer Settlers*, 174).

29. Handman, "Economic Reasons for the Coming of the Mexican Immigrant," 606–7; Peteet, *Farming Credit in Texas*, 55; Warner, *Oral Memoirs*, 32, Texas Collection.

30. James Tull Richardson, "Social Changes in Hunt County," 29.

31. Moir and Jurney, *Pioneer Settlers*, 176; Carroll interview number 2, IOH.

32. Matthews and Dart, *Welfare of Children*, 38; Dodd interview number 2, IOH.

33. Weir interview number 2, IOH.

34. Almanza interview number 1, IOH.

35. Dodd interview number 2, IOH.

36. James Conrad, "Mrs. Tucker Remembers Life before Conveniences," *Commerce Journal*, 24 June 1987.

37. Navarro interview number 1, IOH.

38. Carroll interview number 2, IOH.

39. Jurney and Moir, *Historic Buildings*, 47.

40. Locke, *Action on Bullhide Creek*, 12–13.

41. Matthews and Dart, *Welfare of Children*, 38, 40–41.

42. Dodd interview number 1, IOH.

43. Hurtado interview number 1, IOH.

44. Campbell, "Country Life in Mooreville Texas," Texas Collection; Locke, *Action on Bullhide Creek*, 178; Weir interview number 4, IOH.

45. Carroll interview number 2, IOH.

46. Matthews and Dart, *Welfare of Children*, 66. They conclude that the average number of people in migrant households was nine. Half of families were living in houses with one or two rooms. Fifteen out of thirty-five Anglo families had only one sleeping room, and only eight had three or four sleeping rooms. African American families tended to be larger, with smaller quarters. Half of the Anglo families and 70 percent of the black migrant families were living with three or more persons per room. See also Menefee, *Mexican Migrant Workers*, 33–34.

47. Weir interview number 2, IOH; Locke, *Action on Bullhide Creek*, 63–64.

48. Crenshaw, *Texas Blackland Heritage*, 15.

49. Hurtado interview number 1, IOH.

50. Rice, "Memories of Mama Rice" and "Some Highlights in the Life of Lee Rice, Part 1," Rice Papers, Archives, Gee Library.

51. Locke, *Action on Bullhide Creek*, 178.

52. Weir interview number 4, IOH.

53. Dodd interview number 3, IOH.

54. Washington, *Oral Memoirs*, 25, Texas Collection.

55. Jurney and Moir, *Historic Buildings*, 20; Bourne, *Pioneer Farmer's Daughter*, 157; Weir interview number 4, IOH.

56. Directions for making several versions of homemade whitewash are found in the Conner Papers, folder 134, Texas Collection.

57. Fordyce Sims, unpublished memoirs on file at Old City Park, Dallas, quoted in Jurney, Lebo, and Green, *Historic Farming*, 28.

58. Allen, *Labor of Women*, 238.

59. Crenshaw, *Texas Blackland Heritage*, 49.

60. Grier, *Culture and Comfort*, 15.

61. Jupe, *History of Tours*, 601, 734.

62. Weir interview number 4, IOH.

63. Folley interview number 2, IOH.

64. Caufield interview number 2, IOH.

65. Locke, *Action on Bullhide Creek*, 58; Caufield interview number 2, Almanza interview number 1, and Hurtado interview number 1, IOH.

66. Weir interview number 2, IOH.

67. Campbell, "Country Life in Mooreville Texas," Texas Collection.

68. Dodd interview number 1, IOH.

69. McBride, *"Filosofer" of "Kukel-bur" Flat*, 78, 81–82.

70. Weir interview number 2, IOH.

71. Jupe, *History of Tours*, 804.

72. Weir interview number 4 and Carroll interview number 1, IOH; Lula Kathryn Peacock Jones, *Recollections*, 58, 68.

73. Bourne, *Pioneer Farmer's Daughter*, 178.

74. Dodd interview number 2, IOH.

75. Carroll interview number 3, IOH.

76. Caufield interview number 2, IOH.

77. Rice, "Memories of Mama Rice," 3, Rice Papers, Archives, Gee Library.

78. Bourne, *Pioneer Farmer's Daughter*, 66–68; Joseph Abner Hill, *Autobiographical Notes*, 33.

79. Carroll interview number 3, IOH.

80. Everett, *Among the Salt*, 28.

81. Letha Jumper, "Little Money in Pockets Helps Everyone," *Tawakoni News*, 6 September 1990, 3.

82. Weir interview number 4, IOH.

83. Dodd interview number 2, IOH.

84. Jurney and Moir, *Historic Buildings*, 97, 99, 105, 111.

85. Dodd interview number 2 and Hurtado interview number 1, IOH.

86. Matthews and Dart, *Welfare of Children*, 66.

87. Templin and Marshall, *Soil Survey of Hunt County*, 8.

88. McBride, *"Filosofer" of "Kukel-bur" Flat*, 147–48.

89. Dodd interview number 1, IOH.

90. Jurney and Moir, *Historic Buildings*, 73; Carroll interviews 2 and 1, IOH.

91. Almanza interview number 1, IOH; Allen, *Labor of Women*, 181, 217.

92. Stimpson, *My Remembers*, 89.

93. Gordon, "Negro in McLennan County," 73; Matthews and Dart, *Welfare of Children*, 39, 66.

94. Humphrey, *Farther Off from Heaven*, 56.

95. Carroll interview number 1, IOH.

96. Dodd interviews 2 and 1, IOH.

97. James Conrad, "Hunt Countians Used Many Means to Battle Bugs, Flies," *Commerce Journal*, 15 June 1988.

98. Caufield interview number 2, IOH.

99. Everett, *Among the Salt*, 22.

100. Locke, *Action on Bullhide Creek*, 120.

101. Stimpson, *My Remembers*, 29.

102. Jurney and Moir, *Historic Buildings*, 17.

103. Jupe, *History of Tours*, 567.

104. Simcik, *Oral Memoirs*, 51, Texas Collection.

105. Sadie Hatfield, *Conservation and Landscaping the Rural Home*, in Conner Papers, folder 125, Texas Collection.

106. Stimpson, *My Remembers*, 30.

107. Weir interview number 4, IOH.

108. Locke, *Action on Bullhide Creek*, 59, 63–64; Matthews and Dart, *Welfare of Children*, 66.

109. Moir and Jurney, *Pioneer Settlers*, 176.

110. Jurney, Lebo, and Green, *Historic Farming*, 357.

111. Weir interview number 2, IOH.

112. Dodd interview number 3, IOH.

113. Allen, *Labor of Women*, 45, 178, 275. These percentages far exceed the national average; ten years earlier, only 79 percent of farm women nationwide had used kerosene lamps. See Ward, *Home Demonstration Work*, 15.

114. Clark, *Quick History of Boyce*, 22.

115. Rice, "Making Hay on the Paul Mathews Meadow at Floyd (and nine other stories)," Rice Papers, Archives, Gee Library.

116. McRae interview, 29, Archives, Gee Library.

117. Dodd interview number 2, IOH.

118. Weir interview number 2, IOH.

119. Bolton, *Electricity in the Country Home*, 18.

120. Garnett, *Some Socially Significant Rural Conditions*, 13; Matthews and Dart, *Welfare of Children*, 38; Waggoner, *Electricity on Texas Farms*, 12, 14.

121. Rice, "Making Hay," 3, Archives, Gee Library.

122. Flowers, "Impact of the New Deal on Hunt County, Texas," 28–29.

123. Lewis, *On the Edge of the Black Waxy*, 30; Brophy, "Black Texan," 75.

124. Major floods occurred in the Blacklands in June 1899, December 1913, April 1915, and September 1921 (*Texas Almanac* [1988–89], 110).

125. Only one oral history interviewee, Ray Summers, recalls having springs as a source of water. Two tenant farms on which he lived in Collin County had spring water (Summers, *Oral Memoirs*, 18, Texas Collection).

126. Bedichek, *Adventures with a Texas Naturalist*, xiii.

127. See Rogers, " 'I Am Tired Writing,' " 186–87, for an account of the scarcity of water by Hugh Harmon McElvy, who emigrated from the East to Collin County about 1870.

128. Matthews and Dart, *Welfare of Children*, 42.

129. Leonard and Naugle, "Recent Increase in Tenancy," 21.

130. Caufield interview number 2, IOH.

131. Moir and Jurney, *Pioneer Settlers*, 176; Matthews and Dart, *Welfare of Children*, 38, 66; Gordon, "Negro in McLennan County," 73.

132. Matthews and Dart, *Welfare of Children*, 43; Cohen, *Rural Water Supply*, 3, 5.

133. M. R. Bentley, *Waterworks for Texas Homes*, 2.

134. Folley interview number 1, IOH.

135. Matthews and Dart, *Welfare of Children*, 38.

136. Jurney, Lebo, and Green, *Historic Farming*, 221–22; Jurney and Moir, *Historic Buildings*, 235–36; Matthews and Dart, *Welfare of Children*, 39.

137. Locke, *Action on Bullhide Creek*, 15.

138. Matthews and Dart, *Welfare of Children*, 43.

139. Rampy, *Choice and Chance*, 5; Weir interview number 1, IOH. See also Simcik, *Oral Memoirs*, 25, Texas Collection.

140. James Conrad, "Keeping Water Plentiful Was Part of the Chores," *Greenville Herald-Banner*, 25 January 1987, A-10.

141. Locke, *Action on Bullhide Creek*, 177.

142. Conrad, "Keeping Water Plentiful."

143. Templin and Marshall, *Soil Survey of Hunt County*, 2.

144. Jurney and Moir, *Historic Buildings*, 27; Weir interview number 1, IOH.

145. Locke, *Action on Bullhide Creek*, 177.

146. Folley interview number 1, IOH.

147. *Report by the Commission on Industrial Relations*, 9032; Conrad, "Keeping Water Plentiful"; Rice, "Some Highlights in the Life of Lee Rice, Part 2," Rice Papers, Archives, Gee Library.

148. Locke, *Action on Bullhide Creek*, 73; Templin and Marshall, *Soil Survey of Hunt County*, 2.

149. Jupe, *History of Tours*, 801.

150. Allen, *Labor of Women*, 218–19; Matthews and Dart, *Welfare of Children*, 66.

151. Dodd interview number 1, IOH.

152. Weir interview number 4, IOH.

153. Brophy, "Black Texan," 75. Again, Texas compares unfavorably to the national average, for 32 percent of farm families nationwide had running water just after World War I (Ward, *Home Demonstration Work*, 15).

154. Cohen, *Rural Water Supply*, 2.

155. For a poignant look at the efforts of African American extension workers to bring sanitation standards to their clients, see Conner speeches "Household Arts" (n.d.) and "My Experience as an Extension Worker" (1925), in Conner Papers, folder 132, Texas Collection.

156. Locke, *Action on Bullhide Creek*, 178.

157. Matthews and Dart, *Welfare of Children*, 41, 66; Gordon, "Negro in McLennan County," 73.

158. Cohen, *Rural Water Supply*, 4.

159. Jurney, Lebo, and Green, *Historic Farming*, 221–22; Jurney and Moir, *Historic Buildings*, 235–36.

160. Weir interview number 1, IOH.

161. Jurney, Lebo, and Green, *Historic Farming*, 357; Jurney and Moir, *Historic Buildings*, 203.

162. Jurney and Moir, *Historic Buildings*, 203.

163. Weir interview number 4, IOH.

164. Lewis, *On the Edge of the Black Waxy*, 30.

165. McGee, "Hog Killing Day," 8.

166. Brophy, "Black Texan," 75.

167. Weir interviews 1 and 2, IOH; Locke, *Action on Bullhide Creek*, 178.

168. "Recollections of Geneva Kahlish," in Jupe, *History of Tours*, 445.

169. Dodd interview number 1, IOH.

170. Folley interview number 2, IOH.

171. Dodd interview number 1, IOH.

172. Caufield interview number 3, IOH; *Waco Daily Times-Herald*, 4 October 1915, 5; 1 April 1917, 9.

173. McGee, "Hog Killing Day," 10.

174. McBride, *"Filosofer" of "Kukel-bur" Flat*, 158.

175. Weir interview number 2, IOH.

176. Dodd interview number 1, IOH.

177. Locke, *Action on Bullhide Creek*, 40; Rice, "Railroad Days Remembered," *Greenville Herald-Banner*, 18 April 1988; Rice, "Memories of Mama Rice," Rice Papers, Archives, Gee Library; Carroll interview number 2, IOH.

178. Dodd interview number 1, IOH.

179. Weir interview number 3, IOH.

180. Personal conversation with Inez Adams Walker, 23 October 1992; Hurtado interview number 1, IOH.

181. Matthews and Dart, *Welfare of Children*, 46, 64.

182. Personal conversation with Inez Adams Walker, 23 October 1992; Weir interview number 2, IOH.

183. Rice, "Memories of Mama Rice," Rice Papers, Archives, Gee Library.

184. Dodd interview number 1, IOH; Allen, *Labor of Women*, 183.

185. Kramarae, "Talk of Sewing Circles and Sweatshops," 150, 153–54.

186. Simcik, *Oral Memoirs*, 71, Texas Collection.

187. Weir interview number 2, IOH; Crenshaw, *Texas Blackland Heritage*, 48.

188. *Report by the Commission on Industrial Relations*, 9041.

189. McRae interview, 15, Archives, Gee Library; Dawson, *Oral Memoirs*, 3, Texas Collection; McBride, *"Filosofer" of "Kukel-bur" Flat*, 158.

190. Matthews and Dart, *Welfare of Children*, 6.

191. Locke, *Action on Bullhide Creek*, 99; Weir interview number 2, IOH.

192. Simcik, *Oral Memoirs*, 77, Texas Collection.

193. Dodd interview number 3, IOH.

194. Folley interview number 1, IOH.

195. Carroll interview number 2, Dodd interview number 3, and Weir interview number 1, IOH; Campbell, "Country Life in Mooreville Texas," Texas Collection.

196. *Waco Daily Times-Herald*, 3 October 1915, 3.

197. Folley interview number 1, IOH.

198. Matthews and Dart, *Welfare of Children*, 31.

199. Personal conversation with Inez Adams Walker, 28 October 1992.

200. Ruth Allen reported that two-thirds of the Anglo women whom she interviewed had made at least one quilt in the last year. Ten percent of those reporting had made six or more quilts in the last year, and almost one-half had made four or more. Fewer than 10 percent of Mexican women, on the other hand, had made even one quilt the previous year (Allen, *Labor of Women*, 87).

201. Yabsley, *Texas Quilts, Texas Women*, 44–45.

202. Carroll interview number 2, IOH.

203. Dodd interview number 1, IOH.

204. Dodd interview number 3, IOH.

205. Bresenhan and Puentes, *Lone Stars*, 18.

206. Yabsley, *Texas Quilts, Texas Women*, 59.

207. Carroll interview number 2, IOH.

208. Bourne, *Pioneer Farmer's Daughter*, 144.

209. Caufield interview number 6, IOH.

210. Weir interview number 2, IOH.

211. Ibid.

212. Hurtado interview number 1, IOH.

213. Jupe, *History of Tours*, 721.

214. Bresenhan and Puentes, *Lone Stars*, 130.

215. Carroll interview number 2, IOH.

216. Weir interview number 1, IOH.

217. Jupe, *History of Tours*, 584, 723.

218. Almanza interview number 2, IOH.

219. Dodd interview number 1, IOH.

220. Lula Kathryn Peacock Jones, *Recollections*, 24; McBride, *"Filosofer" of "Kukel-bur" Flat*, 164–65.

221. According to Allen, 60 percent of Anglo families made soap, while less than 4 percent of Mexican families did (Allen, *Labor of Women*, 87, 220).

222. Caufield interview number 3, IOH.

223. Ibid.; Bourne, *Pioneer Farmer's Daughter*, 70; Crenshaw, *Texas Blackland Heritage*, 35; Carroll interview number 3, IOH.

224. Hurtado interview number 1, IOH; Simcik, *Oral Memoirs*, 69–70, Texas Collection; McGee, "Hog Killing Day," 11.

225. Almanza interview number 1, IOH.

226. Bourne, *Pioneer Farmer's Daughter*, 179; Humphrey, *Ordways*, 122.

227. McRae interview, 16, Archives, Gee Library; Bourne, *Pioneer Farmer's Daughter*, 166.

228. Norma Miller Langford, "Daughter of Early Settlers Recalls Life in Quinlan," *Tawakoni News*, 4 July 1991, 17.

229. Bourne, *Pioneer Farmer's Daughter*, 165; McRae interview, 16, Archives, Gee Library; Weir interview number 2, IOH.

230. Stimpson, *My Remembers*, 46.

231. Weir interview number 2, IOH.

232. Rice, "Recollection of Other Highlights in My Life," Rice Papers, Archives, Gee Library.

233. Stimpson, *My Remembers*, 44.

234. Hurtado interview number 1, IOH; Locke, *Action on Bullhide Creek*, 67; Allen, *Labor of Women*, 218.

235. Summers, *Oral Memoirs*, 48, Texas Collection.

236. Dodd interviews 2 and 1, IOH.

237. Caufield interview number 3, IOH.

238. Allen, *Labor of Women*, 46.

239. Westbrook, *Oral Memoirs*, 32, Texas Collection.

240. Weir interviews 1, 2, and 3.

241. Allen, *Labor of Women*, 45, 182; Matthews and Dart, *Welfare of Children*, 46; Carroll interview number 4, IOH; Jupe, *History of Tours*, 709; Weir interview number 3, IOH.

242. Jurney, Lebo, and Green, *Historic Farming*, 356.

243. Rice, "True Memories," Rice Papers, Archives, Gee Library.

244. Jurney and Moir, *Historic Buildings*, 203; Jurney, Lebo, and Green, *Historic Farming*, 356; McRae interview, 16, Archives, Gee Library.

245. James Conrad, "Doing Laundry Likely Not Part of the Good Old Days," *Greenville Herald-Banner*, 24 February 1991, A5.

246. Carroll interview number 4, IOH.

247. Folley interview number 2, IOH.

248. According to Ruth Allen, 63 percent of Anglo women, 97 percent of African American women, and 85 percent of Mexican women used flatirons in 1930. The relatively low number of Mexican women using flatirons is explained by the fact that 12 percent of them had no ironing equipment at all (Allen, *Labor of Women*, 45, 182, 218).

249. Dodd interview number 3, IOH; Bourne, *Pioneer Farmer's Daughter*, 179; Humphrey, *Ordways*, 122.

250. Caskey, *One Hundred and Twenty Years in Florence, Texas*, 27.

251. Mrs. Nat P. Jackson, "June 30, 1917, Annual Report," Texas Agricultural Extension Service Papers, Box 2, file 32, Archives, Sterling C. Evans Library, Texas A&M University, College Station (hereafter Archives, Evans Library).

252. Weir interview number 3 and Carroll interview number 4, IOH; Allen, *Labor of Women*, 44. Weir was more fastidious than many wives. Mary Ann Collier Campbell specifically recalled that her family did not iron clothes worn to the field (Campbell, "Country Life in Mooreville Texas," Texas Collection).

Chapter Three

1. Dillow and Carver, *Mrs. Blackwell's Heart-of-Texas Cookbook*, xiv; Dillow and Carver's italics.

2. Taylor, *Eating, Drinking, and Visiting in the South*; Hilliard, *Hog Meat and Hoe Cake*.

3. Farb and Armelagos, *Consuming Passions*, 97. Anthropologists stress the efficacy of studying food as a means of understanding a regional culture. See, for example, Brown and Mussell, "Introduction," 5–9, and Farb and Armelagos, *Consuming Passions*, 1–7. Former University of Texas at Austin folklorist Roger Abrahams, however, observes that "there has been little systematic work done on Southern culinary practices, black or white" (Abrahams, "Equal Opportunity Eating," 33–34).

4. For a discussion of women's psychological and anthropological identification with food, see Kaplan, "Introduction: Beauty and the Feast," 13.

5. Dillow and Carver, *Mrs. Blackwell's Heart-of-Texas Cookbook*, xvi.

6. Dawson, *Oral Memoirs*, 3, Texas Collection.

7. Taylor, *Eating, Drinking, and Visiting in the South*, 4, 10; Hilliard, *Hog Meat and Hoe Cake*, 8, 95.

8. See, for example, Bradbury, *Working Families*, 90–92, and Ross, *Love and Toil*, 27–55.

9. Leonard and Naugle, "Recent Increase in Tenancy," 21. According to home economist Jessie Whitacre, the diets of wage laborers were inferior even to those of renters. See Whitacre, *Food Supply of Texas Rural Families*, 10.

10. Matthews and Dart, *Welfare of Children*, 6. This finding mirrors that of social workers in the Yazoo-Mississippi Delta in the 1920s, cited in Fite, *Cotton Fields No More*, 116.

11. Weir interview number 4, IOH.

12. Willard, *Farm Management Study*, 15; Bennett, Burke, and Lounsbury, *Soil Survey of Ellis County*, 10.

13. Rinzler, *Complete Book of Food*, 55, 89.

14. Dodd interview number 2, IOH.

15. Carroll interview number 3, IOH.

16. Personal conversation with Inez Adams Walker, 23 October 1992.

17. Dodd interview number 1, IOH.

18. Dodd interview number 2, IOH.

19. Bourne, *Pioneer Farmer's Daughter*, 72–73.

20. Dillow and Carver, *Mrs. Blackwell's Heart-of-Texas Cookbook*, xxii.

21. Rinzler, *Complete Book of Food*, 354.

22. Washington, *Oral Memoirs*, 6, Texas Collection.

23. Personal conversation with Inez Adams Walker, 28 October 1992; Bourne, *Pioneer Farmer's Daughter*, 150; McRae interview, 18, Archives, Gee Library; Carroll interview number 6, IOH.

24. Weir interview number 1, IOH; Lula Kathryn Peacock Jones, *Recollections*, 21; Jupe, *History of Tours*, 440, 647; James Conrad, "Mother, Daughter Shared Way of Life Fast Disappearing," *Greenville Herald-Banner*, 24 August 1987.

25. Caufield interview number 2, IOH.

26. McRae interview, 33–34, Archives, Gee Library.

27. Washington, *Oral Memoirs*, 27, Texas Collection.

28. Rinzler, *Complete Book of Food*, 280.

29. Jurney and Moir, *Historic Buildings*, 153.

30. Machann and Mendl, *Krásná Amerika*, 140.

31. Dodd interview number 1, IOH; Simcik, *Oral Memoirs*, 22, Texas Collection.

32. Dodd interview number 2, IOH; Jurney, Lebo, and Green, *Historic Farming*, 358; Hazel Beauton Riley, *Washing on the Line*, 4.

33. Locke, *Action on Bullhide Creek*, 94.

34. Personal conversation with Garland Sharpless, 5 December 1991.

35. Owens, *Tell Me a Story*, 69–70.

36. R. W. Williams, "Backward Glances," *Wolfe City Sun*, 8 September 1950.

37. Matthews and Dart, *Welfare of Children*, 54.

38. Carroll interview number 2, IOH; Agricultural Adjustment Agency, *Feeding Farm Folks*, 8.

39. Bourne, *Pioneer Farmer's Daughter*, 70; Folley interview number 2, IOH.

40. McGee, "Hog Killing Day," 11.

41. Folley interview number 2, IOH.

42. Washington, *Oral Memoirs*, 9, Texas Collection.

43. Carroll interview number 3 and Folley interview number 2, IOH.

44. McGee, "Hog Killing Day," 11.

45. One of the most dramatically written accounts of hog killing is in Humphrey, *Farther Off from Heaven*, 76–78. See also "Hog-Killing Time on the Burns Farm in Miller Grove," Agriculture Vertical File, Hunt County Museum, Greenville; and Carroll interview number 3, IOH, for thorough descriptions.

46. Lula Kathryn Peacock Jones, *Recollections*, 24; Simcik, *Oral Memoirs*, 69, Texas Collection.

47. Dodd interview number 1, IOH; Rice, "Memories of Mama Rice," Rice Papers, Archives, Gee Library; Carroll interview number 3, IOH.

48. McGee, "Hog Killing Day," 8–9; Folley interview number 2, IOH; Jurney, Lebo, and Green, *Historic Farming*, 355; Campbell, "Country Life in Mooreville Texas," Texas Collection.

49. McGee, "Hog Killing Day," 8–9.

50. Taylor, *Eating, Drinking, and Visiting in the South*, 112–13; Dodd interview number 1, Carroll interview number 3, and Folley interview number 2, IOH; Jurney, Lebo, and Green, *Historic Farming*, 355; Dillow and Carver, *Mrs. Blackwell's Heart-of-Texas Cookbook*, 12.

51. Machann, *Krásná Amerika*, 140.

52. Folley interview number 2, IOH; Everett, *Among the Salt*, 22; Jurney, Lebo, and Green,

Historic Farming, 355; Simcik, *Oral Memoirs*, 65, Texas Collection; Carroll interview number 3, IOH; Dillow and Carver, *Mrs. Blackwell's Heart-of-Texas Cookbook*, 12–13.

53. Hurtado interview number 1 and Carroll interview number 3, IOH.

54. Almanza interview number 1, IOH.

55. James Conrad, "Hard Work, Planning Kept Food on the Shelves," *Greenville Herald-Banner*, 31 October 1988.

56. Jurney, Lebo, and Green, *Historic Farming*, 355; Dodd interview number 1, IOH; Taylor, *Eating, Drinking, and Visiting in the South*, 25.

57. Simcik, *Oral Memoirs*, 67, Texas Collection.

58. Dodd interview number 1, IOH.

59. Malone, *Oral Memoirs*, 20, Texas Collection. Taylor describes skipper flies in *Eating, Drinking, and Visiting in the South*, 25.

60. Dodd interview number 2, IOH.

61. Carroll interview number 3, IOH.

62. Weir interview number 1, IOH.

63. Dodd interviews number 1 and 2, IOH.

64. Weir interview number 1, Carroll interview number 3, and Dodd interview number 2, IOH.

65. Weir interview number 1, IOH; "Hog-Killing Time on the Burns Farm," Agriculture Vertical File, Hunt County Museum, Greenville; Carroll interview number 3, IOH.

66. Almanza interview number 1 and Hurtado interview number 1, IOH.

67. McGee, "Hog Killing Day," 11; Locke, *Action on Bullhide Creek*, 33; "Hog-Killing Time on the Burns Farm," Agriculture Vertical File, Hunt County Museum, Greenville; Carroll interview number 3 and Folley interview number 2, IOH; Dillow and Carver, *Mrs. Blackwell's Heart-of-Texas Cookbook*, 2, 13.

68. Humphrey, *Farther Off from Heaven*, 78.

69. Almanza interview number 1, IOH.

70. Rinzler, *Complete Book of Food*, 116, 280.

71. Etheridge, *Butterfly Caste*, 42, 154.

72. Carroll interview number 1, IOH.

73. William A. Owens collected a folk song, called "The Grumbler's Song," that demonstrates the importance of Texas farm women. The song reflected the reality of gender roles in the Blackland Prairie. The wife demonstrated competence in every aspect of farmwork, and the husband quickly gave up trying to produce food (see Owens, *Texas Folk Songs*, 228–29).

74. Sanders, *Farm Ownership and Tenancy*, 54; Peteet, *Farming Credit in Texas*, 58; Leonard, "Economic Aspects of the Tenant Problem," 122. In 1914, Levi T. Steward, living temporarily near Savoy, Fannin County, told the U.S. Senate Commission on Industrial Relations that landlords in Lamar County would not permit him to keep a cow or hogs. See *Report by the Commission on Industrial Relations*, 9033.

75. Leonard, "Economic Aspects of the Tenant Problem," 122.

76. Allen, *Labor of Women*, 89, 179, 219.

77. Caufield interview number 2, IOH.

78. Matthews and Dart, *Welfare of Children*, 67; Rinzler, *Complete Book of Food*, 33, 285.

79. Dodd interview number 2, IOH. Interviews from southern Dallas County corroborate Dodd's statement. Researchers there found that men usually broke the ground for the

garden; after that, responsibility for the garden was "primarily that of the woman of the house. She supervised planting and care of the garden although it was agreed that everyone was expected to help with planting, weeding, and cultivating as needed" (Jurney, Lebo, and Green, *Historic Farming*, 355). See also Almanza interview number 1, IOH.

80. Weir interview number 2 and Carroll interview number 3, IOH.

81. Stimpson, *My Remembers*, 95.

82. Dodd interview number 2, IOH.

83. Folley interview number 1, IOH.

84. Weir interview number 1, IOH.

85. Almanza interview number 1 and Hurtado interview number 1, IOH. The tiny peppers were probably of the variety commonly known as chiltecpin. See Andrews, *Peppers*, 119–20.

86. Calvert, "Cotton Fields No More."

87. Dodd interview number 2, IOH. See also Lula Kathryn Peacock Jones, *Recollections*, 19–20, for her discussion of planting procedures on her family farm.

88. Jupe, *History of Tours*, 801; Jurney, Lebo, and Green, *Historic Farming*, 358.

89. Weir interview number 2, IOH.

90. Joseph Abner Hill, *Autobiographical Notes*, 10; Conrad, "Hard Work, Planning Kept Food on the Shelves"; James Conrad, "Early Farm Families Seldom Wanted for Fresh Vegetables," *Greenville Herald-Banner*, 12 August 1990; James Conrad, "Mrs. Tucker Remembers Life before Conveniences," *Commerce Journal*, 24 June 1987; Jurney, Lebo, and Green, *Historic Farming*, 355; Lula Kathryn Peacock Jones, *Recollections*, 24; Dodd interview number 1, IOH. Home demonstration agents urged their clients to plant larger gardens with more variety. Jeffie O. A. Conner recommended planting eighteen or twenty kinds of vegetables for an increased range, and the home demonstration agents devised a twelve-month plan for keeping gardens going year-round (Conner Papers, file 125, Texas Collection).

91. Dodd interview number 2, IOH. Bertha Blackwell, from Navarro County, shared the grandfather's belief that collards would "counteract all of the rich food consumed on Christmas Day," and the Blackwell family always ate collards on December 26 (Dillow and Carver, *Mrs. Blackwell's Heart-of-Texas Cookbook*, 36).

92. Jurney, Lebo, and Green, *Historic Farming*, 355. Blacklands houses typically have no cellars because of the extreme slickness of the clay soil, which is prone to slumps and cave-ins.

93. Dodd interview number 2, IOH.

94. In Hill County in the early autumn of 1920, only 14 percent of white families and 10 percent of black families reported eating any kind of fruit—fresh, dried, or canned—the day before (Matthews and Dart, *Welfare of Children*, 53).

95. Agricultural Adjustment Agency, *Feeding Farm Folks*, 8.

96. Jupe, *History of Tours*, 442.

97. Rice, "Some Highlights in the Life of Lee Rice, Part 2," Rice Papers, Archives, Gee Library.

98. Dodd interview number 2, IOH.

99. Weir interview number 2, IOH. See also Hazel Beauton Riley, *Washing on the Line*, 5; Weir interview number 1, IOH; and Jupe, *History of Tours*, 473.

100. Carroll interview number 3 and Dodd interview number 2, IOH.

101. Rice, "Memories of Mama Rice," Rice Papers, Archives, Gee Library.

102. McRae interview, 14, Archives, Gee Library.

103. Weir interview number 1, IOH.

104. Dodd interview number 2, IOH.

105. Dillow and Carver, *Mrs. Blackwell's Heart-of-Texas Cookbook*, 78.

106. Malone, *Oral Memoirs*, 19, Texas Collection.

107. Jurney, Lebo, and Green, *Historic Farming*, 355; Dodd interviews 1 and 2.

108. Allen, *Labor of Women*, 87, 179, 219. Adelaida Torres Almanza was among the rare Mexican women who canned. See Almanza interview number 1, IOH.

109. Dodd interview number 2, IOH.

110. Weir interview number 2, IOH; Locke, *Action on Bullhide Creek*, 58.

111. Lula Kathryn Peacock Jones, *Recollections*, 22; Locke, *Action on Bullhide Creek*, 58; Dillow and Carver, *Mrs. Blackwell's Heart-of-Texas Cookbook*, 40.

112. Folley interview number 1 and Carroll interview number 3, IOH.

113. Personal conversation with Inez Adams Walker, 28 October 1992. For a detailed explanation of open-kettle, cold-pack, and pressure-cooker methods of canning, see Gleason, *Food Preservation*.

114. Bear, *Care and Preservation of Food in the Home*, 11; Carroll interview number 3, IOH.

115. Gleason, *Food Preservation*, 19.

116. Texas Agricultural Extension Service Papers, Historical Notes, 1912, Archives, Evans Library.

117. Texas Agricultural Extension Service Historical Notes, 1917, Archives, Evans Library.

118. Weir interview number 2, IOH. For step-by-step canning instructions from the World War I period, see Carter, *Canning, Preserving, Pickling*, and Simpson, *Food Saving in Texas*.

119. Conrad, "Hard Work, Planning Kept Food on the Shelves."

120. Caufield interview number 2, IOH.

121. Peteet, Merwin, and Simpson, *Community Canning Plants*; "A Brief Resumé of Home Demonstration Work in Texas," Texas Agricultural Extension Service Historical Notes, 1939, Archives, Evans Library.

122. "1917 and 1918 Projects: Cooperative Community Canners," Texas Agricultural Extension Service Papers, file number 2-34, Archives, Evans Library. Home demonstration clubs in Texas are a worthy subject for much detailed analysis. Several recent doctoral dissertations discuss home demonstration in the South. See Hoffschwelle, "Rebuilding the Southern Rural Community"; Lu Ann Jones, "Re-visioning the Countryside"; and Rieff, " 'Rousing the People of the Land.' " For a cogent critique of the national Home Demonstration Service, see Jellison, *Entitled to Power*, chs. 1 and 2.

123. Carroll interview number 3, IOH.

124. Jurney and Moir, *Historic Buildings*, 204.

125. Hale, *Oral Memoirs*, 5, Texas Collection.

126. Everett, *Among the Salt*, 10.

127. McRae interview, 14–15, Archives, Gee Library.

128. Carroll interview number 3 and Folley interview number 1, IOH.

129. Allen, *Labor of Women*, 179, 219, 255.

130. Matthews and Dart, *Welfare of Children*, 52; Allen, *Labor of Women*, 219.

131. Carroll interview number 2, IOH.

132. Folley interview number 2 and Dodd interview number 2, IOH; Dillow and Carver, *Mrs. Blackwell's Heart-of-Texas Cookbook*, 58.

133. Almanza interview number 1 and Hurtado interview number 1, IOH. The Sanchez family moved every three or four years, and they sold their entire chicken flock and all of their cows prior to each move.

134. McBride, *"Filosofer" of "Kukel-bur" Flat*, 165; Dillow and Carver, *Mrs. Blackwell's Heart-of-Texas Cookbook*, 58.

135. R. W. Williams, "Backward Glances," *Wolfe City Sun*, 18 March 1949.

136. Bedichek, *Adventures with a Texas Naturalist*, 99; Dodd interview number 1, IOH.

137. Washington, *Oral Memoirs*, 4, Texas Collection.

138. Dodd interview number 1, IOH.

139. Dodd interview number 2, IOH; Rinzler, *Complete Book of Food*, 134–35.

140. Dillow and Carver, *Mrs. Blackwell's Heart-of-Texas Cookbook*, 50.

141. Dodd interview number 2, IOH; Dillow and Carver, *Mrs. Blackwell's Heart-of-Texas Cookbook*, 1, 7. Reserving the best pieces of meat for the men is the only direct evidence of Blackland Prairie women depriving themselves of food to feed others. This practice, common in other regions, undoubtedly occurred.

142. Dodd interviews 2 and 1, and Weir interview number 2, IOH. Dillow and Carver give detailed instructions on how to wring a chicken's neck and pick off its feathers in *Mrs. Blackwell's Heart-of-Texas Cookbook*, 4.

143. Dillow and Carver, *Mrs. Blackwell's Heart-of-Texas Cookbook*, 6–7.

144. Dodd interview number 2, IOH. In their study of Navarro County, Jurney and Moir found that "surplus eggs were sold whenever possible, otherwise given to neighbors"; possibly in this context "neighbors" may actually be tenants and the eggs part of their provisions (Jurney and Moir, *Historic Buildings*, 205).

145. Jensen, "Cloth, Butter, and Boarders," 21. Women's production for the market has sometimes been sentimentalized. In Dorothy Scarborough's 1929 novel, *Can't Get a Red Bird*, the heroine borrows cows and makes good butter, which her husband fortuitously sells to the wife of the mayor of Dallas. The mayor's wife is so impressed by the quality of the butter that she asks for eggs and lamb and tells all of her friends. In this way the farm couple makes enough money to pay off the grocery debt (255–72).

146. Locke, *Action on Bullhide Creek*, 40.

147. Bourne, *Pioneer Farmer's Daughter*, 179; Crenshaw, *Texas Blackland Heritage*, 28; James Conrad, "Chicken Peddler's Arrival Was a Most Welcome Sight," *Greenville Herald-Banner*, 10 January 1988.

148. Crenshaw, *Texas Blackland Heritage*, 29.

149. Hurtado interview number 1, IOH.

150. Rice, "Memories of Mama Rice," Rice Papers, Archives, Gee Library.

151. Allen, *Labor of Women*, 255.

152. Weir interview number 2, IOH.

153. Jupe, *History of Tours*, 804.

154. Ward, "Farm Woman's Problems," 445.

155. Carroll interview number 2, IOH.

156. Weir interview number 2, IOH.

157. Dodd interview number 2 and Almanza interview number 1, IOH.

158. Personal conversation with Inez Adams Walker, 28 October 1992.

159. Allen, *Labor of Women*, 219, 255, 257. Statewide, the average was approximately 75 percent (Matthews and Dart, *Welfare of Children*, 52; Agricultural Adjustment Agency, *Feeding Farm Folks*, 8).

160. Caufield interview number 2, IOH.

161. Weir interview number 4, IOH.

162. Dillow and Carver, *Mrs. Blackwell's Heart-of-Texas Cookbook*, 57.

163. Carroll interview number 2, IOH.

164. Weir interview number 2, IOH.

165. Sanders, *Farm Ownership and Tenancy*, 54.

166. Caufield interview number 2, IOH.

167. Jurney and Moir, *Historic Buildings*, 205; Jupe, *History of Tours*, 440; Dodd interview number 2, IOH. Luz Sanchez Hurtado discussed keeping milk in a cistern (Hurtado interview number 1, IOH). The archives at Texas A&M University–Commerce contain plans for a tin cooler to be kept in the well, given to archivist James Conrad by Helen M. Douglas, whose father was a tinsmith. The drawing in the file shows a vertical container in which jars with tight-fitting lids, holding milk and other foods, could be stacked. These coolers came in various sizes: those holding three, four, or five one-quart fruit jars; or two or three half-gallon fruit jars. The smallest cost $1.75 and the largest, $2.00 (Water/Cistern Vertical File, Archives, Gee Library).

168. Everett, *Among the Salt*, 8.

169. Weir interview number 2, IOH.

170. Dodd interview number 1, IOH.

171. Weir interview number 3, IOH.

172. By 1940, 35 percent of white Texas tenants and 15 percent of black Texas tenants had iceboxes. According to a survey by anthropologist Oscar Lewis, in Bell County, in the central Blackland Prairie, approximately 53 percent of all farm families had iceboxes (Brophy, "Black Texan," 75; Lewis, *On the Edge of the Black Waxy*, 30). It should be noted, however, that, just prior to World War II, 54.8 percent of white tenants and 83.7 percent of black tenants had no refrigeration in their homes at all (Brophy, "Black Texan," 75). In contrast, 18 percent of the women in Haskell County, Kansas, had mechanical refrigeration by 1940. See Jellison, *Entitled to Power*, 126.

173. Weir interview number 3, IOH.

174. Weir interview number 2, IOH.

175. Rinzler, *Complete Book of Food*, 93.

176. Weir interview number 2 and Folley interview number 2, IOH.

177. Hurtado interview number 1 and Almanza interview number 1, IOH.

178. Simcik, *Oral Memoirs*, 63–65, Texas Collection.

179. Rinzler, *Complete Book of Food*, 67.

180. Dodd interview number 1 and Carroll interview number 3, IOH.

181. Dillow and Carver, *Mrs. Blackwell's Heart-of-Texas Cookbook*, 56.

182. Dodd interview number 4, IOH.

183. Dillow and Carver, *Mrs. Blackwell's Heart-of-Texas Cookbook*, 56.

184. Weir interview number 3, IOH.

185. Simcik, *Oral Memoirs*, 60–61.

186. Personal conversation with Inez Adams Walker, 28 October 1992; Dodd interview number 2, IOH; Rice, "Memories of Mama Rice," Rice Papers, Archives, Gee Library.

187. No statistics exist for the number of women in the Blackland Prairie who sold butter, but Florence Ward's 1920 survey revealed that nationwide, only 33 percent of the women sold butter and only 11 percent realized "butter money" from it (Ward, "Farm Woman's Problems," 444). Presumably, the number of women who sold butter in the Blacklands would be even smaller, since only a fraction of the population had cows.

188. Caufield interview number 2, IOH.

189. Rice, "Memories of Mama Rice," Rice Papers, Archives, Gee Library (Rice's italics).

190. Folley interview number 1, IOH.

191. Weir interview number 3, IOH.

192. Ibid.

193. Dodd interview number 2, IOH.

194. Folley interview number 1, IOH. Some women, like Hattie Schorn Straten, sold fruit as well (Jupe, *History of Tours*, 708).

195. Stimpson, *My Remembers*, 9.

196. Carroll interview number 3, IOH.

197. Weir interview number 1, IOH; Locke, *Action on Bullhide Creek*, 33.

198. Machann and Mendl, *Krásná Amerika*, 84; Simcik, *Oral Memoirs*, 22, Texas Collection.

199. Simcik, *Oral Memoirs*, 62–63, Texas Collection.

200. Personal conversation with Inez Adams Walker, 28 October 1992.

201. Hurtado interview number 1, IOH.

202. Carroll interview number 3, IOH.

203. Whitacre, *Food Supply of Texas Rural Families*, 14, 18.

204. Personal conversation with Inez Adams Walker, 28 October 1992; Simcik, *Oral Memoirs*, 22, Texas Collection; James Abner Hill, *Autobiographical Notes*, 10; Whitacre, *Food Supply of Texas Rural Families*, 17; Humphrey, *Ordways*, 122; Bourne, *Pioneer Farmer's Daughter*, 49, 150; Jurney, Lebo, and Green, *Historic Farming*, 355; McRae interview, 15, Archives, Gee Library; Conrad, "Mrs. Tucker"; Carroll interview number 6, IOH; Jupe, *History of Tours*, 440, 804.

205. Dillow and Carver, *Mrs. Blackwell's Heart-of-Texas Cookbook*, 72–73.

206. Weir interview number 1, IOH.

207. Carroll interview number 6, IOH.

208. Dodd interview number 2, IOH.

209. Weir interview number 2, IOH.

210. Taylor, *Eating, Drinking, and Visiting in the South*, 107, 140.

211. Brophy, "Black Texan," 75; Dodd interview number 2, IOH.

212. Weir interviews 1 and 2, IOH. Jurney and Moir note that Navarro County farmers never used coal because "fires were often extinguished immediately after a task was done" and coal was too difficult to light. Wood came from the Richland Creek "floodplain and slope forests" (Jurney and Moir, *Historic Buildings*, 243).

213. Dodd interview number 2, IOH.

214. Carroll interview number 2, IOH.

215. Dodd interview number 2, Folley interview number 2, and Hurtado interview number 1, IOH. Levi Steward, testifying before the U.S. Senate Industrial Relations Committee in 1914, complained of having to haul wood eight or ten miles, paying "fifty cents for it cut or a quarter if I cut it myself" (*Report by the Commission on Industrial Relations*, 9032–33).

216. Stimpson, *My Remembers*, 32.

217. Dodd interview number 2, IOH; Rice, "Memories of Mama Rice," 5, Rice Papers, Archives, Gee Library.

218. McRae interview, 39–40, Archives, Gee Library; Folley interview number 2, IOH.

219. Brophy, "Black Texan," 75.

220. Lewis interview, 6–7, Archives, Gee Library.

221. Rice, "More Memories," Rice Papers, Archives, Gee Library.

222. Dodd interview number 3, IOH.

223. Weir interview number 1, IOH.

224. Dillow and Carver, *Mrs. Blackwell's Heart-of-Texas Cookbook*, xvii, xx.

225. Dodd interview number 4, IOH.

226. Whitacre, *Food Supply of Texas Rural Families*, 7–8; Locke, *Action on Bullhide Creek*, 65.

227. Stimpson, *My Remembers*, 40; Dillow and Carver, *Mrs. Blackwell's Heart-of-Texas Cookbook*, 65.

228. Taylor, *Eating, Drinking, and Visiting in the South*, 20; Hilliard, *Hog Meat and Hoecake*, 49.

229. Allen, *Labor of Women*, 220; Locke, *Action on Bullhide Creek*, 67.

230. Navarro interview number 3 and Almanza interview number 3, IOH.

231. Dodson, "Tortilla Making," 137–41; Navarro interview number 3 and Almanza interview number 3, IOH.

232. Locke, *Action on Bullhide Creek*, 62, 74.

233. Dodd interview number 2, IOH.

234. Ibid.

235. Rice, "Memories of Mama Rice," Rice Papers, Archives, Gee Library; Jupe, *History of Tours*, 522; Dodd interview number 2, IOH.

236. Jupe, *History of Tours*, 610.

237. Dillow and Carver, *Mrs. Blackwell's Heart-of-Texas Cookbook*, xvi.

238. Weir interview number 1, IOH.

239. Stimpson, *My Remembers*, 117.

240. Carroll interview number 4, IOH.

241. Dillow and Carver, *Mrs. Blackwell's Heart-of-Texas Cookbook*, xviii–xix.

242. Rice, "Memories of Mama Rice," 4, 6, Rice Papers, Archives, Gee Library.

243. Humphrey, *Ordways*, 35.

244. Everett, *Among the Salt*, 19.

245. On the nature of southern meals, see Taylor, *Eating, Drinking, and Visiting in the South*, 120. For specific breakfast foods, see Locke, *Action on Bullhide Creek*, 3, 34, 64–65; Weir interview number 2, IOH; Conrad, "Mrs. Tucker"; and Dodd interview number 1 and Folley interview number 1, IOH.

246. Owens, *Season of Weathering*, 13; Folley interview number 2, IOH.

247. Weir interview number 1, IOH.

248. Ibid.

249. Dodd interview number 1, IOH. Dillow and Carver give recipes for potatoes fried with ample amounts of grease and, for times when grease was in short supply, for those fried with a minimum of grease and then steamed (*Mrs. Blackwell's Heart-of-Texas Cookbook*, 19–20).

250. Carroll interview number 2, IOH.

251. Simcik, *Oral Memoirs*, 58–59, Texas Collection.

252. Machann and Mendl, *Krásná Amerika*, 140–41; Jupe, *History of Tours*, 667.

253. Jeffries, "Cotton Picking," 63.

254. Weir interview number 3, IOH.

255. Washington, *Oral Memoirs*, 14, Texas Collection.

256. McRae interview, 17, Archives, Gee Library.

257. Campbell, "Country Life in Mooreville Texas," Texas Collection.

258. Dodd interview number 1, IOH.

259. Coltharp, "Reminiscences of Cotton Pickin' Days," 540–41.

260. Owens, *Season of Weathering*, 16.

261. Letha Jumper, "Little Money in Pockets Helps Everyone," *Tawakoni News*, 6 September 1990, 3.

262. Simcik, *Oral Memoirs*, 65–66, Texas Collection.

263. Almanza interview number 2, IOH.

264. Owens, *Season of Weathering*, 15.

265. Locke, *Action on Bullhide Creek*, 64.

266. Ibid., 64, 67; Hurtado interview number 2, IOH.

267. Jumper, "Little Money in Pockets Helps Everyone," 3.

268. Weir interview number 2, IOH.

269. Conrad, "Mrs. Tucker"; Simcik, *Oral Memoirs*, 60–61, Texas Collection; Weir interview number 2, IOH; Crenshaw, *Texas Blackland Heritage*, 61; Folley interview number 1, IOH.

270. Conrad, "Early Farm Families Seldom Wanted for Fresh Vegetables."

271. Dodd interview number 2, IOH.

272. Locke, *Action on Bullhide Creek*, 64, 67.

273. Dillow and Carver, *Mrs. Blackwell's Heart-of-Texas Cookbook*, 8.

274. Locke, *Action on Bullhide Creek*, 33–34.

275. Dillow and Carver, *Mrs. Blackwell's Heart-of-Texas Cookbook*, 35.

276. Dodd interview number 2, IOH.

277. Weir interview number 1, IOH.

278. Caskey, *One Hundred and Twenty Years in Florence, Texas*, 27; Bourne, *Pioneer Farmer's Daughter*, 50; Hurtado interview number 1, IOH.

279. Weir interview number 2, IOH; Jupe, *History of Tours*, 671.

280. Jumper, "Little Money in Pockets Helps Everyone," 3.

281. Dodd interview number 1, IOH.

282. Aubrey Garrett oral history interview (interviewed by Howard Garrett on 11 April 1990, in Emory, Texas) in Cemetery Workday Vertical File, Archives, Gee Library.

283. Dodd interview number 1 and Carroll interview number 3, IOH.

284. Navarro interview number 3 and Almanza interview number 3, IOH.

285. Stimpson, *My Remembers*, 42.

286. Machann and Mendl, *Krásná Amerika*, 141; Jupe, *History of Tours*, 473.

287. Carroll interview number 4, IOH.

288. Dillow and Carver, *Mrs. Blackwell's Heart-of-Texas Cookbook*, 71.

289. Dodd interview number 2, IOH.

290. Weir interview number 2 and Carroll interview number 4, IOH.

291. Machann and Mendl, *Krásná Amerika*, 140; Simcik, *Oral Memoirs*, 58, Texas Collection.

292. Navarro interview number 3, Almanza interview number 3, and Hurtado interview number 1, IOH.

Chapter Four

1. Dodd interview number 1, IOH; Locke, *Action on Bullhide Creek*, 55–56; Letha Jumper, "Little Money in Pockets Helps Everyone," *Tawakoni News*, 6 September 1990, 3.

2. *Semi-Weekly Farm News*, 8 February 1910, 7.

3. Fox-Genovese, *Within the Plantation Household*, 195. Stephanie McCurry explores the work patterns of antebellum yeoman women in South Carolina and concludes that the field work of women did nothing to alter the patriarchal views of their men. Many northern and European visitors were horrified at southern yeoman women's field work, and upper-class white southerners politely ignored it. McCurry makes no comment on how yeoman farmers or their wives viewed their field work. See her "Politics of Yeoman Households in South Carolina," 22–38, and *Masters of Small Worlds*, 79–85.

4. Scott, *Southern Lady*, 228. For an excellent discussion of the meaning and implications of southern ladyhood, see Anne Goodwyn Jones, *Tomorrow Is Another Day*, ch. 1. She details the persistence of the southern lady myth to the late 1970s (18–19). See also Cook, "Growing Up White, Genteel, and Female," 9 and 44.

5. Personal conversation with Genevieve Westbrook Charlton, December 1990, Corsicana, Texas.

6. *Farm and Ranch*, 19 March 1910, 25.

7. Ibid., 15 February 1910, 7.

8. *Waco Daily Times-Herald*, 5 November 1911, 6.

9. Most societies worldwide have traditionally followed a division of labor. For discussions of the division of labor, see Flora, "Public Policy and Women in Agricultural Production," 268; Cloud, "Farm Women and the Structural Transformation of Agriculture," 285–87; and Boserup, *Woman's Role in Economic Development*, 15.

10. Lewis, *On the Edge of the Black Waxy*, 24–25. These comments resonate strongly with the findings of Boserup, *Woman's Role in Economic Development*, 31, 66–67.

11. Machann and Mendl, *Krásná Amerika*, 78.

12. Jupe, *History of Tours*, 659.

13. *Semi-Weekly Farm News*, 30 August 1910, 7.

14. Gibbons, *Child Labor among the Cotton Growers of Texas*, 49.

15. Matthews and Dart, *Welfare of Children*, 45; Allen, *Labor of Women*, 271, 274, 275.

16. Matthews and Dart, *Welfare of Children*, 44. See also Chambers, "Life in a Cotton Farming Community," 143, for his class-prejudiced account of Red River County, and Machann and Mendl, *Krásná Amerika*, 78, for comments on Czech attitudes toward Anglos' "shiftlessness."

17. Ward, "Farm Woman's Problems," 444.

18. Allen, *Labor of Women*, 79.

19. Matthews and Dart, *Welfare of Children*, 45.

20. Allen, *Labor of Women*, 186, 189; Matthews and Dart, *Welfare of Children*, 45.

21. Allen, *Labor of Women*, 224, 225.

22. Hurtado interview number 1, IOH.

23. Ward, "Farm Woman's Problems," 444.

24. Gibbons, *Child Labor among the Cotton Growers of Texas*, 49.

25. Jeffries, "Cotton Picking," 63.

26. Carroll interview number 2, IOH.

27. Weir interview number 1, IOH.

28. Matthews and Dart, *Welfare of Children*, 44. In Dallas County, researchers found that "although the usual sexual divisions of labor prevailed in regard to daily and weekly chores such as cooking and laundry[,] planting and harvest were times when those customs and traditions changed and division lines became blurred" (Jurney, Lebo, and Green, *Historic Farming*, 358). These figures roughly parallel those found in 185 societies by ethnologists George P. Murdock and Catarina Provost, who constructed an index of the average percentage of male participation in fifty tasks. The figures include soil preparation, 73.1 percent; crop planting, 54.4 percent; harvesting, 45.0 percent; and crop tending, 44.6 percent. Texas women participated more in agriculture than does the average woman worldwide, but the view of certain activities—especially plowing—as acceptable or ill-advised for women remains constant (Murdock and Provost, "Factors in the Division of Labor by Sex," 207).

29. Jupe, *History of Tours*, 685.

30. Ibid., 442, 585, 784.

31. Jeffries, "Cotton Picking," 63.

32. Matthews and Dart, *Welfare of Children*, 47.

33. Gibbons, *Child Labor among the Cotton Growers of Texas*, 49.

34. Allen, *Labor of Women*, 138.

35. James Conrad, "Early Hunt County Families Endured Hardships," *Commerce Journal*, 6 August 1986, 3A.

36. McDaniel, *Oral Memoirs*, 14, Texas Collection.

37. Allen, *Labor of Women*, 121; Elbert, "Farmer Takes a Wife," 185.

38. McBride, *"Filosofer" of "Kukel-bur" Flat*, 114, 199–200; Almanza interview number 2, IOH.

39. Matthews and Dart, *Welfare of Children*, 49; Gibbons, *Child Labor among the Cotton Growers of Texas*, 49; Jupe, *History of Tours*, 676, 685.

40. Carroll interview number 1, IOH.

41. Jupe, *History of Tours*, 481; Humphrey, *Ordways*, 138.

42. Stimpson, *My Remembers*, 69.

43. Folley interview number 1, IOH; Jeffries, "Cotton Picking," 63; Jupe, *History of Tours*, 714.

44. Jupe, *History of Tours*, 570.

45. Washington, *Oral Memoirs*, 13–14, Texas Collection. "Cooling the breast" was a practice carried over from slavery. For a discussion of this practice, see Schwartz, " 'At Noon, Oh How I Ran,' " 245–46.

46. U.S. Department of Agriculture, *Cotton Plant*, 243; Evans, "Texas Agriculture, 1865–1880," 26; Crenshaw, *Texas Blackland Heritage*, 93.

47. Carroll interview number 1, IOH.

48. Morgan, *Fieldcrops for the Cotton-Belt*, 105–6.

49. Jupe, *History of Tours*, 708; personal conversation with Garland Sharpless, 9 February 1992; Allen, *Labor of Women*, 142. Boserup finds the cause of male control of plowing in

developing countries to be men's domination of new technology (*Woman's Role in Economic Development*, 24, 33, 53, 57).

50. Dorothy Scarborough, *Can't Get a Red Bird*, 46.

51. Sitton, "Mule, Man and Bull Puncher"; Hurtado interview number 1, IOH; personal conversation with Dorothy Woods Moore, Commerce, Texas, 18 July 1991.

52. Caufield interview number 4, IOH.

53. Folley interview number 1, IOH. In the family of Annie and Robert Sharpless, the four oldest daughters plowed because the three male children were at first too young and then the older two boys were killed in separate accidents in 1925 and 1926 (personal conversation with Garland Sharpless, 9 February 1992). See also Jupe, *History of Tours*, 734, and Hardeman interview, 7, Archives, Gee Library. The equipment that farm families used varied widely. By the turn of the century, the equipment list for prosperous farmers included a cotton stalk cutter (walking or riding), turning plow, a disc plow, a middle buster, a sweep, a cotton seed planter, cultivators (walking or riding), a steel-tooth drag harrow, hoes, scales, cotton sacks, and cotton wagons (Locke, *Action on Bullhide Creek*, 47; Carroll interview number 1, IOH). But for many in the 1920s, "the horse, mules, single buster, and walking cultivator make up most of their equipment" (James Tull Richardson, "Social Changes in Hunt County," 34).

54. Jupe, *History of Tours*, 619.

55. Morgan, *Fieldcrops for the Cotton-Belt*, 108; Evans, "Texas Agriculture, 1865–1880," 29–31.

56. Alford, *Oral Memoirs*, 23–24, Texas Collection.

57. Evans, "Texas Agriculture, 1865–1880," 31. Almost all of the cotton planted in Texas was American upland cotton (*Gossypium hirsutum*) (Morgan, *Fieldcrops for the Cotton-Belt*, 33). The most popular varieties for Texas in the 1920s included Mebane's Triumph, Kasch, Lone Star, Bennett, Rowden, Belton, Truitt, Acala, and Durango (Brown, *Cotton*, 52).

58. Evans, "Texas Agriculture, 1865–1880," 31, and "Texas Agriculture, 1880–1930," 38. Heavy rains made the work harder; Bernice Weir recalled that about 1903, "It rained so much that year that Papa had cotton out north of the house and the rows were about a mile long and it took the hands a half a day to chop one row of cotton—clean that one row out" (Weir interview number 1, IOH).

59. Lewis, *On the Edge of the Black Waxy*, 103. Rural sociologist Cornelia Butler Flora comments that family labor is uniquely flexible in maximizing survival strategies and minimizing risk: "Labor can be mobilized when it is needed and sustained when it is not." Some family members' needs, however, may be in conflict with others', and benefits for some may be costs for others (Flora, "Public Policy and Women in Agricultural Production," 267).

60. Allen, *Labor of Women*, 100, 191, 227. Ester Boserup cites a startlingly similar study from southeast India in which the four primary social groups were divided according to field work: one in which neither the women nor the men performed any manual work; one in which the men worked their own fields and the women occupied "mainly domestic duties"; one in which the women worked mainly "within the family framework and in their own fields, although they might work for a wage in the busy season"; and one in which the women "were expected regularly to seek paid work for the support of their families" (Boserup, *Woman's Role in Economic Development*, 69–70).

61. Jupe, *History of Tours*, 610, 671.

62. Lula Kathryn Peacock Jones, *Recollections*, 22. See also Jerome Kearby Bentley, *Spring and Autumn*, 22.

63. Weir interview number 2, IOH.

64. Carroll interview number 1, IOH.

65. Personal conversation with Garland Sharpless, December 1991.

66. Carroll interview number 1, IOH.

67. Matthews and Dart, *Welfare of Children*, 14.

68. Dodd interview number 1, IOH.

69. Folley interview number 1, IOH.

70. Stimpson, *My Remembers*, 32.

71. Ischy interview number 2, A. Frank Smith Jr. Library Center, Southwestern University, Georgetown, Tex.

72. Evans, "Texas Agriculture, 1880–1930," 53; Templin and Marshall, *Soil Survey of Hunt County*, 3.

73. Weir interview number 3, IOH.

74. Owens, *A Season of Weathering*, 117.

75. Owens, *Texas Folk Songs*, 15.

76. Stimpson, *My Remembers*, 103–4.

77. Locke, *Action on Bullhide Creek*, 52; Morgan, *Fieldcrops for the Cotton-Belt*, 111, 113–14.

78. See Parker, "Cotton Seed," 163; Willard, *Farm Management Study*, 37; and Morgan, *Fieldcrops for the Cotton-Belt*, 81–82, 94–96, on the use of fertilizer. For discussions of various pests and their remedies, see Bourne, *Pioneer Farmer's Daughter*, 151; Sanderson, *Miscellaneous Cotton Insects in Texas*, 8; Dodd interview number 1 and Carroll interview number 1, IOH; Evans, "Texas Agriculture, 1880–1930," 59–67, 73–75, 87–88; Morgan, *Fieldcrops for the Cotton-Belt*, 127–34; and Bennett, Burke, and Lounsbury, *Soil Survey of Ellis County*, 11.

79. Evans, "Texas Agriculture, 1865–1880," 33; Crenshaw, *Texas Blackland Heritage*, 27; McBride, *"Filosofer" of "Kukel-bur" Flat*, 153. A good representation of the cotton plant in its stages from bloom to open boll is Otis Dozier's 1936 oil painting *Cotton Boll*. The painting is reproduced in Stewart, *Lone Star Regionalism*, 64.

80. Carroll interview number 1, IOH.

81. Brown, *Cotton*, 45.

82. Crenshaw, *Texas Blackland Heritage*, 28; Weir interview number 2, IOH.

83. Crenshaw, *Texas Blackland Heritage*, 28.

84. Dodd interview number 1, IOH.

85. Carroll interview number 2, IOH.

86. Jeffries, "Cotton Picking," 66.

87. Letter from Cass Nation, Greenville, Texas, to James Conrad, Commerce, Texas, 13 September 1991, in James Conrad's possession; Coltharp, "Reminiscences of Cotton Pickin' Days," 540; Jeffries, "Cotton Picking," 66.

88. Locke, *Action on Bullhide Creek*, 67.

89. Dodd interview number 1 and Hurtado interview number 1, IOH; McGee, "Hog Killing Day," 8; Jumper, "Little Money in Pockets Helps Everyone," 3.

90. Folley interview number 1, IOH.

91. Pitcock, "Voices of Experience"; Alford, *Oral Memoirs*, 15–16, Texas Collection.

92. Folley interview number 2, IOH. For a drawing and description of the slat or "slit" bonnet, see Jeffery, "Sunbonnet as Folk Costume," 214–15.

93. Carroll interview number 1, IOH.

94. Simcik, *Oral Memoirs*, 78, Texas Collection; Jeffries, "Cotton Picking," 71.

95. Jeffries, "Cotton Picking," 63.

96. Folley interview number 1, IOH. See also Rice, "Recollection of Other Highlights in My Life," Rice Papers, Archives, Gee Library. For an excellent account of picking cotton, see Owens, *Season of Weathering*, 13–19.

97. James Conrad, "Blackland Memories," typescript in Archives, Gee Library.

98. Pitcock, "Voices of Experience."

99. Nation to Conrad, 13 September 1991; Lula Kathryn Peacock Jones, *Recollections*, 11.

100. Summers, *Oral Memoirs*, 83, Texas Collection.

101. R. W. Williams, "Backward Glances," *Wolfe City Sun*, 15 September 1950.

102. R. W. Williams, "Backward Glances," *Wolfe City Sun*, 22 January 1951.

103. Jupe, *History of Tours*, 584.

104. Personal conversation with Inez Adams Walker, 23 October 1992.

105. Locke, *Action on Bullhide Creek*, 55; Carroll interview number 1, IOH; Coltharp, "Reminiscences of Cotton Pickin' Days," 541; Couch, "Agriculture," 308.

106. Ischy interview number 2, A. Frank Smith Jr. Library Center, Southwestern University, Georgetown, Tex. The Calvert family bought protective oil for their hands from peddlers (Dodd interview number 1, IOH).

107. Coltharp, "Reminiscences of Cotton Pickin' Days," 539.

108. Burkett, *Cotton*, 195; Collings, *Production of Cotton*, 167. Collings also provides a discussion of the "grading and classification of American upland cotton lint" (165–74).

109. Dodd interview number 1, IOH; Locke, *Action on Bullhide Creek*, 55–56.

110. Jumper, "Little Money in Pockets Helps Everyone," 3.

111. Eugene Hollon, "Growing Up in East Texas during the Depression," in Commerce, Depression Vertical File, Archives, Gee Library; Morgan, *Fieldcrops for the Cotton-Belt*, 117; Evans, "Texas Agriculture, 1865–1880," 38.

112. Bomar, *Texas Weather*, 145, 148, 149.

113. Oscar Adams, "File 13" column, *Commerce Journal*, 28 September 1955; Jeffries, "Cotton Picking," 62, 69.

114. Folley interview number 2, IOH; Locke, *Action on Bullhide Creek*, 60 n. 14; McBride, *"Filosofer" of "Kukel-bur" Flat*, 137.

115. U.S. Department of Agriculture, *Cotton Plant*, 245; Jeffries, "Cotton Picking," 71.

116. Jeffries, "Cotton Picking," 68; Coltharp, "Reminiscences of Cotton Pickin' Days," 539–40; Evans, "Texas Agriculture, 1865–1880," 39.

117. Dodd interview number 1 and Carroll interview number 1, IOH; Owens, *Season of Weathering*, 16.

118. Dodd interview number 1, IOH.

119. Adams, "File 13"; Dorothy Scarborough, *Can't Get a Red Bird*, 59; Hazel Beauton Riley, *Washing on the Line*, 11.

120. Bourne, *Pioneer Farmer's Daughter*, 152.

121. Willard, *Farm Management Study*, 8–9; Jeffries, "Cotton Picking," 64–65; Jupe, *His-*

tory of Tours, 643; Evans, "Texas Agriculture, 1880–1930," 40; McDaniel, *Oral Memoirs*, 11, Texas Collection.

122. Personal conversation with Inez Adams Walker, 28 October 1992.

123. Hardeman oral history interview, 6, 11, Archives, Gee Library; Washington, *Oral Memoirs*, 44, Texas Collection. E. E. Davis documents the shortening of school terms to accommodate the cotton crop. In 1921–22, the average term length for a rural school in Williamson County averaged 131 days, while the term in Taylor was 166 days, in Granger, 169 days, and in Georgetown, 159 days (Davis, *Study of Rural Schools in Williamson County*, 18–19).

124. Owens, *Season of Weathering*, 13.

125. James Conrad, "Cotton Harvest," typescript in "Blackland Memories" file, Archives, Gee Library.

126. Adams, "File 13"; Rampy, *Choice and Chance*, 11.

127. Weir interview number 2, IOH.

128. McDaniel, *Oral Memoirs*, 12, Texas Collection.

129. Weir interview number 1, IOH.

130. Locke, *Action on Bullhide Creek*, 65.

131. Templin and Marshall, *Soil Survey of Hunt County*, 9; Matthews and Dart, *Welfare of Children*, 61; Summers, *Oral Memoirs*, 25, Texas Collection.

132. Evans, "Texas Agriculture, 1880–1930," 39; Reisler, *By the Sweat of Their Brow*, 14–16. Accurate statistics on Mexican immigration are impossible to obtain because the U.S. Census Bureau classified Mexicans as "white."

133. Reisler, *By the Sweat of Their Brow*, 14–15.

134. Locke, *Action on Bullhide Creek*, 65; Handman, "Economic Reasons for the Coming of the Mexican Immigrant," 611. One of the best-known *jefes* in Central Texas was named Cruz. See Almanza interview number 1, IOH, for a discussion of Cruz and his arrangements with his tenants.

135. U.S. Department of Agriculture, *Cotton Plant*, 245.

136. Lomax and Lomax, *Negro Folk Songs as Sung by Lead Belly*, 92–94.

137. Locke, *Action on Bullhide Creek*, 56.

138. Podsednik interview, 6, Texas Collection.

139. Cooper, *Oral Memoirs*, 20, Texas Collection.

140. Folley interview number 1, IOH.

141. Hardeman interview, 7–8, Archives, Gee Library.

142. Caufield interview number 4, IOH.

143. Coltharp, "Reminiscences of Cotton Pickin' Days," 540–41.

144. Personal conversation with Inez Adams Walker, 23 October 1992.

145. *Pea* refers to the sixteen-pound weight on the scale known as a pea weight after the abbreviation of avoirdupois, the American system of weight (personal conversation with David O. Lintz and Calvin B. Smith, Waco, Texas, 30 November 1992).

146. Carroll interview number 1, IOH.

147. Weir interview number 2, IOH.

148. Evans, "Texas Agriculture, 1880–1930," 41; Allen, *Labor of Women*, 109, 197.

149. Personal conversation with Inez Adams Walker, 28 October 1992.

150. Hardeman interview, 10, Archives, Gee Library.

151. Anne Goodwyn Jones, *Tomorrow Is Another Day*, 13.

152. For a discussion of the cotton-ginning procedure and its history, see Britton, *Bale o' Cotton*.

153. Carroll interview number 1, IOH.

Chapter Five

1. Personal conversation with Inez Adams Walker, 23 October 1992.

2. Washington, *Oral Memoirs*, 49, Texas Collection.

3. St. Paul Home Demonstration Club Bicentennial Committee, *History of St. Paul Community*, 1.

4. Matthews and Dart, *Welfare of Children*, 2.

5. Wehrwein, "Social Life in Southern Travis County," 500, 505; Matthews and Dart, *Welfare of Children*, 68. According to Wehrwein, white farm owners made the most frequent visits; a majority reported that they visited frequently and none reported never going visiting. White tenants, conversely, were much less sociable, with only a third visiting frequently, the majority visiting "rarely," and almost 5 percent never going visiting. African American owners proved less sociable than either their white counterparts or other black tenants, with a majority of owners declaring frequent visits but almost half reporting rare visits. Like white owners, all black owners revealed at least some visiting. Black tenants visited most frequently, as only a third told of rare visits and only a handful reported no visits. Mexican farmers fared the worst socially in this sample, as only a quarter reported frequent visits, the majority described rare visits, and 17 percent reported that they never visited with neighbors. Wehrwein concluded that blacks who socialized less "were those living more or less isolated and who therefore could not visit very often." White owners proved more outgoing than tenants, having lived in the area longer and "had time to get acquainted" (Wehrwein, "Social Life in Southern Travis County," 500–501).

6. Allen, *Labor of Women*, 37.

7. James Tull Richardson, "Social Changes in Hunt County," 126.

8. Bateson, *Composing a Life*, 181.

9. Wehrwein, "Social Life in Southern Travis County," 500–501.

10. Matthews and Dart, *Welfare of Children*, 58.

11. Locke, *Action on Bullhide Creek*, 89.

12. Rampy, *Choice and Chance*, 4.

13. Weir interview number 2, IOH.

14. Folley interview number 3, IOH.

15. Simcik, *Oral Memoirs*, 20, Texas Collection; Jupe, *History of Tours*, 601.

16. Jupe, *History of Tours*, 601, 687.

17. Weir interview number 1.

18. Locke, *Action on Bullhide Creek*, 90.

19. Bourne, *Pioneer Farmer's Daughter*, 138.

20. Clara Jones, *Pillars of Faith*, [13].

21. Sowell, *Girl Named Laura*, 39; Matthews and Dart, *Welfare of Children*, 59; Simcik, *Oral Memoirs*, 28, Texas Collection.

22. Dodd interview number 3, IOH.

23. Caufield interview number 6, IOH.

24. Wehrwein, "Social Life in Southern Travis County," 505.

25. Jurney, Lebo, and Green, *Historic Farming*, 359.

26. Humphrey, *Farther Off from Heaven*, 137–39.

27. Jupe, *History of Tours*, 658.

28. Allen, *Labor of Women*, 221.

29. *Welcome to Celeste*, 22; Locke, *Action on Bullhide Creek*, 138; Wehrwein, "Social Life in Southern Travis County," 508.

30. Rampy, *Choice and Chance*, 4–5. Unfortunately, I have discovered no collections of personal correspondence from or between rural women.

31. Matthews and Dart, *Welfare of Children*, 56–57. Higher literacy rates among women reflect the fact that rural women in Texas generally received more education than rural men. For a detailed discussion, see Ullrich, *Farm Operator*, 12–13.

32. Matthews and Dart, *Welfare of Children*, 68.

33. Allen, *Labor of Women*, 56.

34. Ibid., 153; James Conrad, "Filling Leisure Time Wasn't Difficult," Blackland Memories Collection, Archives, Gee Library.

35. Allen, *Labor of Women*, 185.

36. Carroll interview number 6, IOH.

37. Weir interviews 1 and 3.

38. Conrad, "Filling Leisure Time Wasn't Difficult," Blackland Memories Collection, Archives, Gee Library; Clara Stearns Scarborough, *Land of Good Water*, 262.

39. Machann and Mendl, *Krásná Amerika*, 185; Allen, *Labor of Women*, 223.

40. Allen, *Labor of Women*, 58.

41. Carroll interview number 6, IOH.

42. James Tull Richardson, "Social Changes in Hunt County," 62.

43. Allen, *Labor of Women*, 59, 185, 223. See also Locke, *Action on Bullhide Creek*, 75; McBride, *"Filosofer" of "Kukel-bur" Flat*, 92–93; and Weir interview number 1, IOH. In their reading habits, the people of the Blacklands resembled the working-class people of Muncie, Indiana, in the 1920s, who bought few books outside of schoolbooks and Bibles and read periodicals "primarily for the vicarious living in fictional form they contain" (Lynd and Lynd, *Middletown*, 230, 241).

44. *Texas Almanac* (1939), 327; Allen, *Labor of Women*, 63, 185.

45. Dodd interviews 3 and 4.

46. Barnes, *Oral Memoirs*, 23–24, Texas Collection.

47. *Texas Almanac* (1927), 269. In 1930, Ruth Allen found that only 8.1 percent of white women had radios, and no African American or Mexican women had them (*Labor of Women*, 41, 183, 219). The urban populations proved far more likely to have radios. In 1930, 38.7 percent of the households in Dallas County, for example, owned radios. In Hunt County, 21 percent of families did so, as did 22.1 percent in McLennan County. Relatively more rural Ellis County, which could receive Dallas stations, had radios in 19.9 percent of its households, while in Williamson County only 14.7 percent of families owned receivers. The statistics, based on the 1930 federal census, are quoted in *Eliminating Advertising Waste in Texas*, plate 2. In June 1931, Price-Waterhouse conducted a survey for Columbia Broadcasting System, asking recipients to tell which radio stations they listened to most. In Waco, the urban response was 9 percent above the national average, but the rural response was 22.9 percent below the national average (*Eliminating Advertising Waste in Texas*, 44).

48. Rice, "Some Old Stories," Rice Papers, and McRae interview, 40–41, Archives, Gee Library.

49. Lewis interview, 35, Archives, Gee Library.

50. *Texas Almanac* (1941), 247.

51. Rice, "Some Old Stories," Rice Papers, Archives, Gee Library; Weir interview number 3, IOH; Terrace, *Radio's Golden Years*, 167.

52. Machann and Mendl, *Krásná Amerika*, 163.

53. *Texas Almanac* (1941), 247. By 1940, the number of white tenants with radios had risen to 46.5 percent, but only 10.5 percent of black tenants possessed them (Brophy, "Black Texan," 75).

54. For a discussion of radio in other parts of the nation, see Wik, "Radio in Rural America," 339–50.

55. Dillow and Carver, *Mrs. Blackwell's Heart-of-Texas Cookbook*, 73.

56. McRae interview, 29, Archives, Gee Library; Jurney, Lebo, and Green, *Historic Farming*, 359; R. W. Williams, "Backward Glances," *Wolfe City Sun*, 30 January 1948; Jupe, *History of Tours*, 804; Wehrwein, "Social Life in Southern Travis County," 509; Matthews and Dart, *Welfare of Children*; 60; Allen, *Labor of Women*, 42, 183, 219. This statistic points to the relative poverty of the rural South; by 1919, 85 percent of the farm families in the Midwest had telephone service. See Jellison, *Entitled to Power*, 35. See also Rakow, "Women and the Telephone," 210–11, on the limited effectiveness of the telephone for farm women.

57. Dodd interview number 3, IOH.

58. Templin and Marshall, *Soil Survey of Hunt County*, 4; Weir interview number 4, IOH.

59. Crenshaw, *Texas Blackland Heritage*, 59.

60. Carroll interviews 1 and 2, and Weir interview number 2, IOH.

61. Dodd interview number 3, IOH.

62. Folley interview number 3, IOH.

63. Carroll interview number 5, IOH.

64. Caufield interview number 6, IOH.

65. Aubrey Garrett oral history interview (interviewed by Howard Garrett on 11 April 1990, in Emory, Texas) in Cemetery Workday Vertical File, Archives, Gee Library.

66. *Lift High the Cross, 1882–1982. Zion Lutheran Church, Walburg, Texas*, in Zion Lutheran Church and School History, Walburg, Texas, Vertical File, Georgetown Public Library.

67. Jupe, *History of Tours*, 473.

68. *Lift High the Cross*, 12.

69. Barnes, *Oral Memoirs*, 28–29, Texas Collection.

70. Hazel Beauton Riley, *Washing on the Line*, 3–4.

71. Weir interview number 3, IOH.

72. Stimpson, *My Remembers*, 124.

73. Folley interview number 3 and Dodd interview number 3, IOH.

74. U.S. Department of Commerce, Bureau of the Census, *Religious Bodies 1916*, 83, 100, 475, 497; *Religious Bodies 1926*, 103, 130, 961, 995; and *Religious Bodies 1936*, 114, 143, 1134, 1187, 1528.

75. Folley interview number 3, IOH.

76. Allen, *Labor of Women*, 53, 184; map appended to DuPuy, "Social Trends in McLennan County."

77. Allen, *Labor of Women*, 184.

78. Carroll interview number 5 and Dodd interview number 3, IOH.

79. Dodd interview number 3, IOH.

80. Carroll interview number 5, IOH.

81. Stimpson, *My Remembers*, 118.

82. Allen, *Labor of Women*, 222. On the paucity of Roman Catholic services for Mexican immigrants, see Hinojosa, "Immigrant Church," 38–41.

83. Almanza interview number 2, IOH.

84. Locke, *Action on Bullhide Creek*, 75; McBride, *"Filosofer" of "Kukel-bur" Flat*, 92–93; Weir interview number 1, IOH.

85. Allen, *Labor of Women*, 61.

86. Caufield interview number 1, IOH.

87. Dodd interview number 3, IOH.

88. Caufield interview number 1, IOH.

89. Carroll interview number 5, IOH.

90. Stimpson, *My Remembers*, 59–60.

91. Jupe, *History of Tours*, 593, 656; Almanza interview number 2, IOH.

92. Simcik, *Oral Memoirs*, 32, 34, Texas Collection.

93. A very large body of literature exists on southern and Texas religion. For a brief introduction, see Samuel S. Hill, "Religion," in *Encyclopedia of Southern Culture*. A 1934 survey of McLennan County revealed that outside of the urban center of Waco there were 103 churches in the county. Of those, 31 were white Baptist (mostly Southern Baptist), 25 were white Methodist (Methodist Episcopal, South), 16 were "Colored Baptist" (most likely National Baptist), and 8 were Colored Methodist Episcopal (a segregated division of Methodism formed in 1870)—a total of 80 Baptist or Methodist churches representing 78 percent of all rural churches in the county. The Disciples of Christ and the Church of Christ, who split around the turn of the century, held their own ground with 5 churches each in rural McLennan County. Other Protestant denominations represented in the countryside included Presbyterian (4), Lutheran (3), and "Colored Presbyterian" (2). Many of these were located in small towns such as Riesel and Mart, which also had Baptist and Methodist churches. The three Roman Catholic churches in the county outside of Waco were located in the Czech communities in the eastern part of the county (map appended to DuPuy, "Social Trends in McLennan County").

For discussions of the various denominations in the South, see the following entries in the *Encyclopedia of Religion in the South*: Winthrop S. Hudson, "Baptist Denomination"; A. V. Huff Jr., "Methodist Church"; William B. Gravely, "Christian Methodist Episcopal Church"; Samuel C. Pearson, "Disciples of Christ"; and Richard T. Hughes, "Churches of Christ."

94. Hughes, "Churches of Christ," in *Encyclopedia of Religion in the South*; Lewis, *On the Edge of the Black Waxy*, 73–74.

95. Bourne, *Pioneer Farmer's Daughter*, 124.

96. "Rural Williamson Rich in Churches," *San Antonio Express*, 30 October 1933.

97. Map appended to DuPuy, "Social Trends in McLennan County."

98. Allen, *Labor of Women*, 222.

99. Carroll interview number 6, IOH.

100. Personal conversation with Inez Adams Walker, 23 October 1992.

101. Jordan, *Texas*, 119; Hunt County Baptist Association Minutes, 1924, Texas Collection; Everett, *Among the Salt*, 1–2.

102. Stimpson, *My Remembers*, 89.

103. Poage, *McLennan County before 1980*, 262; Beach, *Souvenir of Golden Jubilee*, 17, 19.

104. Simcik, *Oral Memoirs*, 80–81, Texas Collection.

105. Carroll interview number 5, IOH.

106. Folley interview number 3, IOH.

107. Carroll interview number 5, IOH.

108. Jupe, *History of Tours*, 804.

109. Simcik, *Oral Memoirs*, 7–8, Texas Collection.

110. Friedman, *Enclosed Garden*, 69.

111. Stimpson, *My Remembers*, 119, 121.

112. Ibid., 118, 121.

113. In southern Travis County, almost one-half of the blacks, one-third of white owners, and one-fifth of white tenants and Mexicans reported that at least one member of their family belonged to a church society (Wehrwein, "Social Life in Southern Travis County," 508).

114. Beach, *Souvenir of Golden Jubilee*, 28; James Tull Richardson, "Social Changes in Hunt County," 60.

115. Perry United Methodist Church, *Century of Methodism*, [30].

116. Ibid., [31].

117. Folley interview number 3, IOH.

118. Everett, *Among the Salt*, 11.

119. Victoria Fritz Richardson, *History of the Immanuel Lutheran Church*, 9.

120. Folley interview number 3, IOH.

121. Stimpson, *My Remembers*, 150.

122. Caufield interview number 6, IOH.

123. Dodd interview number 3, IOH.

124. Folley interview number 3, IOH.

125. "Rural Williamson Rich in Churches"; *Lift High the Cross*, 14.

126. *Membership and Official Directory of Maypearl Circuit*, [7].

127. Burnett interview, 31, Archives, Gee Library; Carroll interview number 4, IOH.

128. Locke, *Action on Bullhide Creek*, 30–31; Carroll interview number 4 and Weir interview number 3, IOH.

129. Simcik, *Oral Memoirs*, 75, Texas Collection.

130. Jupe, *History of Tours*, 671.

131. Isaac, *Transformation of Virginia*, 85, 161, 301–2; Heyrman, *Southern Cross*, 144, 233–34.

132. Wehrwein, "Social Life in Southern Travis County," 506.

133. Owens, *Season of Weathering*, 242. See also Weir interview number 2, IOH.

134. Hale, *Oral Memoirs*, 10, Texas Collection.

135. Owens, *Texas Folk Songs*, 110–11.

136. Dodd interview number 3, IOH.

137. Caufield interview number 6, IOH.

138. Summers, *Oral Memoirs*, 36, Texas Collection.

139. Bourne, *Pioneer Farmer's Daughter*, 143–44.

140. Folley interview number 3, IOH.

141. "Rural Williamson Rich in Churches."

142. Stimpson, *My Remembers*, 123–24.

143. Ibid., 120.

144. Hardaway, "Sacred Harp Traditions in Texas."

145. Lewis interview, 53, Archives, Gee Library. The Stamps-Baxter Music Company of Dallas enjoyed wide popularity in the 1930s, spreading gospel music through male quartets on radio and in recordings. See Harry Eskew, "Shape-note Hymnody," in *The New Grove Dictionary of Music and Musicians*.

146. Weir interview number 3, IOH.

147. Crenshaw, *Texas Blackland Heritage*, 65.

148. Folley interview number 3, IOH.

149. Stimpson, *My Remembers*, 120.

150. Hazel Beauton Riley, *Washing on the Line*, 25.

151. Dodd interview number 3, IOH.

152. McBride, *"Filosofer" of "Kukel-bur" Flat*, 162.

153. Carroll interview number 5, IOH.

154. Goff, "Rev. Culpepper in Greenville," *Newspaper Columns of C. W. Goff*, 2:89, Archives, Gee Library.

155. Bourne, *Pioneer Farmer's Daughter*, 86, 96.

156. Folley interview number 3, IOH.

157. Stimpson, *My Remembers*, 118.

158. Carroll interview number 5, IOH.

159. Allen, *Labor of Women*, 63.

160. *Semi-Weekly Farm News*, 8 February 1910, 7, and 15 March 1910, 7.

161. Caufield interviews 5 and 6, IOH.

162. Ibid.

163. Stimpson, *My Remembers*, 102–3.

Chapter Six

1. Telephone conversation with Garland Sharpless, Waco, Texas, 8 July 1992.

2. Lewis interview, 36, Archives, Gee Library.

3. Locke, *Action on Bullhide Creek*, 126.

4. Dodd interview number 3, IOH.

5. S. G. Reed, "Interurban Lines in Texas," in Webb and Carroll, eds., *Handbook of Texas*.

6. Simcik, *Oral Memoirs*, 49, Texas Collection.

7. Campbell, "Country Life in Mooreville Texas," Texas Collection.

8. Bourne, *Pioneer Farmer's Daughter*, 126–27, 212; McRae interview, 38, Archives, Gee Library.

9. McBride, *"Filosofer" of "Kukel-bur" Flat*, 166; Locke, *Action on Bullhide Creek*, 114; Perkins interview, 2, Archives, Gee Library; Jupe, *History of Tours*, 760.

10. Interrante, " 'You Can't Go to Town in a Bathtub,' " 160–61; Almanza interview number 2, IOH.

11. Locke, *Action on Bullhide Creek*, 137. See also McBride, *"Filosofer" of "Kukel-bur" Flat*, 230; Owens, *This Stubborn Soil*, 42; Owens, *Season of Weathering*, 240–41; Crenshaw, *Texas Blackland Heritage*, 24.

12. Humphrey, *Ordways*, 114; James Conrad, "Mrs. Tucker Remembers Life before Conveniences," *Commerce Journal*, 24 June 1987.

13. Dodd interview number 3, IOH.

14. Spain, *Gendered Spaces*, xiv.

15. By 1914, 20 percent of the farmers in Ellis County had replaced their horses and buggies with the new machines (Willard, *Farm Management Study*, 8). By 1920, 57 percent of the Anglo Hill County families surveyed owned cars, and by 1929, 85 percent of the Anglo families in the lower Blacklands had acquired autos (Matthews and Dart, *Welfare of Children*, 60; Allen, *Labor of Women*, 41). These figures are significantly below the average in the rural North and West, where 62 percent of the farm families owned automobiles as early as 1920. See Ward, "Farm Woman's Problems," 446. Even among poorer ethnic groups, auto ownership became important; in 1930, 53.8 percent of the black women and 45.4 percent of the Mexican women with whom Ruth Allen spoke lived in families who owned cars (Allen, *Labor of Women*, 183, 219).

16. Carroll interview number 6, IOH. For a general discussion of the impact of the automobile on rural women, see Scharff, *Taking the Wheel*, 142–45.

17. Allen, *Labor of Women*, 40.

18. Weir interview number 3 and Carroll interview number 6, IOH.

19. Caufield interview number 7, IOH.

20. Campbell, "Country Life in Mooreville Texas," Texas Collection.

21. Allen, *Labor of Women*, 40; Everett, *Among the Salt*, 16–17; Templin and Marshall, *Soil Survey of Hunt County*, 4.

22. *Texas Almanac* (1941), 438, 462, 481, 520.

23. Webb and Carroll, eds., "Moody, Texas," and "Temple, Texas," in *Handbook of Texas*; *Texas Almanac* (1992–93), 177, 178. For an excellent account on how small towns such as Moody came into being, see Ayers, *Promise of the New South*, ch. 3.

24. Dodd interview number 3, IOH.

25. Carroll interview number 3, IOH. A study of Hunt County revealed that farmers reported going to town much more frequently in 1930 than in 1920. In 1920, only 39 percent had gone to town more than once a week, but in 1930, 58 percent went more than once a week. The number of Blacklands farmers who went as rarely as once a month dropped by half (James Tull Richardson, "Social Changes in Hunt County," 124).

26. M. B. Newton Jr., "First Monday Trades Day," in *Encyclopedia of Southern Culture*.

27. Rice, "Stories of Events I Remember," Rice Papers, Archives, Gee Library; Lewis, *On the Edge of the Black Waxy*, 33; Locke, *Action on Bullhide Creek*, 113.

28. Matthews and Dart, *Welfare of Children*, 59.

29. Owens, *Season of Weathering*, 46.

30. Seaholm, "Earnest Women," 412.

31. Maude Wilson, *Highlights of Fifty-Two Years, Shakespeare Club, Waxahachie*, Clubs—Women—Waxahachie Vertical File, Sims Library, Waxahachie.

32. Seaholm, "Earnest Women," 413; *Dallas Morning News*, 17 October 1915, Section 1, p. 9.

33. Allen, *Labor of Women*, 52–53, 222.

34. Ibid., 138, 183–84, 219.

35. Carroll interview number 2, IOH.

36. Rice, "Five Final Stories," Rice Papers, Archives, Gee Library.

37. Lewis interview, 42, Archives, Gee Library.

38. Owens, *A Season of Weathering*, 17.

39. W. Eugene Hollon, "Growing Up in East Texas during the Depression," Commerce, Depression Vertical File, Archives, Gee Library.

40. Perkins interview, 24–25, Archives, Gee Library.

41. Caufield interview number 7, IOH.

42. Perkins interview, 26, Archives, Gee Library; Winn, "Chautauqua—1912," 22.

43. Benjamin W. Griffith, "Chautauqua," in *Encyclopedia of Southern Culture*.

44. Lewis interview, 19–20, Archives, Gee Library.

45. Winn, "Chautauqua—1912," 21.

46. McRae interview, 31, and James Conrad, "Filling Leisure Time Wasn't Difficult," Blackland Memories Collection, Archives, Gee Library.

47. Caufield interview number 7, IOH.

48. Almanza interview number 2, IOH. While the Waco newspaper does not verify the availability of Spanish-language movies in the 1920s, Luz Sanchez Hurtado believes that the movies began showing about 1927 (personal conversation, 2 August 1995).

49. Allen, *Labor of Women*, 54.

50. Carroll interview number 6, IOH.

51. Matthews and Dart, *Welfare of Children*, 59.

52. Wehrwein, "Social Life in Southern Travis County," 505.

53. Rice, "Remembering Highlights," Rice Papers, Archives, Gee Library.

54. James Conrad, "Hunt County Fair Has Long History," *Greenville Herald-Banner*, 7 August 1989; Douglas, "History of the Agricultural Fairs of Texas," 34, 188–201; *Mart Herald*, 18 August 1977, 7; *Texas Almanac* (1912), 113.

55. Conrad, "Hunt County Fair Has Long History."

56. James Tull Richardson, "Social Changes in Hunt County," 47–49; Conrad, "Hunt County Fair Has Long History"; "Fairs, Commerce Tri-County," in *Handbook of Commerce, Texas, 1872–1985*.

57. "New and Larger Exhibits to Be Shown at Ennis at 1925 Ellis County Fair," *Waxahachie Daily Light*, 24 August 1925.

58. *Catalogue and Premium List, Ellis County Fair, Golden Jubilee Year, Sept. 27 to Oct. 2, 1937*, in Ellis County Fair Vertical File, Sims Library, Waxahachie.

59. Ibid.

60. Barnes, *Texas Cotton Palace*, 20.

61. Dorothy Scarborough, *In the Land of Cotton*, 121–22.

62. Dodd interview number 3, IOH.

63. Weir interview number 4, IOH.

64. Estes, *Oral Memoirs*, 36, Texas Collection.

65. Caufield interview number 7, IOH. Newspaper research fails to reveal whether blacks were banned outright from the Cotton Palace.

66. Dodd interview number 3, IOH. See also James Tull Richardson, "Social Changes in Hunt County," 37; McRae interview, 37, Archives, Gee Library, on the decline of Cumby,

Hunt County; Johnson, *City on a Hill*, 13, on the decline of Coupland, Williamson County; and Chambers, "Life in a Cotton Farming Community," 146–47, on the decline of White-rock, Red River County.

67. Wehrwein, "Social Life in Southern Travis County," 501–2. The Hoover Research Commission in 1933 described this process of a "large center" extending "the radius of its influence" as "metropolitanism" (Interrante, " 'You Can't Go to Town in a Bathtub,' " 158–59).

68. Allen, *Labor of Women*, 49, 51. In contrast to Allen's assessment, William Owens, in the early 1930s, found the play-party continuing (Owens, *Swing and Turn*, xix).

69. E. T. Dawson, "E. T. Dawson Gives History of Greathouse," *Waxahachie Daily Light*, 8 June 1978; Clara Jones, *Pillars of Faith*, [20].

70. Weir interviews 1 and 3, IOH.

71. Jaffe, "Rural Women in Unskilled Labor," 22; Rice, "A Success Story," Rice Papers, Archives, Gee Library.

72. Jaffe, "Rural Women in Unskilled Labor," ix; Motheral, *Recent Trends in Land Tenure*, 22, 32.

73. Jaffe, "Rural Women in Unskilled Labor," 20, 22. Researchers from the Works Progress Administration found that in the 1930s females left the country in greater proportions than males and tended to predominate in the cities (Lively and Taeuber, *Rural Migration in the United States*, 122). See also National Youth Administration, *Cotton Growing in Texas*, 5.

74. Owens, *Season of Weathering*, 38. See also Yeary, *Cotton*, 5; Humphrey, *Farther Off from Heaven*, 56; and Rampy, *Choice and Chance*, 13.

75. Caufield interview number 7, IOH.

76. Coltharp, "Reminiscences of Cotton Pickin' Days," 539.

77. Contemporary observers in Texas were well aware of the impact of the new programs. For their comments, see Hamilton, *Social Aspects of Recent Trends in Mechanization*, 1; Lewis, *On the Edge of the Black Waxy*, 11–12; Barns, "Employment in Texas," 300; and Motheral, *Recent Trends in Land Tenure*, 5, 9.

78. Skrabanek, *Characteristics and Changes in the Texas Farm Population*, 6.

79. National Youth Administration, *Cotton Growing in Texas*, 57; Steen, *Twentieth Century Texas*, 50.

80. Dodd interview number 2, IOH. Some reformers decried this awareness as leading to discontent without providing any remedies. University of Texas sociologist Ruth Allen observed that going to town had bad effects on rural women: "Has she not gained a discontent which can hardly be classed as divine and an unwillingness to perform the old tasks with neither the willingness, the knowledge, nor the opportunity of performing new ones?" (Allen, *Labor of Women*, 41).

81. Dodd interview number 3, IOH.

82. Yeary, *Cotton*, 6; Lewis, *On the Edge of the Black Waxy*, 36–37.

83. Jaffe, "Rural Women in Unskilled Labor," 25; Owens, *Season of Weathering*, 44. For a comparison to Jaffe, see the study of rural young women in Richmond, Virginia, and Durham, North Carolina, found in Hatcher, *Rural Girls in the City for Work*.

84. Caufield interview number 7, IOH.

85. Allen, *Labor of Women*, 36.

86. Weir interview number 4, IOH. For examples of individuals' moves to town from the rural Blackland Prairie, see Jupe, *History of Tours*, 565, 598, 651, 691; Owens, *Season of*

Weathering, 40; Rampy, *Choice and Chance*, 22, 28, 39, 51; McBride, *"Filosofer" of "Kukelbur" Flat*, 191, 216; Crenshaw, *Texas Blackland Heritage*, 29; Estes, *Oral Memoirs*, 15, Texas Collecton; Folley interviews 1 and 3; Goff, *Newspaper Columns of C. W. Goff*, 1:164, and McRae interview, 21–22, Archives, Gee Library; and Springer, *Oral Memoirs*, 11, Texas Collection.

87. *Texas Almanac* (1941), 108–10.

88. Skrabanek, *Characteristics and Changes in the Texas Farm Population*, 4–9.

89. *Georgetown, Texas, Illustrated* (Citizens Club, Georgetown[?], n.d.) in Georgetown, Texas, Vertical File, Georgetown Public Library.

90. In the 1920s, the mills included Belton, Bonham, Corsicana, Dallas, Hillsboro, Itasca, McKinney, Mexia, New Braunfels, San Antonio, San Marcos, Sherman, Waco, and Waxahachie (*Texas Almanac* [1927], 230).

91. "Cotton Mills in the Fields," undated clipping (ca. 1908) in Cotton Mills and Compresses Vertical File, Sims Library, Waxahachie.

92. *Texas Department of Agriculture Yearbook*, 204, 206.

93. Thomas T. West, "A History of Celeste, Texas," in Celeste—History, Hunt County Vertical File, Archives, Gee Library.

94. Elmer Fincher, "Old Waxahachie Cotton Mill," *The [Ennis, Texas] Weekly Local*, 19 August 1977, 1. See also "City Former Site of Cotton Mill," *Waxahachie Daily Light*, 5 September 1976, and Sneed, "Waxahachie Cotton Mills," 15.

95. *Texas Almanac* (1927), 230; Bizzell, *Rural Texas*, 262.

96. "Oil, Discovery and Production of," "Mexia Oil Field," and "Luling, Texas," all in *Handbook of Texas*.

97. Carroll interviews 2 and 4.

98. Rice, "Stories Poems Songs," Rice Papers, Archives, Gee Library.

99. Mantor, *Our Town*, 15, 23; James Conrad, "Towns Grew in Century's First Decade," *Greenville Herald-Banner*, 11 May 1987, A3.

100. Jaffe, "Rural Women in Unskilled Labor," iv–v.

101. Jupe, *History of Tours*, 524. See Interrante, " 'You Can't Go to Town in a Bathtub,' " 164, for a comparison to commuting in the Midwest.

102. Washington, *Oral Memoirs*, 44, Texas Collection.

103. Allen, *Labor of Women*, 37.

104. Humphrey, *Ordways*, 10–11. For discussions of urban-rural contrast and conflict, see Lewis, *On the Edge of the Black Waxy*, 37, and Dykstra, "Town-Country Conflict," 195–204.

105. Everett, *Among the Salt*, 23.

106. Alford, *Oral Memoirs*, 46–47, Texas Collection.

107. Barns, "Employment in Texas," 301.

108. Weir interview number 4, IOH. For an excellent overview on the impact of World War II on the rural South, see Daniel, "Going among Strangers," 886–911.

109. Lewis, *On the Edge of the Black Waxy*, 57–59; Aderholt, "Education in Williamson County," 37.

110. James Conrad, "Rural School Districts Proliferated in 1899," *Commerce Journal*, n.d.; Matthews and Dart, *Welfare of Children*, 32.

111. Davis, *Study of Rural Schools in Williamson County*, 21; Bowers, *Country Life Movement*, 81.

112. Turley interview, 53, Archives, Gee Library; Bowers, *Country Life Movement*, 108–9.

113. Weir interview number 3, IOH.

114. James Tull Richardson, "Social Changes in Hunt County," 84, 89, 90.

115. Allen, *Labor of Women*, 40.

116. Lewis, *On the Edge of the Black Waxy*, 73.

117. Hunt County Baptist Association Minutes, 1924, 1930, 1944, Texas Collection.

118. Everett, *Among the Salt*, 33, 35. For a general discussion of the problems associated with the decline of the rural church, see *Function, Policy and Program of the Country Church*.

119. Allen, *Labor of Women*, 51.

120. Dodd interview number 3, IOH.

121. Owens, *Season of Weathering*, 119, 162–63.

122. Caufield interview number 6, IOH.

123. Owens, *Tell Me a Story*, 303.

124. Bill Neely, "Deep Ellum Blues," on *Blackland Farm Boy*, recording 5014, Arhoolie, 1974.

125. Weir interview number 3, IOH.

126. Jupe, *History of Tours*, 517.

127. Owens, *Season of Weathering*, 74.

128. Ibid., 158, 160.

129. Daniel, "Transformation of the Rural South," 232.

130. Hairston, "Cotton Comes to Williamson," 33.

131. Carroll interview number 7, IOH.

bibliography

Manuscript Collections and Oral History Interviews

College Station, Tex.

    Archives, Sterling C. Evans Library, Texas A&M University

        Texas Agricultural Extension Service Historical Files.

        Texas Agricultural Extension Service Papers.

        Texas Extension Service Historical Notes and Staff Lists by year, 1903–19.

Commerce, Tex.

    Archives, James Gee Library, Texas A&M University, Commerce

        Blackland Memories Collection.

        Burnett, Flake, oral history interview. Interviewed by James H. Conrad on 10 January 1986, in Greenville, Texas.

        C. G. Butler, Hunt County History Vertical File.

        Celeste—History. Hunt County Vertical File.

        Cemetery Workday Vertical File.

        Commerce, Depression Vertical File.

        Goff, C. W. *Newspaper Columns of C. W. Goff*. Compiled by the Commerce [Texas] Public Library, 1982. 2 volumes.

        Hardeman, Julia Roberts, oral history interview. Interviewed by Corrinne Crow on 15 May 1975, in Commerce, Texas.

        Lewis, Lois Lacy, oral history interviews. Interviewed by James H. Conrad and Mary Jane Seigler on 8 April and 29 April 1985, in Celeste, Texas.

        McRae, Bessie Winniford, oral history interview. Interviewed by James Conrad on 29 March 1982, in Cumby, Texas.

        Perkins, Lucille Mora, oral history interviews. Interviewed by Judy Rudoff on 5 September, 17 September, and 19 September 1980, in Commerce, Texas.

        Rice, Lee. Papers.

        Turley, Lucille, oral history interview. Interviewed by James H. Conrad and Mary Jane Seigler on 12 November 1984, in Commerce, Texas.

        Water/Cistern Vertical File.

Georgetown, Tex.

A. Frank Smith Jr. Library Center, Southwestern University

Ischy, Tullia Hall, oral history interviews. Interviewed by John Martin on 2 April, 7 April, and 12 April 1986, in Georgetown, Texas.

Georgetown Public Library

Georgetown, Texas, Vertical File.

Zion Lutheran Church and School History, Walburg, Texas, Vertical File.

Greenville, Tex.

Hunt County Museum

Agriculture Vertical File.

Waco, Tex.

Baylor University

Institute for Oral History

Almanza, Adelaida Torres, oral history interviews. Interviewed by M. Rebecca Sharpless with simultaneous Spanish-English translation by Lelis Idalia Nolasco on four occasions from 8 March to 7 July 1995, in Waco, Texas.

Carroll, Dovie Lee, and Etta Lillian Hardy Carroll, oral history interviews. Interviewed by M. Rebecca Sharpless on seven occasions from 21 September 1990 to 11 July 1991, in Waxahachie, Texas.

Caufield, Alice Owens, oral history interviews. Interviewed by M. Rebecca Sharpless on seven occasions from 22 January to 1 March 1993, in Waco, Texas.

Dodd, Myrtle Irene Calvert, oral history interviews. Interviewed by M. Rebecca Sharpless on four occasions from 14 August to 19 September 1990, in Waco, Texas.

Folley, Della Inez, oral history interviews. Interviewed by M. Rebecca Sharpless on four occasions from 4 September to 17 October 1990, in Mart, Texas.

Hurtado, Luz Sanchez, oral history interviews. Interviewed by M. Rebecca Sharpless with simultaneous Spanish-English translation by Lelis Idalia Nolasco on 27 July and 2 August 1995, in Waco, Texas.

Navarro, Cayetana Martinez, oral history interviews. Interviewed by M. Rebecca Sharpless with simultaneous Spanish-English translation by Lelis Idalia Nolasco on 16 June, 30 June, and 7 July 1995, in Waco, Texas.

Weir, Bernice Porter Bostick, oral history interviews. Interviewed by M. Rebecca Sharpless on four occasions from 9 July to 6 August 1990, in Liberty Hill, McLennan County, Texas.

Willis, Nancy Stricklin, oral history interview. Interviewed by Daryl Fleming on 1 July 1990, in Johnson County, Texas.

The Texas Collection

Alford, Lillian Jane. *Oral Memoirs of Lillian Jane Alford*. Interviewed by Anne Radford Phillips on 5 December 1991 in Burton, Texas.

Barnes, Lavonia Jenkins. *Oral Memoirs of Lavonia Jenkins Barnes*. Interviewed by Pamela Bennett Crow on 8 March, 15 March, and 22 March 1976, in Waco, Texas.

Campbell, Mary Ann Collier. "Country Life in Mooreville Texas in the Thirties." Typescript.

Conner, Jeffie Obrea Allen. Papers.

Cooper, Marguerite Ethel Webb. *Oral Memoirs of Marguerite Ethel Webb Cooper*. Interviewed by Kay Clifton on 25 March 1977, in Waco, Texas.

Dawson, Joseph Martin. *Oral Memoirs of Joseph Martin Dawson*. Interviewed by Thomas L. Charlton, Rufus B. Spain, and Kay Nowlin on eight occasions from 18 January 1971 to 7 January 1972, in Corsicana and Waco, Texas.

Estes, Elizabeth Williams. *Oral Memoirs of Elizabeth Williams Estes*. Interviewed by Margaret Mills on 5 May and 4 June 1976, in Waco, Texas.

Gunn Family Papers.

Hale, Alma Stewart. *Oral Memoirs of Alma Stewart Hale*. Interviewed by Doni Van Ryswyk on eight occasions from 27 January to 28 March 1988 in Waco, Texas.

Hatch, Roy Hamlin. *Oral Memoirs of Roy Hamlin Hatch*. Interviewed by Thomas L. Charlton and Dial Moffatt on 6 March, 19 April, and 3 May 1973, in Waco, Texas.

Hunt County Baptist Association Minutes.

McDaniel, Douthit Young. *Oral Memoirs of Douthit Young McDaniel*. Interviewed by Thomas L. Charlton on eight occasions from 15 May to 24 June 1975, in Waco, Texas.

Malone, Vera Allen. *Oral Memoirs of Vera Allen Malone*. Interviewed by LaWanda Ball on 5 December 1975, in Waco, Texas.

Podsednik, Frances Bartek. Interviewed by Henry Apperson on 25 September 1969, in West, Texas.

Simcik, Mary Hanak. *Oral Memoirs of Mary Hanak Simcik*. Interviewed by La-Wanda Ball on 24 November 1975, in Waco, Texas.

Springer, R. A. *Oral Memoirs of R. A. Springer*. Interviewed by Rufus B. Spain and Thomas L. Charlton on 6 August 1971, 10 May 1972, and 4 August 1972, in Dallas and Waco, Texas.

Summers, Ray. *Oral Memoirs of Ray Summers*. Interviewed by Daniel B. McGee on eighteen occasions from 11 August to 29 August 1980, in Waco, Texas.

Warner, Anna Mae Bell. *Oral Memoirs of Anna Mae Bell Warner*. Interviewed by LaWanda Ball on 13 February and 16 February 1976, in Waco, Texas.

Washington, Maggie Langham. *Oral Memoirs of Maggie Langham Washington*. Interviewed by Doni Van Ryswyk and Marla Luffer on six occasions from 10 March 1988 to 13 March 1989, in Waco, Texas.

Westbrook, Marguerite Thompson. *Oral Memoirs of Marguerite Thompson Westbrook*. Interviewed by Kay Clifton on 16 February and 22 February 1977, in Marlin, Texas.

Waxahachie, Tex.
  Nicholas P. Sims Memorial Library
    Clubs—Women—Waxahachie Vertical File.
    Cotton Mills and Compresses Vertical File.
    Ellis County Fair Vertical File.

Newspapers

Commerce [Texas] Journal, 1955, 1986–88.
Dallas Morning News, 1915.

Farm and Ranch (Dallas), 1910.

Greenville Herald-Banner, 1987–91.

Mart Herald, 1977.

San Antonio Express, 1933.

Semi-Weekly Farm News (Dallas), 1910.

Tawakoni News, 1990–91.

Waco Daily Times-Herald, 1911, 1915, 1917.

Waxahachie Daily Light, 1925, 1976, 1978.

Weekly Local (Ennis, Texas), 1977.

Wolfe City Sun, 1948–51.

Government Publications

U.S. Government Documents

Agricultural Adjustment Agency, Southern Division. *Feeding Farm Folks Through the Farm's Own Program*. Washington, D.C.: Government Printing Office, 1939.

Bennett, Frank, R. T. Avon Burke, and Clarence Lounsbury. *Soil Survey of Ellis County, Texas*. Washington, D.C.: Government Printing Office, 1911.

Lively, C. E., and Conrad Taeuber. *Rural Migration in the United States*. Works Progress Administration Research Monograph 19. Washington, D.C.: Government Printing Office, 1939.

Matthews, Ellen Nathalie, and Helen Maretta Dart. *The Welfare of Children in Cotton-Growing Areas of Texas*. U.S. Department of Labor, Children's Bureau Publication no. 134. Washington, D.C.: Government Printing Office, 1924.

Menefee, Selden C. *Mexican Migrant Workers of South Texas*. Washington, D.C.: Government Printing Office, 1941.

Motheral, Joe R. *Types of Farm Tenancy in Texas*. U.S. Department of Agriculture in cooperation with the Texas Agricultural Experiment Station, Austin, 1941.

National Youth Administration. *Cotton Growing in Texas*. Austin: National Youth Administration of Texas, 1939.

Report by the Commission on Industrial Relations. U.S. 64th Congress, 1st session. Sen. Doc. 415 (1916), 9 and 10.

Sanderson, Ezra Dwight. *Miscellaneous Cotton Insects in Texas*. Washington, D.C.: Government Printing Office, 1905.

Templin, E. H., and R. M. Marshall. *Soil Survey of Hunt County, Texas*. Washington, D.C.: Government Printing Office, 1939.

Ullrich, C. E. *The Farm Operator in the Texas Rural and Town Relief Population, October 1935*. College Station, Tex.: Federal Works Progress Administration, Texas Relief Commission, 1936.

U.S. Department of Agriculture. *The Cotton Plant: Its History, Botany, Chemistry, Culture, Enemies, and Uses*. Washington, D.C.: Government Printing Office, 1896.

U.S. Department of Commerce and Labor, Bureau of the Census. *Special Reports: Mortality Statistics, 1900 to 1904*. Washington, D.C.: Government Printing Office, 1906.

U.S. Department of Commerce, Bureau of the Census. *Fourteenth Census of the United States*. Vol. 6, Part 2, *Agriculture, the Southern States*. Washington, D.C.: Government Printing Office, 1922.

——. *Fifteenth Census of the United States.* Vol. 2, Part 2, *Agriculture, the Southern States.* Washington, D.C.: Government Printing Office, 1932.

——. *Mortality Statistics, 1910.* Washington, D.C.: Government Printing Office, 1913.

——. *Mortality Statistics, 1920.* Washington, D.C.: Government Printing Office, 1922.

——. *Mortality Statistics, 1930.* Washington, D.C.: Government Printing Office, 1932.

——. *Religious Bodies, 1916, Part II, Separate Denominations: History, Description, and Statistics.* Washington, D.C.: Government Printing Office, 1919.

——. *Religious Bodies, 1926, Part II: Statistics, History, Doctrine, Organization, and Work.* Washington, D.C.: Government Printing Office, 1929.

——. *Religious Bodies, 1936: Statistics, History, Doctrine, Organization, and Work.* Washington, D.C.: Government Printing Office, 1941.

——. *Thirteenth Census of the United States.* Vol. 7, *Agriculture.* Washington, D.C.: Government Printing Office, 1912.

——. *Vital Statistics of the United States, 1940.* Washington, D.C.: Government Printing Office, 1943.

U.S. Department of the Interior. *Population of the United States.* Vol. 1, *Eighth Census of the United States.* Washington, D.C.: Government Printing Office, 1864.

——. *Twelfth Census of the United States, 1900.* Vol. 5, *Agriculture, Part I.* Washington, D.C.: Government Printing Office, 1902.

U.S. Department of Agriculture Bulletins

Sanders, Jesse Thomas. *Farm Ownership and Tenancy in the Black Prairie of Texas.* U.S. Department of Agriculture Bulletin no. 1068, 12 May 1922. Washington, D.C.: Government Printing Office, 1922.

Ward, Florence E. *Home Demonstration Work under the Smith-Lever Act, 1914–1924.* U.S. Department of Agriculture circular no. 43, June 1929. Washington, D.C.: Government Printing Office, 1922.

Willard, Rex E. *A Farm Management Study of Cotton Farms of Ellis County, Texas.* U.S. Department of Agriculture Bulletin no. 659. Washington, D.C.: Government Printing Office, 1918.

Books

Agee, James, and Walker Evans. *Let Us Now Praise Famous Men: Three Tenant Families.* Boston: Houghton Mifflin Company, 1941.

Allen, Ruth. *The Labor of Women in the Production of Cotton.* University of Texas Bulletin no. 3134, 8 September 1931.

Andrews, Jean. *Peppers: The Domesticated Capsicums.* Austin: University of Texas Press, 1995.

Aptheker, Bettina. *Tapestries of Life: Women's Work, Women's Consciousness, and the Meaning of Daily Experience.* Amherst: University of Massachusetts Press, 1989.

Ayers, Edward L. *The Promise of the New South: Life after Reconstruction.* New York: Oxford University Press, 1992.

Bailey, Beth L. *From Front Porch to Back Seat: Courtship in Twentieth-Century America.* Baltimore: Johns Hopkins University Press, 1989.

Barkley, Mary Starr. *A History of Central Texas.* Austin: Austin Printing Co., 1970.

Barnes, Lavonia Jenkins. *The Texas Cotton Palace*. Waco: Heritage Society of Waco, 1964.

Barr, Alwyn. *Black Texans: A History of Negroes in Texas, 1528–1971*. Austin: Jenkins Publishing, 1973.

Bateson, Mary Catherine. *Composing a Life*. New York: Penguin Books, 1989.

Beach, Walter G., trans. and comp. *Souvenir of Golden Jubilee, Church of the Visitation, Westphalia, Texas*. Austin: Capital Printing Company, 1933.

Bear, Jennie R. *Care and Preservation of Food in the Home*. University of Texas Bulletin no. 69, 10 December 1915.

Bedichek, Roy. *Adventures with a Texas Naturalist*. Austin: University of Texas Press, 1947.

Bentley, Jerome Kearby. *Spring and Autumn: Footprints of a Texas Octogenarian*. Dallas: Temple Publishing Co., ca. 1977.

Bentley, M. R. *Waterworks for Texas Homes*. Texas Agricultural Extension Service Bulletin no. B-67, May 1926.

Berger, Michael L. *The Devil Wagon in God's Country: The Automobile and Social Change in Rural America, 1893–1929*. Hamden, Conn.: Archon Books, 1979.

Bizzell, William Bennett. *Rural Texas*. New York: Macmillan, 1924.

Bolton, F. C. *Electricity in the Country Home*. Bulletin of the Agricultural and Mechanical College of Texas, 3rd series, vol. 1, no. 9, September 1915.

Bomar, George W. *Texas Weather*. Austin: University of Texas Press, 1983.

Boserup, Ester. *Woman's Role in Economic Development*. London: Allen and Unwin, 1970.

Bourne, Emma Guest. *A Pioneer Farmer's Daughter of Red River Valley, Northeast Texas*. Dallas: The Story Book Press, 1950.

Bowers, William L. *The Country Life Movement in America, 1900–1920*. Port Washington, N.Y.: Kennikat Press, 1974.

Bradbury, Bettina. *Working Families: Age, Gender, and Daily Survival in Industrializing Montreal*. Toronto: McClelland and Stewart, 1993.

Bresenhan, Karoline Patterson, and Nancy O'Bryant Puentes. *Lone Stars: A Legacy of Texas Quilts, 1836–1936*. Austin: University of Texas Press, 1986.

Britton, Karen Gerhardt. *Bale o' Cotton: The Mechanical Art of Cotton Ginning*. College Station: Texas A&M University Press, 1992.

Brooks, Gwendolyn. *Maud Martha*. New York: Harper & Brothers, 1953.

Brown, Harry Bates. *Cotton: History, Species, Varieties, Morphology, Breeding, Culture, Diseases, Marketing, and Uses*. New York: McGraw-Hill Book Company, 1927.

Burkett, C. W. *Cotton: Its Cultivation, Marketing, Manufacture, and the Problems of the World Market*. New York: Doubleday, Page & Company, 1908.

Calvert, Robert A., and Arnoldo De León. *The History of Texas*. Arlington Heights, Ill.: Harlan Davidson, 1990.

Campbell, Randolph B. *An Empire for Slavery: The Peculiar Institution in Texas, 1821–1865*. Baton Rouge: Louisiana State University Press, 1989.

Campbell, Randolph B., and Richard G. Lowe. *Wealth and Power in Antebellum Texas*. College Station: Texas A&M University Press, 1977.

Carter, Bernice. *Canning, Preserving, Pickling*. Texas Agricultural Extension Service Bulletin no. B-26, July 1916.

Cashin, Joan. *A Family Venture: Men and Women on the Southern Frontier*. New York: Oxford University Press, 1991.

Caskey, Eleanor Adeline McCaskill. *One Hundred and Twenty Years in Florence, Texas*,

1851–1970. Georgetown, Tex.: Heritage Printing Co., 1970 (located at The Texas Collection, Baylor University, Waco, Tex.).

Chipman, Donald E. *Spanish Texas, 1519–1821*. Austin: University of Texas Press, 1993.

Clark, Edward R. *A Quick History of Boyce: A Texas Pioneer Community*. Waxahachie, Tex.: Edward R. Clark, 1983.

Cohen, Chester. *Rural Water Supply*. Austin: Texas State Department of Health, 1934.

Collings, Gilbert H. *The Production of Cotton*. New York: Wiley, Chapman & Hall, 1926.

Cotton, Walter F. *History of Negroes of Limestone County from 1860 to 1939*. Mexia, Tex.: J. A. Chatman and S. M. Meriwether, News Print Co., 1939.

Crenshaw, Troy. *Texas Blackland Heritage*. Waco, Tex.: Texian Press, 1983.

Davis, Edward Everett. *A Study of Rural Schools in Williamson County*. University of Texas Bulletin no. 2238, 8 October 1922.

D'Emilio, John, and Estelle B. Friedman. *Intimate Matters: A History of Sexuality in America*. New York: Harper and Row, 1988.

Deutsch, Sarah. *No Separate Refuge: Culture, Class, and Gender on an Anglo-Hispanic Frontier in the American Southwest, 1880–1940*. New York: Oxford University Press, 1987.

Dillow, Louise B., and Deenie B. Carver. *Mrs. Blackwell's Heart-of-Texas Cookbook*. San Antonio: Corona Publishing Company, 1980.

Egerton, John. *Southern Food: At Home, on the Road, in History*. New York: Alfred A. Knopf, 1987.

Eliminating Advertising Waste in Texas. Dallas: Texas Daily Press League, 1932.

Ellis County History Workshop. *History of Ellis County, Texas*. Waco, Tex.: Texian Press, 1972.

Etheridge, Elizabeth W. *The Butterfly Caste: A Social History of Pellagra in the South*. Westport, Conn.: Greenwood Publishing Company, 1972.

Everett, Mrs. J. D. (Gladys). *Among the Salt: Matthew 5:13*. Waco, Tex.: Texian Press, 1985.

Farb, Peter, and George Armelagos. *Consuming Passions: The Anthropology of Eating*. Boston: Houghton Mifflin Company, 1980.

Fass, Paula. *The Damned and the Beautiful: American Youth in the 1920s*. New York: Oxford University Press, 1977.

Fink, Deborah. *Agrarian Women: Wives and Mothers in Rural Nebraska, 1880–1940*. Chapel Hill: University of North Carolina Press, 1992.

———. *Open Country, Iowa: Rural Women, Tradition, and Change*. Albany: State University Press of New York, 1986.

Fite, Gilbert C. *Cotton Fields No More: Southern Agriculture, 1865–1980*. Lexington: University Press of Kentucky, 1984.

Flynt, Wayne. *Poor but Proud: Alabama's Poor Whites*. Tuscaloosa: University of Alabama Press, 1989.

Fox-Genovese, Elizabeth. *Within the Plantation Household: Black and White Women of the Old South*. Chapel Hill: University of North Carolina Press, 1988.

Friedman, Jean E. *The Enclosed Garden: Women and Community in the Evangelical South, 1830–1900*. Chapel Hill: University of North Carolina Press, 1985.

Function, Policy and Program of the Country Church. Report of the Committee of the Rural Ministers' Conference, Agricultural and Mechanical College of Texas, 16–26 July 1923. Bulletin of the Agricultural and Mechanical College of Texas, 3rd series, vol. 9, no. 8, 1 August 1923.

Gabbard, L. P., and H. E. Rea. *Cotton Production in Texas*. Texas Agricultural Experiment Station Bulletin no. 39, 1926.

Garnett, William Edward. *Some Socially Significant Rural Conditions*. Bulletin of the Agricultural and Mechanical College of Texas, 3rd series, vol. 9, no. 9, 1 September 1923.

Gibbons, Charles E. *Child Labor among the Cotton Growers of Texas: A Study of Children Living in Rural Communities in Six Counties in Texas*. New York: National Child Labor Committee, 1925.

Gleason, Margaret. *Food Preservation, Canning, Preserving, Jelly Making*. Texas State College for Women, College of Industrial Arts Bulletin no. 88, 1 April 1921.

Gluck, Sherna Berger, and Daphne Patai, eds. *Women's Words: The Feminist Practice of Oral History*. New York: Routledge, Chapman and Hall, 1991.

Graham, Don. *No Name on the Bullet: A Biography of Audie Murphy*. New York: Viking Press, 1989.

Gray, Lewis Cecil. *History of Agriculture in the Southern States to 1860*. Washington, D.C.: The Carnegie Institution of Washington, 1933.

Grier, Katherine C. *Culture and Comfort: People, Parlors, and Upholstery, 1850–1930*. Rochester, N.Y.: The Strong Museum, 1988.

Hamilton, C. Horace. *The Social Aspects of Recent Trends in Mechanization of Agriculture*. College Station: Texas Agricultural Experiment Station, 1938.

Handbook of Commerce, Texas, 1872–1985. Commerce, Tex.: Friends of the Commerce Public Library, 1985.

Haney, Lewis H., ed. *Studies in the Land Problem in Texas*. University of Texas Bulletin no. 39, 1915.

Hatcher, O. Latham. *Rural Girls in the City for Work: A Study Made for the Southern Woman's Educational Alliance*. Richmond, Va.: Garrett & Massie, 1930.

Heyrman, Christine Leigh. *Southern Cross: The Beginnings of the Bible Belt*. New York: Alfred A. Knopf, 1997.

Hill, Joseph Abner. *Autobiographical Notes on the Life of Joseph Abner Hill*. N.p., 1971.

Hill, Samuel S., ed. *Encyclopedia of Religion in the South*. Macon, Ga.: Mercer University Press, 1984.

Hilliard, Sam Bowers. *Hog Meat and Hoe Cake: Food Supply in the Old South, 1840–1860*. Carbondale: Southern Illinois University Press, 1972.

Hoy, Suellen. *Chasing Dirt: The American Pursuit of Cleanliness*. New York: Oxford University Press, 1995.

Humphrey, William. *Farther Off from Heaven*. New York: Alfred A. Knopf, 1977.

———. *The Ordways*. New York: Alfred A. Knopf, 1965.

Isaac, Rhys. *The Transformation of Virginia, 1740–1790*. Chapel Hill: University of North Carolina Press, 1982.

Jellison, Katherine. *Entitled to Power: Farm Women and Technology, 1913–1963*. Chapel Hill: University of North Carolina Press, 1993.

Jensen, Joan M. *Loosening the Bonds: Mid-Atlantic Farm Women, 1750–1850*. New Haven: Yale University Press, 1986.

———. *Promise to the Land: Essays on Rural Women*. Albuquerque: University of New Mexico Press, 1991.

Johnson, Charles S., Edwin R. Embree, and W. W. Alexander. *The Collapse of Cotton Tenancy*. Chapel Hill: University of North Carolina Press, 1935.

Johnson, Jewel R. *A City on a Hill: A Story of a Community, a Church, a People.* N.p.: [1974?].

Jones, Anne Goodwyn. *Tomorrow is Another Day: The Woman Writer in the South, 1859–1936.* Baton Rouge: Louisiana State University Press, 1987.

Jones, Clara. *Pillars of Faith: First Christian Church, Taylor, Texas.* Taylor, Tex.: Clara Jones, 1964.

Jones, Jacqueline. *Labor of Love, Labor of Sorrow: Black Women, Work, and the Family from Slavery to the Present.* New York: Basic Books, 1985.

Jones, Lula Kathryn Peacock. *Recollections of Lula Kathryn (Kate) Peacock Jones.* Amarillo, Tex.: Coltharp Printing, 1979.

Jordan, Terry G., with John L. Bean Jr., and William M. Holmes. *Texas: A Geography.* Boulder, Colo.: Westview Press, 1984.

Jupe, Mary Elizabeth. *A History of Tours, Texas.* San Antonio: n.p., 1988.

Jurney, David H., and Randall W. Moir. *Historic Buildings, Material Culture, and People of the Prairie Margin: Architecture, Artifacts, and Synthesis of Historic Archaeology.* Dallas: Archaeology Research Program, Institute for the Study of Earth and Man, Southern Methodist University, 1987.

Jurney, David H., Susan A. Lebo, and Melissa M. Green. *Historic Farming on the Hogwallow Prairies: Ethnoarchaeological Investigations of the Mountain Creek Area, North Central Texas.* Dallas: Archaeology Research Program, Institute for the Study of Earth and Man, Southern Methodist University, 1988.

Kirby, Jack Temple. *Rural Worlds Lost: The American South, 1920–1960.* Baton Rouge: Louisiana State University Press, 1987.

Lewis, Oscar. *On the Edge of the Black Waxy: A Cultural Survey of Bell County, Texas.* St. Louis: Washington University, 1948.

Locke, Frank M. *Action on Bullhide Creek, 1897–1908: A Socio-Historical Narrative.* Waco, Tex.: Texian Press, 1970.

Lomax, John A., and Alan Lomax. *Negro Folk Songs as Sung by Lead Belly.* New York: Macmillan, 1936.

Lynd, Robert S., and Helen Merrell Lynd. *Middletown: A Study in American Culture.* New York: Harcourt, Brace and Company, 1929.

McBride, Alma McKethan. *The "Filosofer" of "Kukel-bur" Flat.* Waco, Tex.: Texian Press, 1975.

McCurry, Stephanie. *Masters of Small Worlds: Yeoman Households, Gender Relations, and the Political Culture of the Antebellum South Carolina Low Country.* New York: Oxford University Press, 1995.

McGinnes, Jeannette Hatter, and Hazel Alexander Potter. *They Found the Blacklands: A Genealogical History of Moody Area People, 1850–1950.* Waco, Tex.: Texian Press, 1977.

Machann, Clinton, and James W. Mendl. *Krásná Amerika: A Study of the Texas Czechs, 1851–1939.* Austin: Eakin Press, 1983.

McMurry, Sally. *Families and Farmhouses in Nineteenth Century America: Vernacular Design and Social Change.* New York: Oxford University Press, 1988.

Mantor, Ruth. *Our Town: Taylor.* N.p., 1983.

May, Elaine Tyler. *Barren in the Promised Land: Childless Americans and the Pursuit of Happiness.* New York: Basic Books, 1995.

Membership and Official Directory of Maypearl Circuit, Methodist-Episcopal Church, South, 1904 (located at Nicholas P. Sims Memorial Library, Waxahachie, Tex.).

Midlothian Methodist Heritage, 1847, 1976. N.p., [ca. 1976] (located at Nicholas P. Sims Memorial Library, Waxahachie, Tex.).

Moir, Randall W., and David H. Jurney. *Pioneer Settlers, Tenant Farmers, and Communities*. Dallas: Archaeology Research Program, Institute for the Study of Earth and Man, Southern Methodist University, 1987.

Montejano, David. *Anglos and Mexicans in the Making of Texas, 1836–1936*. Austin: University of Texas Press, 1987.

Moore, Gary L., and Harry J. Shafer. *Archeological Test Excavations at 41WM21 in Granger Reservoir, Williamson County, Texas*. College Station, Tex.: Texas A&M University, Department of Anthropology, 1978.

Morgan, James Oscar. *Fieldcrops for the Cotton-Belt*. New York: Macmillan, 1927.

Motheral, Joseph. *Recent Trends in Land Tenure in Texas*. Texas Agricultural Experiment Station Bulletin no. 641, June 1944.

Neth, Mary. *Preserving the Family Farm: Women, Community, and the Foundations of Agribusiness in the Midwest, 1900–1940*. Baltimore: Johns Hopkins University Press, 1995.

Newcomb, W. W., Jr. *The Indians of Texas: From Prehistoric to Modern Times*. Austin: University of Texas Press, 1961.

Norvell, Estelle May. *Student's History of Williamson County*. [Georgetown, Tex.?]: n.p., [ca. 1926].

Osterud, Nancy Grey. *Bonds of Community: The Lives of Women in Nineteenth-Century New York*. Ithaca, N.Y.: Cornell University Press, 1991.

Owens, William A. *A Season of Weathering*. New York: Charles Scribner's Sons, 1973.

——. *Swing and Turn: Texas Play-Party Games*. Dallas, Tex.: Tardy Publishing Co., 1936.

——. *Tell Me a Story, Sing Me a Song. . .: A Texas Chronicle*. Austin: University of Texas Press, 1983.

——. *Texas Folk Songs*. Austin: Texas Folklore Society, 1950.

——. *This Stubborn Soil: A Frontier Boyhood*. New York: Charles Scribner's Sons, 1966.

Perry United Methodist Church. *A Century of Methodism: Perry United Methodist Church, Centennial Celebration, June 25–July 2, 1972*. Perry, Tex.: Perry United Methodist Church, 1972.

Personal Narratives Group, eds. *Interpreting Women's Lives: Feminist Theory and Personal Narratives*. Bloomington: Indiana University Press, 1989.

Peteet, Walton. *Farming Credit in Texas*. Texas Agricultural Extension Service Bulletin no. B-34, February 1917.

Peteet, Walton, Chauncey Merwin, and Cornelia Simpson. *Community Canning Plants*. Texas Agricultural Extension Service Bulletin no. B-48, 1919.

Poage, William Robert. *McLennan County before 1980*. Waco, Tex.: Texian Press, 1981.

Rampy, Thomas Randall. *Choice and Chance: The Life of T. R. Rampy*. Falls Church, Va.: n.p., 1971.

Reisler, Mark. *By the Sweat of Their Brow: Mexican Immigrant Labor in the United States, 1900–1940*. Westport, Conn.: Greenwood Press, 1976.

Richardson, Victoria Fritz. *History of the Immanuel Lutheran Church, Taylor, Texas: Williamson County; With Two Pioneers: Alexander Anderson and Henry Fritz, Sr.* South Pasadena, Calif.: V. F. Richardson, 1973 (located at A. Frank Smith Jr. Library Center, Southwestern University, Georgetown, Tex.).

Riley, Glenda. *The Female Frontier: A Comparative View of Women on the Prairie and the Plains*. Lawrence: University Press of Kansas, 1988.

Riley, Hazel Beauton. *Washing on the Line*. Quanah, Tex.: Nortex Press, 1973.

Rinzler, Carol Ann. *The Complete Book of Food: A Nutritional, Medical, and Culinary Guide*. New York: World Almanac, 1987.

Ross, Ellen. *Love and Toil: Motherhood in Outcast London, 1870–1918*. New York: Oxford University Press, 1993.

Rothman, Ellen K. *Hands and Hearts: A History of Courtship in America*. New York: Basic Books, 1984.

Sadie, Stanley, ed. *The New Grove Dictionary of Music and Musicians*. London: Macmillan Publishers Inc., 1980.

Saville, Julie. *The Work of Reconstruction: From Slave to Wage Laborer in South Carolina, 1860–1870*. New York: Cambridge University Press, 1994.

Scarborough, Clara Stearns. *Land of Good Water: Takachue Pouetsu. A Williamson County, Texas, History*. Georgetown, Tex.: Williamson County Sun Publishers, ca. 1973.

Scarborough, Dorothy. *Can't Get a Red Bird*. New York: Harper and Brothers, 1929.

———. *In the Land of Cotton*. New York: Macmillan, 1923.

Scharff, Virginia. *Taking the Wheel: Women and the Coming of the Motor Age*. New York: Free Press, 1991.

Scott, Anne Firor. *The Southern Lady: From Pedestal to Politics, 1830–1930*. Chicago: University of Chicago Press, 1970.

Simpson, Cornelia. *Food Saving in Texas: Drying, Brining, Canning, Curing*. Texas Agricultural Extension Service Bulletin no. B-38, June 1, 1917.

Skrabanek, Robert L. *Characteristics and Changes in the Texas Farm Population*. Texas Agricultural Experiment Station Bulletin no. 825, December 1955.

Sowell, Jimmie Elizabeth. *A Girl Named Laura*. N.p., 1984 (located at S. M. Dunlap Library, Italy, Texas).

Spain, Daphne. *Gendered Spaces*. Chapel Hill: University of North Carolina Press, 1993.

Sparkman, R. E. *Souvenir of Historic Ellis County, Texas*. Italy, Tex.: n.p., 1938.

St. Paul Home Demonstration Club Bicentennial Committee. *History of St. Paul Community*. N.p., 1976 (located at Nicholas P. Sims Memorial Library, Waxahachie, Tex.).

Steedman, Carolyn. *Landscape for a Good Woman: A Story of Two Lives*. New Brunswick, N.J.: Rutgers University Press, 1987.

Steen, Ralph W. *Twentieth Century Texas: An Economic and Social History*. Austin: The Steck Company, 1942.

Stewart, Rick. *Lone Star Regionalism: The Dallas Nine and Their Circle, 1928–1945*. Austin: Texas Monthly Press, 1985.

Stimpson, Eddie ("Sarge"), Jr. *My Remembers: A Black Sharecropper's Recollections of the Depression*. Denton: University of North Texas Press, 1996.

Studies in Farm Tenancy in Texas. University of Texas Bulletin no. 21, 10 April 1915.

Taylor, Joe Gray. *Eating, Drinking, and Visiting in the South: An Informal History*. Baton Rouge: Louisiana State University Press, 1982.

Terrace, Vincent. *Radio's Golden Years: The Encyclopedia of Radio Programs, 1930–1960*. San Diego: A. S. Barnes and Co., Inc., 1981.

Texas Almanac and State Industrial Guide. Dallas: A. H. Belo and Company, 1904–43, 1988–89, 1992–93.

Texas Department of Agriculture Yearbook, 1908. Austin: Von Boeckmann-Jones, 1908.

Vaughan, G. L. *The Cotton Renter's Son*. Wolfe City, Tex.: Henington Publishing Company, 1967.

Waggoner, J. E. *Electricity on Texas Farms*. Bulletin of the Agricultural and Mechanical College of Texas, 3rd series, vol. 14, no. 2, 1 February 1928.

Wallace, Ernest, and E. Adamson Hoebel. *The Comanche: Lords of the South Plains*. Norman: University of Oklahoma Press, 1952.

Webb, Walter Prescott, and H. Bailey Carroll, eds. *The Handbook of Texas*. Austin: Texas State Historical Association, 1952.

Welcome to Celeste, Texas: Small Town, Big Heart. Celeste, Tex.: Historical Committee, 1976.

Whitacre, Jessie. *The Food Supply of Texas Rural Families*. Texas Agricultural Experiment Station Bulletin no. 642, October 1943.

White, Deborah Gray. *Ar'n't I a Woman?: Female Slaves in the Plantation South*. New York: W. W. Norton and Company, 1985.

Wilson, Charles Reagan, and William Ferris, eds. *Encyclopedia of Southern Culture*. Chapel Hill: University of North Carolina Press, 1989.

Yabsley, Suzanne. *Texas Quilts, Texas Women*. College Station: Texas A&M University Press, 1984.

Yeary, W. B. *Cotton: The South's Greatest Asset, Its Troubles and Their Remedies*. Farmersville, Tex.: W. B. Yeary, 1915.

Articles and Essays

Abrahams, Roger. "Equal Opportunity Eating: A Structural Excursus on Things of the Mouth." In *Ethnic and Regional Foodways in the United States: The Performance of Group Identity*, edited by Linda Keller Brown and Kay Mussell, 19–36. Knoxville: University of Tennessee Press, 1984.

Adams, Jane. "Resistance to 'Modernity': Southern Illinois Farm Women and the Cult of Domesticity." *American Ethnologist* 20 (February 1993): 89–113.

Aderholt, Bess. "Education in Williamson County." In *Student's History of Williamson County*, comp. Estelle May Norvell, 36–37. [Georgetown, Tex.?]: n.p., [ca. 1926].

Amsbury, David L. "Spanish and French Nonsettlement of the Blacklands." In *The Texas Blackland Prairie: Land, History, and Culture*, edited by M. Rebecca Sharpless and Joe C. Yelderman Jr., 122–35. Waco, Tex.: Baylor University, 1993.

Barns, Florence E. "Employment in Texas—A Survey." In *Texas Almanac and State Industrial Guide, 1941–1942*, 299–302. Dallas: A. H. Belo and Company, 1941.

Billson, Marcus C., and Sidonie A. Smith. "Lillian Hellman and the Strategy of the 'Other.'" In *Women's Autobiography: Essays in Criticism*, edited by Estelle C. Jellinek, 163–79. Bloomington: Indiana University Press, 1980.

Borland, Katherine. "'That's Not What I Said': Interpretive Conflict in Oral Narrative Research." In *Women's Words: The Feminist Practice of Oral History*, edited by Sherna Berger Gluck and Daphne Patai, 63–76. New York: Routledge, Chapman and Hall, 1991.

Britton, Karen Gerhardt. "Infections." In *Common Bonds: Stories by and about Modern Texas Women*, edited by Suzanne Comer, 222–27. Dallas: Southern Methodist University Press, 1990.

———. "Notes on the Authors and the Stories." In *Common Bonds: Stories by and about*

Modern Texas Women, edited by Suzanne Comer, 326–27. Dallas: Southern Methodist University Press, 1990.

Broughton, T. L. "Women's Autobiography: The Self at Stake?" In *Autobiography and Questions of Gender*, edited by Shirley Neuman, 76–94. London: Frank Cass and Co., 1991.

Brown, Linda Keller, and Kay Mussell. "Introduction." In *Ethnic and Regional Foodways in the United States: The Performance of Group Identity*, edited by Linda Keller Brown and Kay Mussell, 3–15. Knoxville: University of Tennessee Press, 1984.

Cauley, T. J. "Agricultural Land Tenure in Texas." *Southwestern Political and Social Science Quarterly* 11 (1930): 135–47.

Chambers, William T. "Life in a Cotton Farming Community." *Journal of Geography* 28 (1930): 141–47.

Cloud, Kathleen. "Farm Women and the Structural Transformation of Agriculture: A Cross-Cultural Perspective." In *Women and Farming: Changing Roles, Changing Structures*, edited by Wava G. Haney and Jane B. Knowles, 281–99. Boulder, Colo.: Westview Press, 1988.

Collins, Patricia Hill. "Shifting the Center: Race, Class, and Feminist Theorizing about Motherhood." In *Mothering: Ideology, Experience, and Agency*, edited by Evelyn Nakano Glenn, Grace Chang, and Linda Rennie Forcey, 45–65. New York: Routledge, 1994.

Coltharp, J. B. "Reminiscences of Cotton Pickin' Days." *Southwestern Historical Quarterly* 73 (1970): 539–42.

Couch, Everett. "Agriculture." In Ellis County History Workshop, *History of Ellis County, Texas*. Waco, Tex.: Texian Press, 1972.

Daniel, Pete. "Going among Strangers: Southern Reactions to World War II." *Journal of American History* 77 (1990): 886–911.

——. "The Transformation of the Rural South, 1930 to the Present." *Agricultural History* 55 (1981): 231–48.

Dodson, Ruth. "Tortilla Making." In *In the Shadow of History*, edited by J. Frank Dobie, Mody C. Boatright, and Harry H. Ransom, 137–41. Austin: Texas Folklore Society, 1939.

Dykstra, Robert R. "Town-Country Conflict: A Hidden Dimension in American Social History." *Agricultural History* 37 (1964): 195–204.

Elbert, Sarah. "The Farmer Takes a Wife: Women in America's Farming Families." In *Women, Households, and the Economy*, edited by Lourdes Benería and Catharine R. Stimpson, 173–97. New Brunswick, N.J.: Rutgers University Press, 1987.

——. "Women and Farming: Changing Structures, Changing Roles." In *Women and Farming: Changing Roles, Changing Structures*, edited by Wava G. Haney and Jane B. Knowles, 245–64. Boulder, Colo.: Westview Press, 1988.

Flora, Cornelia Butler. "Public Policy and Women in Agricultural Production: A Comparative and Historical Analysis." In *Women and Farming: Changing Roles, Changing Structures*, edited by Wava G. Haney and Jane B. Knowles, 265–80. Boulder, Colo.: Westview Press, 1988.

Fox-Genovese, Elizabeth. "Between Individualism and Community: Autobiographies of Southern Women." In *Located Lives: Place and Idea in Southern Autobiography*, edited by J. Bill Berry, 20–38. Athens: University of Georgia Press, 1990.

Fuller, Roden. "Occupations of the Mexican-Born Population of Texas, New Mexico and Arizona, 1900–1920." *Journal of the American Statistical Association* 23 (March 1928): 64–67.

Gonzalez, Rosalinda M. "Chicanas and Mexican Immigrant Families, 1920–1940: Women's Subordination and Family Exploitation." In *Decades of Discontent: The Women's Movement, 1920–1940*, edited by Lois Scharf and Joan Jensen, 59–84. Westport, Conn.: Greenwood Press, 1983.

Hairston, Charles L. "Cotton Comes to Williamson." In *Williamson County Centennial, 1848–1948*, 31–33. Georgetown, Tex.: n.p., 1948.

Hampsten, Elizabeth. "Considering More than a Single Reader." In *Interpreting Women's Lives: Feminist Theory and Personal Narratives*, edited by Personal Narratives Group 129–38. Bloomington: Indiana University Press, 1989.

Handman, Max Sylvius. "Economic Reasons for the Coming of the Mexican Immigrant." *American Journal of Sociology* 35, no. 4 (1930): 601–11.

Healey, Jane F. "Privately Published Autobiographies by Texans: Their Significance for Scholars." *Southwestern Historical Quarterly* 95 (1992): 497–510.

Hinojosa, Gilberto M. "The Immigrant Church, 1910–1940." In *Mexican Americans and the Catholic Church, 1900–1965*, edited by Jay P. Dolan and Gilberto M. Hinojosa, 31–83. Notre Dame, Ind.: University of Notre Dame Press.

Interrante, Joseph. " 'You Can't Go to Town in a Bathtub': Automobile Movement and the Reorganization of American Rural Space, 1900–1930." *Radical History Review* 21 (1979): 151–68.

Jameson, Elizabeth. "Women as Workers, Women as Civilizers: True Womanhood in the American West." In *The Women's West*, edited by Susan Armitage and Elizabeth Jameson, 145–64. Norman: University of Oklahoma Press, 1987.

Jeffery, Janet K. "The Sunbonnet as Folk Costume." In *Corners of Texas: Publication of the Texas Folklore Society LII*, edited by Francis Edward Abernethy, 209–19. Denton: University of North Texas Press, 1993.

Jeffries, Charlie. "Cotton Picking." *Southwest Review* 21 (Autumn 1934): 61–73.

Jehlen, Myra. "Archimedes and the Paradox of Feminist Criticism." *Signs* 6, no. 4 (1984): 575–601.

Jensen, Joan M. "Cloth, Butter, and Boarders: Women's Household Production for the Market." *Review of Radical Political Economics* 12 (Summer 1980): 14–24.

——. "The Death of Rosa: Sexuality in Rural America." *Agricultural History* 67 (1993): 1–12.

——. " 'I've Worked, I'm Not Afraid of Work': Farm Women in New Mexico, 1920–1940." In *New Mexico Women: Intercultural Perspectives*, edited by Joan M. Jensen and Darlis A. Miller, 227–55. Albuquerque: University of New Mexico Press, 1986.

Jordan, Terry G. "The Imprint of the Upper and Lower South on Mid-nineteenth-century Texas." *Annals of American Geographers* 57 (December 1967): 667–90.

——. "Population Origins in Texas, 1850." *The Geographical Review* 59 (1969): 82–103.

Kaplan, Jane Rachel. "Introduction: Beauty and the Feast." In *A Woman's Conflict: The Special Relationship between Women and Food*, edited by Jane Rachel Kaplan, 2–14. Englewood Cliffs, N.J.: Prentice-Hall, 1980.

Kerr, Homer L. "Migration into Texas, 1860–1880." *Southwestern Historical Quarterly* 70 (1966): 184–216.

Kniffen, Fred. "On Corner-Timbering." *Pioneer America* 1 (January 1969): 1.

Kramarae, Cheris. "Talk of Sewing Circles and Sweatshops." In *Technology and Women's Voices: Keeping in Touch*, edited by Cheris Kramarae, 147–60. New York: Routledge and Kegan Paul, 1988.

Lawless, Elaine J. " 'I Was Afraid Someone Like You . . . an Outsider . . . Would Misunderstand': Negotiating Interpretive Differences between Ethnographers and Subjects." *Journal of American Folklore* 105 (1992): 302–14.

Leonard, W. E., and E. B. Naugle. "The Recent Increase in Tenancy, Its Causes and Some Suggestions as to Remedies." In *Studies in the Land Problem in Texas*, edited by Lewis H. Haney, 12–33. University of Texas Bulletin no. 39, 1915.

Leonard, William E. "The Economic Aspects of the Tenant Problem in Ellis County." In *Studies in Farm Tenancy*, University of Texas Bulletin no. 21, April 10, 1921, 103–24.

McCurry, Stephanie. "The Politics of Yeoman Households in South Carolina." In *Divided Houses: Gender and the Civil War*, edited by Catherine Clinton and Nina Silber, 22–38. New York: Oxford University Press, 1992.

McGee, Pat. "Hog Killing Day." *Harvest Magazine* 2, no. 3 (September–October 1989): 7–11.

McKay, Nellie C. "Race, Gender, and Cultural Context in Zora Neale Hurston's *Dust Tracks on a Road*." In *Life/Lines: Theorizing Women's Autobiography*, edited by Bella Brodzki and Celeste Schenck, 175–88. Ithaca: Cornell University Press, 1988.

Marks, Shula. "The Context of Personal Narratives: Reflections on 'Not Either an Experimental Doll'—The Separate Worlds of Three South African Women." In *Life/Lines: Theorizing Women's Autobiography*, edited by Bella Brodzki and Celeste Schenck, 39–58. Ithaca: Cornell University Press, 1988.

Mercier, Laurie K. "Women's Role in Montana Agriculture: 'You Had to Make Every Minute Count.' " *Montana* 38 (Autumn 1988): 50–61.

Murdock, George P., and Catarina Provost. "Factors in the Division of Labor by Sex: A Cross-Cultural Analysis." *Ethnology* 12 (1973): 203–25.

Neighbours, Kenneth F. "Indian Exodus Out of Texas in 1859." *West Texas Historical Association Yearbook* 36 (1960): 80–97.

Osterud, Nancy Grey. "Land, Identity, and Agency in the Oral Autobiographies of Farm Women." In *Women and Farming: Changing Roles, Changing Structures*, edited by Wava G. Haney and Jane B. Knowles, 73–87. Boulder, Colo.: Westview Press, 1988.

Parker, D. "Cotton Seed—Its Value, and How to Obtain It." In *Proceedings of the Third Annual Session of the Texas Farmers' Congress*, edited by B. C. Pittuck, 160–63. Houston: The Literary Bureau, [1900?].

Pittenger, Mark. "A World of Difference: Constructing the 'Underclass' in Progressive America." *American Quarterly* 49 (March 1997): 26–65.

Rakow, Lana F. "Women and the Telephone: The Gendering of a Communications Technology." In *Technology and Women's Voices: Keeping in Touch*, edited by Cheris Kramarae, 207–28. New York: Routledge and Kegan Paul, 1988.

Rogers, William Warren, ed. " 'I Am Tired Writeing': A Georgia Farmer Reports on Texas in 1871." *Southwestern Historical Quarterly* 87 (1983): 183–88.

Sachs, Carolyn. "Women's Work in the U.S.: Variations by Region." *Agriculture and Human Values* 2 (1985): 131–39.

Schwartz, Marie Jenkins. " 'At Noon, Oh How I Ran': Breastfeeding and Weaning on Plantation and Farm in Antebellum Virginia and Alabama." In *Discovering the Women in Slavery: Emancipating Perspectives on the American Past*, edited by Patricia Morton, 241–59. Athens: University of Georgia Press, 1996.

Shaw, Stephanie. "Mothering under Slavery in the Antebellum South." In *Mothering: Ideol-*

ogy, Experience, and Agency, edited by Evelyn Nakano Glenn, Grace Chang, and Linda Rennie Forcey, 237–58. New York: Routledge, 1994.

Shostak, Marjorie. " 'What the Wind Won't Take Away': The Genesis of *Nisa—The Life and Words of a !Kung Woman*." In *Interpreting Women's Lives: Feminist Theory and Personal Narratives*, edited by Personal Narratives Group, 228–40. Bloomington: Indiana University Press, 1989.

Smith, Sidonie. "The Autobiographical Manifesto: Identities, Temporalities, Politics." In *Autobiography and Questions of Gender*, edited by Shirley Neuman, 186–212. London: Frank Cass and Co., 1991.

Sneed, Greg. "Waxahachie Cotton Mills." In Waxahachie High School Junior Historians, *This Was Ellis County*. Waxahachie: Waxahachie High School Junior Historians, 1981.

Sommer, Doris. " 'Not Just a Personal Story': Women's *Testimonios* and the Plural Self." In *Life/Lines: Theorizing Women's Autobiography*, edited by Bella Brodzki and Celeste Schenck, 107–30. Ithaca: Cornell University Press, 1988.

SoRelle, James M. " 'The Waco Horror': The Lynching of Jesse Washington." *Southwestern Historical Quarterly* 86 (1983): 517–36.

Spacks, Patricia Meyer. "Selves in Hiding." In *Women's Autobiography: Essays in Criticism*, edited by Estelle C. Jellinek, 112–32. Bloomington: Indiana University Press, 1980.

Strong-Boag, Veronica. "Pulling in Double Harness or Hauling a Double Load: Women, Work, and Feminism on the Canadian Prairie." *Journal of Canadian Studies* 21 (Fall 1986): 32–52.

Toelken, Barre. "Folklore and Reality in the American West." In *Sense of Place: American Regional Cultures*, edited by Barbara Allen and Thomas J. Schlereth (Lexington: The University Press of Kentucky, 1991), 15.

Ward, Florence E. "The Farm Woman's Problems." *Journal of Home Economics* 12 (October 1920): 437–57.

Wehrwein, George S. "Housing Conditions among Tenant Farmers." In *Studies in the Land Problem in Texas*, edited by Lewis H. Haney, 41–45. University of Texas Bulletin no. 39, 1915.

———. "Social Life in Southern Travis County." In *The Rural Community, Ancient and Modern*, edited by Newell Leroy Sims, 498–509. New York: Charles Scribner's Sons, 1920.

White, Deborah Gray. "Female Slaves: Sex Roles and Status in the Antebellum Plantation South." In *Half Sisters of History: Southern Women and the American Past*, edited by Catherine Clinton, 56–75. Durham, N.C.: Duke University Press, 1994.

Wik, Reynold M. "The Radio in Rural America during the 1920s." *Agricultural History* 55 (1981): 339–50.

Winn, Roger. "Chautauqua—1912." In Waxahachie Junior High School Historians, *This Was Ellis County*, 71–75. Waxahachie: Waxahachie High School Junior Historians, 1981.

Unpublished Materials

Brophy, William Joseph. "The Black Texan, 1900–1950: A Quantitative History." Ph.D. diss., Vanderbilt University, 1974.

Calvert, Robert A. "Cotton Fields No More." Paper presented at "The Community That Cotton Made: An Historical Exploration," Greenville, Texas, April 1997.

Cook, Florence Elliott. "Growing up White, Genteel, and Female in a Changing South, 1865 to 1915." Ph.D. diss., University of California, Berkeley, 1992.

Douglas, Louva Myrtia. "The History of the Agricultural Fairs of Texas." M.A. thesis, University of Texas, 1943.

DuPuy, Louisa Romans. "Social Trends in McLennan County." M.A. thesis, Baylor University, 1934.

Evans, Samuel L. "Texas Agriculture, 1865–1880." M.A. thesis, University of Texas, 1955.

———. "Texas Agriculture, 1880–1930." Ph.D. diss., University of Texas, 1961.

Flowers, N. Charlene. "The Impact of the New Deal on Hunt County, Texas, 1933–1936." M.A. thesis, East Texas State University, 1973.

Gordon, J. R. "The Negro in McLennan County." M.A. thesis, Baylor University, 1932.

Grundy, Pamela. "Alabama Landmarks: History, Identity and Landscape in Clay County, Alabama." Paper presented at the Oral History Association Annual Meeting, Philadelphia, Pa., October 1996.

Hardaway, Lisa Carol. "Sacred Harp Traditions in Texas." M.A. thesis, Rice University, 1989.

Healey, Jane Frances. "An Annotated Bibliography of Privately Published Autobiographies Gathered by the Baylor University Texas Collection." M.A. thesis, Baylor University, 1986.

Hoffschwelle, Mary. "Rebuilding the Southern Rural Community: Reformers, Schools, and Homes in Tennessee, 1914–1929." Ph.D. diss., Vanderbilt University, 1993.

Jaffe, Madeline. "Rural Women in Unskilled Labor: A Study of Women from Country Districts in Unskilled Wage-earning Groups, Austin, Texas." M.A. thesis, University of Texas, 1931.

Jones, Lu Ann. "Re-visioning the Countryside: Southern Women, Rural Reform, and the Farm Economy in the Twentieth Century." Ph.D. diss., University of North Carolina at Chapel Hill, 1996.

Pazdral, Olga. "Czech Folklore in Texas." M.A. thesis, University of Texas, 1942.

Pitcock, Margaruite. "Voices of Experience." Paper presented at "The Community That Cotton Made: An Historical Exploration," Greenville, Texas, April 1997.

Ramey, Daina L. "From Seamstress to Field Hand: Female Slave Labor in Georgia, 1820–1860." Paper presented at the Fourth Southern Conference on Women's History, Charleston, South Carolina, June 1997.

Richardson, James Tull. "Social Changes in Hunt County, Texas, for the Decade 1920 to 1930 and Their Sociological Significance." M.A. thesis, University of Texas, 1933.

Rieff, Lynne Anderson. " 'Rousing the People of the Land': Home Demonstration Work in the Deep South, 1914–1950." Ph.D. diss., Auburn University, 1995.

Seaholm, Megan. "Earnest Women: The White Woman's Club Movement in Progressive Era Texas, 1880–1920." Ph.D. diss., Rice University, 1988.

Sitton, Thad. "Mule, Man and Bull Puncher: Work Stock in the Cotton Countryside." Paper presented at "The Community That Cotton Made: An Historical Exploration," Greenville, Texas, April 1997.

Wilkison, Kyle Grant. "The End of Independence: Social and Political Reactions to Economic Change in Texas, 1870–1914." Ph.D. diss., Vanderbilt University, 1995.

index

Adams family, 99; food and, 113, 140. *See also* Walker, Inez Adams

African Americans: discrimination against, 13, 148; immigration to Blackland Prairie, 13–14; marriage to other African Americans, 26; courtship among, 26, 27–28; wedding rituals, 32; childbearing, 39–40; child care sharing, 51–52; household sharing, 55–56; housing conditions, 75–76; alcohol abuse, 64–65; employment as domestics, 70–71, 148, 244; gardening, 122; food preservation, 127, 130; poultry production, 131; gender conventions among, 162, 170; field work, 163–66, 167, 170, 171–72, 174, 180–83; communities of, 189–90; literacy among, 193–94; church attendance, 201, 207; prayers against racism, 215; trips to town, 226; and segregation of movie theaters, 228; employment for women, 239, 244. *See also* Caufield, Alice Owens; Langham, Leta Taylor; Stimpson, Millie Birks; Walker, Inez Adams; Washington, Maggie Langham

Agricultural Adjustment Administration, 233–34

Agricultural labor by women, 1; racial divisions in, 2; historical development of, 2–3; national trends in, 4. *See also* Field work: division of labor by gender

Alcohol, 156; abuse, 64–65; disapproval of consumption, 210

Alford, Lillian Jane, 170–71, 176–77, 240–41

Allen Baptist Church (Collin County, Texas), 211

Almanza, Adelaida Torres, xv; marriage, 27; sewing, 102; cooking, 154, 157; church attendance, 202

Almanza, Juan, 27

Almanza family housing, 74–75, 85

Assistance, community, 197–200. *See also* Charity

Austin, Texas, 237; employment for women in, 239

Austin family, 80

Autobiography as historical source, xiii

Automobiles: effect on courtship, 22–23. *See also* Transportation: automobiles

Baptists: compared to Methodists, 205–6; disapproval of alcohol, 210; disapproval of dancing, 210–11

Baptist Young Peoples Union (BYPU), 209

Bartering. *See* Peddlers

Bealls Chapel Baptist Church (Milam County, Texas), 204–5

Bean, Narcissus, 137

Beef, 142–43

Bell County, Texas, 242

Benton, Bertie, 28

Berger, Anna, 34

Berger, Katherine Schneider, 156, 199

Berger, Rosie Filer, 34, 168

Berry family, 57, 192

Bird, Bob, 61

Birth control. *See* Contraception

Blackland Prairie of Texas: physiography, 3–4, 5–6; cotton agriculture in, 4; poverty in, 7; crop-lien system in, 7–12; racism in, 12–13; settlement patterns in, 13–15, 160; wood supplies in, 75, 145–46; water supplies in, 90–91; climate in, 99; religious denominations in, 204; urbanization of, 236–37

Blackwell, Bertha, 109, 137

Blackwell family, xii, 42, 49

Blended families, 57–58, 61–62

Bluebonnet Ordnance Plant (McGregor, Texas), 241

Bostick, Bonnie Nell, 48, 235

Bostick, June, 235

Bostick, Pat, 22–23, 38, 96, 125; treatment of field workers, 181–82

Bostick, Texanna Eleanor White, 33–34, 58, 79–80, 83

Bostick family, 81, 94, 191; death of children, 48, 200; housing, 74, 76, 78, 90, 93. *See also* Weir, Bernice Porter Bostick

Bourne, Emma Guest, 83, 192; religious practices, 204, 211, 214

Brazos Valley Cotton Mill (West, Texas), 237

Breast-feeding, 48–49, 110, 169

Brown, Matilda, 100

Burnett, Jim, 65

Butter. *See* Dairy products; Petty commodity production

Calvert, Hester, 102, 167; sewing, 24, 97, 175; childbearing, 44; quilting, 100; cooking, 113, 119–20, 124, 126, 127, 149

Calvert, Robert, 37–38, 135–36, 147, 179

Calvert family, 53, 66, 70, 78, 115, 135, 197; clothing, 24; balance of power within, 37–38, 147; family size, 42; housing and housewares, 76, 81, 84, 86, 89, 93, 95; purchasing goods, 95; house fire, 147, 197–98; trips to town, 221, 224; move to town, 243. *See also* Calvert, Hester; Dodd, Myrtle Calvert

Campbell, Mary Ann Collier, 222

Canning. *See* Food: preservation of

Carroll, Etta (Dovie Carroll's stepmother), 34, 58, 224

Carroll, Etta Hardy and Dovie, xv, 34, 48, 75, 113; courtship, 26; marriage, 29–30; interpersonal relationship, 38, 63; parenthood, 45; discipline of children, 51; housing and household furnishings, 82, 84, 85–86, 107; quilting, 100, 101–2; purchase of household goods, 105, 129; gardening, 123; food preparation and preservation, 129, 142, 152; petty commodity production, 135; field work, 165, 172, 185; church attendance, 201–2; religious beliefs, 203, 215; trips to town, 224–25, 229; move to town, 238, 247

Carroll family, 54, 56, 117, 174–75; housing, 76; death of son Stacy Lee, 198

Carver, Deenie Blackwell, xii, 148. *See also* Blackwell family

Caufield, Alice Owens, 211, 228; discipline as a child, 24, 51–52, 211; housing, 87, 91; clothing, 96; petty commodity production, 140; field work, 184; religious beliefs, 215–16; driving, 223; segregated entertainment, 228, 230–31; move to town, 232–33, 235

Celeste, Hunt County, Texas, 226–27; cotton mill, 237

Charity, 58, 116, 117, 137. *See also* Assistance, community

Chautauqua shows, 228

Chickens. *See* Poultry production: chickens

Childbearing, 39–41, 255 (n. 82); negative effects of, 43, 54. *See also* Pregnancy

Childbirth, 17, 42–47, 255 (n. 96); physician-assisted, 44–45

Child care, 48–52, 56–57; field work and, 168–69

Children: economic significance of, 3, 39; deaths of, 47–48, 104; food for, 48–49, 150–51, 156; care of siblings by, 56, 150–51, 168; housework assistance by, 70, 139, 147–48, 152, 224; field work, 172–73, 177; religious instruction of, 203, 206

Churches, 200–202, 204–7; racial segregation of, 204–5; half-time Baptist and Methodist, 205–6; women's organizations in, 207–8, 286 (n. 113); young peoples' organizations in, 208–9; music in, 211; impact of urbanization on, 242–43

Church of Christ, 204

Circuses, 227–28

Clothing: morality and, 23–24; children's, 98–99; shoes, 99; for field work, 176–77. *See also* Sewing: clothing

Cochran, Vina, 160

Collier family, 76, 223

Coltharp, J. B., 233

Comanche Indians, 13

Comfort Magazine, 195

Commerce, Texas: growth of, 236

Communities: division by class and ethnicity, 189–90

Contraception, 43–44

Cooking. *See* Food preparation

Cooper, Henry and Sarah, 87

Cooper, Marguerite, 184

Corn, 111–14

Corporal punishment, 51–52

Cotton farming: labor by women, 2, 3, 12. *See also* Field work

Cotton gin, 187

Cotton Palace. *See* Texas Cotton Palace

Cotton prices, 12, 98

Courtship, 18–23, 26–29; effects of transportation on, 22–23

Cows, 136–37. *See also* Dairy products

Credit, 11; for household goods, 105, 129; for food, 110, 121–22, 143–44

Crenshaw, Josie Henderson, 25, 48, 98, 175; poultry bartering, 134

Crenshaw family, 48, 66–67

Crop-lien system, xii, 7–12, 69–70, 232–33; economic impact of, 7; mobility within, 9–10, 69; social stratification within, 11–12; impact on diet, 110, 111, 121–22, 125, 131, 136–37, 143, 268 (n. 74); gender and, 159; religion and, 204, 205; effect of Agricultural Adjustment Administration on, 233–34

Curanderas (folk healer), 45

Czechoslovakians: discrimination against, 13, 55; immigration to Blackland Prairie, 13–15; courtship rituals among, 23; dances, 30, 31, 193, 210; wedding rituals among, 30–32; power of women among, 32, 38–39; alcohol, use and abuse, 64, 210; foodways, 118, 139, 152–53, 157; gender conventions among, 162, 170; field work, 163, 170, 178; meals, 191. *See also* Simcik, Mary Hanak

Dairy products: shortages of, 136–37; milk, 137; preservation of, 137–38; clabber and cottage cheese, 138–39; butter, 139–40

Dallas, Texas: rural migration to, 220, 240–41, 243–45; growth of, 237

Dallas Federation of Women's Clubs, 225

Dancing, 192–93; disapproval of, 209–11

Dawson, Joseph Martin, 110

Debbendener, Elizabeth Maler, 63–64

Desertion by husbands, 62–63, 64

Diet: pork, corn, and syrup base, 110–11, 112–21. *See also* Food

Dillow, Louise Blackwell, xii, 42, 51, 109. *See also* Blackwell family

Divorce, 63–64

Dodd, Myrtle Calvert, 37, 230; education, xv; moral instruction of, 23, 24, 211; clothing, 24, 99; attitude toward younger siblings, 42; housework, 70; field work, 172, 176, 179; reading, 195; move to town, 234. *See also* Calvert family

Domestic abuse, 59–60, 61–62

Domestic labor: by African American women, 70–71, 102, 104–5, 148, 244

Domestic production: by women, 3, 4. *See*

also Gardens; Petty commodity production; Poultry production; Sewing

Dulock, Sophie, 245

Earle, Hallie, 195

Elderly: treatment of, 17, 65–67; movement from farms, 34, 232, 245–46

Electrification, 88, 90

Ellis County, Texas, 250 (n. 6); wages in, 7; tenancy in, 11–12, 234; urbanization of, 236

Ellis County Fair, 230

Employment: in town, 237–41

Ennis, Texas: growth of, 236

Entertainment: in town, 226–31; rural (*see* Dancing; Parties; Play-parties; Singings and singing schools; Visiting)

Epworth League, 209

Estes, Elizabeth Williams, 43, 230

Fairs, 229–31

Family relationships: among generations, 33–35, 54–55, 66, 77, 79–80

Family size. *See* Household and family size

Family wages: for field work, 3, 181, 186–87

Farm and Ranch, 195

Farm laborers, 7

Farm size, xi

Field work: objections to, 35, 160–63, 169–70, 276 (n. 3); division of labor by gender, 35–36, 159, 165–66, 169–70, 183–86, 276 (n. 9), 277 (nn. 28, 49), 278 (n. 53); meals during, 153–55; hired labor for, 159, 171–72, 180–83, 278 (n. 60); tenure status and, 163–64; ethnicity and, 163–66; motherhood and, 164–65, 167; chopping and cultivating, 165, 166, 171–75, 278 (n. 58); picking, 165, 175–84; plowing, 166, 169–70; wages for, 166, 171–72, 186–87, 239–40; housework balanced with, 167–68; child care and, 167–69; laying by, 174–75; clothing for, 176–77; disability and, 177–78; migrant laborers, 182–83; weighing, 184–86

Fires, house, 146–47

Firewood, 75, 145–46, 273 (nn. 212, 215)

Florence, Julia Savannah Beaty, 101

Floyd, Hunt County, Texas, 213

Folley, Inez, xv; housework, 91–92, 146; clothing, 99; field work, 170, 172–73, 184; religious beliefs, 206

Folley, Lou Thomas: childbearing, 44; midwifery, 45; widowhood, 58; food preparation, 123, 127, 152; petty commodity production, 140; field work, 166, 184; sewing, 176; nursing the sick, 198; singing, 211–12

Folley family, 42, 58, 80, 117; housing, 92–93

Food: celebrations with, 31, 120–21, 150–51, 191; for children, 48–49, 150–51, 156; shortages of, 51, 111–12, 113, 115–16, 124, 125, 130, 132–33, 266 (n. 10); importance of, 109–10, 121, 266 (n. 3); sharing, 111, 116, 117, 125–26, 136–37; effects of poverty on, 111–12, 120, 122, 124; gender division in providing, 112, 114, 117–18, 119, 121, 122, 129–30, 131; preservation of, 118–19, 126–31, 142–43; purchase of, 124–25, 141–42, 143–44, 149, 153, 154; fruits, 125–26; beverages, 156. *See also* Corn; Diet; Fruits; Gardens; Meals; Pork; Sausage; Syrup; Vegetables

Food preparation, 34, 144–45, 148–57; ruined by children, 50–51; lard, 119–20; breads, 148–50, 152; condiments, 155–56; beverages and alcohol, 156; sweets, 156–57. *See also* Meals

Freeman, Frances, 162

Friendship Baptist Church (McLennan County, Texas), 208

Fruits, 125–31, 269 (n. 94); shortages of, 125; preservation of, 126–31

Funeral practices, 48, 199–200

Gardens, 122–25, 269 (n. 90); gender division in working, 123, 268–69 (n. 79)

Gardner, Lorena, 47

Geese. *See* Poultry production

Gender conventions, 35–39, 160–63

Georgetown, Texas, 236

Germans: discrimination against, 13; immigration to Blackland Prairie, 13–15; beef sales, 142; gender conventions among, 162, 170; field work, 163, 170; dances, 193, 210; funeral practices, 199; use of alcohol, 210

Greenville, Texas, 236

Grellhesl family, 63

Guest family, 26, 54. *See also* Bourne, Emma Guest

Gunn family, 61–62

Hale, Alma Stewart, 210

Hanak family, 87; Roman Catholicism and, 203–4, 206–7

"Happy Belle," 161

Hardeman, Julia: death of mother, 56; field work, 181, 184, 186–87

Harkey, Gillie, 129

Health care, 46, 52–54, 86, 93; impact of poverty on, 121

Hegler, Jewel Peacock, 33

Hennig, Elisabeth Jupe, 87

Heroines of Jericho, 52, 101, 198, 208

Hewitt, Texas, 231

Hilger, Mary Hollie Hayes, 178

Hlavenka, Marie Vrba, 102, 166

Hoelscher, Elsie, 168

Hog killing, 116–21. *See also* Pork

Holidays, 123, 175

Hollands Magazine, 195

Home, concepts of, 69–70

Home demonstration, 101, 106–7, 230; canning demonstrations, 128–29

Household and family size, 39–41, 42–43, 54, 55–58, 65–66, 255 (n. 82)

Household technology: refrigeration, 38, 272 (nn. 167, 172); plumbing, 93; sewing machines, 97–98; washing machines, 105; irons, 106–7, 265 (n. 248); canning equipment, 126–30; butter making, 139–40; stoves, 144, 145–47. *See also* Lighting

Housewares and linens, 81–84

Housework: significance of, 69–70; effect of economic status on, 70–71; house cleaning, 78; field work balanced with, 167–68

Housing: styles and construction, 71, 258 (n. 3), 259 (n. 14); additions to, 71–72, 75; quality and size of, 72–74, 75–77, 259 (nn. 10, 16), 260 (n. 46); decoration and weatherproofing, 74, 77–80; heat sources, 74–75; furnishings, 80–82; exterior finishes, 84; windows and screens, 84–86; landscaping, 86–88; outbuildings, 88. *See also* Lighting; Sanitation; Water supplies

Hunt County, Texas, 250 (n. 6); tenancy in, 9, 11, 234; motion pictures in, 228; urbanization of, 236; churches in, 242

Hunt County Fair, 229

Hurtado, Luz Sanchez, xv. *See also* Sanchez, Refugia; Sanchez family

Instruction: of young women by other women, 17, 46, 99–100, 106, 139, 148–49

Ironing, 106–7, 266 (n. 252)

Irons, 106–7, 265 (n. 248)

Ischy, Tullia Hall, 173

Isolation, rural, 190, 222, 224, 226

Itasca Manufacturing Company (Hill County), 237

James, Lula, 161

Jenkins, Cecil Mae, 199

Jenkins family, 195–96

Jones, Enos, 12

Jones, Lula Kathryn Peacock: sisters' marriages, 1, 33; setting up household, 12, 72–73; courtship, 29

Jones, Mattie, 173

Jumper, Letha, 83, 179

Jupe, Caroline Gast, 63

Jupe, Gertrude Holocek, 79

Kasberg, Agnes Straten, 150, 171

Kin networks, 17, 54–57

Kirk, Limestone County, Texas, 213

Labor: division of by gender, 4, 35–36, 70, 268 (n. 73). *See also* Field work; Housework

Ladies Aid, 207

Ladies Society, 207

Land, purchase of, 38

Landowners, 7–12

Langford, Norma Miller, 103

Langham, Leta Taylor, 168–69

Langham family, 78, 153, 189–90, 239–40; poultry production, 132

Lard, 119–20

Laundry, 102–6. *See also* Domestic labor: by African American women; Ironing; Soap

Laying-by time, 174–75

Lewis, Lois Lacy, 196, 221, 228

Liberty Hill, McLennan County, Texas, 223, 241–42

Libraries, 195–96

Lighting, 88–90; kerosene, 88–89; carbide, 89; Delco systems, 90

Limestone County, Texas, 213

Literacy, 193–94

Locke, Frank, 98–99

Locke family, 37, 190–91; housing, 76, 78, 92, 93

Lubbock, Texas: rural migration to, 220

Lutheran church, 204; music in, 212

Luther's League, 209

Lynching, 25–26

Ma Perkins radio show, 196

McBride, Alma McKethan, 167

McDaniel, Claude, 182

McGregor, Texas: growth of, 236

McKethan family, 81, 96, 167–68

McLennan County, Texas, 11, 250 (n. 6); churches in, 204; tenancy in, 234; urbanization of, 236

McRae, Bessie Winniford, 126, 222

Mail: delivery of, 193

Malone, Vera Allen, 64–65, 119

Marriage, 17; exogamy, 1, 26, 32–35, 54; during field work, 1–2; expectation of, 17, 18–21; ages of women at, 17–18; creation of households within, 32–33, 72–73, 81–82, 83; gender relations within, 33, 35–39; unhappy, 59–65. *See also* Courtship; Desertion by husbands; Divorce; Weddings; Widowhood

Mart, Texas: growth of, 236

Mattresses: manufacture and care, 80–81, 82–83

Mayfield, Emma Owens, 18

Meals, 112, 150–55; during field work, 152–55; as social events, 150–51, 190

Medicines, 52–54

Medicine shows, 227

Merchants, 11, 105, 121–22, 143–44, 239–40. *See also* Peddlers

Methodists: compared to Baptists, 205–6; disapproval of alcohol, 210; disapproval of dancing, 210–11

Mexicans: discrimination against, 13; immigration to Blackland Prairie, 15; marriage to other Mexicans, 26–27; gender attitudes among, 43, 162, 170, 254 (n. 66); medicines, 53; household sharing, 56; housing conditions, 74, 93; wood chopping by, 75; gardening, 122; food preservation, 127, 130; poultry production, 131; field work, 163, 164, 171–72, 182–83; communities of, 190; literacy, 193–94; church attendance, 202; dances, 210; trips to town, 226; Spanish-language motion pictures, 228; employment for women, 239

—foodways, 118, 120–21, 139, 154, 155; spices, 123–24; sweets, 156, 157; tamales, 120–21; tortilla making, 148–49. *See also* Almanza, Adelaida Torres; Hurtado, Luz Sanchez; Navarro, Cayetana Martinez

Midlothian, Texas: growth of, 236

Midwives, 44–45

Migrant workers, 155; housing for, 76–77, 88

Migration: rural to urban, 219–21, 231–41, 235–36; chain migration, 220–21, 240–41

Milk. *See* Dairy products

Moody, Texas, 223–24

Moore, Bird, 57

Moore, Dorothy Woods, 170

Morality: clothing and, 23–24; sexual, 23–26; alcohol consumption and, 209–10; dancing and, 209–11

Mortality: children's, 47–48

Motherhood, expectation of, 39. *See also* Childbearing

Motion pictures, 228–29

Murphy, Audie, 42

Murphy family, 42, 64

Music, sacred, 211–13

Musical events, 22, 192–93, 212, 231

Narrative, xii

Nash, Ellis County, Texas: churches around, 204

Native Americans, 13

Navarro, Cayetana Martinez, xv; childbearing, 42; tortilla making, 148–49

New Deal. *See* Agricultural Adjustment Administration; Rural Electrification Administration

Newspapers, 194–95

Nursing the sick, 198

Oil production in Texas, 238–39

Oral history interviewing, xiii-xvii

Orchards, 125

Orphans, care of, 41, 56–57

Owens, Eliza, 103, 203; discipline of children, 24, 51–52; work as laundress, 104

Owens, Howard, 136, 184, 211, 232

Owens, Monroe and Mae, 232

Owens, Ruthie, 47

Owens, William, family, 173–74, 210–11; move to town, 245–46

Paris, Lamar County, Texas, 225

Parties, 192

Peddlers, 53, 82, 98, 144, 196; barter system, 134, 143, 175

Perkins, Louis John, 22

Perkins, Lucille Mora, 22

Perry, Falls County, Texas, 243

Petty commodity production, 3, 4, 143, 271 (n. 145); poultry, 134–36; butter, 140–42, 273 (n. 187)

Pickling, 127

Pitcock, Margaruite, 177

Play-parties, 18–19

Podsednik, Frances, 183

Pork, 114–21

Porter family, 55, 145, 150, 245; housing, 92, 94. *See also* Weir, Bernice Porter Bostick

Poultry production: geese, 82–83; chickens, 131–35, 271 (n. 144); turkeys, 135–36. *See also* Petty commodity production

Poverty, 7, 11–12; effects on diet, 111–12, 120, 121–22, 124, 130–31, 136–37; effects on health care, 121. *See also* Crop-lien system; Food

Pregnancy: attitudes toward, 41; prenatal care, 44. *See also* Childbirth

Quilting, 99–102, 264 (n. 200)

Race relations, 26–27

Racism, 12–15; prayers against, 215–16

Radio, 196, 283 (n. 47), 284 (n. 53)

Railroads. *See* Transportation: trains

Rape family, 24

Rauschhuber, Maria Mousberger, 45

Reading, 194–96, 283 (n. 43)

Refrigeration, 137–38, 272 (nn. 167, 172)

Religious beliefs, 66–67, 213–16, 285 (n. 93); consolation on death of children, 47–48; household prayer and worship, 150, 202, 203–4; as sustenance during work, 174, 205, 212, 244; Bible reading, 195, 202–3; church attendance, 200–202; knowledge of Scripture, 203; and smoothing of class differences, 204, 205; intercessory prayer, 205, 215; revivals, 213–14

Remarriage, 57–58

Rest rooms, 225–26

Revivals, 213–14

Rice, Lee, 229

Rice family, 82–83, 104; relocations of,

9–10; housing, 77–78, 146–47; petty commodity production, 140
Richardson, Ada, 104
Roberts family, 56
Roman Catholicism, 202, 203–4, 205; influence of local priest, 206–7
Rural Electrification Administration, 90
Rural Welfare Association, 225

St. Clair, Ruth, 167
Salem Methodist Church, Perry, Texas, 207
San Antonio, Texas, 237
Sanchez, Refugia: quilting, 101; laundry, 104; food preservation, 142
Sanchez family, 76; housing, 77, 84
Sanitation, 93–94, 263 (n. 155)
Sartain, Ruth Peacock, 1
Sausage, 117–18
Schneider, Clara Wachsman, 171
Schools: cultural impact of, 24; consolidation of, 241–42
Schroeder, Clara Wolf, 166
Schroeder family, 55
Semi-Weekly Farm News, 195
Sewing, 95–98; linens and towels, 82; clothing, 96–97, 176–77; for "outsiders," 98; fancy work, 102, 229, 230; cotton sacks, 175–76. See also Quilting
Sewing machines, 97–98
Sex: community mores regarding, 23–26; instructions for young women about, 25, 41–42
Sharecropping, xii, 7–12. See also Crop-lien system
Sharpless family, 219–20
Shepton Baptist Church (Collin County, Texas), 207, 212
Shopping: men as family shoppers, 96, 144, 222, 224; trips to town, 223, 224–27, 231, 288 (n. 25)
Simcik, Mary Hanak, 18, 154, 205, 221; discipline as a child, 25; clothing, 99; food production, 115, 118–19
Sims, Fordyce, 79
Singings and singing schools, 22, 212, 231

Single parents, 56
Slavery: and cotton agriculture, 2; movement to Blackland Prairie, 13–14, 252 (n. 37)
Slemmons, Effie, 58–59
Soap, 95, 102–3
Sociological reports, xvii–xviii
Southern ladyhood, 160–63
Space: indoor and outdoor, 69, 72; separated by gender, 222, 224, 258 (n. 5)
Spanish settlement in Texas, 13
Spouse abuse. See Domestic abuse
Stamps-Baxter Music Company, 212–13, 287 (n. 145)
Steward, Beulah, 98
Steward, Levi, 93
Stimpson, Eddie, Sr., 27–28
Stimpson, Millie Birks, 73, 104; courtship, 27–28; child rearing, 49, 52; marital discord, 60–61; work as domestic, 70–71; field work, 168; religious practices, 203, 212
Stimpson family: housing, 73, 87, 88; field work, 173
Stoves, 144, 145–47
Strawn, Bea, 99–100
Syrup, 114

Taylor, Texas: growth of, 236
Taylor Bedding Company (Taylor, Texas), 239
Telephones, 196–97, 284 (n. 56)
Temple, Texas, 224
Tenant farming, 7–12. See also Crop-lien system
Texas Blackland Prairie. See Blackland Prairie of Texas
Texas Cotton Palace, 221, 230–31
Textile mills, 237–38, 291 (n. 90)
Textiles and sewing materials, 82, 96–97, 175, 176
Tonkawa Indians, 13
Tours, McLennan County, Texas: wedding practices in, 30–31. See also Czechoslovakians; Germans

Transportation, 190; automobiles, 22–23, 221–23, 288 (n. 15); animal-powered, 202, 221–22; trains, 221; gender divisions in, 222–23

Travis County, Texas: entertainment in, 210, 229; urbanization, 231, 235

Turkeys. *See* Poultry production: turkeys

Turley, Lucille, 241

Uptmor, Anna Jupe, 64, 79

Uptmor, Josephine Schroeder, 34

Uptmor, Mary Jupe, 101, 102

Uptmor, Mary Olsovsky, 65

Uptmor, Otillia Guggenberger, 57

Uptmor family, 79

Urbanization, xviii, 231–37. *See also* Employment: in town; Schools: consolidation of

Urban women: productivity among, 4, 247

Valley View Baptist Church (McLennan County, Texas), 242–43

Vaughan family, 37

Vegetables, 122–25

Visiting, 190–92, 282 (n. 5)

Vrba, Rosina Macicek, 57

Waco, Texas: rural migration to, 220; as market center, 224; growth of, 236, 237; employment for women in, 239

Walker, Inez Adams: courtship, 27; childbirth, 44–45; field work, 179, 180–81, 186. *See also* Adams family

Walker, W. T., 27

Walther League, 209

Washing machines, 105

Washington, Jesse: lynching of, 25–26

Washington, Maggie Langham, 189–90, 239–40; labor, 114, 153, 168–69. *See also* Langham family

Water supplies, 90–93, 95, 103; wells, 91–92; tanks, 92; cisterns, 92–93

Waxahachie, Texas: chautauqua shows in, 228; growth of, 236

Waxahachie Cotton Mill, 238

Waxahachie Shakespeare Club, 225

Weddings, 29–32; Czech practices, 30–32

Weinberger, Pauline Wanke, 65

Weir, Bernice Porter Bostick, xi, 38, 41, 138, 157, 230, 235; courtship, 22; marriage, 30; pregnancy, 39, 44; religious beliefs, 48; child care, 48–49, 50; housekeeping, 79–80, 81–82, 104, 105, 107; sewing, 97, 98, 102; quilting, 97, 101; clothing, 98–99; gardening, 123; poultry production, 134–35; petty commodity production, 140; field work, 165, 186; driving, 223–24. *See also* Bostick family; Porter family

Westbrook family, 46, 73, 105

Wichita Indians, 13

Widowhood, 58–59, 166–67

Willenborg, Annie Uptmor, 166–67

Williams, R. W., 178

Williams family, 73

Williamson County, Texas, 250–51 (n. 6); churches in, 204; tenancy in, 234; urbanization of, 236

Winkler, Janie Kasberg, 124

Woman's Missionary Union, 207–8

World War II, 241

XLI Club (Gainesville, Texas), 225

Zotz, Mary, 81, 135